SANCTIONED SAVAGERY

SANCTIONED SAVAGERY

A HISTORY OF VIOLENCE IN AMERICAN FOOTBALL

MICHAEL ORIARD

THE UNIVERSITY OF NORTH CAROLINA PRESS
CHAPEL HILL

This book was published with the assistance of the Thornton H. Brooks Fund
of the University of North Carolina Press.

Manufactured in the United States of America

Designed by Lindsay Starr
Set in Charis and Irby
by codeMantra
Cover art © Adobe Stock / matrosovv.

LIBRARY OF CONGRESS CATALOGING-IN-PUBLICATION DATA
Names: Oriard, Michael, 1948– author.
Title: Sanctioned savagery : a history of violence in American football / Michael Oriard.
Description: Chapel Hill : The University of North Carolina Press,
2025. | Includes bibliographical references and index.
Identifiers: LCCN 2025013867 | ISBN 9781469690643 (cloth ; alk. paper) |
ISBN 9781469690650 (epub) | ISBN 9781469690667 (pdf)
Subjects: LCSH: Violence in sports—United States—History. | Football—United States—History. | Football injuries—United States. | Football injuries—Social aspects—United States. | Masculinity in sports—Health aspects—United States. | BISAC: SPORTS & RECREATION / History | SOCIAL SCIENCE / Ethnic Studies / American / General
Classification: LCC GV706.7 .O75 2025 | DDC 796.33209—dc23/eng/20250512
LC record available at https://lccn.loc.gov/2025013867

For product safety concerns under the European Union's General Product
Safety Regulation (EU GPSR), please contact gpsr@mare-nostrum.co.uk or
write to the University of North Carolina Press and Mare Nostrum Group
B.V., Mauritskade 21D, 1091 GC Amsterdam, The Netherlands.

FOR CLYDE

CONTENTS

FIGURES

PREFACE

While trying to minimize repeating what I had previously written in *Reading Football*, *King Football*, and *Brand NFL*, I have more freely used passages from my 2013 e-book, *The Head in Football*. I wrote that essay at the invitation of the publisher Ivan Dee and was drawn to the prospect because it would be too long for a journal, and I wanted it to be heavily illustrated. I also somehow imagined that it might reach a large readership, but it remained a well-kept secret from the moment it went online. Because the copyright reverted to me after five years, I do not need to thank Ivan Dee for permission to use passages from it here, but I am grateful to him for the opportunity to write the piece that now informs sections of this book.

For my earlier books on football's cultural history, I was hugely dependent on microfilm, most of which was unavailable at my university. For this one, the archives of newspapers.com made the hard work of research immensely easier and simpler. Its archives are not unlimited, but its resources made it possible to reconstruct a close approximation of the national conversation on the subject at hand. Microfilm remained necessary at times, as did much other material available to me only through interlibrary loans at Oregon State University. As always, I am grateful to Deborah Carroll and her colleagues for regularly going above and beyond to track down needed materials, even during the pandemic, when many institutions were not fully functioning or functioning at all. I also thank Gregory Bond, curator of the University of Notre Dame's Joyce Sports Research Collection, for his responses to my repeated requests for information from the collection and reproductions of materials. And I am indebted to the anonymous readers of my manuscript for the University of North Carolina Press, particularly for insisting that it needed much more attention to the medical literature on football and for providing references that pointed me in the right directions to navigate through it. Also, to Lucas Church and the many people at the Press who made this book a reality, thank you.

Sometime in 2009, a videographer in Portland, Todd Trigsted, contacted me out of the blue with a proposal to collaborate on a documentary on the cultural history of football, based on my books. We became a two-man team: I wrote the script and conducted the interviews; Todd filmed and edited (in a Ken Burns-y style). With chronic traumatic encephalopathy emerging as a major national story, it inevitably came to shape the trajectory of our film. We interviewed former players (some with symptoms, others not), journalists, scholars, and parents, along with Steve Sabol at NFL Films (just months before his shocking death), the groundbreaking researchers Ann McKee and Chris Nowinski at the Center for the Study of Traumatic Encephalopathy, Kevin Guskiewicz at the University of North Carolina, and members of the team at Purdue University. When we finished the film, Todd and his business partners were unsuccessful in marketing it, but after screenings at a couple of film festivals, Todd placed it on Vimeo in April 2015 under the title *Gridiron Gladiators: The History and Uncertain Future of American Football*, where it continues to languish, presumably unwatched. But making the documentary introduced me to several of the people whom I write about in this book. I thank Todd for that experience.

I carry some reminders of my football career in a bad back and the lingering effects from my pinched nerve, but I am among the fortunate ones, unlike my Chiefs teammate Clyde Werner, a linebacker and special-teams player and a large-souled man off the field, who has had twenty orthopedic surgeries since he retired, including a half dozen on his Achilles tendon and multiple fusions of his spinal vertebrae from S1 to T12, without relieving his constant pain. Clyde is paying a higher price for his football career than anyone should have to pay. I dedicate this book to him.

Corvallis, Oregon
February 2025

SANCTIONED SAVAGERY

INTRODUCTION

On September 24, 2002, the Pittsburgh Steelers' Hall of Fame center Mike Webster died from heart failure at the age of fifty, twelve years into retirement. Initially, the news was shocking but not unexpected. Before his induction, newspapers around the country had carried the story that "Iron Mike," after seventeen NFL seasons, most notably as anchor of the Steelers' offensive line during the Super Bowl years of the 1970s, was now bankrupt, homeless, depressed, and racked by convulsions and spasms. The *New York Times* reported that his death followed "more than a decade of physical and psychological turmoil apparently brought on by repeated blows to the head on the field" and cited a clinical psychologist who "said Webster had 'the football version of punch drunk.'"[1]

The pathologist on duty in the coroner's office in Pittsburgh when Mike Webster's body was brought in was a Nigerian immigrant, Dr. Bennet Omalu, who had no formal neurological training but an interest in head trauma and a familiarity with Webster's story. After performing the autopsy, Omalu kept Webster's brain for several months to pursue his suspicions, slicing off sections to view under a microscope and then showing them to his more experienced colleagues. By early 2003 they had all agreed: The tangles and brown stains in Webster's brain tissues were tau proteins that indicated chronic traumatic encephalopathy (CTE), so-called punch-drunk syndrome, first identified in boxers back in 1928 but, until now, long rumored but never confirmed in a football player. Within a few years of Omalu publishing his findings in July 2005, the rationale that had justified the injuries from football's violence since the late nineteenth century—that the game's benefits outweighed its physical harm—would be in serious jeopardy. Football players risked damage not just to their bodies but to their brains as well.

I was paying attention when Mike Webster died because I was writing a book about the modern National Football League, and Webster seemed the worst wreck in the NFL's "Wrecking Yard," as *Sports Illustrated* had titled a cover story on damaged former players a little over a year earlier. In concluding *Brand NFL* in February 2007 and looking to pro football's future, I emphasized the game's transformation since the 1960s from a *sport* to *entertainment* and wondered whether the league's leaders risked misreading their public, for whom football mattered as much more than *mere* entertainment. In one chapter, discussing the NFL's "dark side," I had briefly described the reports in the press about Webster's grotesquely deteriorating physical and mental condition around the time of his induction into the Pro Football Hall of Fame and then his death five years later. By the time I finished the book, Omalu had published his findings, but his discovery had not yet been widely reported in the press, and its significance was not yet understood—at least not by me, and I was paying attention, as I say. By that time, Omalu had also found CTE in the brain of another former Steeler, Terry Long, who had killed himself by drinking antifreeze at the age of forty-five, and had again published his findings, in November 2006. In January 2007, the *New York Times*'s Alan Schwarz had published the first of what would become more than 100 stories about the "concussion crisis," this one about the suicide of former Philadelphia Eagles defensive back Andre Waters, in which Schwarz also mentioned Webster and Long. I missed that story, and I finished my book with speculations about the NFL's future, still oblivious to the significance of what Bennet Omalu had discovered.

For a paperback edition three years later, I appended an afterword (written in May 2010) in which I addressed what I saw as the two most significant developments in the NFL since my book's original publication: yet another eruption of labor conflict, which was putting in jeopardy the collective bargaining agreement by which everyone was getting rich; and the emerging evidence that *all* football players might be at risk for the long-term consequences of brain trauma from head blows. Between February 2007 and May 2010, the "concussion crisis" had commenced, more precisely in the fall of 2009, when, after a steady drumbeat of reports from Alan Schwarz in the *New York Times*, blockbuster stories in *GQ* and the *New Yorker* and the televised skewering of NFL commissioner Roger Goodell in a congressional hearing had made the risk of CTE a truly national issue.

Like all former NFL players, I assume, I immediately conducted a private inventory of whatever concussions I could recall (none in which I remembered losing consciousness) and concluded that I was likely OK. But football was not OK, and as the author of four books on the cultural history of American football by that time, I followed the unfolding of the concussion crisis with increasing amazement, as football players from my youth died, one by one, ravaged by CTE, with each death seeming to put the future of the game a little more in jeopardy. I thought that, when the crisis was finally resolved, one way or another—football made safe enough to continue playing or deemed *too* dangerous—I would attempt to make sense of it in another book. I would reconsider all that I had written about the role of violence in the sport's history since the late nineteenth century in light of the discovery of the long-term risks not just to knees and hips and shoulders but to former players' very selfhood. This book is that reconsideration, somewhat premature, because that final resolution is not yet known. (By the time the risks of CTE are fully understood, I may be too old to write about it.)

So, among other things, this book is a belated acknowledgment of the overwhelming significance of Bennet Omalu's discovery of CTE in Mike Webster's brain. It necessarily draws on all that I have written about football over the past forty-some years. After publishing a study of American sports fiction in 1982 from my Stanford dissertation (which I had written in the offseasons while playing for the Kansas City Chiefs), my first book on football, also in 1982, offered "reflections" (at thirty-four, I was too young for a "memoir") on my own experiences playing the game from the fourth grade at Sacred Heart Grade School in Spokane, Washington, through high school at Gonzaga Prep and then college at Notre Dame, to four years in the NFL with Kansas City (and part of a fifth with the Canadian Football League's Hamilton Tiger-Cats after being cut by the Chiefs at the end of a players' strike). *The End of Autumn* was the story of an ordinary player, not a star. I can look back at it now as a historical document, or case study, detailing one football player's experiences, neither typical nor unique, from the late 1950s into the 1970s.

As a case study, the book described a boy's growing up big enough to compete with his older brother but never good enough to beat him, finding in football his own world, separate from his brother's, in which being *tough* was the first requirement. It described the tackling drills, in which the boy discovered whether *he* was tough enough (a discovery that would have to be repeated in blocking and tackling drills at the next levels, too). It described doing neck-bridges, beginning in high school, to build up muscles against spinal cord fractures. It described first the boy's and then the young man's two serious injuries in his eighteen years of tackle football (putting him among the fortunate ones): torn cartilage in his left knee in the first game of his senior season in high school and a pinched nerve ("stinger") in the left side of his neck in a spring practice before his senior year in college. In high school, he hobbled through the rest of the season on his heavily wrapped knee, with no less effort but considerably less grace, and then had surgery in February. With his pinched nerve, he had to change the way he blocked for the next six seasons. He could not use his helmeted head as a weapon without the risk of excruciating pain and numbness shooting down his left arm. (Protecting his too-long neck, which seemed a liability at the time, ended up protecting his head, too, without his realizing it.)

In the chapters on his Chiefs years, the former player described his teammate E. J. Holub's knee, after nine operations, looking like "well-marbled meat at the butcher shop." He wrote about the Chiefs' middle linebacker, Willie Lanier, a rival to Dick Butkus as the hardest hitter in the NFL, who wore a helmet thickly padded on the outside and tackled with his chest and shoulders, not his head, after nearly dying from a subdural hematoma his rookie year. He wrote about a rookie defensive end and special-teams player, John Lohmeyer, breaking his neck on a kickoff and being sent back into the game by the team doctor after twisting John's head back and forth by the face mask to confirm that he was OK. An X-ray in the doctor's office the next day revealed the break (and startled the doctor). He wrote about injury and pain as basic realities of pro football players' lives, and he titled one of the chapters "The End of Toughness," about his own slow realization that being tough could have unhappy consequences and that he had to take care of his own body for the sake of its future, because he could no longer trust the adults in his football life to do it for him.

Those chapters resonate with me more powerfully since CTE was found in Mike Webster's brain. I already understood that playing football could exact a steep price, aside from physical disability. My title called attention to the *end* of football, and the book came about when an editor at Doubleday saw a piece in the *New York Times* that I wrote about my Kansas City teammate Jim Tyrer's shocking murder-suicide in September 1980. I was an English professor by then, much aware of the literary tradition of the former athlete haunted by his lost youthful glory. In the book, I cast Jim as a tragic case of the ex-athlete. I realize now that his tragedy was most likely a case of undiagnosed CTE.

Those experiences from playing organized tackle football for eighteen of my first twenty-six years inevitably informed my understanding of the game when I began writing about its cultural history, beginning with *Reading Football* in 1993. Summarizing that history here will make it unnecessary to repeat it for background in the following chapters. The first American intercollegiate football game, between Princeton and Rutgers in 1869, was a soccer-type game won by Rutgers, 6 goals to 4. Subsequent contests among a handful of elite universities in the Northeast over the next few years eventually led to a meeting of students from Harvard, Yale, Princeton, and Columbia in Springfield, Massachusetts, in November 1876, at which Harvard's representative persuaded the others to adopt the running game (rugby) over the kicking game (soccer). The transformation of English rugby into American football then came about from two radical rule changes, in 1880 and 1882, proposed by Yale's representative, Walter Camp (long known as the "Father of American Football"). The rule in 1880 assigned possession of the ball to one team at a time, through a "scrimmage" (rather than by the randomness of the rugby *scrum*mage). The rule in 1882 then required the team in possession to advance the ball five yards in three tries or surrender it to the other side.

Camp's innovations created the framework for what would quickly become the two most distinctive features of American football, making it a "scientific" game on the one hand and a "collision sport" on the other. Possession of the ball meant opportunities for strategy, predetermined plays, signals to call them, and differentiated responsibilities among the eleven players in distinctively named positions. At the same time, separating the two teams meant lining up on opposing sides of an invisible line, confronting each other as if to do battle, and it led inevitably to everything that made American football violent, "a game of blocking and tackling," as a once-common cliché put it. Camp's interest was in the scientific game, which supposedly would produce the nation's future leaders by demanding and developing quick thinking, judgment, and command. The collision sport would produce *men*, men who could "take it." The collision sport is what this book examines, but Camp also matters importantly as football's First Coach (initially in an unofficial capacity at Yale): the first adult who took over control of the game from the boys, the forefather of all the men who drove their players to prove they could "take it."

Reading Football also explored numerous other aspects of the early game: the role of the modern newspaper, developed in New York by Joseph Pulitzer in the 1880s, in making college football a major American spectator sport; the attention in early newspaper coverage to the social elite (including, conspicuously, the women) among those spectators at the season's big games played by Harvard, Yale, and Princeton; the transformation of Thanksgiving into a day of football; the weekly columns in *Harper's Weekly* in the 1890s written by the Anglophile sports journalist Caspar Whitney and the dozens of articles in magazines and intellectual journals attacking or defending the game; the startling invasion in 1895 of a team from the Carlisle Indian Industrial School into a football world ruled by the nation's Anglo-Saxon elite.

But *violence* was fundamental to American football from the beginning. Rugby had been rough. The American game that Walter Camp and his fellow rule makers created was rougher, and both the players and the public embraced it, not *despite* but *because of* its violence, for the game's "*necessary* roughness" that made it a "manly game." That embrace of violence was somehow related to a national history deeply steeped in violence—its birth in revolution, its brutal conquest of the continent, its pervasive gun culture. It was also somehow related to the disruptions and dislocations of American life and American men's lives wrought by urbanization and industrialization, as they left farms and small towns, where they had to be self-sufficient, for meaningless labor in factories and businesses in burgeoning cities. The traditional elite (whose sons went to Harvard, Yale, and Princeton) faced their own disruptions, as the rise of self-made new wealth increasingly usurped their power and influence. Football somehow compensated for what had been lost in the advance of civilization. At the deepest, unarticulated level, anxieties about manliness and masculinity were fundamental to football's astonishingly rapid rise in these early years from an informal game played by schoolboys to a national sporting spectacle.

King Football (2001) took the story of college football from the 1920s through the 1950s, as the game spread from the Northeast to the rest of the country, became rooted in community and regional identities, was democratized by farmers' and coal miners' sons and by second-generation immigrants from southern and eastern Europe, produced its first true celebrity player in Red Grange and celebrity coach in Knute Rockne, became absorbed into college social life, and was riven by continual controversies over "commercialism," "professionalism," and "overemphasis." Bowl games—Orange, Sugar, and Cotton, joining the long-established Rose—made New Year's a day of football in the 1930s, like Thanksgiving since the 1890s. The Prep Bowl in Chicago, matching the public high school and Catholic league champions, regularly drew as many as 75,000 spectators to Soldier Field, topped by an astonishing 120,000 in 1937. The National Football League restructured itself, in 1933, as a big-city organization (with only Green Bay as a vestige from its small-city beginnings), positioning itself to become a truly national sport, through television, by the end of the 1950s.

The sport celebrated as "King Football" was the *college* game throughout this period. It saturated both local and national media, which in the 1920s included radio and film as well as print. Sports coverage in daily newspapers doubled over the 1920s, and by the '30s, local radio stations and three national networks were broadcasting college games all day on Saturdays every week in the fall. The newsreels that accompanied feature films were showing college football highlights every week in the fall, and about five of those features each year in the 1930s were football movies. The most popular general-interest weekly magazines, the *Saturday Evening Post* and *Collier's*, began regularly publishing articles on college football and football coaches in the late 1920s and never stopped. Those two magazines alone also published forty-six football covers over the 1930s, while football fiction, which had begun as a trickle in the first two decades of the 1900s, became a deluge, with forty-two stories and six novel-length serials in the '30s. From late September into December, college football had become virtually unavoidable.

Alongside the daily "mainstream" press, by the 1930s a thriving (mostly weekly) Black press, Polish press, Italian press, Jewish press, Catholic press, and varied other ethnic presses were covering *their* players and teams and selecting *their* All-Americans. Besides football at Black colleges, the Black press, led by the *Chicago Defender* and *Pittsburgh Courier*, covered the excruciatingly slow desegregation of college football outside the South: the solitary Black player on a handful of "mixed" teams in the North and West; the benching of those players against Southern opponents; the unprecedented four (!) Black players on the 1939 UCLA team—including Jackie Robinson and Kenny Washington, the best player in the country but left off the All-America team and not drafted by the NFL, due to a "gentlemen's agreement" among the owners that lasted from 1933 through 1945. By the 1950s, with Black players increasingly conspicuous on college teams outside the South, both in numbers and as stars, the mainstream press, too, was covering them, along with the two major racial incidents of that decade, the slugging of Drake's Johnny Bright in 1951 (captured in a series of graphic stop-action photographs published in *Life* magazine for all the country to see) and the attempt by the segregationist governor of Georgia to keep Georgia Tech from playing Pitt in the 1956 Sugar Bowl because Pitt had one Black player.

King Football described the major developments in college football in the 1950s as the National Collegiate Athletic Association's resistance to television, in order to protect attendance and gate receipts, and its internal battles over payments to supposed "amateur" athletes that culminated in the adoption of the athletic scholarship and the implosion of the Pacific Coast Conference over booster slush funds. While briefly noting the postwar/Cold War era's cult of toughness, *King Football* all but ignored the ascendance of the "hard-nosed" brutal coaches who are at the very heart of this new book.

The 1950s was also the decade in which pro football reached a national audience for the first time through television. Pro football into the 1950s had not been just ignored but scorned by the college football establishment because of its brutality—it was violent, as football must be, but also *dirty*—and because it was played for money rather than for character building and Alma Mater. America's embrace of pro football since the 1960s for its *extreme* violence became a major part of the story in *Brand NFL* (2007), and that obviously remains central to this new book. Of necessity, the story told in *Brand NFL* about the transformation of pro football's image in the 1960s from "savagery" to "*sanctioned* savagery" (the term from an essay by the journalist Thomas Morgan in *Esquire* in November 1959) I repeat in this new book, because it became the foundation of the NFL that is now confronting its concussion crisis.

For well over a century, a belief that football, through its violence, builds character has coexisted with regular calls to eliminate foul play. A belief that injuries, however common, were incidental to football (unlike in prizefighting, where they were the primary purpose) coexisted with an unofficial but common practice of going after the other team's best player, to get him out of the game. A rarely challenged claim that football made "men out of boys" coexisted with the fact that only a small minority of boys played football at any time in the game's history. *Sanctioned Savagery* explores those conflicts and contradictions, without presuming to resolve them.

I have narrowed the broader sweep of my previous books to focus on the core issue of football violence, in light of what we now know about its potential long-term consequences. Football violence was always understood to have its costs, in injuries and even occasional fatalities, but the benefits of the game, and of the violence itself as a test and proof of toughness, of manliness, were always seen to outweigh them. The discovery that football has ravaged players' core identities, not just their bodies, has forced a reconsideration of that long-standing cost-benefit analysis. No serious new attempt to abolish football has yet emerged out of the concussion crisis, but that possibility is still pending.

Reading Football and *King Football* focused on college football; *Brand NFL*, on the pros. I paid little attention to the high school game, beyond its importance to community identity, in *King Football* and virtually none at all to youth football (which began to be seriously organized only in the 1950s). From the perspective of the crisis threatening football's future today, with the game's survival partly dependent on parents' continuing to let their sons play the game, the history of football for boys becomes an important part of the story. For that history, I am particularly indebted to the work of the public health scholar Kathleen Bachynski, whose *No Game for Boys to Play* (2019) was an indispensable resource.

In this new book I examine the long history of football violence in relation to what I now see, partly in response to Bachynski's work, as a fundamental tension between *health* concerns and *cultural* values—between the game's inevitable injuries (and occasional fatalities) and the values that have justified them. ("Culture" is perhaps an unfortunate term to stand for the personal, social, political, even religious motives for watching football, playing football, or letting one's sons play it, but I can think of no other. "Culture" stands for all of the nonrational reasons that the game has survived despite a wholly rational concern for the players' physical well-being.) From the perspective of physical health, there is no such thing as "*necessary* roughness." A broken collarbone is bodily damage, not an acceptable cost for playing a "manly" game. The continuing tension between football violence as a health issue and as a cultural issue over the course of the game's history (with culture invariably trumping health) is the underlying subject of all the chapters that follow. My desire would be to discover how actual players, parents, and fans thought about football's violence over the past 125 years or so. The closest I can come to that is to reconstruct as well as I can the culture in which the game was played through what was written in newspapers and magazines. That is what this book attempts to do.[2]

That the justifications for football's violence changed so little from one generation to the next, even the language itself, was one of my major surprises in reconstructing that history. This discovery led me to a sense that football's history in the United States since the 1890s—including what we think of as the Progressive Era, Jazz Age, Depression, Cold War, and so on as distinct "moments" in American history—has itself been a single "moment," marked most significantly by a radical undermining of traditional masculinity by the forces of urbanization, industrialization, and technology and of white masculinity by integration and immigration. Trying to account for the appeal of football in any particular era bumped up against the reality that arguments in defense of football violence in 2013 were the same ones made in 1894, however much circumstances changed.

The following chapters are roughly chronological, structured in part around what I see as three pivotal episodes in football history, when health and culture most directly collided, and which now appear as preludes to the concussion crisis that threatens the game's future. The first two were a full-blown crisis and a potential one, both of which college football survived. The first has become widely known in recent years by the general public as well as by historians through reporting on the concussion crisis: the threat, following the death of Harold Moore at the end of the 1905 season, to abolish football altogether that instead led to major rule changes (including the adoption of the forward pass), which seemed to make the game safer (with President Theodore Roosevelt in an overstated starring role in some accounts), and to the creation of the NCAA to govern the sport. The second, well known to historians but not the general public, came in 1931, when army cadet Richard Sheridan died from a cervical fracture in making a tackle on a kickoff in the game against Yale. The uproar this time was intense but brief; it led again to more rule revisions but no movement to abolish a game that by that time had become too big to fail, as it were.

For the third episode, less dramatic but ultimately more consequential, I would nominate a development over the course of a few years, rather than a specific event: the development in the mid-1950s of the hard-shell plastic helmet and its adoption by a generation of "hard-nosed" coaches, led by Bear Bryant, as their players' primary weapon in blocking and tackling. Before the hard-shell helmet, there had been (undiagnosed) cases of CTE, but only with the hard-shell helmet and coaches to teach its use as a weapon could CTE become an epidemic. It made the "collision sport," the "game of blocking and tackling," immeasurably more destructive; and college coaches' techniques quickly filtered down to high school and youth football, too.

Exploring the history of football as a public health issue, as documented by Kathleen Bachynski and others, I discovered that concern in the medical establishment about football injuries simply *as injuries* dates back at least to the early twentieth century but also that it has consistently been overridden by the popular view of injuries as an acceptable cost for the game's cultural benefits, by the idea that "taking it" made boys into men and weak males into strong ones. The following chapters, then, will trace the history of that tension more or less chronologically, with particular attention to the three episodes mentioned above. Chapter 1 retraces ground covered in *Reading Football* on the game's beginnings as a collision sport through the crisis of 1905–6. Chapter 2 considers the aftermath of that crisis and the emergence of college football as the country's greatest popular spectacle in the 1920s, until the death of Cadet Sheridan in 1931 forced a new reckoning with football violence. Chapters 3 and 4 examine that reckoning in the initiation of an annual report on the year's fatalities and catastrophic injuries to the American Football Coaches Association; the first comprehensive studies of football injuries, including concussions; and the steady stream of articles in women's magazines addressing the fundamental question of whether football was safe enough for their sons to play. These chapters also consider the high school football culture that emerged in the 1930s and 1940s from unconventional sources, ranging from boys' pulp stories to a popular skit on "sissy football," to the anti-football rants of a prominent newspaper health columnist; all of which effectively shifted the question from whether football was safe enough to why boys wanted to play it.

Chapters 5 and 6 turn to the post–World War II generation of "hard-nosed" college coaches, most fully embodied in Bear Bryant, who transformed football from a sport with violent elements to a violent sport, closer to war, with the hard-shell plastic helmet as the principal weapon (and NCAA Rules Committees complicit in the transformation). The more violent football of the postwar era produced the players who would become the first generation of CTE casualties, and the way that their coaches taught them to play would require the dramatic rule changes, enacted since 2010 or so, to de-weaponize the helmet. For understanding how football has found itself in a *concussion* crisis—and not just a piling up of more damaged bodies as players became bigger, faster, and stronger—these chapters are the heart of the book. Chapters 7 and 8 then shift the focus to the National Football League, where the concussion crisis originated and has most conspicuously played out. Chapter 7 revisits the account in my earlier *Brand NFL* of the NFL's embrace in the 1960s of its once notorious "savagery" as the essence of what was now "America's Game," reconsidered here from the perspective opened up by the discovery of CTE in Mike Webster's brain. Chapter 8 traces the emergence of the concussion crisis following that discovery and the so-called war on football that ensued, as this latest crisis has played out in a country more conspicuously divided than ever by class, race, geography, and politics. Finally, a brief epilogue assesses where parents, players, and fans find themselves today, knowing what they now know about the potential long-term ravages of brain damage from football but not knowing just how dangerous football remains after all of the efforts to make it safer. In covering the NFL's denials of concussions' seriousness from 1994 to roughly 2007 and the early unfolding of the "concussion crisis" in the years following, I am of course indebted to the extraordinary reporting of Mark Fainaru-Wada and Steve Fainaru in *League of Denial* in 2013.

Although the chapters are roughly chronological, they yield no overriding narrative to explain an evolving public understanding of football violence but rather a series of loosely related episodes, a mosaic with disparate parts. As noted above, the arguments for and against football's violence have remained remarkably consistent for over a century. Nor do I attempt to explain the relation of football violence to the vastly more complicated history of American violence, to what the historian Drew Gilpin Faust, in a completely different context, has called the "violence . . . at the heart of our national mythology" and "our national creed."[3] To make sense of such a complex topic is not just beyond this book but beyond my capacity to explain.

CHAPTER 1

NECESSARY ROUGHNESS

On November 27, 1884, Yale and Princeton played their Thanksgiving Day football game at the Polo Grounds in New York, before 25,000 fans—a huge crowd for a schoolboys' game that just a few years earlier would have interested almost no one beyond the players' classmates and girlfriends. With Yale leading 6–4, the referee suspended the contest, due to darkness, and then reluctantly declared it a 0–0 draw (as it remains in the record books) because it ended short of the required two forty-five-minute halves due to a forty-minute delay while the teams disputed over the referee. All the major New York newspapers covered the game, some on the front page, including the *New York Sun*. Reporting on a "foot-ball" game when it was still a novelty, the *Sun*'s anonymous writer offered readers little more than impressions of violent chaos, with little attempt to explain the overall confusion.

I pick up the account with Yale leading 6–0, having just scored a touchdown (four points) in the opening three minutes and added the goal kick

6 NEW YORK HERALD SUNDAY, NOVEMBER 29, 1896. COLORED SUPPLEMENT.

THE MODERN GLADIATORS.

Figure 1.1. C. R. McCauley cartoon, "The Modern Gladiators," in *New York Herald*, Colored Supplement, November 29, 1896. San Francisco Academy of Comic Art Collection, The Ohio State University, Billy Ireland Cartoon Library and Museum.

(two points): "The ball was taken back to the centre of the field and the fight went on."[1] Spectators could see "writhing heaps" of players and "threatening attitudes, fists shaken in front of noses, dartings hither and thither as when hounds are after a fox, throttling, wrestling, and the pitching of individuals headlong to the earth." Those on the field (including the reporters) "saw something more. They saw real fighting, savage blows that drew blood, and falls that seemed as though they must crack all the bones and drive the life out of those who sustained them; and eyes were getting wilder all the time, and the work was waxing every moment hotter." After Princeton scored but missed the goal kick, narrowing Yale's lead to 6–4,

> the sides relinquished the last of such restraint as may up to this time have remained with them, and let themselves out utterly. There came a crush on one of the edges of the field about midway between the goals. All the maddened giants of both the teams were in it, and they lay heaped, kicking, choking, hitting, gouging, and howling. One smaller man lay under them. He held the ball hugged to his breast and pressed it to the ground. His chin rested upon it, and his white face looked out from the ruck as the face of a man might look who was on the rack.

The writer dwelled on this scene as if it were the chief drama of the game. The players of both teams, "their dirty canvas-jackets and knickerbockers . . . streaked and flecked with blood," stood around, aimlessly, until they removed the young man, Captain Richards of Yale, from the field, to be put to bed and attended by surgeons. Play then resumed, with more impressions of random violence, including what sounds like a Princeton player's concussion—lying motionless for a minute after his "head seemed to have been driven into the earth"—and the same player's dislocated shoulder five minutes later. Also, a Yale player dropped to the turf, "as though he had been shot," after a Princeton man slugged him in the face. The account concluded, anticlimactically, with that forty-minute delay that led to the suspension of play.

CREATING A COLLISION SPORT

That 1884 Yale–Princeton game, as described in the *New York Sun*, reads today more like a rough-and-tumble brawl than a sport that anyone would recognize as football, and it appears to have seemed that way to the reporter as well. From this account, it is frankly difficult to understand how football became so popular, so quickly. This contest was just the third between the two rival schools since Walter Camp's proposals of 1880 and 1882 completed the decisive break from the British Rugby Union Code. Most of the initial code's sixty-one rules involved technical details about goals and fair catches, place kicks, punt-outs, and the like. But Rule 57 read, "No hacking or hacking over [the difference not explained] or tripping up shall be allowed under any circumstances." And Rule 59 specified that there "shall be two judges, one for each side, and also a referee, to whom disputed points shall be referred, and whose decisions shall be final." Parke Davis, the chief chronicler of football's early history, found this rule significant enough to warrant an asterisk, with an explanation at the bottom of the page: "Entirely new. Under the Rugby Union Code the captains acted as officials."[2]

From the beginning, then, American football was a rough, physical sport that required an impartial judge to assure that it did not become *too* rough, because the players could not be trusted to govern themselves (as young British gentlemen playing Rugby Union could). The annual conventions of the member institutions repeatedly tried to limit the new game's violence. Amendments approved in October 1880 (in addition to the more momentous creation of the "scrimmage," assigning possession of the ball to one side) added a penalty for "fouls when judged to be intentional by a referee." At the October 1882 convention (more important for the down-and-distance rule), the representatives instructed referees to disqualify anyone warned twice for tripping or "foul tackling" (again unexplained). No more rules regarding contact fouls were added until February 1885, when, after a long debate, the members rejected Walter Camp's proposal for a five-yard "neutral zone" between the rush lines, to reduce "slugging," but agreed to penalize slugging with two points for "the offended side." The following October, a second warning for "unnecessary roughness" was made grounds for disqualification. In March 1887, the captains from Harvard, Yale, Princeton, Pennsylvania, and Wesleyan signed a pledge "to use all means in our power to coach our teams to stop holding in the rush line, slugging, and all other objectionable features of the game." At a second meeting two months later, the rules committee added an additional referee for better enforcement.[3]

Clearly, "unnecessary roughness" and "slugging" were problems in American football from the very beginning, which successive revisions of the rules failed to eliminate. The overriding problem lay partly in the players' disdain for inconvenient rules (thus the need for impartial referees) but also in the game itself, which was created with the possession and five-yard rules. Assigning possession of the ball to one team set up players from the opposing sides across from each other, like rival armies, instead of huddled in a "scrum," scrambling for the ball. It also created a problem of determining how the team with the ball could advance it. Rugby rules required players on the side possessing the ball to remain *behind* the ball in order to be "on-side." By the original scrimmage rule of 1880, when the man with the ball "snapped" it back to the "quarter-back," the other players on the offense had to be lined up behind him. (That's how the *quarter*-back got his name.) The man receiving the ball could advance it or pass it off, but only if his teammates all remained behind him or behind the man who ended up with the ball. Offside play became an immediate problem, requiring the October 1881 convention to decree a handful of new rules: Should a player be offside when the ball was snapped, it would be snapped again; three offsides on the same down would lose the ball to the other team; a player would be disqualified on his third warning for "intentional off-side playing." In October 1883, the convention agreed to allow a third warning before disqualification, and then two months later it reimposed disqualification after two.[4]

Offside play led inevitably to what everyone now knows as *blocking*, one of the fundamental elements of American football. Writing in 1911 about the early rule against offside play, Parke Davis explained that "custom gradually had been nullifying this rule with the evolution of 'guarding' and 'warding' into 'interference.' The interferers originally were restrained at the side of the runner, but as officials relaxed in enforcing the rule against off-side play the interferers gradually moved more and more forward until finally they preceded the runner and the rule against such a formation was considered dead."[5] Davis used words like "custom," "evolution," and "relaxed" enforcement to describe as a natural process what, in fact, was systematic violation of a fundamental rule, abetted by lax officiating, which was finally rescinded because it was unwanted and unenforceable. Finally, in 1888, when players were expressly forbidden to interfere with their "hands or arms," but nothing was said about shoulders or torsos, blocking became tacitly legalized, and the offensive and defensive rush lines became the shock troops of opposing armies.

A second major rule revision in 1888, to allow low tackling, was more intentional. Here, the rationale was less urgent but the consequences equally profound. The original rule that required tackling above the hips gave an advantage to speedy ball carriers, able to elude defenders who had to get close enough to grasp their upper torsos securely. After the decisive rule changes in 1880 and 1882, rugby-style "open" play continued: backs running wide (with technically offside blockers clearing the way) and throwing long lateral passes to teammates. (That 1884 Yale–Princeton game was played under these rules, despite the conspicuous absence of "open" play in the account in the *Sun*.) With the 1888 rule permitting tackles between the hips and knees, tacklers could launch their bodies from farther away and more easily bring down speedy backs. At the same time, the prohibition against interfering with the hands and arms meant that the offensive rush line, which typically spread itself nearly across the breadth of the field with arms extended, was now packed closer together, shoulder to shoulder, with the backs bunched close behind them, "for the quick plunges into the line that the new game required," as Parke Davis explained.[6] Pounding the ball into the middle of the defense (behind those now legal blockers) became the most efficient way to advance the ball five yards in three tries. I belabor these details because they illustrate how football evolved partly by accident and unintended consequences. "Mass" football replaced "open" football almost overnight: maximum offensive weight and force directed at a single point of attack in the defense, with all of the resulting damage to unpadded faces, heads, and bodies that one would expect. As Parke Davis put it in 1911, "And thus passed the beautiful, open style of game recalled so fondly by the older generation of collegians, and in its place came the mass play, ugly and uncouth in construction, but which, designed to be useful rather than handsome, overcame the low tackle and won its long list of victories."[7]

Within a decade, American football had become fundamentally neither a kicking (soccer) nor a running and lateral-passing (rugby) game but a blocking and tackling game. A *collision* sport. And with "mass" football came the challenge that would haunt the game down to the present day: to determine how much violence was tolerable, even necessary, for football to be football.

GAMBOLING PRIZEFIGHTERS

"Capt. Richards of Yale," the young man badly injured in the 1884 Yale–Princeton game, was Eugene L. Richards Jr., who five months later wrote an impassioned defense of football in the sporting monthly *Outing*, challenging the game's detractors for being merely "jealous" or "ignorant" of the game. The ignorant ones, mostly "gray-haired" professors, according to young Richards, declared football "dangerous and brutal" without ever having witnessed a contest. (He likely had in mind the Harvard faculty, who, the day before the Yale–Princeton game, had voted overwhelmingly to abolish football after the school's own recent game with Princeton had degenerated into a "slugging match."[8] That ban would last for one year.) Richards considered the jealous ones to be the "more dangerous," because "wiser," critics. They were chiefly prizefighters and the "sports" (gamblers) who followed them, who "pretend to decry [football] because it is rough," as if they were allies of the religious press on a "crusade against immorality," when their true concern was simply the competition for customers. According to Richards, the game of football that "reporters have portrayed as the playful gamboling of twenty-two prize-fighters" was, in fact, "the most manly and the most scientific sport in existence." "Manly" and "scientific" denoted two very different dimensions of American football. The "scientific" game was Walter Camp's chess-like match of wits and strategies. It was the "manly" game that young Richards emphasized when he wrote that, in a civilization that cared more "for the development of our pockets" than for "the development of our bodies," it made no sense "to be squeamish about a broken collar-bone," when "the majority . . . are receiving lasting benefits from athletics, which will insure us, as a nation, against physical degeneration."[9]

Richards offered no novel ideas here but rather summed up what was already an entrenched debate between those who declared football no better than prizefighting and those who declared it essential for personal and national manhood. Support for the argument that the game was "dangerous and brutal," like prizefighting, came not just from supposedly clueless professors but also from the game itself, in the ubiquitous "slugging" that was openly visible to everyone watching. As the account in the *Sun* made clear, to understand, or even just to see clearly, what was happening on the field was a major challenge for football's early spectators, but "slugging"—fists cocked and flying—was conspicuous. Newspapers began to report on slugging in games at least by 1883, when Joseph Pulitzer's *New York World* titled its account of the Yale–Princeton game "Fighting at Football" and noted a recently published "Harvard edict" that declared "college foot-ball . . . but a sort of disguised series of 'slugging' encounters."[10] (Harvard's faculty and its president, Charles W. Eliot, were football's chief institutional critics over the 1880s and 1890s, while Yale backed whatever Walter Camp wanted, usually with Princeton's support.)[11]

An editorial in the *New York Times* condemned that 1884 Yale–Princeton contest as nothing more than "a rough-and-tumble fight."[12] Two years later, another Yale–Princeton game was marked by "the roughest kind of 'slugging.'"[13] In 1887, the *Times* denounced "Wesleyan's Football Sluggers" for seeming to play by the principle "Slug all you can; throw the men on their head and jump on them."[14] And so on and so on. By the 1890s, slugging had become virtually a distinctive style of play for some teams or in some games, sometimes announced in such headlines as these in 1890 and 1891: "Rough Play at Football" (Penn's "exhibition of 'slugging'" against Columbia), "Fighting Football Players" (Williams College's "exhibition of 'muckerism,'" with "low tricks, kicking,

Figure 1.2. Victor Gillam cartoon, "A Slugger's Comment on College Foot-Ball," in *Judge*, November 30, 1889.

and slugging in general"), "Rough Play Won the Game" (after Chicago beat Cornell "by individual play and 'slugging'").[15] New York papers sometimes highlighted the *absence* of slugging as a game's remarkable feature.[16]

As Captain Richards complained, football slugging brought comparisons to prizefighting in arguments both for and against the game that would continue sporadically into the 1950s. The justification *for* football was that damaging the opponent was incidental, not its sole purpose, as in prizefighting. The charge *against* football was that supposed "gentlemen" who slugged were behaving no better than lowborn prizefighters. "Football or Prize Fights?" asked a headline in the *New York Evening World* in 1889 and then again in 1891.[17] "This Was Not Football" ("it looked more like a prize fight") declared the *New York Times* in 1891.[18] A full-page cartoon in the humor magazine *Judge* in 1889 (fig. 1.2) had John L. Sullivan offering "A Slugger's Comment on College Foot-Ball" to a battered young player: "If that kind of work is eddication, young feller, I orta be a perfesher at Yale, m'self." (Sullivan was reputed to have declared after watching Harvard play Yale, "There's murder in that game.")[19]

While agreeing with critics that slugging had no place in football, defenders of the sport blamed the press for exaggerating the violence. Captain

Richards's complaint about reporters' portraying college football as "the playful gamboling of twenty-two prize-fighters" developed into a more general denunciation of "newspaper sensationalism,"[20] which poses an obvious question here: Was the game truly brutal, not just rough, or did the press amplify the violence out of proportion to the reality? The most plausible answer would have to be *both*. Injuries and fatalities reported in the press were real, not made up. But the rhetorical excesses and ghoulish illustrations of the modern newspaper developed in the 1890s by Joseph Pulitzer and his imitators and rivals (preeminently, William Randolph Hearst after purchasing the *New York Journal* in 1895) highlighted and exaggerated the violence, for the sake of circulations, the way television would do a century later, for the sake of ratings. In either case, whether real or exaggerated, the violence *appealed* to readers and spectators.

MASS + MOMENTUM = MAYHEM

Condemnations and advocacy did not echo in a vacuum; games were played, and players were injured and occasionally died, though usually far removed from the lives of those reading about it. Football's formative years were marked by a single continuing crisis over its violence, which swelled and subsided like an irregular tide until the tsunami of 1905. *Or*, its seasons played out in relative calm, interrupted by crises in 1893–94, 1897, and finally 1905. In either case, those were the particular seasons when newspaper coverage of the game's violence was most sensational and football came closest to self-immolation.

The too-frequent slugging in early football violated rules that were inadequately enforced. At the same time, some of the violence was the unintended consequence of strategic innovations—the *scientific* rather than the *manly* game. The "famous 'V Trick,' the original wedge and forerunner of the mass play," as Parke Davis characterized it, was conceived by a Princeton player in 1884 but did not come into "general use" until 1888 (when efforts to ban off-side interference were finally abandoned). Initially, the V Trick was used as the opening play of the game, when the team in possession had a choice to put the ball in play by either snapping it back to a teammate or kicking it away to the opponents (this option would continue for decades). As described by Davis in 1911, the V was formed ten yards from the opponents' rush line "by the eleven players taking positions in a solid V-shaped mass, apex forward, the arms of the players encircling the bodies of one another," with the player who would put the ball in play at the apex of the V. "When all were ready the ball was technically kicked off by being touched to the toe and ground simultaneously, but without being released. The mass then started heavily forward, the player who picked up the ball disappeared within it, and the opponents charged."[21] (No paraphrase could capture the strangeness of that play.)

As Davis noted without comment, "Such a play was in direct disregard of the old rule on off-side play."[22] After 1888, with blocking fully legal, variations on the V Trick became basic running plays from scrimmage: masses of players lined up in the backfield and leading the ball carrier into the opposing line. Such plays depended on the absence of a rule requiring seven players (or *any* number of players) on the line of scrimmage when the ball was put in play. (The rules also allowed the ball carrier in the V to link arms with his blockers or even hold onto straps attached to their jerseys, as they all plunged into the line.)[23] Yet another missing rule was the one that now would declare the ball carrier "down" when he was on the ground or when his forward progress had been stopped., as in the game today. The players in the V were to push and pull until the entire mass came to a stop in a huge pileup, and even then, the man with the ball was not "down" until he could no longer crawl or squirm forward and finally called himself "Down." This meant that a runner on the ground was to be jumped on by as many defenders as needed to keep him from moving and to make him surrender.

Such "mass" plays produced piles of crushed bodies, broken collarbones and noses, and wrenched and twisted limbs. They were also rather boring to watch. To these routine *mass* plays, *momentum* was added in 1892 with the "flying wedge," the lastingly famous mass-momentum play that has come to stand for all of them in popular football history. An amateur scholar of the Napoleonic wars named Lorin F. Deland devised the play for Harvard, whose players unveiled it for the opening of the second half against Yale in November 1892. Deland's stratagem, in effect, moved the conventional V several yards farther back and sent it rushing toward Yale's stationary defense *before* the ball was put in play—to reach the defense while already moving at full speed. This is how the *Boston Globe* described it (with its one-sentence paragraphs merged into a single one). Again, a paraphrase would not do it justice:

> Capt. Trafford's men gather about him, apparently to form the orthodox V. But suddenly his 10 men leave him standing alone with the ball on the line and break into three detachments. The four biggest men on the team, Waters, Mackie, Lewis and Emmons, drop back about eight yards to the right. Lake takes his position all alone several yards in a direct line back of Trafford, and the remaining five players are grouped at the left about five yards back of the kick-off line. Through the mind

> of every Harvard man at the game there flashed the thought, "Now we are to have a Deland play." Capt. Trafford nods his head and the four big fellows at the right come tearing down toward him. . . . They are met just as they reach their captain by Lake, who comes straight down the field, and the other five men, who came at an angle. The ball is passed to Lake; he hands it to Brewer, and, the 11 men having acquired a tremendous momentum, go tearing around Yale's right end for 20 yards. It is the longest single gain Harvard has made, and there is pandemonium in the crimson grand stand.[24]

It was Harvard's longest gain in losing to Yale, 6–0. The *New York Times* concluded its account, "This is the only Harvard trick during the game which amounted to anything. It is a new wrinkle, however, and may be developed into an effective play."[25]

This "new wrinkle" was *momentum*, which was made possible by the absence of anything like today's rules on "forward motion," which allow *one* player to be moving *away* from the line of scrimmage at the snap of the ball. Deland's flying wedge to open the second half against Yale became widely adapted as a play from scrimmage the following season, and it established a template for offensive strategies over the next few years, limited only by coaches' imaginations. Against Yale in 1893, Harvard debuted its "turtle-back" play, a weirdly complicated-sounding affair described by Parke Davis as "a play executed by forming the eleven men in the shape of a solid oval against a selected point in the rush-line, usually the tackle, and at the snap of the ball into the interior of the oval rolling the mass out around the end, thus unwinding the runner into a clear field." (Try to picture *that.*) The "push-play," again as Davis explained, was "a formation similar to the turtle-back, but in which the runner was lifted on top of the mass and pushed over the opposing rush-line." Yale's mass-momentum play had just the center and two guards on the line and the remaining eight players in a wedge fifteen yards deep in the backfield, all running toward the "objective point" in the line just as the ball was snapped. Davis dryly commented that "it is needless to say that the impact was such that the objective point usually remembered it for years." Princeton lined up its ends behind the tackles; Harvard's "tackles-back" formation did just that; Penn dropped the guards back. (Davis credited Penn's coach George Woodruff more generally for "introduc[ing] the flying principle into all interference.") According to Davis, writing in 1911 about these innovations since 1894, "From that day to this the tandem-tackle principle has been the chief feature in the invention of offensive tactics."[26]

Within the confusion of nomenclature and technical details, attacking an "objective point" in the defense with a mass of moving bodies followed a brutally simple principle. Mass-momentum plays were obviously dangerous to heads, necks, and faces at the moment of impact and to limbs, ribs, and internal organs in the crush of bodies that followed. All the while, "slugging" continued to add a dollop of open brutality. Football players were "gladiators" in the 1890s in one of the era's favorite clichés (as it was for prizefighters, too), sometimes in passing ("Princeton's gladiators," "the gladiators of Harvard and Yale"), occasionally spun out in wildly extended metaphors that now read more like parody.[27] Writers could use the figure of the gladiator either to glorify or to denounce football: thumbs up or thumbs down on the game's violence. (Is the conquering gladiator from the *New York Herald* in November 1896 in figure 1.1 heroic or barbaric?) For some, football marked a regression into barbarism; for others, a reclamation of primitive manhood threatened by modern civilization.

PERSONAL ENCOUNTERS

Football became more violent in the 1890s partly because players simply ignored the ban on slugging; partly as an unintended consequence of the rules that legalized blocking and low tackling; partly from strategic innovations, beginning with the V and then the flying wedge, which added mass and momentum to routine plays; and partly from the absence of rules (limiting mass and momentum or declaring a runner down) that have long seemed fundamental. The resulting violence always had its fierce critics but also its equally impassioned defenders who decried slugging and other forms of foul play but, above all, wanted a *manly* game. Against the persistent attacks by distinguished critics such as Harvard president Charles W. Eliot and editor of the *New York Evening Post* E. L. Godkin, and as violence was becoming more graphic in Pulitzer's *World* (fig. 1.3) and other large-circulation daily newspapers, writers continued to rise to the game's defense.[28] Describing his "First Glimpse at Football," in *Frank Leslie's Illustrated Newspaper* after the 1892 season, a journalist named Philip Poindexter stated the case simply: "To bear pain without flinching, and to laugh at the wounds and the scars of a hotly-contested game, is very good discipline, and tends to develop manliness of character."[29]

A year later in *Harper's Weekly*, a young Theodore Roosevelt, currently serving as commissioner of the US Civil Service, proclaimed "The Value of an Athletic Training" for young men and for the country. In the first of his many pronouncements on rough sports like football with which he would be identified as president, Roosevelt denounced "slugging" and "kindred brutality" but insisted that, "after every precaution has been taken, then it is mere unmanliness to complain of occasional mishaps." From the "mishaps," in fact, came the manly qualities: "resolution, courage, endurance, and capacity to hold one's own and to stand up under punishment." Roosevelt himself had been too small and sickly for football at Harvard, but after his own man-making adventure in

Figure 1.3. "What the Public Sees of the College Course," *New York World,* November 26, 1893. The central image of Death gathering its victims is captioned "The Main Study."

the Dakota Badlands after college, he could now more confidently declare that "the sports especially dear to a vigorous and manly nation are always those in which there is a certain slight element of risk. Every effort should be made to minimize this risk, but it is mere unmanly folly to try to do away with the sport because the risk exists."[30]

University professors and presidents echoed Roosevelt's views in prestigious journals.[31] The father of the young man who was battered in the Yale–Princeton game in 1884, a professor of mathematics at Yale, captured most clearly the cultural argument for football in *Popular Science Monthly* in October 1894. In his article for *Outing*, Richards Jr. had praised football as a "manly" sport for its "development of our bodies." Nine years later, Richards Sr. praised it for developing "manly *character*" (my emphasis). "If there is one virtue most to be desired in a manly character—without which, indeed, it ceases to be manly—that virtue is courage," Professor Richards declared. "And of the college sports there is not one which cultivates this manly virtue more than football." Junior had simply loved the rough-and-tumble of a football game (likely its primary appeal, with no loftier purpose, for most of the boys and young men who played football in its early years). Senior insisted that in the game's routine collisions, which might seem brutal to "timid people" but were "tame fun" to schoolboys, there was more than fun at stake. "Personal encounters of some kind seem absolutely necessary to the education of young men," wrote the professor (of mathematics, not of medicine or philosophy), "especially young men of the strongest characters. Such young men, judiciously trained, constitute the best citizens of a State. A State full of such citizens becomes thereby the safest to live in, for such men are the best defense."[32]

Personal encounters were the essence of football, the "gamboling of twenty-two prize-fighters" viewed heroically. Eight months earlier, in his annual report to the Board of Overseers, as excerpted in the press, President Eliot had declared that "the natural tendency of all sports which involve violent personal collision between the players, as in foot-ball," was to become "brutal and brutalizing."[33] Richards, however, insisted that "personal encounters" produced "young men of the strongest characters," not by inflicting violence on opposing players but by *restraint*: "If violent encounters on the football field do lead to the temptation of inflicting needless personal injuries on an opponent, they also give opportunities for resisting this temptation, and consequently for the development of the highest forms of courage and self-control."[34] (In December, E. L. Godkin wrote an editorial explicitly mocking Professor Richards's claims for "personal encounters.")[35] Here was the most fundamental justification for football violence in the game's formative period: *taking it*, to use the colloquial term, built character (and distinguished football from the brutality of prizefighting). Football's violence required, and therefore fostered, not more violence but *restraint*. This give-and-take over personal collisions/personal encounters summed up the competing views on football violence that would mark the game's history for the next half century.

A WASP GENTLEMAN'S GAME

These competing ideas were published in 1894, following the introduction of mass-momentum plays from scrimmage in 1893 that elevated the game's routine violence. In May 1894, a newly formed rules committee consisting of representatives from just Harvard, Yale, Princeton, and Penn responded with several revisions to make the game safer: shortening the contest from ninety to seventy minutes, divided into two halves (for the players to recuperate); requiring that the ball be kicked at least ten yards forward on a kickoff, rather than snapped back to a teammate (to eliminate the flying wedge); penalizing any "piling up upon a runner after he has cried down or the referee has blown his whistle." (The runner would still have to cry, "Down," not just *be* down, for piling on to stop.) The new rules also decreed, "No momentum mass play shall be allowed," but they defined such a play as "one in which more than three men start before the ball is put in play" or "more than three men group for that purpose more than five yards back of the point where the ball is put in play."[36] Whether to placate critics or to make the game truly safer, mass momentum would survive, but with somewhat less mass and momentum.

Walter Camp was the architect of that compromise, and just as he had been the driving force in devising the rules that created American football, he became the driving force in preserving it from reformers' tampering. In the winter and spring of 1894, Camp assembled a committee of distinguished representatives from Harvard, Yale, Princeton, and one secondary school to lend their authority to a survey of former and current players about their experiences and injuries. The compiled results from nearly a thousand respondents, along with reprinted articles such as Professor Richards's on "personal encounter," were published as *Football Facts and Figures* in November, just in time for the season's big games. All but 9 of 337 former players at the three universities reported that they had benefited from playing football, as did 357 of the 359 current players at all colleges. Just three from the former group and one from the latter claimed to have suffered a permanent injury.[37]

The book also reprinted letters sent to Camp with survey responses, most of them echoing the usual arguments about broken bones being a small price, the valuable lessons of self-control, and the like.[38] The majority of these men had played before the rules on blocking and low tackling in 1888 transformed their cherished "open" game into "mass" play. (Several of them urged reforms to bring back the football they remembered so warmly.) Whether any *current* players had received a "permanent" injury could hardly be known.

It turns out that Camp did not report *all* the facts and figures. The sports historian Ronald Smith discovered that Camp had omitted comments from his correspondents that reflected badly on football.[39] Even altered, Camp's book did nothing to settle the debate. The ineffectiveness of the reforms adopted in May became painfully evident in the Harvard–Yale game on November 24, 1894, which featured, in the words of Caspar Whitney, the influential sports editor at *Harper's Weekly* (and author of its Amateur Sport column from 1891 through 1899), "the best football, the most perfectly drilled eleven [Yale's], the most telling team-play Harvard has yet shown, and the most vicious spirit I have **ever** seen displayed in a contest between the two elevens" (boldface in original).[40] Like Roosevelt, Whitney viewed "professionalism" as football's greater problem, and he scorned criticism of football's fundamental roughness.[41] His ideal was the British gentleman sportsman, who would rather lose than sully his honor (and who, having won at birth, had no need to win at mere games). Professionalism and brutality were equally affronts to the "gentlemen's game." In a column earlier that season, Whitney had insisted that the first key to preserving "hard, clean football" from becoming "a foul, 'dirty'" game lay primarily in "getting gentlemen on the team, and men who have an honest right to be there" (as opposed to ringers recruited for their physical prowess). Whitney's second requirement was for an additional umpire, "to rule men off on the very first evidence of slugging," a strange necessity for a game supposedly played mostly by "gentlemen."[42]

"Gentlemen" was a pervasive term in the justifications for football in this era, and whether it referred to behavior or to social position was not always clear, since they were assumed to be linked. Over time, as the game became democratized at public colleges and universities, the term would necessarily refer to behavior—a measure of the social respectability available to ordinary boys and young men through college football in an era when just a tiny percentage of the citizenry attended college (around 2 percent in 1920). A gentleman would "take it" and show restraint; a brute would "slug."

The toll from the Harvard–Yale game that provoked Whitney's outrage included a dislocated collarbone, a broken nose, two head injuries (presumably mild concussions), a "contusion of the brain" (a more serious concussion, perhaps a subdural hematoma) that left a Yale player still unconscious as the newspapers went to press. Also, two disqualifications for slugging. The press, conspicuously including the religious press, was scathing.[43] In his column a week later, Whitney offered his most extended reflections on football violence. Responding to the criticism aroused by the contest, Whitney acknowledged that "the game permits unnecessary roughness and occasional brutal exhibitions," but he insisted that brutality was "by no means an essential of football play," only "a quality of personal instinct." In other words, only brutes were brutal. To critics who declared football "too dangerous to life and limb," Whitney answered this way: "First of all, the history of the world over reveals the fact that those games with a certain element of danger have been the most fascinating and the most popular, and this will remain true so long as the Anglo Saxon race inhabits the globe."[44]

Whitney made explicit the racial chauvinism that champions of "manly" football usually just implied, though he was not alone. Senator Henry Cabot Lodge, Theodore Roosevelt's Harvard classmate, would echo Whitney in a talk at Harvard's commencement dinner in June 1896, when he told the graduates, "The time given to athletic contests and the injuries incurred on the playing-field are part of the price which the English speaking race has paid for being world-conquerors."[45] Writing in *Outing* in December 1900, near the onset of the United States' imperial adventures, yet another Harvard man, W. Cameron Forbes (once player and coach, future governor-general of the Philippines and ambassador to Japan), would call football "the expression of the strength of the Anglo-Saxon . . . the dominant spirit of a dominant race."[46]

Though usually unspoken, writing about "manliness" was *always* about white manliness, because that was what the writers assumed in an era when a mere handful of young Black men played at supposedly integrated colleges, and immigrants of questionable whiteness from southern and eastern Europe had not yet transformed (and democratized) the game.[47] The appearance in New York, in 1895, of a team representing the Carlisle Indian Industrial School thus registered a profound shock to the football world. In 1893, students at the boarding school (part of the federal government's effort to erase Indigenous cultures) asked the superintendent, Captain R. H. Pratt, to restore football after he had dropped it the previous year when a player's leg was broken. Pratt agreed, but on two conditions: first, "that you will never under any circumstances, slug. That you will play fair straight through, and if the other fellows slug you will in no case return it. Can't you see that if you slug, people who are looking on will say, 'There, that's the Indian of it. Just see them. They are savages and you can't get it out of them.'" (The second condition was that they would one day "whip the biggest football team in the country." They would fulfill both demands.)[48]

After playing a couple of local high schools in 1893 and then a handful of small Pennsylvania colleges, plus Navy, in 1894, Carlisle joined the big time in 1895 by adding Penn and Yale on their home fields, along with a team representing the Manhattan YMCA after Thanksgiving, in the presence of the New York press. The *World* reported afterward that the Indians disappointed spectators who expected them to show up "in a few stripes of warpaint, waving tomahawks and knives." The writer himself was most struck by "the spirit with which they played," particularly when they protested so little the three obviously "unfair decisions by the referee." The writer decided that the Indians needed "more aggressiveness," not less. "They play fast and hard football, but that recklessness to tackling and danger so essential to success is lacking. To speak plainly, the Indians play too fair. It would naturally be supposed that desperate vindictiveness would be their strong point. When Metoxen was carried off the field with a wrenched knee he surprised everybody by blubbering with pain. So much for the inherent stoicism of the race."[49]

The Indians who invaded Manhattan Field in 1895 were assumed to be savages but instead played like gentlemen, confounding the white Anglo spectators who expected players on *their* teams to *be* gentlemen but play *like* savages. Though unstated in this account, lacking aggressiveness implicitly also made Carlisle less "manly," but Pratt was surely right that overaggressiveness would be construed as "savagery." Carlisle could not win on these terms, but its team went on to become a sentimental favorite among New York fans for several more seasons, easy to romanticize as a "vanishing race" that posed no threat to white dominance.[50]

PROTECTING THE HEAD

Football's roughness was not just an idea over which opposing sides argued; it was also a reality that players had to deal with, however much they might claim to relish it. The advent of flying tackles and mass-momentum plays made protecting the head particularly urgent and a particular challenge. While players could sew a bit of padding into the shoulders of their sweaters, the best they could do initially for their exposed heads was grow their hair long, resulting in the mop-topped football player who became the delight of cartoonists in the 1890s.[51] According to Parke Davis, players' long hair "was defended at the time by the assertion that it was done for protection" but was, in fact, simply a Princeton player's joke in 1890 that caught on and became the fashion for four years, ending when Yale showed up close-shorn against Princeton in 1895 but lingering on as "the comic type of the football player." (See fig. 1.4.)[52]

Joke or not, players increasingly felt a need to protect themselves. The first piece of manufactured protective equipment (apart from canvas jackets and moleskin pants) was a "nose mask" produced around 1890 by A. G. Spalding & Co. (fig. 1.5): a rubber cup strapped over the nose, with holes for breathing (another easy target for cartoonists).[53] Spalding brought out its first "football caps" (similar to modern stocking caps) in 1891, made from either silk or knitted wool, plain or striped (and one model with a tassel at the end of a flopped-over top for the fashion-conscious gladiator), which purportedly provided "absolute protection" for players "suffering with sore ears."[54]

Noses and ears, not heads, were clearly the body parts initially most felt at risk by the players themselves. (Prizefighters were not the only ones concerned about developing cauliflower ears.) Credit for the first helmet worn

Figure 1.4. Samuel D. Erhard's cover for *Puck*, November 23, 1898, showing both mop-top and nose guard. Library of Congress.

in a football game has been given to James Naismith (better known as the inventor of basketball), while playing for the YMCA Training School in 1891, and to Navy's Joseph Mason Reeves (a future admiral) in 1893. Naismith's was simply a wide band of flannel worn around his head and ears, with a strap to secure it, for protecting a damaged ear. Reeves's was a thickly padded cap that a local shoemaker constructed for him after he suffered serious head injuries the previous season, making it football's first actual head (rather than ear) protection.[55] Spalding's first commercial "head harness," in 1894, was also designed more for protecting ears than heads: just four leather straps, attached to a band around the head, with leather flaps to protect either one ear or two

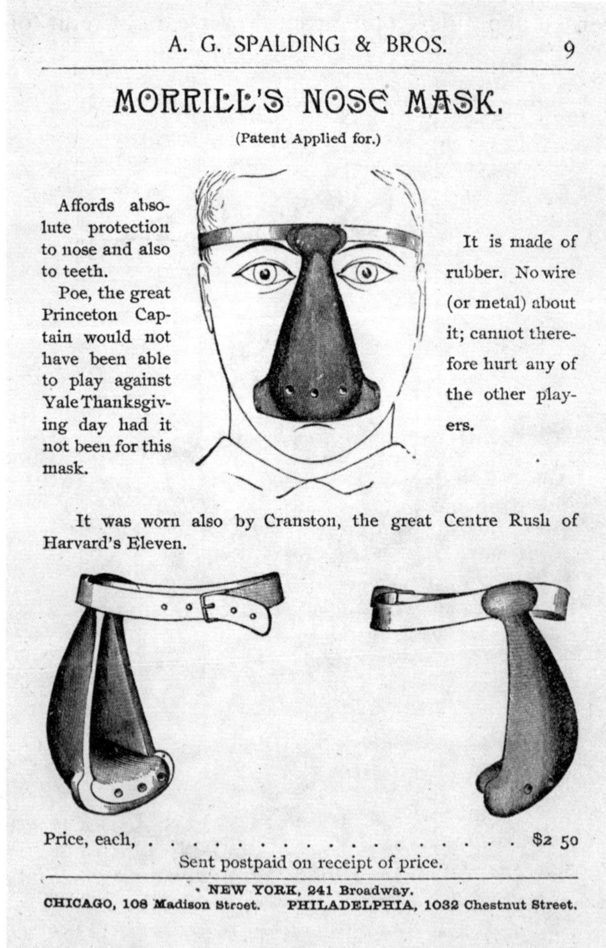

Figure 1.5. Ad in *Spalding's Official Foot Ball Guide*, 1891. Reproduced from the original held by the Department of Special Collections of the Hesburgh Libraries of the University of Notre Dame. Spalding continued to market the nose mask through the 1910s.

Figure 1.6. Ad in *Spalding's Official Foot Ball Guide*, 1894. Reproduced from the original held by the Department of Special Collections of the Hesburgh Libraries of the University of Notre Dame.

(fig. 1.6). These early efforts are most striking today for their comic inadequacy, but they are important for signaling players' felt need for protection. Spalding brought out its first hard-leather, cap-style head harness in 1899, and the company would continue to introduce new models in variations of both types—straps or caps, hard or soft leather, padded or unpadded—over the next several years.[56] These were the helmets worn by nostalgically remembered "leatherheads."

Players' efforts to protect themselves in order to play what was, after all, a *game* were immediately seized on by cartoonists. In 1891 and 1893, Grant Hamilton imagined the armored player of the future in two brilliant cartoons for *Judge*, one a double-page centerfold and the other a full-page back cover (figs. 1.7a–b). Cartoonists, of course, depend on viewers to be familiar with their subjects in order to get the joke. These cartoons make it clear that the public understood violence to be a distinctive feature of the game, perhaps the *most* distinctive feature (as opposed, say, to the disputes over eligibility and professionalism that roiled universities and amateur purists like Caspar Whitney but did not matter to the general public at all).

By 1897, a fully padded football player could wear a primitive helmet with ear shields, nose guard, mouth protector, shoulder braces, wrist supporters, and shin guards. It cannot be known how the public felt about the need for all of this "football armor," or whether it offered reassurance that players were safe, but at least one former star of the 1880s saw it as an affront to the game he cherished. Harry Beecher (grandson of the famous clergyman Henry Ward Beecher and grandnephew of the author of *Uncle Tom's Cabin*) had been a freshman teammate of Captain Richards in 1884 and was himself Yale's captain in 1887. Now a journalist for the *New York World*, Beecher mourned the passing of the exhilarating "open" play of his own era, when no such "armor" was required. The game that he knew rewarded speed and quickness, not brute strength, and every player was so carefully trained "that each muscle and bone of his body would be able to bear its shocks without unnatural guards." (Beecher had obviously not been a medical student.) He charged that the new protective equipment "coddles the muscles" and makes

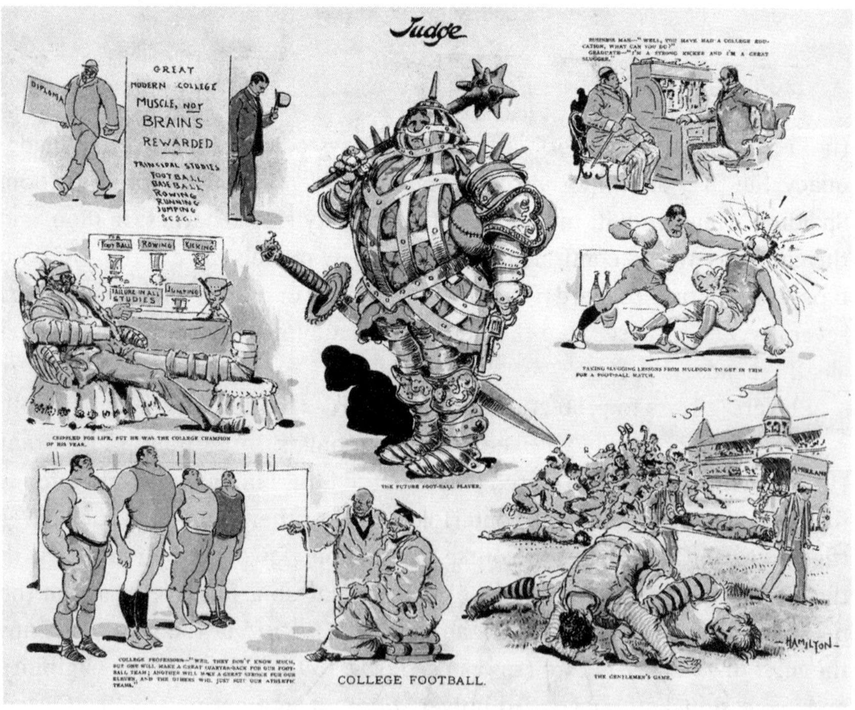

Figure 1.7a. Grant Hamilton, "College Football," cartoon in *Judge*, November 21, 1891.

Figure 1.7b. Grant Hamilton, "College Foot-Ball Craze," cartoon in *Judge*, November 30, 1893.

them "unable to bear their share of strain when unguarded." Implicitly, that would undermine the manliness of the player who "must take his chances in a game which by nature is conceded to be rough." In other words, players' pads and shields were not objectionable because the game's increased violence had made them necessary but because they undermined the players' challenge to *take it*, unaided. Beecher acknowledged that getting rid of modern football armor would require changing the rules, so as to eliminate mass play, but in the meantime, he was adamantly opposed to "this kindergarten show of protection in a game that requires no protection."[57] How ironic that the mass play assailed for brutality was "kindergarten football" to an advocate for open play.

Figure 1.8. Cartoon accompanying Harry Beecher, "Football Player of '97 Armored Like a Knight of Old," from *New York World* Sunday magazine, October 17, 1897.

Everyone who valued football agreed on wanting a rough and "manly" game but not on what that entailed or on the rules to maintain it.[58]

VON GAMMON, RIP

Beecher's complaints about football armor appeared in the *World*'s Sunday magazine on October 17, 1897. Two weeks later, a player for the University of Georgia, Richard Von Albade Gammon (known to all as Von Gammon) died from a fractured skull suffered in a routine pileup (not a mass-momentum play) in a game against the University of Virginia. Georgia immediately disbanded its football team, as did George Tech and Mercer University, while both houses of the Georgia General Assembly, already in session, passed bills to ban football in the state. Gammon's death was a fatality far from the center of the football world, but it fueled the ongoing controversies there. None of the major contests among Harvard, Yale, Princeton, and Penn had yet been played (they always came in November), but football violence had already become an issue in New York newspapers. On October 13, prompted by no specific event, the *New York Evening World* had invited readers to respond to a question, "Do You Think Football a Brutal Sport?" and published letters from readers, pro and con, on four subsequent days. On October 23, in reporting on the Yale–Carlisle game, the *Evening World* prominently featured a tally of the injured players from each team, under the provocative headline, "The Injured Players—None of Them Will Die."[59] A week later, Von Gammon *did* die.

After another week passed, Hearst's *American Magazine* Sunday supplement published a spectacularly graphic illustration of the fatal injuries of Gammon in Georgia and two young men in the New York area, accompanied by statements from the author of the anti-football bill in Georgia and a medical doctor calling on college authorities to intervene (fig. 1.9a). On Monday, the *New York Herald* began publishing daily reminders of football lethality leading up to the Harvard–Yale game on Saturday, concluding on the day of the game with a "List of Victims of Savage Tackling and Brutal Mass Play during Part of the Seasons of 1896 and 1897." (The *Herald* listed the nine deaths and twenty-six serious injuries "with the sole purpose of arousing public spirit to reform a noble sport and rescue it from a brutality which is only paralleled by the exhibitions in the Coliseum of ancient Rome, where men died to gratify the savage instincts of onlookers.")[60]After all of this, the Harvard–Yale game itself was anticlimactic, a scoreless tie and a "Clean and Manly Contest from Beginning to End."[61] But the *Herald* nonetheless identified the three players injured in the game (all from Harvard). The *World* named six; the *Evening*

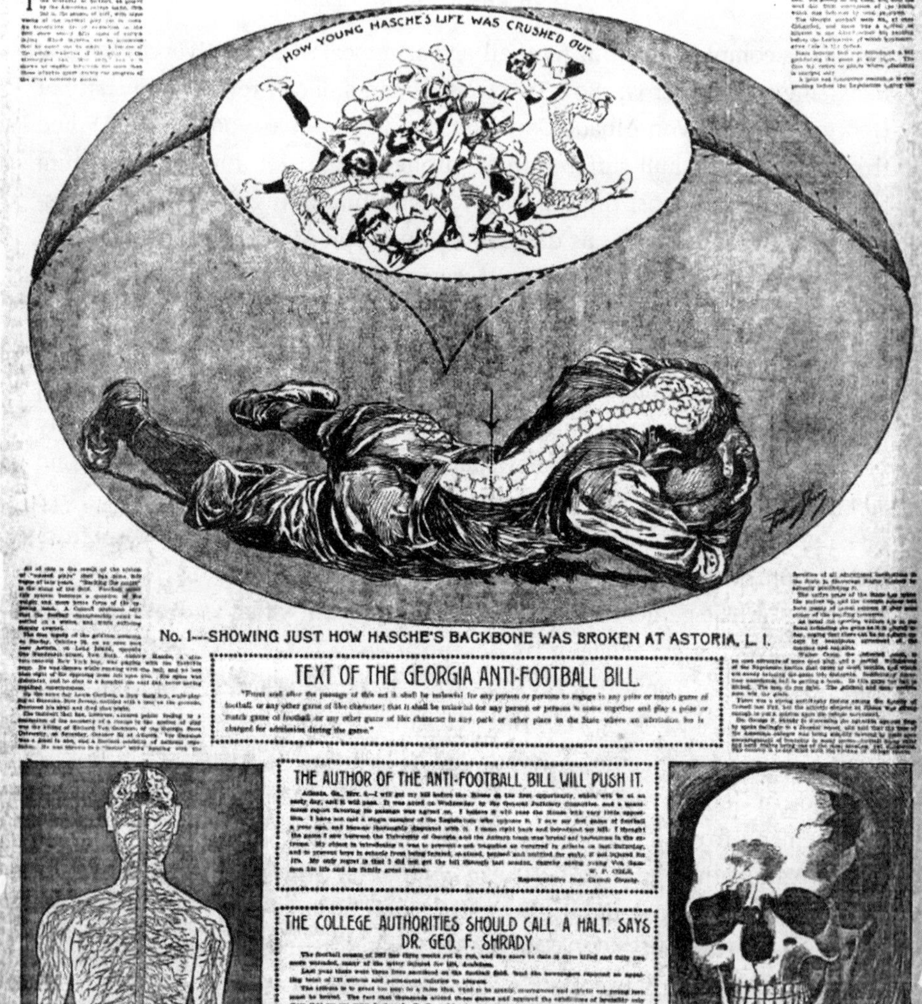

NEW YORK JOURNAL, SUNDAY, NOVEMBER 7, 1897.

A LAW TO MAKE FOOTBALL A CRIME!

The Three Recent Deaths on the Football Field Result in a Bill in Georgia's Legislature Forbidding the Game as Brutal and Barbarous.

No. 1---SHOWING JUST HOW HASCHE'S BACKBONE WAS BROKEN AT ASTORIA, L. I.

TEXT OF THE GEORGIA ANTI-FOOTBALL BILL.

THE AUTHOR OF THE ANTI-FOOTBALL BILL WILL PUSH IT.

THE COLLEGE AUTHORITIES SHOULD CALL A HALT, SAYS DR. GEO. F. SHRADY.

No. 2—How Von Gammon Was Killed by Concussion of the Brain—Complete Paralysis.

No. 3—How Cordona Was Killed at Bayonne, N. J., by a Fracture of the Skull.

Figure 1.9a. The deaths of Andrew Hasche from a spinal injury, Von Gammon from a concussion, and Louis Cordona from a skull fracture, as dramatized in *American Magazine* (Sunday supplement of the *New York Journal*), November 7, 1897.

World, nine. And the *World*'s front page (not to be outdone by Hearst's *American Magazine*) was dominated by a cartoon of Death as "The Twelfth Player in Every Football Game" (fig 1.9b). For its coverage of the game, the *World* solicited testimony from the recent heavyweight champion: "James J. Corbett Declares That Football Is More Brutal and Dangerous Than Prize-Fighting."[62] A week later, for Yale–Princeton, the expert critic from another dangerous sport was a Spanish matador: "'Cruel,' Says a Bull-Fighter."[63] Both the *World* and the *Evening World* began listing "Maimed and Injured" or "The Injured Players" or "Accidents" among the cascading subheads in reports on the big games involving Harvard, Yale, Princeton, and Penn. To regard all of this as an anti-football crusade by Pulitzer's morning and evening papers, rather than a strategy for building circulation during a "yellow journalism" war, would be mistaken. Three days before the Harvard–Yale game, on the same page as a story about a club player in Pittsburgh dying after being crushed in a pileup, the *Evening World* printed a cartoon mocking the legislative efforts in Georgia to ban football after the death of Von Gammon. "Kind of Football

THE TWELFTH PLAYER IN EVERY FOOTBALL GAME.

Figure 1.9b. Cartoon, "The Twelfth Player in Every Football Game," from *New York World*, November 14, 1897. Note the "score" on the football.

Which Would Be Popular with Georgia Legislators" portrayed gentlemen in top hats and waistcoats, sipping tea and relaxing on a large cushion at a sort of Edwardian football tailgate.[64]

The *World*'s cartoon put the season's death toll at eight, while another ghoulish cartoon in the *Herald* the week before claimed nine.[65] Whatever the correct number, while the cartoons and illustrations were "newspaper sensationalism," the death counts were simply news.

1905: ABOLISH OR REFORM?

That football survived the 1897 season might seem baffling on the evidence of this newspaper onslaught. It survived, in part, because Gammon was the only collegian killed on the field—the others were supposedly too young or not properly trained for the full rigors of the sport—and because fatalities and political decisions in Georgia did not truly matter in New York, Boston, or Philadelphia. In Georgia, after the House of Representatives on November 4 voted 91–3 to ban football in the state, the state senate approved the same bill, 31–3, on November 18 and sent it to the governor, who had attended the fatal game with his wife and had initially been inclined to approve the ban. The local press and the Georgia public also widely supported abolition, but possibly moved by a published letter from Gammon's mother, urging that football be saved on behalf of her son, because "it would be inexpressibly sad to have the cause he held so dear injured by his sacrifice," the governor vetoed the bill on December 8. The legislature immediately voted to override the veto but lacked the necessary two-thirds majority. Georgia and Georgia Tech would resume football in 1898.[66]

For all of the journalistic uproar, no major rule changes followed the 1897 season, just some tinkering with the number of men allowed in the backfield—another adjustment to the amount of mass allowed in "mass play." For 1898, two of the six players still permitted behind the line were required to position themselves outside the ends. For 1899, "outside" was specified to mean both feet outside the outside foot of the end (as always, anticipating efforts to evade the intention of the rules). For 1903, seven players were required on the line of scrimmage when the ball was between the twenty-five-yard lines but still only five when the ball was inside the twenty-five. (Mass play would be less dangerous closer to the goal line?) The rules committee in 1903 also banned head protectors made from "sole leather, papier-mâché, or other hard or unyielding substances" and required "shoulder guards" to be padded on the outside as well as the inside. A half century before the hard-shell plastic helmet would revolutionize blocking and tackling, football men already recognized the helmet's potential use as a weapon. For 1904, six men were required on the line for all plays, and one of the five in the backfield had to line up outside the end.[67]

While rule makers, in effect, calibrated the amount of permissible violence, critics and defenders repeated the usual arguments about either football's brutality or its invaluable roughness. In November 1900, a decline in fatalities so far that season prompted a remarkable editorial in the *New York Tribune* welcoming that news. "Football is one of the finest sports that the wit of man has ever hit upon," the writer declared, "and minor wounds and bruises are of little account in comparison with the noble emulation, spirit and zest of the contests. A broken leg or two, a twisted spine, a fracture of the skull or a concussion of the brain do not dull the zeal of the brave boys who carry the colors and emit the yells of our colleges and universities." The writer added that it would be a terrible shame to lose "these young heroes. Those who fight so gallantly on the football field are needed to fight the forces of wrong and evil on every front."[68] If the writer intended this to be bitterly ironic, that intention was not clear.

In 1901, at least one traditionalist was still celebrating football as a school for gentlemen by fostering self-restraint. In 1901, the Reverend Charles F. Thwing, president of Adelbart College and Case Western Reserve in Cleveland, laid out "the five points of the ethical Calvinism of foot-ball" in the venerable *North American Review*. Thwing's first "point" was the game's "mighty *musts*," all the things that a player *must* do: train, practice, obey the captain (writing when the captain, not a coach, still ran the team), and "keep his temper" (implicitly in the heat of rough play), which also stood alone as Thwing's fifth "point": the "self-restraint" which football developed in young men by demanding it. The game "teems with temptations to be mean" and "opportunities to do nasty things," Thwing wrote; yield to those temptations, and "character becomes mean and nasty." But resisting those temptations makes a true Christian gentleman. He recalled a student at his university in Cleveland who was about to quit the team because "he could not keep himself from doing mean things to the man opposite." President Thwing had asked him, "But don't the officials keep you from breaking the rules? 'Oh,' said he, 'I can slug the fellow or kick him, or do him up easily enough, and no official ever be the wiser.'" Reverend Thwing advised him not to quit but instead to "make himself a man worthy to play the game." Captain Richards in 1885 had viewed the violence in football as a bulwark against "physical *de*generation." Thwing saw it as an opportunity for moral *re*generation. After deciding to stay on, the student later reported that he was doing better.

Somewhat remarkably, Reverend Thwing expressed no concern about the sorry state of football, as his student described it, but rather saw the game as "a moral apprenticeship, an ethical practice school" for young men that "helps to make the finest type of the gentleman." Football "is subject to very serious evils," Thwing conceded, but due to "the conduct of the game and its incidental conditions," not to "its essential elements. Before and above these evils I would emphasize its functions in developing the gentleman of ethical character and conduct."[69] Thwing's tortuous reasoning—that football was a better game for building character because of its constant temptations to "evil" (*un*necessary roughness) than it would be without those temptations—does in fact follow from placing high value on self-restraint, on "taking it." No pain, no gain! Calvinism indeed!

No major new crises erupted in the early years of the new century, just the usual calls for eliminating, or at least reducing, routine brutality. In his annual January assessments of the 1901, 1902, and 1903 seasons, Caspar Whitney (now writing for the monthly *Outing*) reiterated his long-standing distaste for what he called "battering ram" football while affirming his tolerance for "bruised muscles, even occasional broken bones," because "we would not have it emasculated." Whitney also repeated the contempt, which he had frequently expressed in *Harper's Weekly* in the 1890s, for the "dirty players" who were "the thugs of society" rather than the "gentlemen" they ought to be, along with his pleas for better officiating to eliminate the "unchecked foul play," which "does more harm to football than a dozen broken legs."[70] Like Reverend Thwing, Whitney expected football players to be gentlemen, but he seems to have had more confidence in better officiating than in self-restraint as the key to producing them.

The 1905 season opened like any other in recent years, but it closed with football on life support. On June 28, 1905, in what would turn into a prelude to the football season, now President Theodore Roosevelt, the nation's chief spokesman for rough sport and the "strenuous life," delivered an address at his alma mater's commencement dinner on "The Harvard Spirit."[71] The president's comments about football were a small part of his talk but the part that the press would repeatedly quote over the coming football season. "I believe heartily in sport," Roosevelt told Harvard's new graduates. "I believe in outdoor games, and I do not mind in the least that they are rough games, or that those who take part in them are occasionally injured. I have no sympathy whatever with the overwrought sentimentality which would keep a young man in cotton wool, and I have a hearty contempt for him if he counts a broken arm or collar bone as of serious consequence when balanced against the chance of showing that he possesses hardihood, physical address, and courage."[72]

The sentiment was long familiar (Eugene Richards Jr. had invoked the same collarbone in 1885), and Roosevelt himself had been proclaiming it for years, but the man expressing it was now the president of the United States. As always, Roosevelt was less concerned about brutality in football than about "professionalism," that is, the "furtive" professionalism (recruiting and subsidizing players) in a supposedly amateur sport rather than the honest professionalism of prizefighters like John L. Sullivan and Mike Donovan (his own sparring partner in the White House).[73] When the president spoke at Harvard, the muckraking magazine *McClure's* was publishing a two-part series on professionalism in college football, with details about the ringers, tramp athletes, and subsidized working-class athletes at elite Northeastern colleges and even prep schools.[74] Renewed calls for reform were thus already in the air when a brutal early-season game between Penn and Swarthmore prompted the president to summon representatives from Harvard, Yale, and Princeton to the White House—including, most importantly, Yale's Walter Camp and Harvard coach William T. "Bill" Reid. At the meeting on October 9, as the *Washington Post* reported, Roosevelt impressed upon the sport's leaders to amend the rules in order "to do away with much of the brutality which makes the game objectionable to many people."[75]

Camp drafted the group's response for publication, which read in its entirety, "At a meeting with the President of the United States it was agreed that we consider an honorable obligation exists to carry out in letter and in spirit the rules of the game of foot ball relating to roughness, holding, and foul play, and the active coaches of our Universities being present with us pledge themselves to so regard it, and to do their utmost to carry out these obligations."[76] The press applauded yet another triumph for the roughriding, trust-busting president with a big stick who (after subduing the Russian Bear, the Democratic Donkey, the Government Grafter, and the Spanish Monkey) had now tamed the "Football Slugger," too (fig. 1.10). On November 5, a graphic full-page layout in the magazine section of Pulitzer's *World* posed a familiar question, "Can a Gentleman Play Football?" and tabulated "Football's Harvest of Death and Wounds since 1900": forty-five deaths, fourteen broken collarbones, ten broken legs, four skull fractures, and so on.[77] The game needed reforming, and the leading football men, at the president's urging, had pledged to do so.

TAMING THE FOOTBALL SLUGGER.

Figure 1.10. Emil Flohri cartoon, "Taming the Football Slugger," in *Judge*, November 4, 1905.

But after signing their pledge, the representatives from Harvard, Yale, and Princeton returned to their campuses and the business of winning football games. Among the Big Three (or Four now, with Penn), only Harvard harbored deep and long-standing ambivalence about football. Now, rumors that Harvard's Board of Overseers had secretly voted to abolish the game prompted what a historian of the episode termed a "preemptive strike" from Bill Reid to preserve it: a statement to the Harvard Graduates' Athletic Association, released to the press, calling for radical reform. It declared, in part, "Although I am willing to admit that the necessary roughness of the game may be objectionable to some people, that appears to me to be much less serious than the fact that there is a distinct advantage to be gained by brutality and evasion of the rules. . . . For these reasons I have come to believe that the game ought to be radically changed." Reid called on the Graduates' Athletic Association "immediately to appoint a committee whose duty it shall be to make a careful investigation of the subject, and to report such thoroughgoing alterations in the game as will remove the unfair advantage now obtained from violation of the rules."[78]

The rules were the problem, not the game itself. Reid effectively set the agenda for reform rather than abolition as events would play out. The following Saturday, the annual game between the Harvard and Yale freshmen featured an undersized end named Theodore Roosevelt Jr., adding family drama to the ongoing debates about brutality. By all reports, young Ted acquitted himself well, but "the repeated hammering of the Yale plays sent at him" forced him to the sidelines, "groggy" and "exhausted," before the end of the game.[79] The next day, the *World* put an illustration of the "President's Son as Sample 'Victim' of Football Game" on its front page, with arrows pointing to the injured parts of his body and a box of text ("What the President Said of the Game His Son Plays") containing the lines from his June address at Harvard.[80] The unstated question was obvious: How did the defender of broken collarbones in a noble cause feel when they belonged to his own child? A week later, the Harvard–Yale varsity game featured a Yale player's vicious hit on a Harvard man in the act of making a fair catch, breaking his nose, as the referee stood nearby and did nothing. A *Boston Globe* photographer captured the moment of impact for the next day's front page, and an outraged Roosevelt summoned Reid to the White House to explain this betrayal of their October agreement.[81]

For all of their drama, the uproar over these incidents would have passed without major consequence had a halfback for Union College, Harold Moore, not died from a cerebral hemorrhage after a head-on collision on the same day that the Harvard varsity played Yale. The game in Boston drew the top reporters from New York newspapers, but Union's opponent was New York University in a game played in the city and covered by the major papers, too. The next day in chapel, NYU chancellor Henry MacCracken told the students that he would urge the trustees to drop football. Uptown, Columbia's president and faculty committee made the same decision. The *Chicago Daily Tribune*, after polling college presidents from around the country on the nineteen deaths and 138 serious injuries recorded for the 1905 season, published their responses on Monday. Presidents from Minnesota, Northern Illinois, Cornell, Iowa State, Notre Dame, and California agreed that football must be either reformed or abolished. Responding for the University of Chicago, whose president was ill and unavailable, the dean of the Divinity School, Shailer Mathews, called football a "boy killing, man mutilating, money making, education prostituting, gladiatorial 'sport'" that taught virility and courage, but so did war.[82] Mathews's comments were reprinted in the *New York Times* and papers around the country, and then in the weekly *Nation* and *Literary Digest* over the next two weeks, to become an enduring statement from the crisis.[83]

The hit on the Harvard man broke a rule; Harold Moore died from a fully legal collision. On Tuesday, Columbia president Nicholas Murray Butler officially abolished football at the school. Meanwhile, NYU's MacCracken had invited all of his university's football opponents from recent years to send representatives to a conference on December 8, to determine a course of action. Twelve showed up, making thirteen with NYU; five voted to abolish football, eight to reform it. With Harvard, Yale, Princeton, and Penn absent, the fate of football in America was not truly at stake in that narrow majority, but had the vote gone the other way, whatever football survived would have been seriously diminished. On December 28, MacCracken convened representatives from sixty-two institutions (again without the Big Four, or many colleges outside the East) for a second meeting, out of which came the Intercollegiate Athletic Association of the United States (which in 1910 would be renamed the National Collegiate Athletic Association). Out on the West Coast, against the vociferous objection of students, Stanford and Cal in March would abandon football for English rugby (thirteen seasons for Stanford, nine for Cal) and bring along a handful of small California colleges (and high schools) and the University of Nevada with them.[84] A few more colleges besides Columbia would drop the sport altogether, most notably Northwestern (for two seasons, Columbia for nine). Representatives from the rest of the football world set about designing a safer game.

Still committed to preserving Yale's preferred style of mass-momentum play, Walter Camp was openly viewed by this time as an obstacle to any meaningful reform. A front-page story in the *New York Tribune* on the Monday following Harold Moore's death announced a movement to "Oust Camp" by the simple expedient of forming an alternative committee.[85] At the same time, Harvard was threatening to adopt its own set of radically reformed rules. The "amalgamated committee," as the press called what emerged from these rival groups, with representatives from all regions instead of just the traditional handful from the Northeast,[86] met on January 12 and immediately marginalized Camp and maneuvered Harvard's Bill Reid into the leadership position.[87] In a series of publicized meetings over the next two months, the committee eventually agreed on a set of reforms that it released to the public on April 14, 1906.[88] Most radically, a new Rule 14 legalized the forward pass, though with restrictions that virtually guaranteed few schools would embrace it. Any thrown ball that crossed the goal line, that went out of bounds in the air, or that hit the ground before being touched by a player would be lost to the other side. In addition, the ball could be passed no more than twenty yards and had to be thrown from at least five yards outside the center.[89] Such rules seem bizarre, but no ball had ever been thrown forward in any kind of football played anywhere in the world; this was uncharted territory.

Other rule changes were more immediately consequential. The yardage to be gained in three tries was increased from five yards to ten, to force offenses to do something besides hammer at the middle of the defense with mass plays. A runner was declared "down" when any part of his body, other than hands or feet, touched the ground while in an opponent's grasp, which meant no more piling on (or "piling up," as it was termed then), a major source of minor injuries and occasional serious ones. A "neutral zone" the length of the football between the offensive and defensive lines was established, to prevent fisticuffs in close quarters before the ball was put in play and to eliminate interference with the snapback (which was also forbidden by its own new rule). Given the major restrictions on the forward pass, the most innovative new rule for "opening up" the offense was the one that created the "on-side kick," a ball kicked downfield from scrimmage that could be recovered by the offense—kicking to gain yardage, rather than to surrender the ball. For reducing players' exhaustion, the game was shortened from seventy to sixty minutes, in two thirty-minute halves, with a ten-minute intermission. And coaching from the sidelines was penalized fifteen yards (more on that in later chapters).[90]

The new code, as written, was full of fascinating details obviously based on an assumption that players and coaches would try to circumvent the rules put in place. What it meant for an offensive lineman to be on the line of scrimmage, for example, was given additional explanation: "This rule is intended to prevent any player who is supposed to be on the line of scrimmage from taking a position at such an angle to the line of scrimmage whether he faces in toward the centre or away from it as shall enable him the more rapidly to get into the interference." The rule requiring six offensive men on the line permitted one interior lineman to switch places with one of the backs, only if he lined up at least five yards deep. To this, a clarification was added: "Note.—There shall be no shifting of men to evade this rule."[91]

Nearly everything in the new code was intended to make routine play (with its necessary roughness) less dangerous, but it also paid specific attention to acts of brutality and "unnecessary roughness" (while adding another official to detect and penalize them). The long list of specific actions that would mean disqualification and loss of half the distance to the goal line (!) reveals tactics commonly used at that time: "Striking with the fist or elbows, kneeing, kicking, meeting with the knee or striking with the locked hands by the men in breaking through; striking in the face with the heel of the hand the opponent who is carrying the ball . . . or running into the player who has kicked the ball from behind the line of scrimmage" (roughing the punter, that is). Fouls that meant loss of fifteen yards, but no disqualification, included piling up, tripping, tackling the runner out of bounds, hurdling, "or any other acts of unnecessary roughness" (in case additional possibilities had been overlooked).[92]

The final code, when adopted, was broadly applauded but seemed less radical than many of those demanding reform had anticipated. This was football on Bill Reid's and Harvard's terms, rather than on Walter Camp's and Yale's, which would have been even less radical. As the *New York Tribune* put it in yet another defense of necessarily rough football, "There will still be much adverse criticism aimed at football even under the new code. It could not be otherwise, as there are some apparently that expect a parlor game." The *Tribune* approved what the committee had accomplished: "Football will still be a strenuous game, a rough game in which there will be more or less injuries. It could not be otherwise and have the attraction that it does for the players and the onlookers."[93] Assessing the new rules at the beginning of the 1906 season, Caspar Whitney praised the committee for its good work in steering a middle course between extremists on both sides, which he caricatured as one faction "for wiping out the game" and another that "ardently clamored for a game reduced to the innocuous mildness of checkers or croquet."[94]

More inventive pokes at the dreaded emasculation of a manly game came from the great humor magazines. In January, before reformers had even begun meeting, a double-page centerfold in *Puck* imagined "Football in 1906" as played by prancing fops, framing an All-America Team of louche dandies (fig. 1.11a). Then in March, as the rules committee neared the completion of its task, *Judge* envisioned "Football in 1906 under the New Rules" (fig. 1.11b). Two team captains, a beribboned and top-hatted chap in powder blue (for Yale) and his counterpart (bearing a striking resemblance to the current occupant of the White House) in pink (watered-down crimson, for Harvard), bowed to each other at midfield before commencing the contest. The new code by which they will play was written on a scroll lying on the field: "NO PINCHING, NO SLAPPING, HUG EASY, DON'T YELL, NO NOSE PULLING, DON'T BITE."

The joke was serious, of course. The public wanted their football safer, just not *too* safe.

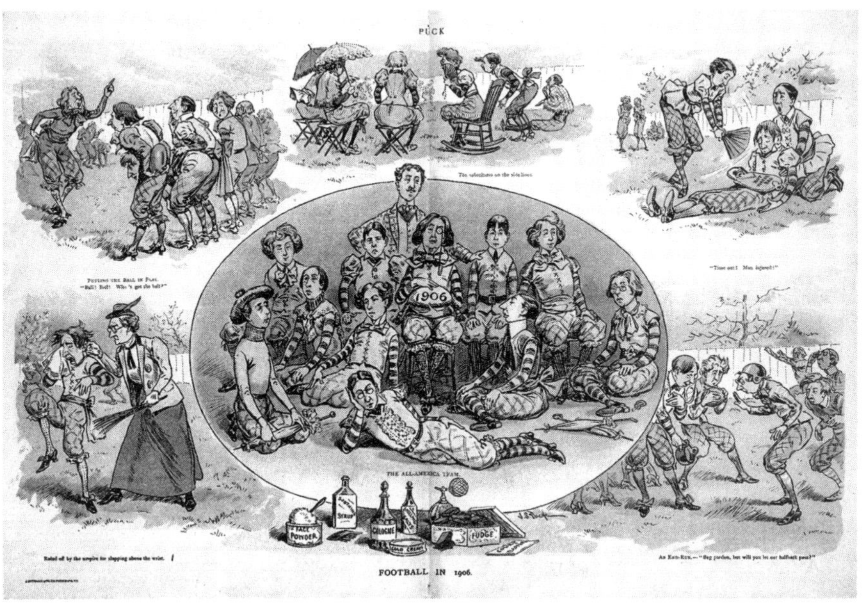

VOL. 50 NO. 1273 MARCH 10 1906 PRICE 10 CENTS

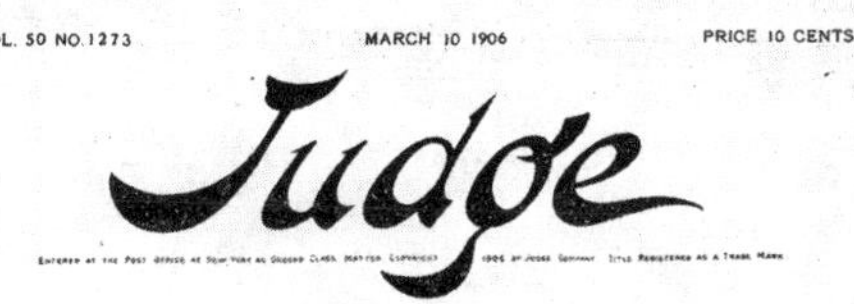

TOP

Figure 1.11a. J. S. Pughe cartoon, "Football in 1906," in *Puck*, January 3, 1906. Library of Congress.

BOTTOM

Figure 1.11b. Emil Flohri's cover for *Judge*, March 10, 1906.

Figure 2.1. George Bellows, illustration for Edward Lyell Fox, "Hold 'Em!," *Everybody's Magazine*, November 1912.

CHAPTER 2

TAKING IT

College football did not face another potential crisis until 1931. On October 24, in New Haven, Connecticut, with the score tied 6–6 in the fourth quarter following Yale's ninety-yard kickoff return, Army elected to kick rather than receive, as the rules allowed. (This was still the era when the common strategy was to try to pin the opponent deep in its own territory for favorable field position after forcing a punt.) Yale's Bob Lassiter ran the kickoff out to the twenty-two-yard line, where Army's 149-pound end, Richard Sheridan, brought him down with a head-first flying tackle. Sheridan's helmet struck Lassiter's knee. As the other players rose from the pile, Cadet Sheridan remained motionless on the turf. In the hush of 70,000 witnesses, Sheridan was removed on a stretcher, to die from a broken neck after two days in a New Haven hospital, without regaining consciousness.

After thoroughly covering Sheridan's condition for three days, newspapers simply went back to the business of covering the weekend's upcoming big games. By this time, 55,000 fans were regularly attending Ohio State home games, 70,000 or more attending Yale's, and over 100,000 filling Soldier Field in Chicago for the biggest games. Football had become too popular and too important to too many powerful institutions even to consider abolishing the game.

FOOTBALL STILL ON TRIAL

This did not happen overnight. In January 1906, before the "amalgamated committee" began meeting to revise the rules, two Boston surgeons who served as Harvard's team doctors, Edward H. Nichols and Homer B. Smith, published an article in the *Boston Medical and Surgical Journal* on the team's injuries over the course of the 1905 season. (Nichols was Harvard's second representative, along with Coach William Reid, at the famous meeting with President Roosevelt the previous October.[1]) Their analysis, written for other medical professionals, reached a wider audience when a long summary in the *Boston Globe* on January 5 reported that the team's 150 players had suffered 145 fractures, dislocations, contusions, and other injuries, most of them by the 70 who saw significant playing time. The doctors observed that "the game appears to breed such a contempt for physical pain that injuries which would appear severe to the ordinary individual were considered trivial by the players." Among those 145 injuries were nineteen concussions. The doctors reported sending all of the concussed players to the infirmary, but they also noted that "concussion was treated by the players in general as a trivial injury and rather regarded as a joke." They also added that "the real seriousness of the injury is not certain. Our own experience with the after effects of the cases is not sufficient for us to draw any definite conclusion, but from conversation with various neurologists we have obtained very various opinions in regard to the possibility of serious after effects." "Various opinions" would persist for decades.

Nichols and Smith ended with nine conclusions (reprinted in the *Globe*), beginning with this one, "The number, severity and permanence of the injuries which are received in playing football are very much greater than generally is credited or believed," and ending with this: "Leaving out all other objections to the game, ethical and practical, the conditions under which the game is played should be so modified as to diminish to a very great degree the number of injuries."[2]

An editorial in the *Journal of the American Medical Association* for January 13 urged all physicians to read Nichols and Smith's article and added that "the fact that 145 injuries . . . occur in one season of play is of itself enough to stamp the game as something that must be greatly modified or abandoned if we are to be considered a civilized people, and if our universities are to be considered centers of influence for good." With so many injuries in a mere game, *JAMA*'s editor wrote, "There must be something in it besides sport, an appeal to the brutal instincts of human nature, or some less worthy incitement even than this, to make young men continue to indulge in a game which is the cause of so many deaths." Regarding concussions, the editor agreed with the two physicians that "at the present time no one is ready to say whether concussion of the brain may or may not have serious consequences in after life."[3]

Here, in a nutshell, was the current medical understanding during the 1905–6 crisis: serious concern about injuries (and fatalities) but uncertainty about their long-term effects, particularly of concussions; and ultimately, a call for reform rather than abolition. Complicating physicians' treatment of injuries, players regarded them as trivial and concussions, specifically, as a joke. Historians of public health in the United States, such as Kathleen Bachynski, Emily Harrison, and Stephen Casper, have been uncovering the history of warnings from the medical establishment about the dangers of football that were consistently ignored by the men charged with keeping players safe.[4] Nichols and Smith pointed to one factor in ignoring warnings: Pain and injury, which for medical experts were solely health problems, meant something different to players (and fans). *JAMA*'s editorial had its own explanation: "the brutal instincts of human nature." Whatever the explanation, while withstanding injuries and even courting pain made no sense whatsoever in medical terms, they were driving forces in preserving the game.

Football in 1906 did, in fact, seem safer under the new rules, though not due to the forward pass, which, for all its upheaval of the game's traditions, was rarely used. That season, Yale threw a pass at a strategic moment in both the Princeton and Harvard games, to the amazement and delight of everyone but the Tigers and the Crimson, but otherwise the eastern football powers kept as close to their regular styles of play as possible.[5] It took a coach in the boondocks with nothing to lose, Eddie Cochems at St. Louis University, and a quarterback with large hands named Bradley Robinson to demonstrate what was possible with the forward pass. Large hands mattered because, with its wide girth and blunt ends, the rugby ball used for American football had to be cradled, not gripped, and launched more like a shotput than with a true overhand throw. (Tossing the ball underhand was even an option.) St. Louis exploited the forward pass in 1906 not as a trick play but as a basic offensive strategy in posting an 11–0 season record while scoring 407 points to opponents' 11.[6] But strong eastern teams wanted no part of the risk.

With no assist from the forward pass, the eighteen deaths in 1905 (revised down from the nineteen, mostly schoolboys, initially reported in the press) dropped to eleven in 1906 and again in 1907, then rose slightly to thirteen in

1908.[7] In his review of the 1906 season for *Outing*, Caspar Whitney saluted a new "spirit of football" after the "brutal exhibition" of 1905; and a year later, he exclaimed that he could not "remember a football season more pleasing than that of 1907."[8] The *Journal of the American Medical Association* was less sanguine, welcoming the reduced fatalities and injuries among college players but adamant that "football is no game for boys to play." "If we must have this gladiatorial 'sport,'" the 1907 editorial concluded, "would it not be better to adopt gladiatorial methods and have the game played only by fully-developed men who had passed a severe physical examination before beginning the course of training?"[9] This was the opening salvo in a decades-long barrage of attacks on the dangers of football for young boys with little effect.

Fatalities soared to twenty-six in 1909, ten of them college players, including Army cadet Eugene Byrne in a game against Harvard on October 30. Army immediately canceled the remainder of its season, including the Navy game. An editorial in the *New York Times* blamed "Deadly Mass Play" and called for its elimination.[10] A more deeply critical editorial in the *Washington Evening Star*, calling football "A National Menace," cut to the heart of the issue of *necessary* roughness. Not only was the American version of football uniquely brutal, but its promoters felt "pride in the fact that it is rough and dangerous. Defenders of the sport declare that it is conducive to the so-called virility of the American character, and that the training in it at our schools and colleges is next to necessity for the development of American youth along national lines." The only solution, given these circumstances, was for mothers and fathers to keep their sons from playing.[11]

Then, on November 13, a halfback at the University of Virginia, Archer Christian, plunged into Georgetown's line and did not rise from the tangle of bodies. Christian died overnight without regaining consciousness, and the singular tragedy of Eugene Byrne now seemed like the onset of another plague like 1897's. The story about Christian in the *Boston Globe* was followed by a series of brief notices of mayhem elsewhere: "Arm Broken in Game" (a six-year-old in Worcester), "School Boy Is Dead" (in Grand Rapids), "Has Brain Concussion" (college player for Ohio Wesleyan), "Two Injured in Pittsburgh" (a broken leg and a dislocated shoulder in the Pitt vs. Washington and Jefferson game), "Leg Broken in Columbus Game" (Ohio State–Vanderbilt).[12] By sheer coincidence, two weeks earlier, a football cover by the great magazine illustrator J. C. Leyendecker that captured football's heroic roughness in a hard tackle had hit newsstands just as Cadet Byrne was fatally injured. Now, two days after Archer Christian died, a cartoonist for the Philadelphia *North American* gave Leyendecker's heroic cover a dark twist (figs. 2.2a–b).

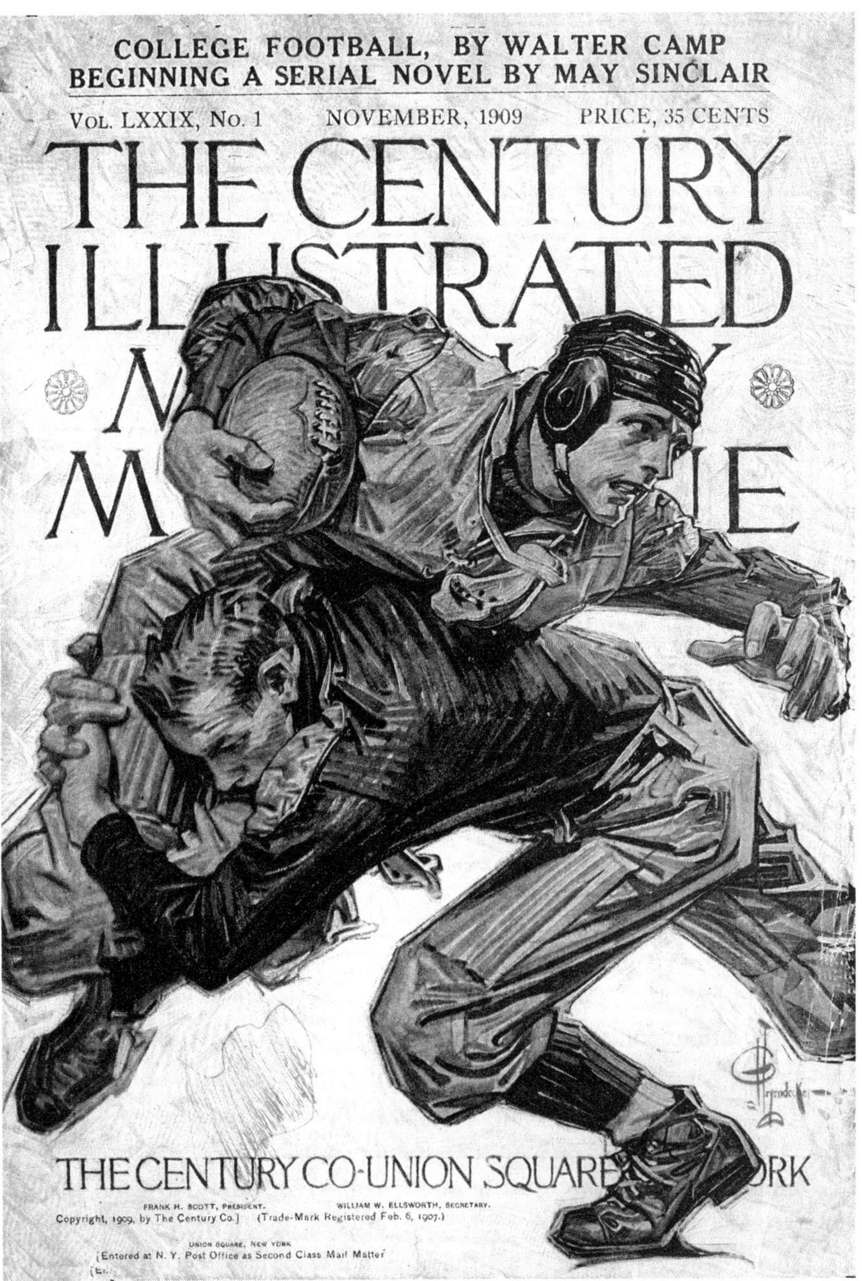

Figure 2.2a. J. C. Leyendecker cover, *Century Illustrated Monthly Magazine*, November 1909.

Figure 2.2b. Herbert Johnson's "Down!," *Philadelphia North American*, November 16, 1909.

Newspaper accounts of Christian's death described the young man's parents and brother keeping vigil at his bedside.[13] Cadet Byrne's grieving father, a former Buffalo police chief, had also been conspicuous in the coverage of that earlier tragedy. The artist who drew the centerfold illustration in *Harper's Weekly* for January 1, 1910, clearly had these events in mind (fig. 2.3). Football deaths had human costs not captured in mere numbers.

Outing's review of the 1909 season listed each name, date, and specific injury (if known) of twenty-five fatalities (missing one in what would become the official count), plus five more that resulted from injuries in 1908 and one back in 1905 (a Cornell player's punctured lung from a broken breastbone that led to pneumonia and finally killed him three years later). Despite these fatalities, the writer judged football "too good a game to be ended; it has too many friends and too many advantages for us to believe that it will not be mended." The writer himself proposed, as a good start, eliminating mass play altogether, and he praised team captains who sent exhausted players to the sidelines before they could become seriously injured, countering the belief that continuing to play when utterly spent was a mark of manliness. "Taking it" could kill you. "Football has been improved, no doubt of it," he concluded. "The slugger no longer reigns and the captains and coaches who would drive their men to the last inch without regard to risk or strain rather than lose are passing out. But the game is not right yet. . . . Football is once more on trial."[14] (The future would show his confidence that hard-driving coaches were "passing out" to have been slightly premature.)

The basic arguments for and against football, and even the proposed solutions, had changed little in twenty years. Legalizing the forward pass in 1906 had not revolutionized the game, as some had hoped and others had feared. For the 1907 season, the rules committee had reduced the penalty for an incomplete pass from loss of the ball to fifteen yards; but a year later, it allowed the defense to recover an incomplete pass, if touched by an offensive player, as if it were a fumble, while permitting only the man who initially touched the ball to recover it for the offense. Passing, unsurprisingly, remained mostly experimental. With the upsurge of deaths in 1909 putting the future of the game at risk again, some in fact thought that passing made the game *more*

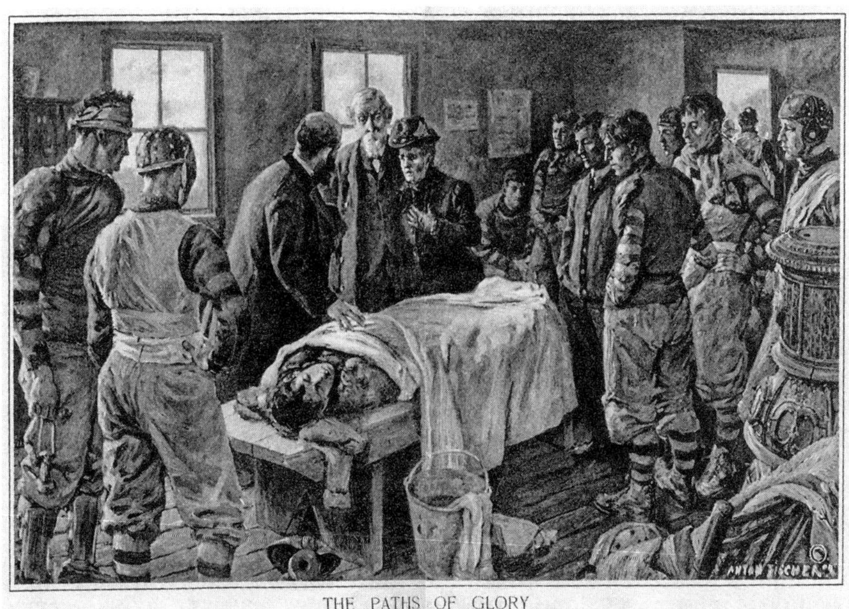

Figure 2.3. Anton Fischer's "The Paths of Glory," *Harper's Weekly*, January 1, 1910.

dangerous, not less—not from pass plays themselves but from the threat of a pass, which forced defenses to drop players back in coverage and leave their linemen unaided against line plunges. Reporting on the rules committee's deliberations in February, the *New York Times* warned that defensive tackles, without their halfbacks behind them, had "been made chopping blocks and mere steps in the 'down-the-field' smashes." (Cadet Byrne was a tackle.) The *Times* proposed forbidding passes to cross the line of scrimmage, in order to keep defensive backs up close.[15]

The rules committee ignored that suggestion but adopted fourteen new rules in May that mostly addressed mass plays one final time: requiring seven men on the line of scrimmage; limiting motion in the backfield before the snap to a single player, away from the line (as in the game to this day); and banning "locked interference" (blockers linking arms and pushing or pulling ball carriers). The committee retained three downs to make ten yards (rejecting a proposal to add a fourth down), widened the neutral zone to a full twelve inches, divided the game into fifteen-minute quarters, and banned "flying tackles" (requiring that a tackler must have at least one foot on the ground). On the forward pass, it ruled an incomplete pass to be a loss of down, no longer a fifteen-yard penalty, and allowed a pass to cross the line of scrimmage at any point, so long as it was thrown from at least five yards behind the line; but it retained the other restrictions.[16]

The revisions seemed to work, as the 1910 and 1911 seasons played out uneventfully, requiring no additional major rule changes. For 1912, the rules committee shortened the field from 110 to 100 yards, with ten-yard end zones into which forward passes could be thrown—a pass over the goal line no longer a turnover—while also eliminating the onside kick adopted in 1906, to leave the forward pass as the sole alternative to running with the ball.[17] The last impediments to the passing game would not be removed until the 1930s and 1940s, but otherwise, after the committee also added a fourth down for making ten yards, football now looked like today's game.[18]

The revisions of 1912 basically completed the creation of American football. And with more teams passing more often but still infrequently, Notre Dame's legendary thrashing of Army at West Point in 1913 on Gus Dorais's passes to Knute Rockne has been widely recognized as the moment when the East finally realized that passing had to be a part of football's future. (It would finally arrive in 1924 with Benny Friedman at Michigan.) There was no mention of injuries, let alone deaths, in these annual reviews. Football seemed safe enough at last.

But still rough enough, too. *Outing*'s review of the 1911 season expressed what the writer took to be an emerging consensus: "The point to be made is simply that properly regulated football is not now an unduly dangerous game—no more so at least than any other vigorous game requiring physical contact. Unnecessary roughness is to be condemned at all times and to be suppressed unmercifully, but the elimination of all risk from football would involve also the elimination of the game itself, and this we do not believe unprejudiced critics are prepared to demand."[19] With unnecessary roughness diminished by harsh penalties and more regulated officiating, slugging and other egregious acts of violence had indeed been mostly eliminated. The physical "risk," whose removal "would involve also the elimination of the game itself," remained a part of football, but it no longer needed to be promoted or justified. The writer simply took for granted that "unprejudiced critics" agreed on this. The idea that "taking it" built character became an unspoken assumption, as football was poised to become the country's major sporting spectacle in the 1920s.

Fatalities were rare, as were catastrophic injuries. Lesser injuries were commonplace, some of them crippling, but the risk of those worst ones and the near inevitability of the others were widely regarded as an acceptable price for the benefits of the game. As the numbers rose and fell, that basic calculus would remain unchanged for nearly 100 years, until the discovery of the damage in Mike Webster's brain would force a nationwide recalculation, whose final resolution remains unsettled.

FOOTBALL FICTION: INSIDE THE GAME

While sportswriters and journalists generated the public conversations around football violence, football fiction offers the historian something different: a glimpse into the more intimate hopes and desires that fueled the popularity of the game, a view from inside rather than outside the game. People are defined by the stories they tell about themselves as well as by what they do. And stories can be less filtered through strictures about what's proper and improper.

Football short stories began appearing in mainstream magazines within just a few years of the game's beginnings—that in itself a sign of its cultural standing as a sport sponsored by elite universities. (Boxing stories would not become common, outside pulp magazines, until the 1920s.) Football episodes appeared in so-called college-life novels as early as the 1870s,[20] but the earliest football short story for adults (rather than boys) that I have identified was published in the *Overland Monthly* (the West Coast magazine that had helped launch the literary careers of Mark Twain and Bret Harte) in January 1894.[21] The author was the future novelist Frank Norris, who had briefly played football in prep school in San Francisco before breaking his arm. In Norris's "Travis Hallett's Half-Back," the star of the football team, a young man named Adler, rescues his girl from a mad panic in a burning theater by relying on the "trained eye" and "coolness of judgment" he had developed on the football field. "The crush and lurch of the crowd was but the old scrimmage of the gridiron field," the narrator explains during the climactic scene, "and the confused, blind rush that enveloped him was no worse than the trained and disciplined charges of the revolving V or the flying wedge, and for one brief instant Adler thanked his God that he was a 'Varsity half-back and knew how to use his weight and wits."[22]

From the beginning, then, the courage and manly character learned on football fields were a foundational theme of football fiction. The *Saturday Evening Post* and *Collier's* both published their first football stories in 1898, the one in *Collier's* written by Walter Camp no less, with a very Campian emphasis on the scientific game But the early magazine stories were mostly about the violent collision sport,[23] and the preeminent writer of that story was the once well-known but now long-forgotten James Hopper, whose twenty football stories between 1904 and 1933 more or less defined the genre for a generation. Norris wrote "Travis Hallett's Half-Back" from an idea. Hopper wrote his most powerful stories out of his own experiences from six seasons (1894–99) of playing football at the University of California (the absence of eligibility rules allowing postgraduate students to keep playing). Hopper thus played during the era of the flying wedge and mass-momentum plays out in California, far from the center of the football world but still the same game. Whether written before or after the 1905 football crisis (after which Cal switched from football to rugby), Hopper's stories remained rooted in the battering-ram game that he had known as a player in the 1890s.

Hopper's quintessential football story, the urtext for many that followed, was published in the *Saturday Evening Post* in October 1904. In "The Strength of the Weak" (subtitled "The Story of the Full-Back Who Got Used to It"), Harley, third substitute fullback (fourth-string, that is), is pressed into play by injuries to his teammates. He is tall but barely 150 pounds, with a flat chest and "no shoulders, no back, no driving power!" "Rather nice legs," though, the assistant reminds the head coach. Plus, "He's got grit." "Yes he has," the coach replies after a pause, "and Jack, he's got to do it on that grit; he's got to do it all, all on that grit."[24]

In practice that week, the coach instructs the scrubs to pound Harley every time he kicks, to "charge him and knock him down. Drive your elbows and knees into him. Any man that misses him goes to the sidelines." (Recall that roughing the punter was not penalized until 1906, two years after this story appeared.) After his first punt in practice, Harley "found himself crumpled to the ground beneath a human avalanche, an avalanche brutal as one of matter, but possessed of a fiendish ingenuity in inflicting torture." To the delight of the coaches, Harley only looks downfield to follow the flight of his ball, a full fifty yards. He kicks again and is again "pounded to earth with a shock that sickened him to the core of his being." The next time, he hesitates, and his kick is blocked. "'That's what you'll have to expect every time you kick in the big game,' said the coach coldly; 'and I'll see that you get it every time till then. Get used to it!' And by the last week of the season Harley was used to it." (George Bellows's opening image for this chapter illustrated an article by another writer, but it captured the central drama of Hopper's story, too.)

When the big game against the superior Red team (Stanford, that is) arrives, it is immediately apparent that Harley at fullback is "the weak cog in the machine," too slow to make long gains, too light to buck for tough yards. Only his punting can prevent disaster for the Blues. The first time he drops back to punt, standing all alone twenty feet behind the line, Harley feels like he is in "a sanctuary where one could recruit one's soul . . . like a young knight at his vigil . . . making his vows."[25] Oblivious to the charging linemen until he gets off the kick, Harley is "hurled to the ground as if the skies had fallen upon him." As he rises, the Red captain mutters, "We're going to break you in two, young fellow." "I'll still have my legs to kick with," Harley answers "with a smile almost feminine," to the other's "frank amazement." With the ball back in its possession, the heavier Red team marches relentlessly down the field, almost to the goal line, but is stopped just short and loses the ball on downs. Harley drops back again. This time the snap is low, and he barely gets the ball off before being "buried as beneath an avalanche of bricks." He rises with a sharp pain in his side, a cracked rib. "But he smiled. 'Not broken yet,' he said to the Red captain." Pure grit.

And so it goes for the rest of the half: the Red team marching with "bulldog ferocity" but stopped short of the goal; Harley punting the ball away, then "pounded to the sod"; the pain in his side "a knife that pulsed, stabbing further and further into his vitals." Again and again, in the same feverish prose. After a brief rest between halves, the coach whispers to Harley as he sends him out for the second half, "It's your punting, remember your punting alone that can save us to-day." The second half proceeds like the first for the Blues:

"A grueling, desperate, teeth grinding effort to keep the Reds from scoring: an effort that took all their physical strength, drained their moral force, strained their spirit in the keeping taut the tremendous determination not to give in, not for a second yield, not for the thousandth part of a second loosen the clutching fingers that held them above the precipice of defeat below them with its hellish promise of rest, peace, renunciation." (Whew!) "The stabbing in Harley's side is piercing him to the very vitals now," but worse, the distance on his punts is diminishing with his exhaustion. First sixty yards, then fifty, then forty, and then, "only with the most bitter effort," barely thirty. (The strategy in a punting duel in this era was to outkick the opponent, to gain five or ten yards on each exchange of punts until within striking distance of the goal line.) Finally, after Harley makes a brilliant touchdown-saving tackle and recovers the fumble, he is too exhausted to handle the center-snap for his punt. The Red team falls on the ball and kicks a field goal for a 5–0 lead. (Field goals counted more than touchdowns until 1897, when both were worth five points. Touchdowns became six points in 1912.)

Facing disaster now, the Blues will not surrender. "The last hope had gone; defeat was irrevocably theirs, but they fought on, impelled by some mad desire of self-sacrifice, an exasperated dissatisfaction with themselves, fighting to fight, to content something indomitable in them that refused to acquiesce." In his own "immense weariness," Harley gets off a punt of only twenty yards, then twenty again, then fifteen, and then zero at last, when the ball goes straight up, drops back to the ground, and rolls to Harley's feet. With "a gulp of eagerness," as "new life thrilled in his veins," Harley grabs the ball and heads upfield, swerving and stumbling, as if in "an illimitable desert," toward the goalpost "fearfully far" away. "It was a run long as death." As Harley crosses the last white line, delirious, he feels himself floating high above the earth, barely attached by "a tenuous silken thread," but knowing that he must come back down to kick the goal for "the sixth point, which effectively made the five of the Reds look, in the words of the coach, like thirty cents."

THE STUFF MEN ARE MADE OF

As Hopper's story suggests, "self-restraint" devolved into "taking it" as football's fundamental challenge, as the game spread from the New England elites to state universities and land-grant colleges around the country, requiring not forbearance but courage and endurance, or "grit." "Taking it" and "grit" were at the center of football fiction in popular magazines into the 1920s, as college football completed its transformation to a thoroughly commercialized popular entertainment.[26] The new college football world no longer had an unequivocal "center" in the Northeast but encompassed the entire country, divided into regional conferences. Following the formation of the Western Conference (forerunner of the Big Nine and Big Ten) in 1896 came the Missouri Valley (the future Big Six, then Big Eight, then Big 12) in 1907, the Southwest in 1914, the Pacific Coast in 1915, and the Southern in 1921 (from which the Southeastern would split off in 1932 and the Atlantic Coast in 1953). By the 1920s, football had distinct regional identities, competing for national prestige through closely followed "intersectional" contests, while closer to home, in-state rivals battled for local bragging rights. Enormous bowl- or horseshoe-shaped stadiums, limited before the First World War to Harvard's and Yale's, sprouted around the country in the 1920s, including the iconic Los Angeles Coliseum and Chicago's Soldier Field (one of several World War I memorial stadiums) and led by the Big Ten, whose members built eight stadiums seating 20,000 or more over the decade, six of them at least 50,000. Football became the center of campus life: the Greek system, homecoming celebrations, mascots and fight songs, pep rallies and bonfires. While baseball remained "the national pastime," college football, with its pageantry of bands and cheerleaders to complement the thrilling action on the field, was "Our Greatest Popular Spectacle."[27]

Brutality was no longer an urgent issue (as seen in figure 2.4), but tying football to masculinity became more explicit than ever in the 1920s. On October 24, 1925, Grantland Rice, the era's foremost sportswriter, titled his weekly column for *Collier's* "The Stuff Men Are Made Of." This "stuff" came not from withstanding foul blows from dishonorable opponents by showing gentlemanly self-restraint but from the routine "weeks of pounding and drudgery" over a long season, "of blocking and tackling, of real physical suffering," that were fundamental to the game. This was not toughness for Christian gentlemen or the privileged sons of the nation's patrician class, threatened by the rise of a new financial and industrial plutocracy, but for young men of all classes, most of them by now in public universities, confronting a "world turning to softness or the comfortable ease that money can buy." College football offered "no financial rewards" (a crucial distinction from professional football, Rice did not need to mention). "Grit Outshines Gold," as one of the section headings put it. Rice described cases of men playing with a "battered right shoulder," a "cracked" ankle, broken bones in both hands. Football offered them and their teammates nothing "luxurious, gentle, fleecy, delicate or dreamy," only "drudgery, discipline, hard work, physical suffering"—and always "constant pressure. . . . If you care to check up a few details, you will find that life itself is largely a matter of facing pressure." For young men living in "an age of greatly extended wealth," there was "still a lot of rough-and-tumble stuff, both mental and physical, left in the hurly-burly, and fortitude still has its part to play."[28] Having the grit to play with such football injuries was ideal preparation.

Rice wrote these lines less than a month before Red Grange shocked the collegiate football world by signing a contract with the Chicago Bears immediately after his final game at Illinois. Following his six-touchdown performance against Michigan in 1924, Grange became college football's first true celebrity player, with newspapers, magazines, and newsreels tracking not just

Figure 2.4. Cartoon in *Judge*, November 10, 1928.

his exploits on the field but also his All-American Boy summer job (as "the Wheaton ice man"), delivering blocks of ice to pay for his college expenses. In signing with the Bears, Grange boldly and baldly pursued football's "financial rewards," Grantland Rice notwithstanding, treating the sport like a potentially lucrative job rather than a sacred calling.

At Illinois, Grange had teammates with names like Kuenzli, D'Ambrosia, and Antonides, sons of the southern and eastern European immigrants ("Mediterraneans" and "Alpines" in the racist terminology of the day) who had been pouring into the United States since the 1890s until a backlash to preserve the purity of the white race ("Nordics," by that terminology) led to the resurgence of the Ku Klux Klan in the 1920s and the shameful immigration quotas imposed by Congress in 1924.[29] College football in the 1920s was no longer the game of the northeastern elite but a sport of the American people, even as the idea of what constituted being an "American" was under extreme pressure.

College football in 1925, then, had a different place in American life from the one that emerged from the shambles of the 1905 season. But if football was more truly national, it was still the same game, and the same one, in fundamental ways, that had evolved in the 1880s and 1890s. "Personal encounters" were valued as highly as ever. Football was no longer a game for "*Christian* gentlemen" but still for *gentlemen*, defined now by sportsmanship rather than by more explicitly moral virtues or class and breeding. It was also, more than ever, a game for making men, not in the older sense of Christian manliness but in the modern sense of masculinity, with its emphasis on force and power. And football players still became men, or proved their manhood, by "taking it."

Knute Rockne, the most-quoted as well as winningest coach of the 1920s (college football's first celebrity coach, as Grange was its first celebrity player), put the players' masculinity at the center of football as a counterforce to the "tea hounds" and "cake-eaters" (also "lounge lizards," "sheiks," "rumble-seat cowboys," "Hollywood athletes," "pastry cutters," "flapper men," "mezzanine floor high-hurdlers," and "the rest of the brood that packs a charlotte russe where a spine should be") who were swarming on college and high school campuses.[30] Rockne's obsession aside, public morals were indeed looser in the Jazz Age, most shockingly among "Flaming Youth," with sex now playing on movie screens and speakeasies offering forbidden pleasures with a hint of danger, as everyone who took an alcoholic drink became an outlaw. That football could be an antidote to all of this would have come as a surprise to Rockne's own George Gipp, no doubt among many others.

The language was jokey, but Rockne was deeply serious. He typically made his comments about "lounge lizards" or "rumble-seat cowboys" at postseason football banquets, often in small towns, but with reporters present who put them on the newswire, to be picked up by papers around the country. One of Rockne's favorite bits was to describe—in greatly overwrought detail—a football game in the near future between daintily attired fops with exquisite manners (like those cartoons in *Puck* and *Judge* in 1906) whose final scores would be reported on the society page rather than in the sports section. In his most elaborate version, which went on for fifteen minutes, Northwestern's players entered the stadium, "gayly clad in purple mauvette tunics," with their fullback, M. Bickerdash Pix III, back to receive the kickoff from Notre Dame's T. Fitzpatrick Murphy, known as "Two Lumps" for his preference in his tea, while Pix III's teammates made "a striking appearance with their green shirtwaists and headgear resembling a woodsman's toque." And on and on. "Two Lumps" saves the game for Notre Dame when Pix III is about to score by calling out that he has a run in his stocking—stopping him dead, to slink off to the locker room in shame.[31] On at least two occasions, five years apart, Rockne turned this silly fantasy into a halftime skit: for the DePauw game in South Bend in 1922 and for USC at Soldier Field before 120,000 in Chicago in 1927.[32]

Football was Rockne's desperately needed cure for the plague of "soft and perfumed" boys. "If I had my way," he told an audience at Iowa State in 1928, "I'd take a boy like that and make him a fullback. Then I would have the quarterback call his signal right over the center where opposition is generally more stubborn. He might not choose to run, but I don't see how he could help it—and contact would do him good."[33] (James Hopper wrote a story in 1912 with that premise.)[34] At a banquet in 1922, Rockne proposed "compulsory football or boxing to bring out manly instinct" and at another in 1927 suggested that compulsory football "would take up slack in hotel lounge rooms." In 1929, he was still offering compulsory football to the Boston City Club "as an antidote for a growing lack of manliness in college men." On this occasion, he added that "young men are either going to get softer and softer, and in larger numbers, or we must get them out on the athletic field and teach them the fighting spirit and the fun of playing the game."[35] In a 1929 magazine article titled "Football . . . a Man's Game" (whose opening, "When, betimes, uproar smote the stately columns of the Acropolis . . . ," points to a ghostwriter), Rockne declared "technic" more important than "toughness" for winning football games, but he also called football "a hard, rough game" to be played "as hard as lies within the power of any team."[36]

In less quirky but no less emphatic language, Rockne's coaching colleague Bill Roper at Princeton also tied football explicitly to manliness. In an article for the *New York Herald Tribune*'s Sunday magazine in 1929, Roper challenged the notion that America's young men were becoming soft by offering the thousands of football teams around the country as his evidence: "For when a game that requires the courage, the stamina, the combativeness, the virility—in a word, the 'hardness'—that is demanded by football, attracts more than 250,000 young men to engage in it actively, day after day, week after week, through the entire fall, then it's going to be pretty hard to convince me that men are getting pallid and namby-pamby, that men are getting 'soft.'" According to Roper, the millions who only watched the games proved *their* "hardness," too. "For football is no game for namby-pambies. Nor is it a sport for namby-pambies to watch."[37]

Injured players staying on the field was a theme for Roper as well as Rice, though with some ambivalence. "The youth who goes out for football today is usually the type who would rather suffer a lifelong injury than be referred to as a quitter," Roper told readers. However admirable for the player, this posed a challenge for the coach. Coaches had to look out for the welfare of players who would not look out for themselves, not for the sake of the player's health, however, but because an injured player could hurt the team by playing below par. For the player, "willingness to stand pain is one of the elements which make competitive sports so worthwhile in developing character and manliness in an age when our youths need something to keep them from becoming 'softies.'" It was up to the coach to prioritize the team's fortunes. According to Roper, what football demanded of those who played it, as did no other modern sport, was "sacrifices of self for the good of the team, complete devotion to a cause and a wholehearted abandon to 'take it.'" As always, tying courage to the withstanding of pain valorized the pain itself as the measure of the courage. That mindset would haunt football into the era of CTE.

DISSENT

Criticism of college football in the 1920s was mostly for its commercialism, professionalism, and distorted educational priorities, not for its violence. Dissent from the popular consensus around character building and man-making through "taking it" was relatively muted, though it did not disappear altogether. A week after Grantland Rice's piece "The Stuff Men Are Made Of" appeared in *Collier's* and two weeks before Red Grange announced turning pro, George Owen, a former Harvard football captain (as well as hockey and basketball captain who earned nine letters from 1921 through 1923), declared in *The Independent* (a weekly journal of opinion), "I believe quite frankly that the majority of college football players do not enjoy playing the game. There are, of course, a certain number of exceptions, but those are the men, I think, who would enjoy any fight. They love the game because of the opportunity it gives them for bodily contact. The real reason for my dislike of football, and I think the dislike of many other players, lies primarily in the terrific grind necessary to keep in the running." To Owen, football was no longer a game but a "stern and relentless business," and he concluded with the negative version of the familiar trope: "I wonder if history is repeating itself. Is the gladiator slave of the Colosseum days of old Rome finding his counterpart in the modern football player? It would certainly seem so."[38]

Owen was not just any old former football captain; he was a *Harvard* man, still the game's aristocracy, and dissatisfaction with Harvard football could not be taken lightly. What Grantland Rice viewed as the "drudgery" of the long season that brought out the stuff that made men, Owen saw as the "grind" that destroyed any pleasure in the game, until after the season when players could look back on what they accomplished. Owen's blasphemy was a mere tremor before Grange's earthquake, but it rattled the football establishment and reverberated for years afterward. Immediate responses came from the *Boston Globe* and the Associated Press (in a story picked up widely).[39] George Trevor, the distinguished sports columnist for the *New York Sun*, applauded Owen's "courage in flaunting hide-bound customs imposed by student opinion" and added, "Many of the greatest stars who ever trod the grid cordially hated the shock of body-to-body contact." (He named George Gipp specifically and noted the chapter in a book published by "Big Bill" Edwards, the former Princeton All-American of the 1890s, devoted to "men who played despite their aversion to the game.")[40] While a *Boston Globe* poll of football captains around the country found that "Every One Plays for the Love of the Game," students at Harvard, Princeton, Dartmouth, Brown, Williams, Wesleyan, and Bowdoin drafted a radical proposal to curb "over-emphasis."[41] A year later, the Harvard psychiatrist Morton Prince, defending football on the question in *The Forum*, "Shall We Abolish Intercollegiate Football?," cited Owen for "express[ing] frankly and publicly what many had been thinking who had not the courage to say it."[42] (Prince called for returning the game to the players, an utterly quixotic idea by this time.) Writers critical of overemphasis in college football in October 1927 and November 1928 continued to cite Owen.[43]

On the other side of that debate over abolishing collegiate football in *The Forum* was Upton Sinclair, the former muckraking journalist and future socialist candidate for governor of California. Sinclair did not name Owen, but he opened his brief against football by adapting the well-worn trope of football "gladiators" to a Marxist argument about manipulating the masses through popular culture. "The masters of ancient Rome provided gladiatorial combats for the purpose of diverting the minds of the populace from the loss of their ancient liberties," Sinclair wrote, "and in the same way the masters of modern America provide gigantic struggles on the football field." To Sinclair, *taking it* was not heroic but self-destructive and perverse. The "enormous mob" in the football stadium "drives the gladiators to more and more frenzied efforts and to brutal treacheries which cripple their rivals. The young heroes break their heart-valves and overstretch their blood vessels and poison their kidneys and weaken themselves for the rest of their lives." Football might make "men," wrote Sinclair, in mockery of Rice and others, but men fit for doing capitalism's dirty work. "Boys who have learned to fight football battles will be prepared to command real armies and send millions of their fellow men to a hideous death." Likewise, "Boys who have slugged their rivals on the football field will be ready as scientists to devise poison gases to wipe out the human race."[44]

And so on, in a tirade that likely lost most readers early on. The socialist Sinclair did not speak for many in the football world by this time. In 1906, abolishing football was unlikely but possible; by 1926, it was inconceivable.

THE STATE OF THE GAME

The year 1929 saw the publication of two major assessments of the state of football in the United States: *The Future of Interscholastic Athletics*, by Frederick Rand Rogers, director of health education for the New York State Education Department; and the long-anticipated report on college athletics from the Carnegie Foundation for the Advancement of Teaching, whose lead author was Howard J. Savage. High school football had developed in tandem with the college game since the late nineteenth century and by the 1920s had become increasingly important in countless communities as a source of local identity and pride. The Public Schools Athletic League, founded in New York in 1903, created a model for state athletic associations or federations that would be established over the next several years, and an oversight body, the forerunner of the National Federation of State High School Athletic Associations, was created in 1920.[45] By the end of the 1920s, intersectional contests, state championships, postseason "bowl" games (beginning in Miami on Christmas Day, 1929), and even a mythical "national champion" (the first one named in 1927) all mirrored the college game.[46] While the national press focused on college football, papers in small towns throughout the country covered their local high school teams as thoroughly and passionately as the metropolitan dailies covered the colleges.

Rogers's report seems to have been largely ignored in the press, but it was directed at the school administrators and athletic associations that had the power to act on its recommendations. (The report was "exciting much comment in the athletic world," according to the one newspaper in which I found it mentioned.[47]) Without singling out football, Rogers's primary concern was high school state championships—for their "emotional overstimulation" and fostering of "overweening ambitions"—which he viewed as an "example of harmful adult interference in schoolboy leisure activities."[48] Among other unfortunate consequences, championships amplified the risk of the inevitable "injuries [that] will occur in any athletic contest," some of which could teach positive lessons, Rogers acknowledged, but only within limits. "Players should learn courage, that is, to 'take chances' in adolescent life, and athletic injuries doubtless form a proper and important part of every normal boy's education. Championships, however, provide artificial stimuli, involving health hazards which are quite unnecessary."[49] Later in the report, Rogers addressed football more directly: "Hazards to life and limb present a most difficult problem. Thus the opinion is growing in some quarters that American football takes too great a physical toll to justify its *unquestioned social value* [my emphasis]. But the game itself is changing rapidly; the dangers may soon be lessened to the point where all but the most sensitive will agree that its advantages outweigh its disadvantages."[50]

Rogers basically reiterated here the consensus regarding college football that had emerged in the 1910s. His only recommendations for addressing the "difficult problem" of injuries, aside from lessening their number by eliminating state championships, were on the need for sound protective equipment. In his conclusion he returned to his primary concern about adult interference. "The present highly organized system of leagues, associations, and championships are almost invariably controlled by non-players whose interests are for protection of players occasionally, mutual gain often, and utilization frequently of pupil players for wholly selfish adult motives almost irrespective of the interest of the players."[51] Like Morton Prince, Rogers saw the adults who controlled the game as the major problem.

The Carnegie report received considerably more public attention when it was released in late October. Its headline-making news about rampant recruiting and subsidizing of athletes in supposedly "amateur" collegiate football (at 84 of 112 institutions examined) was a "bombshell," as Paul Gallico of the *New York Daily News* sarcastically put it, whose "detonation will raise more college professors than newspaper writers from their chairs, since the content of the huge and well-written and arranged report is not exactly unfamiliar material in the various editorial rooms throughout the country."[52] Away from the headline-making news, buried in chapter 7 ("The Hygiene of Athletic Training"), the report addressed athletic injuries in general and "The Serious Dangers of Football" in particular, which included chronic sprains, dislocations, concussions, fractures, collapses, and internal injuries. The Carnegie researchers' survey of 2,978 football players at twenty-two institutions found that 17.6 percent suffered at least one such injury over the course of a season.[53] Their bland conclusion would have surprised no one: "From the point of view of physical injury, it appears that football is the most hazardous of college sports. Current opinion is thus confirmed by statistical analysis."[54] Another dud "bombshell," Gallico might have said.

A separate section of the chapter addressed concussions—which it called "the most difficult, even for the expert and specially trained field physician, to diagnose and to treat"—through a survey conducted by Dr. Edgar Fauver, the athletic director at Wesleyan University, in 1917 of 376 former football players at six institutions. The fact that a survey from 1917 was the best that the Carnegie investigators could find points to the state of medical research on concussions at the time. Forty-four percent of the players (166) reported suffering at least one concussion in their careers, while 32 players had had three or more and as many as twelve, confirming the observation by team physicians "that concussion, once suffered severely, tends to recur the more easily" (a crucial finding that would receive too little attention for decades). The Carnegie authors' own survey of twenty-two institutions over one season found a concussion rate of just 4.4 percent overall, but the range from 2.3 percent at one college (8 of 345 players) to 30 percent at another (30 of 100 players) undermined any definitive conclusions about their frequency.[55]

From interviews with team physicians and coaches, Savage and his colleagues identified five possible causes for football's dangerousness: coaching techniques "that ignore hazards to life and limb and look only to the winning of contests," poor conditioning, playing when "overtired," inadequate medical supervision, and schedules that were too difficult. Once again, the conclusions confirmed "current opinion." Once again, they located football's dangers in its supervision and regulation, not in the game itself.[56] Football itself was safe *enough*.

FOOTBALL FATALITIES IN BLACK AND WHITE

Requiem for Jack Trice

Cadet Richard Sheridan's death in 1931 shocked the football world, but he was not the first collegian from a "major" team to die from a football injury since the evolution of the rules from 1906 to 1912. On October 6, 1923, Jack Trice, a sophomore tackle for Iowa State, was crushed in a pileup on a running play directed at him in the third quarter of a game against Minnesota and died two days later from internal injuries.[57] The *Des Moines Register* did not even mention the injury in its initial account of the game, nor Trice's hospitalization the next day, but it reported his death on the front page (seventh column) on October 9: "John (Jack) Trice, star Negro tackle on the Iowa State college football team died at 3 o'clock this afternoon at the college hospital, as a result of injuries he sustained in the Aggies-Minnesota game at Minneapolis last Saturday." The *Register* called Trice an "all around athlete and student . . . popular among his fellow students and the professors," with a 90 average in the classroom. He had come to Ames from Cleveland with his high school coach, who "regarded him as the best lineman he had ever coached, the strongest man on the Ames line this year, and 'one of the greatest athletes he ever saw.'" On the news of his death, the coach canceled practice for the day, and the school canceled classes.[58]

Following Trice's death, a longer front page (first column) piece in the *Minneapolis Tribune* added more details about the game. Trice had dislocated his left shoulder on the second play but "refused to leave the game." (When later examined in the hospital, his injury proved to be a broken collarbone.) The quality of his play was unaffected, as he repeatedly "stopped the Minnesota plays directed at his position and tore open wide gaps in the Gophers' line to allow the Iowa backs to make gains." Minnesota coach Bill Spaulding was as fulsome in his praise as Iowa State's coach: "I guess he went down fighting, didn't he? And he didn't quit. He was a real football player, a hard hitter, but a clean player, and a thorough sportsman. Our boys commented after the game on his clean and hard play. . . . He was a credit to the game."[59]

Despite the sightly jarring "Negro tackle" and "credit to the game," this all seems much like sportswriters' responses to the deaths of Cadet Eugene Byrne and Archer Christian in 1909—except that newspapers outside Des Moines and Minneapolis (including the *New York Daily News, Boston Globe, Chicago Tribune,* and *Los Angeles Times*) printed only brief wire-service notices (a dozen lines or so) about the "negro tackle's" death, and the *New York Times* was among the papers that published nothing at all. Unlike Von Gammon's and Archer Christian's, Jack Trice's death was not truly newsworthy. But after a handwritten note was discovered in Trice's coat pocket following his death, a longer follow-up story by the Associated Press got fuller and broader coverage. Written to himself the night before the game, what Trice called "My thoughts just before the first real college game of my life" and the AP called "Jack Trice's creed" was reprinted in its entirety:

> The honor of my race, family and self are at stake. Everyone is expecting me to do big things. I will. My whole body and soul are to be thrown recklessly about the field tomorrow.
>
> Every time the ball is snapped, I will be trying to do more than my part. On all defensive plays, I must break through the opponent's line and stop the play in their territory.
>
> Beware of mass interference. Fight low, with your eyes open and toward the play. Roll back the interference. Watch out for crossbucks and reverse end runs. Be on your toes every minute if you expect to make good.[60]

Trice in his room alone at night, consecrating himself to "my race, family and self," was like a "knight" in a James Hopper story, pledged to give all for Alma Mater.[61] From the account of his stellar play in the game the next day, as described in the *Minneapolis Tribune*, Trice had fully internalized the football culture of "taking it," of playing "hard but clean" through the pain of a broken collarbone. But Trice was also the "negro tackle," or "Jack Trice, negro" in the wire-service reports, as if "negro" were either the position he played or what made him a distinct kind of football player. Some columnists were moved by his words that so well expressed football's ideals, but what seemingly made them remarkable was that Trice was a "negro." Three days after his "creed" was published, "The Observer's Column" on the front page of the *Minneapolis Daily Star* addressed that "touching letter which 'Jack' Trice, colored player on the Ames football team, wrote the night before he was killed," which "breathed the spirit of wanting to make good." The writer (unnamed but presumably well-known to his readers as a front-page columnist) was impressed by Trice's "suggestion that he was anxious not for himself so much as for his race," and he confessed that, to his "eternal shame," when he had watched Trice early in the game come to the sidelines, "pointing to his injured shoulder and no one came to help him, I thought he was 'yellow'—not of skin but of heart." The writer was now offering this column as his belated "sincere apology. You went down, playing the game—and I only hope that my spirit has as good a claim to whiteness as yours has Over There."[62]

Full stop.

Not just that chilling line, equating blessedness with whiteness, but the entire statement is horribly revealing. The ignoring of Trice's death by major metropolitan newspapers might be explained by the fact that it came in a game between the state university in Minnesota and the agricultural college in Iowa, before 12,000 spectators and a few wire-service reporters, along with the beat writers for the two teams' hometown papers—a "minor" game, in other words, though between colleges in "major" conferences. But that seems less significant than the fundamental fact that Jack Trice was a "*negro* tackle" in an implicitly but emphatically white college sport. Why did "The Observer" assume that Trice was "yellow," instead of badly hurt, when the medical staff ignored him on the sidelines? Perhaps he had read the recent "Racial Traits in Athletics" articles by Elmer D. Mitchell, a physical educator and former coach at the University of Michigan, that had appeared the previous spring in the *American Physical Education Review*. More likely (and like Mitchell himself), he was simply expressing a widespread racist prejudice and had probably never seen an actual Black football player before Jack Trice. (Minnesota had not had one on its team since Bobby Marshall in 1906.) Much to assume, perhaps, but all too plausible.

In characterizing the "racial traits" of each major ethnic group in the United States, Mitchell was generally patronizing about "the negro," who "mingles easily with white participants, accepting an inferior status and being content with it." He accepts the "pranks" of white teammates with a "good-humored spirit," the "same spirit [that] enables the player of this race to meet intentional rough play and jibes of his opponents with a grin." What Mitchell referred to, in fact, was the appalling racist treatment both by teammates (with their "pranks") and opponents (whose "jibes" were racist epithets, and "rough play" was vicious targeting). Black players' "grins" were Mitchell's invention, likely transposed from the minstrel stage and racist cartoons. As if anticipating "The Observer's" assumption about Jack Trice, Mitchell noted that "many coaches say that the negro is 'yellow,' that he is good only to a certain point and fails in a crisis," a charge that Mitchell magnanimously rejected by explaining that the Black player's apparent lack of the white's "fighting bravery" was actually the "peculiarity of the white to excel and outdo himself in critical strife and to force himself when tired," due to "the surplus of nervous energy with which nature has endowed him." Blacks did not lack courage, in other words; whites just had more of it. According to Mitchell, "Medical studies have shown the black race to have blunted nervous sensibilities as compared to the white," which make Blacks "less affected by stimulants" (which would arouse them to "fighting bravery"). Oh, in addition, by the way, "temperamentally, he is inclined to be lazy."[63]

Encountering the explicit racism of the past is always a shock (for the explicitness, not for the racism). In the context here, what matters is that it utterly excluded Black football players from the purported character-building benefits of their violent sport. Contradictory stereotypes were at play here that would endure for decades: the idea that Blacks did not feel pain as keenly as whites did (their "blunted sensibilities") and the idea that Blacks could not tolerate as much pain as whites could (their lack of "surplus nervous energy").[64] To not feel as much pain meant no virtue in "taking it." To not be able to stand as much pain meant not being able to "take it" at all. The narratives of necessary and unnecessary roughness, underlying football from the beginning, were always, without having to state the self-evident fact, about *white* players.

Cadet Richard Sheridan, RIP

Eight seasons after Jack Trice's fatal injury against Minnesota, Army cadet Richard Sheridan died from a cervical fracture suffered in the Yale game. The response to Cadet Sheridan's death was slightly different. For three days, newspapers throughout the country tracked Sheridan's lingering in the hospital in an iron lung and the wrenching drama of his dying. New York papers carried stories about Army brass and coaches keeping vigil at the hospital, Sheridan's mother and brother driving 1,000 miles from Georgia to be at his bedside, memories of another Army cadet, Eugene Byrne, and another Georgia boy, Von Gammon, fatally injured in football games decades earlier.[65] Over those three days, there was much eulogizing of the popular and talented Sheridan, whose slight body was said to hold a great heart, along with some talk of eliminating the kickoff (the blockers in front of the returner were the sole vestige of the old flying wedge).

Among the era's major sports columnists, both Grantland Rice and Paul Gallico attended the game and could comment on Sheridan's death as first-hand witnesses. Rice saluted "Sheridan's valiant spirit that led to the collision which resulted in a fractured vertebrae [*sic*]," and he called the young man's death "even more regrettable in view of the fact that Sheridan was a 'star' and honor man of high standing and one of the most popular members of the Cadet Corps." What killed him, according to Rice, was "an accident completely unavoidable," but Cadet Sheridan had chosen to put himself at risk: "He evidently had made up his mind that no other Yale back was to run a kick-off for a touchdown that afternoon and he gave all he had in his headlong tackle."[66]

With Sheridan in the hospital in an iron lung, Gallico predicted in his *Daily News* column, "There will be anti-football hysteria in the wake of this tragic accident. I hope it passes over. Football is a good game and a fine thing for the boys of the nation. Not worth the ruining of a fine young life, you say? Perhaps not, but the game has many more pages on the credit than the debit side. Soldiers pause for a brief second at the side of a fallen comrade, grieve and move forward again. Cadet Sheridan met his fate unavoidably, but above all, gallantly and honorably and like a West Pointer."[67]

One must wonder what Rice saw on the field as evidence of Sheridan's resolve not to surrender another touchdown on a kickoff, or what Sheridan did to impress Gallico with his having acted "honorably" and "gallantly." Both columnists simply imagined character traits suitable for a fallen soldier, or for a young man whose character was forged in the violence of football rather than in war. (His race did not matter because it was taken for granted, while the honoring of his humanity was immeasurably greater than for Jack Trice.)

This mix of sentimentalism and fatalism—a fine young life prematurely ended by cruel fate—also characterized other sports columnists' responses. Ed Hughes in the *Brooklyn Daily Eagle*, who also had attended the game, waxed philosophical and literary about Life's "tragic ironies." "Both life and death are a gamble," Hughes wrote, "and the courageous manner in which Sheridan whirled into the proposition that confronted him indicated he was a good gambler. He may have reckoned as Bret Harte's famous Oakhurst that there was 'the usual percentage in favor of the dealer,' but that didn't check his enthusiasm any."[68] Ralph McGill in the *Atlanta Constitution* acknowledged, "No game is greater than a life," but he cautioned that "it was not the game that took the boy away, but that the scheme of things which we cannot comprehend, demanded it, tragic though it seems."[69] Westbrook Pegler in the *Chicago Tribune* weighed the alternative of touch football ("a sissy type of football"), which had been proposed by the Carnegie Foundation's Howard Savage, and concluded, "Football has been indicted by experts on many counts many times ere this, but the indictments always have been tossed out of court and the game goes on, noble, brutal, chivalrous, cruel and altogether gorgeous and daffy."[70] Even the *New York Times*' editorial took a fatalistic view: "There will be an outcry against the perils of football. But the game will go on," safer now than in "the old days of mass play," and "so long as tackling is used in the game, there is danger of such accidents as that which happened to young Sheridan. It is the more lamentable because of the character and promise which he had revealed thus early in his life."[71]

Jack Trice's death caused barely a ripple in the college football world; Cadet Sheridan's rocked it for three days. But for all of the outpouring of shock and sadness in the press, Army did not even cancel the following Saturday's game, let alone suspend the rest of its season and launch an investigation to determine the future of football at West Point. Following a moment of silence throughout the football world for the valiant young cadet, the games went on.

Figure 3.1. Frederic Stanley's cover for the *Saturday Evening Post*, November 13, 1926.

CHAPTER 3

SHOULD YOUR BOY PLAY FOOTBALL?

This is by no means to say that Cadet Sheridan's death had no lasting impact. In addition to a new round of rule revisions, it triggered the first sustained attention from the medical community.

Six weeks after the Sheridan catastrophe, the death of Fordham's Cornelius Murphy ten days after suffering a concussion in a game against Bucknell brought the season's fatalities to forty, doubling the previous high of twenty in 1925.[1] (The death toll for 1931 was later revised to fifty and then subsequently reduced to thirty-three in what became the official count.)[2] Eight of the dead were collegians, another all-time high. The *New York Times* was one of several publications that listed each player by name, locale, and any details known about the injury, assuring that the fatalities were no mere abstraction. "Whether officials will make rule changes which will eliminate some of the roughness of football remains to be seen," the *Times* cautioned. "In some quarters it is felt that almost nothing can be done because the matter of personal contact is highly important to the game."[3]

This "matter of personal contact" ("personal encounter," Eugene Richards Sr. had called it) made explicit the continuing desire to make football no less rough while making it less lethal. As weekly magazines began weighing in, the *Literary Digest* noted, "Wide demand is heard for new rules to outlaw the sort of plays that land players in the morgue—but no demand that the game itself be abolished," due in part to its "character-building aspects."[4] A writer in the *Outlook and Independent* discounted any need for new rules, advocating rather for better enforcement of existing ones. Officials who were lax in their duty were

> the custodians of a game which is the last outpost of virility in a soft, effeminate age. . . . The modern boy needs the Spartan discipline that football gives far more than did his predecessor of pioneer days. Our civilization surrounds him with softening influences. He grows up in a feminine atmosphere. He is nursed, reared and schooled by women. It will be unfortunate if these preventable injuries result in his being denied the hardening of muscle and stiffening of character that football is so well equipped to give him. We talk a lot about glorifying our American womanhood, and rightly, but why do we deny our boys their masculine birthright?[5]

This could have been written in 1894 (or in 1955 or 2013, for that matter). Football was the antidote to softness, from whatever cause, in whatever form. The emphasis on *feminine* softening of American masculinity was a new note that would be increasingly sounded.

In defending the current rules while calling for better enforcement, the writer also declared, "The brutal truth is that misguided or ill-tempered youngsters have been slugging, rabbit punching, hand slashing, and heeling each other along the scrimmage line. Few of these violations, which occur principally in high school games, are detected and few are penalized." How, one might ask, did the "virility" developed through football lead to "slugging, rabbit punching, hand slashing, and heeling"? And it was worse among high schoolers?! Football's man-building and character-building benefits had indeed settled into widely held but rarely examined truisms.

At the annual meeting of the American Football Coaches Association in December 1931, newly elected president Dr. Marvin A. (Mal) Stevens agreed to chair a newly created Committee to Investigate Football Injuries and Fatalities.[6] Stevens was doubly credentialed for the role, as head football coach at Yale since 1928 (which put him on the sidelines when Sheridan was fatally injured) and orthopedic surgeon on the medical faculty at Yale. The committee's initial task was to commission an annual report, to be presented at the meetings of the American Football Coaches Association following each football season. Dr. Floyd Eastwood from the faculty in physical education at NYU (later at Purdue, then Los Angeles State) would oversee these reports from 1932 through 1964, when the task would be taken over by faculty in physical education at the University of North Carolina. Eastwood's report at the coaches' annual meeting would routinely be covered by the wire services—an empirical measure of the state of the game that, over the next thirty years, would never vary sufficiently to spark a new crisis.

For college football's immediate future in the wake of Sheridan's death, the NCAA's rules committee came up with six reforms for 1932:

1. At least ⅜ inch of external padding was required on any equipment with hard surfaces worn by players.
2. At least five players from the receiving team on a kickoff were required to be within fifteen yards of the kickoff line (to reduce the number of bodies that could be in a wedge in front of the receiver).
3. The flying block and flying tackle (such as Cadet Sheridan's when he broke his neck) were banned.
4. A player who was replaced by a substitute would be allowed to return in the following quarter.
5. The ball would be declared dead as soon as any part of the runner (except for hands and feet) touched the ground.
6. Any use of the hands by the defense to strike an opponent's head, neck, or face was forbidden (the penalty to be disqualification and loss of half the distance to the goal line).

The *Literary Digest* called the new rules "the most sweeping revision football has had since 1906."[7] A more recent historian of college football rules called the change to the kickoff "more cosmetic than effective" and the ban on flying blocks and tackles "another public relations move" with little impact on fatalities.[8] But the others made obvious sense in themselves. The substitution rule allowed for an exhausted player to leave the game (rather than risk serious injury by continuing to play) without forfeiting the right to return. The new dead-ball rule reduced piling on. Padding the arms and fists and closely circumscribing permissible use of the hands completed the ban on "slugging" that had first been attempted decades earlier.

An editorial in the *Journal of the American Medical Association* in March (its first on the dangers of football since 1907) was less than enthusiastic, basically asking, Why did all of this take so long? The new rules simply revealed "the extent to which health hazards had been developed and tolerated" for too long. The blows to the head, neck, and face that were finally banned, for example, were not "tolerated even in the prize ring."[9] (The editorial also pointed out that permitting injured athletes to return to play, when they should remain out, increased rather than reduced their risk of serious injury.)

But if the *Journal of the American Medical Association* questioned whether the new rules would actually make football safer, an editorial in the *Yale Daily News* hysterically blasted them for making it *too* safe. Though just an undergraduate's opinion, the editorial caught the attention of the sports editor of the *Birmingham News*, Zipp Newman, who found it "really refreshing" amid the "bitter things" said "in the heat of reform waves last Fall." Newman reprinted roughly half of the *Yale Daily News* editorial, beginning with the entirety of its first paragraph: "Football is no sport for the soft and the yellow. It draws on nerve, determination, and common 'guts.' There is a long grind, a systematic elimination, and a final realization that 'all that glitters is not gold.' That is life. Life is going to be an unpleasant surprise to some sheltered scholars. It is a dirty business that draws on nerve, determination, and common 'guts.'"[10] The grim view of life as a "dirty business" may have owed something to the Depression, but once again the basic ideas had not changed since the 1890s. Zipp Newman was delighted to see it come from elitist Yale of all places. Not so the *Journal of the American Medical Association*, whose follow-up editorial in September also quoted at great length from the undergraduate "outburst," which it found regrettably "reminiscent of statements made by some physicians who urge that sickness and pain develop character in patients." Even critics of college football, Morris Fishbein wrote, "still seem to be less concerned with the sanctity of the healthy body than with the impact of the game, as now conducted, on other human values."[11] Here, distilled, was the perennial tension in football between *health* and *culture*—"the healthy body" in conflict with "other human values"—in regulating a sport that was much more than recreation.

A question of whether the new rules would make football less lethal than in 1931 hovered over the start of the 1932 season—and for some, inevitably, whether the new football would be *too* safe. Writing for *Collier's* in October, the sportswriter Bill Cunningham asked the referee from Cadet Sheridan's fatal game, Edward J. O'Brien, who also happened to be a medical doctor, how he felt about the game's "dangers" and whether it was "worth while." Dr. O'Brien replied that football, "when properly regulated and played with the proper care, is absolutely all right. At one time it was dirty, brutal and dangerous. Players were sent in with explicit instructions to 'get' opposing stars. Injuries were frequent and sometimes ghastly. Coaches were in some cases little better than thugs and they regarded each other with suspicion, distrust and jealousy."[12]

This was a stunning indictment of coaches, but only of coaches in the past. If football was really so much more brutal in some earlier period, one wonders why that brutality was tolerated, even celebrated, as it had been all along. For football's defenders, football was always more brutal in the "old days," whenever those might have been, in order to celebrate the current state of the game. The "new type of man who has gone in for coaching," according to Dr. O'Brien, was utterly different from those in this unspecified previous era. "So far as the game itself goes, as an enthusiast, and as a father of boys, I think I can safely say that from what I've seen close to it on the field it is a splendid builder of character." The value of the lessons in cooperation and self-sacrifice that players learn for "later life is only too obvious. Football, it seems to me, as currently organized, is the finest and the cleanest of training schools." The script had not changed. And Dr. O'Brien was clearly one of those physicians whom the *Journal of the American Medical Association* editorial complained about putting "other human values" ahead of "the sanctity of the healthy body."

After Floyd Eastwood reported to the American Football Coaches Association in December that "direct" and "indirect" deaths declined from fifty to thirty-seven for the 1932 season and collegians' deaths to five, a reporter for the Associated Press credited the new rules for producing "stricter officiating and better coaching" in the "organized college and university conferences," while some of the deaths in high school and sandlot games "might have been avoided if there had been closer adherence to the rules and better medical supervision."[13] This would become a dominant theme in discussions of football's dangers over the rest of the decade in popular magazines. Annual fatalities over the next four years ranged from twenty-five to thirty, but few of them were of college players, a total of just ten in those four years, and none of them from major teams that received national attention.[14] In the absence of open disagreement, an unspoken consensus was emerging among sportswriters and journalists that the rules were working where they were enforced and where the game was properly supervised.

AND WHAT ABOUT CONCUSSIONS?

From the present perspective, as football's future hangs on a satisfactory resolution to its concussion crisis, how concussions were understood and treated over the course of football's history becomes an inevitable question. In the aftermath of Cadet Sheridan's death (and seemingly prompted by that tragedy), physicians published a handful of books on football injuries that reveal what was known about concussions in this period. In 1933, Mal Stevens and Winthrop Morgan Phelps, a colleague in orthopedics at Yale, coauthored *The Control of Football Injuries*, the first comprehensive medical study of the subject. Written for "physicians who may be associated with the development and training of athletes," as the reviewer in the *Journal of the American Medical Association* put it, its chapters addressed every imaginable injury, to body parts ranging from fingers to spines and including concussions. The endorsement by the journal's reviewer would seem to confirm that the authors accurately expressed the state of medical knowledge at this time.[15]

Stevens and Phelps defined a concussion as "the result of a blow on the head which is sufficiently hard to cause a period of temporary disturbance of the proper functioning of the brain." Common symptoms included short-term memory loss, dizziness, ringing in the ears, and brief unconsciousness, with appropriate treatment "depend[ing]" entirely upon the severity of the condition." The authors recommended removing a player from the game, "if there is any evidence of concussion," to undergo "neurological examination" and "a period of rest and quiet" for a length of time at "the discretion of the neurologist." In addition, any "player who receives repeated concussions should consider very seriously withdrawing from football." Stevens and Phelps warned that concussions were more common than generally recognized and advised that a concussed player "should be watched for at least twenty-four or forty-eight hours for any evidence of increased intracranial bleeding." But they also added, "It is well to emphasize the fact that concussions and fractured skulls per se are not particularly dangerous and do not have deleterious after-effects unless there has been brain (cortical) damage with sub-dural or extra-dural hemorrhage." In short, a concussion was potentially a serious traumatic injury, but most had no long-term consequences.[16]

In 1933, the NCAA also commissioned three physicians with university affiliations (Edgar Fauver from Wesleyan, who had conducted the 1917 survey cited by the Carnegie Foundation in 1929; Augustus Thorndike from Harvard; and Joseph E. Raycroft from Princeton) to write a *Medical Handbook for Schools and Colleges*, which reached essentially the same conclusions about concussions, with more detailed recommendations for their treatment by trainers and team doctors, as was appropriate for a "Handbook." While the terms "concussion of the brain" and "fracture of the skull" were "often used in the press," the authors wrote, their seriousness was "often overlooked. When one realizes that 'concussion of the brain' should be defined as 'bruising of the brain tissues' often accompanied with actual bleeding into the tissues, one may realize that the condition should not be regarded lightly." Like Stevens and Phelps, the writers identified the symptoms of memory loss, dizziness, and "a sense of 'daze'" in mild cases. If these symptoms disappeared and the player could correctly answer questions about recent events, he could "return to play under close observation from the sidelines." If he failed the test, he should not continue playing, and "*actual unconsciousness for as long a period as one minute, should preclude further play that day*" (italics in original).[17]

Such guidelines reveal what was most broadly known and unknown about concussions in the 1930s: They could be serious, but most were not, and the difference was clearly indicated by the presence or absence of symptoms. Concussed athletes should not return to play until their symptoms disappeared, but at that point, it was safe to do so. Like Stevens and Phelps, the authors of the handbook tied treatment of concussions to their apparent seriousness. For headache or dizziness lasting over two hours, they recommended hospitalization until the patient was symptom-free for forty-eight hours. For symptoms continuing over forty-eight hours, no more football "for 21 days or longer, if at all." And for individuals "knocked unconscious repeatedly on slight provocation," no more "body-contact sport," ever.[18]

They also added this: "There is definitely a condition described as 'punch drunk' and often recurrent concussion cases in football and boxing demonstrate this."[19] If there were a "smoking gun" in this story, implicating the football establishment in a decades-long conspiracy to ignore evidence of long-term brain damage from concussions, that *punch drunk* would be it. But the term in this period was used for boxers to describe either temporary or permanent states—the wooziness of a battered fighter in the tenth round or the permanent incapacitation of the aging ex-fighter.[20] If Fauver, Thorndike, and Raycroft had themselves witnessed punch-drunkenness as a permanent condition in football players (unlikely in their university settings), they would surely have made much more of it. The passive construction of their statement ("there is . . . a condition described as") suggests that they were referring to possible cases that they had not themselves seen. Hearsay, not evidence. And they approved of players returning to the game in which they were concussed, once their symptoms disappeared. Both the *NCAA Medical Handbook* and

The Control of Football Injuries warned about persisting symptoms, repeated concussions, and serious trauma that might not initially be apparent, but not against returning to play after mild concussions. A concussion was a bruise to the brain, and like a bruise to any other part of the body, in the absence of internal bleeding it would heal without long-term consequences.[21]

In a third key medical text from the 1930s, Augustus Thorndike in 1938 published the first edition of his *Athletic Injuries: Prevention, Diagnosis and Treatment*, based on his medical supervision, as chief of surgery for Harvard's University Health Services, of athletes in all sports at Harvard over five school years, from 1932 to 1937. Subsequent editions (in 1942, 1948, 1956, and 1962) of what became a foundational text in sports medicine would add more athletes to the statistical tables but no changes whatever to the wording about head injuries.

Thorndike addressed concussions in two separate chapters. In chapter 10 ("Internal Injuries"), he identified three classes of concussion: (1) "the mild type in which the patient is momentarily 'knocked unconscious' and immediately recovers or regains all his intellectual functions"; (2) "the mild type in which the individual is 'knocked out on his feet,' but never loses consciousness completely and retains some of his intellectual and all of his vegetative consciousness"; and (3) "the more severe type of concussion in which the period of unconsciousness is obvious and exists for a minute or longer and the patient suffers with the residual symptoms of headache, dizziness, and the complete or incomplete loss of intellect." He also added, "The athlete who suffers from repeated recurrent concussions is referred to as 'punch drunk.' That actual brain pathology exists in this instance, is not yet proven to the author's knowledge."[22] That wording added a more direct qualification than the statement in the 1933 *NCAA Medical Handbook*, confirming that Thorndike (like his earlier coauthors) had heard about punch-drunkenness in football players but not witnessed it himself and that it was still not clinically established. Defining "punch-drunkenness" as susceptibility to "repeated recurrent concussions" was also quite different from the long-term brain damage now identified with chronic traumatic encephalopathy. That understanding was far in the future.

Having defined three classes of concussions in chapter 10, Thorndike in chapter 13 ("Head, Neck and Face") explained the appropriate treatment for each one, guided by a basic principle: "In itself, [a concussion] is not serious, but the complications and sequelae which might follow these cases inadequately treated are the all-important factors facing the athletic surgeon." Players who never lose consciousness "should be permitted to re-enter competition only if they present no residual symptoms or signs." Those who lose consciousness for "at least a minute," or whose symptoms persist after recovering consciousness, "should not be permitted to re-enter competition that day." And those with "residual symptoms" should be hospitalized for at least twenty-four hours.[23]

Athletic Injuries was one of Thorndike's two books (the other was *Manual of Bandaging, Strapping and Splinting*) that the *New York Times* in his obituary called "standards in the field of sports medicine."[24] Along with the *NCAA Medical Handbook* that he coauthored and Stevens and Phelps's *Control of Football Injuries*, it summed up the state of the medical understanding of concussions from the 1930s into the 1960s (with Thorndike's subsequent editions). All three warned sideline physicians to be attentive to persisting symptoms and repeat concussions, but they approved players' returning to play once they were symptom-free, even in the same game. All of these books prioritized players' physical *health*. None of them confronted the fact that health concerns in football butted up against a powerful culture of "taking it" (although, as a football coach as well as a physician, Mal Stevens surely understood that culture well). And none of them knew that concussions could have catastrophic consequences long after symptoms disappeared.

IS FOOTBALL WORTHWHILE?

The authors of these books had very limited data on concussions, as on football injuries generally. Only fatalities were easy to count on a national level. But besides leading directly to Floyd Eastwood's annual reports to the American Football Coaches Association, the death of Richard Sheridan and the rule changes that followed seem to have prompted a handful of more narrowly focused surveys of injuries in high school football. A pair of studies, both published in 1933 in the same issue of the leading professional journal in physical education, tabulated football injuries over four seasons, 1929–32, at two-thirds of the high schools in Massachusetts (by a surgeon at Boston City Hospital, who regularly served as a sideline physician at high school games, and the associate director of physical education for Boston public schools) and at all of the high schools in California over a single season, 1932 (by an administrator in the State Department of Education). The following year, the *Journal of the American Medical Association* published a team physician's study of four seasons (1930–33) at one elite prep school in Michigan.

In the Michigan study, 80 percent of the 200 boys at the Cranbrook School played football, Thomas Horan reported in *JAMA*, and he attributed a dramatic decline in their injuries, from 243 in 1930 to 75 in 1933, to increased strengthening and conditioning. For the public high schools, the rate of "serious" injury was approximately 7 percent in California and ranged from 2.9 to 4.6 percent over the four seasons in Massachusetts. (The data compiled by California's State Department of Education was likely more reliable.) Regarding concussions, the roughly 160 players at the Michigan prep school suffered a total of seventeen over the four seasons, from a low of one to a high of nine. The high school studies found comparable lower rates: one concussion for every 250 players in Massachusetts, one in 234 for California. The physician in Michigan described the usual range of symptoms and, for prevention, stressed the importance of well-fitted headgear and chin straps. While the author of the California study offered no comment on his data, the physician and physical educator in Massachusetts pointedly justified football for boys as "a natural outlet for their nervous energies" and a means for keeping them "off the streets, thereby avoiding other mishaps, such as automobile, motorcycle, and trolley-car injuries, and others too numerous to mention." And they concluded with a summary in bold font: "Under proper supervision, on a good field, with a doctor present to supervise all injured players, with properly arranged schedules under moderately good weather conditions—we believe that football as played in the high schools today is certainly worthwhile and that the personal liability has been reduced to a very low figure."[25]

The public health historian Kathleen Bachynski has termed this approach to injuries a "supervisory imperative": the idea that proper supervision, rather than radical changes to the game itself, would assure that football was safe enough for boys to play. The inherent danger in such a principle was that it could serve the interests of the supervisors above those of the supervised.[26] And it was pervasive in articles by sportswriters in women's and family magazines in the 1930s. After *Ladies' Home Journal* published a small handful of articles during football's crisis-plagued early years, they began pouring out steadily following Cadet Sheridan's death.[27] The stream actually started two months earlier, when *Parents' Magazine* published an article about appropriate sports for adolescents, written by a medical doctor who rejected not only football but every other sport involving "hard impact" or endurance (any foot race over 100 yards), or even intense competition. Football injuries for him were entirely a health issue, without cultural complications—not a very helpful guide to parents whose sons wanted to play on their school teams.[28]

Beginning in October 1932, thirteen articles weighing the benefits and risks of football for boys and written explicitly for parents appeared in *Ladies' Home Journal*, *Woman's Home Companion*, *Parents' Magazine*, *Good Housekeeping*, and *Woman's Day* (with combined circulations of nearly 10 million by the end of the decade).[29] Just four of the articles were written by women; mothers read them, but male "experts" mostly wrote them. The title of every article could have been the one from a handful of articles in the early 1950s, "Should Your Boy Play Football?,"[30] or the one posed by *Woman's Day* in 1937, "Is Football Worth While?"

On balance, the answer to both questions was yes, but with considerable qualification and some strong dissent. The most enthusiastic endorsements came from two of the women who also happened to be wives of college coaches or mothers of players. Mrs. Knute Rockne, the widow of the famous college coach and the subject of an article in *Good Housekeeping* in October 1932, recalled her husband's "contempt for the 'lounge lizards—sissy boys—drug-store cowboys' of the campus" and his desire for "regular he-men" on his teams. ("Not, of course, cave-men," she added.) Having recently lost her husband in a tragic plane crash, Mrs. Rockne was now raising three sons on her own. Two of them were currently playing football with her full encouragement for what it could teach them about "manliness, fairness, determination, perseverance, and above all, courage—invaluable assets in all living." And she urged other mothers to do likewise. "I believe that football is the greatest body and character builder there is," she declared, in a refrain unchanged since the 1890s. "I'm not afraid of its hazards."[31]

Writing in *Ladies' Home Journal* in November 1935, Mrs. Langdon (Biffy) Lea—wife of an 1890s Princeton All-American[32] and mother of three former or current Princeton players—admitted to agonizing about possible injuries to her youngest son, the one still playing, but she ultimately shared Bonnie Rockne's faith in football's positive impact on her boy. "I know that if he does come out physically fit he will be the better for the discipline and the keen competition he has been in, that his body will be stronger and his will to win sharpened to a razor edge, and he will be more of a man than if he had been spending his time at tea fights and on week-end jaunts to New York to fight the battle of the night clubs."[33] "More of a man" was the key phrase here. Mothers as well as fathers wanted manly sons, and football had long promised to develop them.

But "if he does come out physically fit" was another key phrase, and on that count, football offered no guarantees. The other two female authors acknowledged more concern about their sons being hurt, but they also accepted that risk as necessary for their boys' development. A mother of two writing in *Ladies' Home Journal* in January 1938 ("Can He Take It?") described overhearing her children playing with neighbor kids: "I pick up such current expressions as 'Sissy!' or 'You're a panty-waist. You ain't got the nerve.' And later, 'Aw, let him play! He's little but he can take it.' And suddenly it brings home to me, the mother of two, that though the vocabulary of the modern child may strike a low in grammar it shows a high regard for courage and stoic endurance under stress."[34] Another mother, writing in *Parents' Magazine* in August 1939 ("We Must Let Them Go"), urged her readers to let their sons do potentially dangerous things, like climb trees and play football, even though "it's such a rough game, and so many boys are hurt every year!" Her own boy was knocked out one day playing football but was fine the next; another time, he needed four stitches in his chin. "And yet—he learned so many lessons in good sportsmanship, and who was I to have kept him from it?"[35] Being concussed ("knocked out") seemed no more consequential than a cut chin.

The two writers who rejected football outright in these articles were both men, writing in *Parents' Magazine* in 1934 and 1939. The first urged families to play touch football with their friends, as his own did regularly. The other wanted his son to choose a sport that he could play over his lifetime, not just when he was young.[36]

In October 1937, *Woman's Day* posed the question, "Is Football Worth While?" with pro and con views from two former college stars. Speaking against the game was the same George Owen who had rattled the football establishment in 1925 with his indictment of the football "grind" and had more recently been a star for the Boston Bruins in the National Hockey League. Owen repeated that charge now, debunking the idea that football built character and reiterating his distaste for the "drudgery" of "the hours of grueling, smashing contact," which also caused "injuries of some kind to every participant," sometimes for life. Arguing *for* football was Bert Metzger, briefly famous as Knute Rockne's "watch-charm" guard (five-foot-nine, 152 pounds) on his 1930 Notre Dame team, who emphasized the game's lessons in teamwork and self-discipline while also invoking the Rockne credo that football's "hard knocks . . . enabled young fellows to be rugged, to stand up against blows later on." As Metzger put it, Rockne used to charge that, if the critics of overemphasizing football got their wish, "we'd soon be serving tea and lemon at every football game."[37]

None of these arguments were new, but they were now being addressed specifically to the parents of young boys and high schoolers. Football had begun as a college game but immediately spread to high schools, which followed the collegians' lead in all things football. By the 1930s, there were many times more high school players than college players, which meant parents worrying about their sons rather than journalists and eminent spokesmen offering judgments from on high. Without naming a source, one sportswriter in 1932 claimed that 24,000 young men were playing football at roughly 500 colleges, while 350,000 boys played on 10,000 high school teams and another 240,000 on "two thousand organized teams representing church organizations, municipal leagues, athletic clubs and organized sand-lot teams."[38] Another sportswriter in 1937 put the total number of high school football players at 616,000 (roughly the sum of the earlier writer's two non-collegiate groups).[39] Whatever the precise number, these were the boys whose parents were the targets of the articles in women's magazines written by prominent sportswriters in the years following Cadet Sheridan's death.

Edwin B. Dooley, a reporter for the *New York Sun* and former All-American quarterback at Dartmouth (also a future chairman of the New York State Athletic Commission),[40] wrote articles for *Woman's Home Companion* in November 1932 and *Parents' Magazine* in October 1933, in which his primary point was to charge parents with responsibility for assuring that the football their sons played was truly safe. (Dooley cited the 1932 figures noted above.) In the first, he credited Mal Stevens, Floyd Eastwood, and the NCAA Rules Committee's "six drastic rule changes" for the 1932 season with having done everything possible to make college football safer, but it was still up to "intelligent parental interest" to "help safeguard" the boys playing in high schools and on sandlots. "The burden falls on the mothers" (of course), Dooley wrote, to make sure that their sons are "carefully examined by a competent physician" and have regular physical exams during the season.[41]

A year later, Dooley repeated his warning that, while rule changes had made college football safer, the game was "just as dangerous as ever" for "the little fellows on the park lawns and sandlots," and underfunded high schools were "little better off." "How can the parents offset the dangers associated with so vigorous and Spartan a pastime?" he asked. "First, prohibit the extremely young boys from subjecting themselves to the rigors of the game." But if their young sons *must* play, parents had to ensure that they had good equipment and received proper medical care.[42] Most strikingly, Dooley in both articles was eager to disabuse parents of any illusion that playing football would actually benefit their boys beyond whatever pleasure they got from playing. In the first one, he dismissed the idea "that anyone who succeeds on the football field will surely succeed in life. Nothing could be more illogical." In the second, he was even more emphatic: "The archaic notion that football will make a man of a boy is pure fiction. Puny weaklings often have more courage and strength of heart than a big, blustering football player who can tear a line to shreds." One can only wonder how deeply this soaked in.

Dooley's withering scorn for such delusions was unusual, but other sportswriters echoed his warning about football's particular dangers for the very young. Dick Hyland, a former football star at Stanford (and hero of the American rugby team at the 1924 Olympics) on the verge of a long career as a sportswriter and columnist at the *Los Angeles Times*, told readers of *Good Housekeeping* in September 1934 that the overwhelming majority of football deaths and serious injuries occurred in high school or sandlot games and scrimmages. But these could be avoided if boys delayed playing tackle football until they were physically mature and if they were then properly coached and supervised.[43] Two years later, *Good Housekeeping* published a more melodramatic version of the same argument, this time by Bob Considine, a well-known sportswriter in the Hearst newspaper chain. Considine's "Death on the Gridiron" opened with a nightmare scenario of a young boy, "your son, or mine," brutally crushed on a football field and rushed to the hospital, where he will "add his name to the long list of youths of America who have given up their lives in a game long romanticized beyond its intrinsic value." Considine warned parents that this awful drama would play out thirty or forty times that season, with half of the "doomed kids" from the "autumn slaughter" playing in high school (twenty such cases in 1936, according to Floyd Eastwood's figure cited by Considine). For a third of the deaths in this "most scientifically savage" of all sports, Considine blamed unknowledgeable or win-at-all-cost coaches—the ones who praised boys' continuing to play when exhausted as "gameness," rather than denouncing it as "foolhardiness." "Player and public have been well sold on the notion that character is a metal that can be tested only by the acid of excess punishment," Considine wrote. "Most injuries occur when a boy is tottering with fatigue, too weary to duck disaster."[44]

But having thus terrified the mothers and fathers reading this and, like Dooley, challenged football's supposed "intrinsic value," Considine then reassured them that their sons would be just fine, so long as they kept good habits, were properly outfitted and coached, played on well-maintained fields, and had proper medical supervision. A year later, in "No Holiday for Death," again in *Good Housekeeping*, Considine sharpened his criticism of high school football, whose avoidable tragedies made it the "sorriest chapter in the sorriest book on American sporting life." But this time, he shifted primary responsibility from coaches to parents themselves for being "the chief neglectors of high-school football players": fathers too busy with work to oversee their sons' practices, mothers who could but did not.[45] Like Dooley, Considine notably put health concerns above cultural values, but he stopped short of declaring the game itself inherently dangerous.

One final article from the 1930s rejected both "intrinsic" benefits from playing football and supervisory solutions to its potential risks. In "Can the Teens Take It?" in *Parents' Magazine* in February 1939, a father who was also a member of a small-town school board described his community's new coach, who took over a championship team and then finished in last place in his initial season but kept his job after explaining to the board how destructive highly competitive football was for adolescents in the "transitional stage" of their lives. The coach told the board that "already driven by the necessity of proving themselves for their souls' satisfaction, fast-growing Johnny and Joe make the Podunk High School team and are goaded even more mercilessly by social compulsions. They have to reassure themselves in this period of doubt and misgiving by exerting themselves to the limit. They have to show their teammates, the coach, and the stands that they can take it. They have to demonstrate their manhood if it kills them," and, sadly, sometimes it does. "They give prodigally of themselves in the frenzied effort to pile up mountains of evidence in which to bury all suspicion of their being sissies." After hearing this explanation, the board kept the coach and dropped interscholastic athletics altogether.[46]

The debunking of the mystique of "taking it" in these articles is striking, but so is the recognition that it needed debunking. Collectively, they reveal not a general state of uncertainty but rather, as always, of competing certainties about football's benefits and risks.

PUNCH-DRUNK?

While the question of whether football was good for boys' health played out chiefly in women's magazines, the article on the topic that generated the most controversy appeared in 1939 in *Cosmopolitan* (when it was still a general-interest monthly).[47] It was titled "Football—Not for *My* Son" and written by Bill Cunningham, another former All-American—in his case, as a center at Dartmouth in 1920 (six years before Edwin Dooley)—who became a highly respected sportswriter for nearly forty years at the *Boston Post* and *Boston Herald* and a prolific magazine journalist, mostly for *Collier's*, in the 1930s. (He wrote the interview with the doctor/referee mentioned earlier.) In parts of "Football—Not for *My* Son," Cunningham embraced the game more enthusiastically than any of the other sportswriters in the women's magazines did, and he did so on the traditional terms that some of those writers debunked.

"I respect it and salute it as a molder of character," he wrote, "and a teacher of priceless values necessary for living." But in weighing football for his son, rather than as he experienced it, Cunningham was thinking about his boy at age forty:

> That's when he'll need all he has of health and strength and stamina and intelligence. I want him whole and healthy and keenly alert then, unhampered by physical weakness or mental blackouts. . . . His chances won't be improved if he logs into the struggle with arthritic pains in a once-broken shoulder, a spine that keeps sending him back to the doctor, a trick knee that keeps putting him back on crutches, the tortures of sinusitis originating from a smash between the eyes, or a brain that's survived concussion or fracture. Those are the major and inescapable levies of football. Experiences at 20, their shackles at 40.[48]

Cunningham was decades ahead of his time—as if describing former NFL players in the 1990s, struggling with permanent disabilities—and he was writing about football's long-term damage to the bodies of men who did not play beyond college. Approximately one in three players was hurt every year, Cunningham wrote. While there were no data on how many were "permanently" damaged, he suggested that readers "just inquire among the ex-football players you know. You'll discover that practically every one brought some souvenir home from the wars which he'd gladly trade back today." And those souvenirs included brain damage. He had heard about an All-American from his own era who was now "a mental case and has been ever since he got out of college." Although no one knew the cause, "he used to hit a line awful hard, they tell me, and I guess that banging around the head didn't do him any good." Cunningham himself knew a former end, now "a businessman who occasionally has to pull his car in to the nearest curb, take his head in his hands and sit there trying to remember who he is, where he was going and where he lives. . . . Today, at times, he's as punch-drunk as any prize-ring stumble-bum." Another former player, an All-American tackle, "still suffers from the effects of a concussion that had him in the hospital two weeks. There's a jerking in his neck that he can't control; he suffers blinding headaches, and laughter with him is a nervous affliction, not a means of expressing amusement." Cunningham recalled seeing, years ago, yet another "magnificent specimen," two years after his skull was fractured, "stumbling pitifully around with ragged blanks in his mind and faulty co-ordination in his limbs . . . a condition that probably contributed to his death by drowning."

"But that's a sufficient sample," he insisted, after citing several more cases.

> That's mainly why I wouldn't be enthusiastic about seeing a portion of my own flesh and blood hurling his taut young body in the path of fast-forming interference while the thousands cheered.
>
> I'm talking about my boy, you understand, not myself.
>
> Me? Sure, I'd probably play the grand old game again. My shoes hang on the wall on a hook. The battered helmet has swung there beside them for lo, these many years. If the fellow who wore them wanted to get in there and risk his neck, that would seem all right. But when it comes to his replica tackling that Juggernaut, I jump the sights thirty years and simply can't see it. All-America is a lot, but Altogether is more.

The aches and pains of an All-American who parlayed his athletic success into a professional career were an acceptable cost for himself, but none of those rewards was guaranteed for his son, while the costs were almost inevitable and could be much worse than his own. Cunningham was particularly rare among journalists in writing about long-term *brain* damage as one of those costs. As noted previously, Augustus Thorndike and his colleagues reported hearing about punch-drunk football players, but whether they were referring to short-term wooziness rather than a permanent condition is unclear. That condition had been identified in boxers in 1928 by the pathologist Harrison Martland, who confirmed clinically what was already common understanding within the prizefight world. In an article in the *American Journal of the Medical Sciences* in 1936, the psychiatrist Edward J. Carroll built on Martland's work when he warned about "irreparable damage" caused by every knockout. "It is especially important," Carroll wrote, "that athletes entering into competition in which head injuries are frequent and knock-outs are common should realize that they are exposing themselves not only to immediate injury, but also to remote and more sinister effects." Carroll was writing about prizefighters, but he also noted in passing, "Punch-drunk is said to occur among professional football players also."[49] Like Fauver, Thorndike, and Raycroft, Carroll with the passive voice ("is said") alluded to hearsay from the sporting world, not to documented cases.

In 1937, a journalist named Frank Scully claimed in the weekly magazine *Liberty* that dozens of football players ended up as punch-drunk as prizefighters—"stumble-backs" instead of "stumble-bums," he called them, halfbacks who became "half-wits."[50] Scully was mostly known for a popular series of *Fun in Bed* collections of humorous stories for convalescents. His flippant language about "stumble-backs" undercut the seriousness of his subject, for which his evidence, of course, was anecdotal, not clinical (as was Cunningham's).[51] *Liberty* invited readers to reply to Scully's indictment and published a rebuttal from a former assistant coach at Harvard (when George Owen was on the team) who called it "bunk" and asserted, with no explanation, that football was "more needed now than at any previous time in our country's history to do its share in getting the youth of the nation on the right track mentally, physically, and morally."[52] Among the sports columnists who weighed in, Art Cohn of the *Oakland Tribune* accused Scully of "confusing the exception and the rule. For every boy who goes into football and comes out of it an idiot there are ten thousand who enter it as weaklings and emerge from it as MEN."[53] But Jimmy Powers (Paul Gallico's successor as columnist at the *New York Daily News*) seconded Scully's claim: "You'd be surprised at the number of ex-stars now in business in New York who said Frank Scully is right." As Powers put it, the "constant jarring of the brain" had consequences. "The brain is a delicately adjusted bit of mechanism. Look at your great army of slap-happy pugs. They are injured by padded gloves. Imagine what a cleated leather shoe, or an armored shoulder or knee guard can do!?"[54]

As a journalist, Scully was a lightweight. Bill Cunningham was a heavyweight. Scully was mostly ignored, but Cunningham's blasphemy "startled the sports world," as an editorial in one small-town paper put it. "His contemporaries rushed to their typewriters to pound out reams of criticism of Cunningham's statement. They wrote of character building, of sportsmanship, of school spirit and of the opportunities with the professional grid teams."[55] Besides publishing Powers's column, the *Daily News* polled former All-Americans living in the New York area, and a Minneapolis paper solicited reactions from parents of current players at the University of Minnesota. Only one of the parents agreed with Cunningham. Most of both groups downplayed the game's roughness and stressed such benefits as learning "teamwork, resourcefulness, alertness, and sportsmanship." But former Fordham All-American Tony Siano also reaffirmed the value of the game's roughness, at least implicitly, in saying that he wanted his son to play football to "make a man of him." One of the Gopher parents, who had himself played seven years of athletic club football of the "raw-raw, not rah-rah! type," said that he never worried about his son, even after he was injured a year ago. "I knew from experience he had to learn to take it."[56]

The possibility of long-term brain damage from football surfaced in discussions of the game in the 1930s but without clinical evidence or even medical authority to confirm and clarify the risk. It is certainly notable that some prominent national sportswriters in the '30s debunked the cherished belief in football as a character builder, but their scorn was directed at the football played by boys on sandlots and in high schools, not at the football they covered in their day jobs on newspapers, where they wrote about the college game. Collectively, the articles in popular magazines in these years reveal not general uncertainty in the country but the continuation of competing certainties about football's benefits and risks, as old as the game. Limited health data, as always, collided with unexamined clichés and deeply held beliefs.

CHAPTER 4

NO GAME FOR SISSIES

The mother writing in *Ladies' Home Journal* in 1938 who let her son play football after overhearing neighborhood children calling each other "sissy" and "panty-waist" pointed to a reason why boys might want to play football, whether or not they actually enjoyed it. So did the high school coach, described in *Parents' Magazine*, who explained to the school board how high school boys felt driven on the football field "to demonstrate their manhood if it kills them . . . in the frenzied effort to pile up mountains of evidence in which to bury all suspicion of their being sissies."[1]

To one interested outsider, the psychoanalytically trained British anthropologist Geoffrey Gorer, writing in 1948, it was not just American boys who worried about being or not being sissies. In *The American People: A Study in National Character*, Gorer described this obsession as a unique American character trait, which he traced to the rejection of patriarchal authority (beginning with the American Revolution) and to the tyranny of mothers (a favorite scapegoat in the postwar years). "It is the overriding fear of all American parents that their child will turn into a sissy," Gorer wrote in a passage that several reviewers seized on; and "it is the overriding fear of all Americans from the moment that they can understand language that they may be taken for a sissy."[2]

One can doubt the diagnosis but recognize the symptom. The word "sissy" now sounds quaint and juvenile, but it was commonly used in the 1930s and 1940s, including on sports pages, sometimes as a joke (at the expense of

Figure 4.1. Cover photograph by Alfred Eisenstaedt for *Life*, October 9, 1939. Alfred Eisenstaedt/The LIFE Picture Collection/Shutterstock.

non-rugged sports, like golf or tennis or *touch* football; or of a coach's pass-happy "aerial circus" offense that betrayed the essential nature of *real* battering-ram football). But sometimes the word expressed disgust, as in November 1931, when "Lone Star" Dietz, the former Carlisle Indian star and current coach at the Haskell Institute, ranted that the reforms being considered in the aftermath of Cadet Sheridan's death would turn football into a "'sissy' sport" for "a bunch of weak-kneed sisters afraid of their own shadows."[3] Sometimes the term came out defensively, as when a sportswriter, accusing the local high school team's opponent of playing dirty football, felt a need to add, "We are NOT an advocate of 'sissy' football."[4] In 1944, Pitt coach Clark Shaughnessy (the mastermind behind the modern T-formation) felt compelled to defend his limited use of head-on tackling and scrimmaging in practices by insisting that "safe football is not sissy football, it's sensible football."[5]

OF "CHINA DOLLS" AND "SISSY FOOTBALL"

But if Gorer was right that to be or not be a "sissy" was a weirdly American obsession, striking evidence that it had a special urgency for adolescent boys comes from two of the smaller tributaries to the football cultural mainstream in the 1930s. One was the football stories written for teenage boys in the pulp magazine *Sport Story*, published by the firm of Street & Smith in the 1920s and 1930s. Street & Smith was essentially the corporate creator of sports fiction as a distinct popular genre, beginning with the adventures of Frank Merriwell in *Tip Top Weekly* in 1896 and followed by *Popular Magazine* (1903) and *Top-Notch* (1910), whose adventure stories for either older or younger readers included large doses of sport.[6] *Sport Story* arrived in 1923 as the firm's first all-sport magazine, to establish sports fiction as a distinct pulp genre alongside Westerns, detective stories, love stories, sci-fi, and all the rest of the pulp universe. As a semimonthly for seventeen years and then a monthly for four more, *Sport Story* published well over 2,000 stories or installments of serials, covering all the major and several minor sports, including nearly 300 football stories, typically soaked in the game's violence.[7]

It exaggerates little to say that virtually every football story written for boys has had a hero who must overcome some obstacle to win the big game, most obviously a powerful opponent or bitter rival. For all-conquering heroes like Frank Merriwell (in Street & Smith's *Tip Top Weekly*), obstacles might have to come from outside the sport, wholly beyond the flawless hero's control, like gamblers who kidnap him before the big game. In the more respectable middle-class monthly boys' magazines (*American Boy*, *Boys' Life*, *Open Road for Boys*), which churned out football stories in season, the obstacle was often a flaw in the hero himself, his arrogance or selfishness, perhaps, which he had to overcome. These stories were moralistic as well as heroic.

Sport Story strove to thrill its young readers, not instruct them, and its stories, given their plots, were directed at young readers' own desires and anxieties rather than adults' expectations. Pulp stories cannot be taken as some definitive barometer of American boys' inner lives, but in their extravagant actions and emotions they must have touched closer to those lives than the moralistic juvenile magazines did (or than the opinions of sportswriters in women's magazines, certainly). A remarkable number of *Sport Story*'s football tales were simply drenched in violence, and the obstacle that the young hero had to overcome in many of them was his own or others' uncertainty about whether he was tough enough to take it—with or without the word, whether he was a "sissy."

At their most extreme, both the plots and the prose in *Sport Story* epitomized the excesses that came to define the generic term "pulp fiction" (as in the Quentin Tarantino film that it inspired). In "Runcie's Cowardice" (1925), for one rather extreme example, a huge college freshman, despised as a coward because he refuses to play football, turns out to be a brilliant former prep star who gave up the sport after permanently crippling two opponents. When Runcie finally takes to the field, he shocks everyone by playing like "some vampire," "a demon incarnate," a "thing of superhuman strength—savage, tireless, relentless energy, a thing of devilish ingenuity." (For pulp fiction, a half-dozen adjectives or metaphors were always better than one or two.) In the locker room afterward, with "his blood-smeared faced looking repulsively vicious," Runcie tells his teammates that he had indeed been afraid to play, not out of fear for himself but for what he might do to them.[8] The supposed coward turns out to be the most savage of them all.

"Thunderbolt" (1932) by Max Brand (the pen name for Frederick Faust, prolific author of pulp Westerns) used the same plot seven years later, this time concerning a magnificent physical specimen who seems "yellow" on the football field but turns out to be the son of a prizefighter who once killed a man in the ring. Like Runcie, Joe Cochrane fears that, with hands "like the unsheathed claws of a wild beast," he will fulfill his biological destiny by going berserk in a game. The coach/narrator comes up with an ingenious (!) solution: move Joe from defense to offense, where he cannot use his hands. (Brand/Faust was clearly unaware that the substitution rules in the 1930s did not allow separate offensive and defensive units. "Max Brand" was a writer of Westerns, not sport stories, after all. But he did have a rich vocabulary for describing violence.)[9]

This over-the-top violence must have touched the fantasies of young readers or it would not have been injected so often into these stories. The more typical *Sport Story* hero does not have to fear or constrain his savagery but discover or prove that he has it in him. A textbook case of the former was Jackson Scholz's "The Sixth Letter" (1930), which told of Bill Kemper, a great natural athlete who goes out for football as a senior solely to acquire one more varsity letter in a new sport and then proceeds to play utterly without passion. As his coach narrates the story, Bill always stayed down when he was tackled instead of fighting and struggling "for every fraction of an inch" as a "real football player" would do. (Scholz *did* know football; this was two years before the post-Sheridan rule that declared a tackled player *down* before he could keep crawling, while opponents piled on.) Bill also "ran interference in a timid, hesitant manner" because, basically, he "did not like to be hurt" (presumably like many readers of the story). "Don't get the idea that there was anything yellow about the kid," the coach explains, "because there wasn't. He merely did not enjoy being tackled any more than the average person likes having a tooth pulled."[10]

Bill wasn't "yellow," but he didn't like pain. Certainly, many young readers might have identified with that. But then, in the second half of the Thanksgiving Day game, with no warning or explanation, Bill suddenly begs the coach to put him in and proceeds to run wild, "with a savage fierceness that brought a cry of wonder from the stands." As always with *Sport Story*, there was no rule against piling on the overheated prose. Bill plays with an "unnatural savage frenzy" and runs "like a maniac" until he breaks his wrist; even then, he refuses to leave the game. With the ball at midfield and time for one last play, Bill tosses aside his helmet and takes off on one final spectacular dash down the field. As he bears down on the last defender at the goal line, Bill "must have presented a terrible spectacle with his bloody face and burning eyes, running with that fierce high knee action, which is the terror of all football men." When runner and defender collide head-on, "the impact of the two men was a horrible thing." It knocks both of them cold—this may be the only football story to end with a double concussion (clearly no matter of concern for writer or readers or editors of the story). But Bill's momentum carries him, unconscious, across the line, clutching the ball to win the game by one point.

Bill wasn't "yellow," but at first he could not take it, and then he could. This would seem to be a formula that would appeal to boys who were instinctively—or rationally—timid but horrified of being thought "yellow." In another story, a player must overcome his fear of tackling runners from behind, after he once caught a cleated shoe in his face. Yet another learns "that it doesn't hurt to be hurt" when a "savage blow" in a game does not faze him but turns him into a "snarling maniac."[11] It is striking that in none of these stories does anything happen to account for the protagonist's sudden transformation from timidity to recklessness, which marks his rite of passage, his discovery that he has "the stuff men are made of." Such specificity would undermine the basic fantasy of being transformed, however it might happen. The emphasis on *taking it* had been a commonplace in football fiction since James Hopper, but overcoming anxiety was something new.

A specific fear or reluctance, such as tackling from behind, was less typical in these stories than a generic underlying horror of being thought "yellow," or a "sissy," which haunted *Sport Story* throughout its twenty-year run but particularly in the late 1920s and early '30s. Some of the stories had explicit titles—"Angel Face," "Graceful," "Half Pint," "Softy," "Nice Boy!," "China Doll," "Aunty's Boy"—that announced the theme and, of course, turned out to be misleading, or wholly ironic.[12] "Angel Face" has to protect his pretty features for a promised movie career but then runs wild after his contract falls through. "China Doll" has no fear of getting hurt himself but of hurting someone else after his brother has been crippled (a more human-scale version of "Runcie's Coward" and "Thunderbolt"). Sometimes, a visible mark of fragility or effeminacy (blond curls, fine features)[13] or an artistic talent (playing the violin, graceful dancing, a falsetto voice for singing in school plays)[14] has to be proven wholly misleading. The language describing what was at stake was always unambiguous. A boy nicknamed "Lady" for his genius in performing female roles had "nothing sissified about him, as he had proved on the gridiron."[15] A "gridiron dancer" who puts the game in jeopardy by losing thirty-three yards when he instinctively tried to avoid being tackled reenters the game on defense and smashes the ball carrier on his very first play. It was "the first time in his life that he had ever made a deliberate savage attack upon another person," and he is amazed to be unhurt. "It was fun to be a tough guy," he suddenly realizes.[16] Certain writers (all long forgotten)—William Elliott Carleton, Jackson Scholz, T. W. Ford above all—more or less specialized in what might be called this "redeemed sissy" plot.[17]

Bill Kemper's tossing his helmet aside at the crucial moment in "The Sixth Letter," signifying his sudden fearlessness and sense of freedom, was a recurring motif in at least a dozen of these stories in the 1930s.[18] The National Federation of High School Athletic Associations first recommended helmets for all players in 1935.[19] The NCAA did not mandate them until 1939, the National Football League until 1943, and newspaper photographs of college and pro games in the 1930s show a mix of players with or without them, seemingly by choice in weighing comfort against protection. In warning about football's dangers in *Parents' Magazine* in 1933 (as discussed in the previous chapter), Edwin Dooley complained at one point, "Just why so many boys love to hurl aside their helmets in the critical moments of play, or go without them entirely, is more than I can understand."[20] Not wearing one at all might have been for comfort; tossing it aside at the critical moment seems more likely to have been for show. Who knows, maybe some of those boys got the idea from reading *Sport Story*.

A second minor tributary to the mainstream football culture, equally revealing of the game's privileged but fraught place in American boy culture, was first announced (as far as I can tell) in a brief notice on the society page of the *Cincinnati Enquirer* for November 18, 1928, regarding an upcoming "football dinner" at the local YMCA. Among the songs, yells, and skits to be performed, "the main stunt of the party will be 'Sissy Football,' a very feminine interpretation of the game which will bring gales of laughter."[21]

The announcement offered no more details, but a few months later, Harper and Brothers published the collection *Successful Stunts: Fifty Short, Impromptu Dramatic Stunts for Social Occasions*, which included a script for one titled "Sissy Football." Authors were identified for some of the skits but not this one, raising the possibility that it had been circulating for a while without a known origin. Lasting seven minutes with a cast of thirteen (a coach, eleven players, and a waiter), "Sissy Football" opened with the Entire Company "skipping in, singing chorus":

> We will be strong,
> We will be strong,
> Oh, goodness gracious me,
> Our darling coach will make us so,
> S-T-R-O-N-G.

Once assembled, the players pull out handkerchiefs to kneel on while they sing another song, this one about being a "brawny crew," descended from a "great sorority." Next, the Coach sings to the Eleven, then a Guard to the Coach, then the Quarter-back to his Centre:

> Now, Georgette, dear, do pass the ball,
> With vim and lots of pep.
> Be sure and do not muss your hair
> One, two, three, four, five hep.

The Centre, in turn, sings a complaint to the Coach:

> Oh, Coachie, dear, I'm sore and vexed:
> They've trod upon my toes;
> They've slapped my wrist and called me names
> And dirtied all my hose.

After a few more such lines, the skit ends with the entire Eleven serenading their Coach ("hard as nails and soft as pie"), who then announces, "Time out! We must serve tea." After the Waiter serves them and collects the cups, "All then skip out with hands on shoulders, singing chorus again."[22]

Cole Porter, it was not. But whether with this particular script or in alternative versions, "Sissy Football" was performed at school assemblies, church bazaars, YWCA and YMCA parties, school awards banquets, and sorority luncheons many dozens (perhaps hundreds) of times around the country from at least 1928 to at least 1962 (from the known performances reported in local newspapers).[23] The joke was as old as the cartoons in *Puck* and *Judge* in 1906, with their fops and dandies; and Knute Rockne turned it into banquet-circuit schtick around the same time that "Sissy Football" arrived on the scene. *Puck* and *Judge* satirized the efforts to make the game safer. Rockne, in all seriousness, set football against the erosion of masculinity in the Jazz Age. "Sissy Football" did the same thing more obliquely, as a joke on the outrageous idea that a football player could possibly be a "sissy." If that was the case, then any boy could prove he was not a sissy by playing football.

In newspaper accounts, the cast was usually female, though occasionally male. In either case, audiences would have been laughing *with* the football players on their school teams, not *at* them. And the players on those teams would undoubtedly have enjoyed the attention and backhand compliment to their status as anti-sissies. According to the local paper covering a school football rally in Ogden, Utah, in November 1939, a few days after the skit had been performed, when the team captain came out to address the student body, he "advanced to the middle of the gym by gracefully skipping."[24] No anxiety there. The long off-off-Broadway run of "Sissy Football" suggests that playing the game promised immunity against any suspicion of being a sissy.

FOOTBALL TOWNS

But only if one could "take it," of course. The articles in women's magazines in the 1930s invariably noted that football was most dangerous on sandlots and in high schools, where the bodies were less developed and the game less supervised. High school football had developed in tandem with the college game in the late nineteenth century, and over the 1920s and 1930s it became increasingly important in countless communities that lacked a college team as a source of local identity and pride.[25] The Prep Bowl in Chicago between the champions of the Catholic and public high school leagues drew 75,000 or more to Soldier Field in the 1930s and an astonishing 120,000 in 1937; but scholastic football mattered most in small towns with no big-time college team. The fiercest rivalries and biggest games of all were those between neighboring communities that meant nothing, or very little, anywhere else. (By 1929, Frederick Rand Rogers, author of *The Future of Interscholastic Athletics*, was already no fan of the role that high school football had come to play for the adults in small towns everywhere.)

Below the high school level, organized youth football barely existed before the 1950s, almost entirely through local chapters of national groups such as the YMCA, the Boy Scouts, Boys' Clubs, and the Catholic Youth Organization, rather than public school systems. Physical educators (like Rogers) objected to the emphasis on leagues and championships and to limiting the benefits of participation to a select few.[26] Youth football does not seem to have registered in the national media at all until the late 1930s, when *Life* magazine published "Life Goes to a Kids' Football Game" twice, first in November 1938 and then in October 1939. The 1938 story introduced readers to rival teams of ninety-pounders at private academies in Germantown, Pennsylvania, members of "the oldest schoolboy-athletic league in the U.S.," the Interacademic League, founded in 1887 in the Philadelphia area. The boys played for fun and dreamed of being football heroes, while their parents, teachers, and classmates "held their breath for every bruising tackle."[27]

The 1939 story featured Alfred Eisenstaedt's cover photograph (see fig. 4.1) of a young boy in football helmet and uniform, with braces on his teeth and a determined look on his face. The image fell into the long tradition of sentimentalized rough-and-tumble kids on magazine covers dating back to the 1910s (fig. 3.1 is a classic example). The article inside identified the cover boy as eight-year-old Bill Gregory, a fourth-grader in Denver and a member of the Wolf Pack in the Young America League, founded in 1927 for "the world's youngest organized football players," according to the organization. The boys ranged from eight to eighteen, but the four-page photo-essay featured only the youngest ones, with a brief text that focused on their preseason initiation ceremony, where they pledged "to remember that what matters most is courage; that it is no disgrace to be beaten; but that the great disgrace is to turn yellow."[28]

Life offered that pledge to readers within the cute-kid tradition (without acknowledging its dark edge), as it did with another piece titled "Kids' Football" in 1947, as played in Kenilworth, Illinois, where all 167 boys at Joseph Sears public grade school played on intramural teams. "Although the boys frequently come home with black eyes and bloody noses," the text read, "parents are sold on the program. In sharp contrast to the high accident rate in sand-lot football, there has not been a broken bone at Sears in 20 years." Not only that, but "only once in a great while do the boys cry when hit hard."[29]

These were just novelty human-interest stories, before youth football leagues were established in communities around the country beginning in the 1950s. By then, high school football had a distinct place not just in local communities but also in the national football culture, which might be traced to Boys Town, the Catholic orphanage in Omaha, Nebraska, made famous by the 1938 film starring Mickey Rooney and Spencer Tracy (who won a Best Actor Oscar for his performance as Father Flanagan). In November of that year, a football game between teams from Boys Town and Black-Foxe Military Institute, before a celebrity-studded crowd in Los Angeles, with newsreel cameras rolling, launched Boys Town on a thirty-year barnstorming tour against military academies and Catholic prep schools coast-to-coast.[30] (The celebrity of Boys Town also likely prompted a feature story in *Collier's* in 1941 about another orphanage team, the "Mighty Mites" of the Masonic Home in Fort Worth, Texas.)[31]

Orphanage teams were outliers. The norm for the national high school football culture that emerged in the 1940s could be called "Football Town," a generic name for the communities featured in a series of articles and pictorials that cast high school football as a quintessential expression of the "American Way of Life," still thriving despite a World War and then the Cold War that followed. What became a distinct magazine genre began in 1939 in *Life*'s brief (two-page) photo-essay about Massillon, Ohio, where "The Cradle of Pro Football Cheers for a Great High-School Team." The pros had long been gone from Massillon, one of the founding members of the Ohio League in 1902, but the town remained "fanatically interested in football"—high school football now, with a team that had won the last four state championships. *Life* presented its color photographs of the varsity team from Massillon's Washington High scrimmaging against the scrubs (along with one of the marching band) as evidence of "the hard, tough football which is being played at U.S. high schools."[32]

Life was saluting Massillon, Ohio, and Washington High, but it was also saluting high school football throughout the United States, though particularly in smallish towns like Massillon and its bitter rival, Canton, rather than, say, Cleveland and Cincinnati. Over the next ten years, *Life*, *Look*, the *Saturday Evening Post*, and even the monthly magazine *Holiday* published seven more features on high school football in small towns. Massillon itself would remain a storied high school football town into the 1960s (and beyond)[33]—*the* storied football town in many ways, simply "Football Town" as *Holiday* titled its long article in 1949. Legendary coach Paul Brown had created a schoolboy juggernaut in Massillon after arriving in 1932 and proceeding to win six state titles from 1935 through 1940 before departing for Ohio State University (and then, after the war, to the Cleveland Browns). *Holiday*'s final photo showed a newborn boy, still in the hospital, receiving a regulation football from the Booster Club—the consecrating ritual of a true football town. (A photo-essay in *Sports Illustrated* in 1961 showed the same scene but with a peewee football, presumably due to inflation.) According to the various accounts, boys in Massillon did not have the *option* to play football but an expectation to play. No one in these articles seemed to suffer from this demand, though *Sports Illustrated* at least hinted at a possible downside in the caption to one photo: "The young boy with the professional-looking helmet may privately wonder if football is really for him, but in Massillon he has little choice."[34]

That hint of doubt did not enter the Massillon narrative until 1961. The stories of high school football in the 1940s were uncomplicated celebrations of small-town America and the wholesome sport around which local citizens rallied. Whitehall, New York, was a "football-crazy town," in which 100 of the 150 boys in the four-year high school played on the team that had not lost a game in three years.[35] "Moppets" in Amarillo, Texas, "grow up with a football in their hands" and were scouted in grade school.[36] Working-class boys in Everett, Massachusetts, learned "physical fitness" and "mental discipline" through the sport and found "a safety valve for adolescence," while for many of them football was also "the key to college education."[37] In White Plains, New York, "fathers, brothers and uncles pounce upon chubby youngsters almost as soon as they can walk, and school them in the intricacies of a jolting stiff arm and how to toss a bullet or floater pass."[38] In Atchison, Kansas, the coach who inherited an "apathetic and miserable" high school team raised money to give a free uniform to any boy between nine and twelve and a half who wanted one, with the result that Atchison "is full of small fry who never get out of their uniforms." [39] In none of these stories was there any hint of the injuries, either major or minor, let alone any greater risk, addressed in the articles in women's magazines in the 1930s.

But what about the "small fry" who did not want to play football in Football Town? Or in the big city, for that matter? This was a question that came to obsess the syndicated health columnist William Brady over the midcentury portion of a career spanning from 1914 to 1962 (his columns distributed by the National Newspaper Syndicate for most of it). Dr. Brady began attacking high school football at least by December 1931 (immediately following the season when Cadet Sheridan died), when he responded to a mother's letter asking for advice on whether to let her son play football. She explained that she had "read much on the subject, and every article I have read has had a tendency to condemn the game of football as too strenuous for growing boys," but her fifteen-year-old son was eager to play next year. While the boy's father was "bitterly opposed," Mother did not want to thwart her boy's dream of playing on the high school team.[40]

Dr. Brady's response was blunt, nasty even, belittling Mom while praising Dad's good sense. He then laid out the position that would not change in his columns for the next thirty years: that football was "a man's game, a game for university men, and for men who have had proper physical training." No boy should be allowed to play it (the *Journal of the American Medical Association* had taken that position back in 1907). In response to more letters from anxious parents over the next several years, Brady hammered on that fundamental point, singling out not the game's violence as the source of its danger for boys but its strenuousness: the risk of developing an enlarged heart from too intense and sustained physical activity (again echoing concerns expressed in *JAMA* editorials).[41] Each time he addressed the subject, Brady became more adamant and more scornful of anyone who believed otherwise.

Then, in December 1948, Brady wrote a column decrying what he called the "trick employed by the outsiders who exploit grade school and high school boys" by convincing them, or their parents, "that if the youngster doesn't train for football he will be regarded as a 'sissy.'" Brady added, "Too many dim-witted fathers have given in to that."[42] The publication of Geoffrey Gorer's *The American People* earlier in 1948 may or may not be coincidental. In any case, that became Brady's new obsession, to which he returned in no less than nine more columns over the next seven years, using virtually the same language but with increasing exasperation.[43] In February 1949, Brady complained that parents continually ignored his advice because "the other fellows and the coach will brand [their son] a sissy."[44] By July 1951 he had developed a shorthand for this formula, when he described children as "very susceptible to suggestion that one who doesn't subserve the purpose of the town sports, sports writers and their representative, the coach, is yellow, sissy, etc."[45] Just days later, another column elaborated on the particular risk to the underaged boy "who succumbs to the propaganda which brands him as yellow, sissy or unloyal if he does not report for practice when the coach calls for candidates," where he will have to compete with older, heavier, and stronger boys.[46]

Brady's increasing frustration exploded five months later in a column following the death of a high school football player from a head injury, when he mocked parents who seemed more concerned about their sons being "sissies" than living into adulthood. He also asked (rhetorically) if the 75 percent of boys in the high school who did not play football were "sissies, yellow, mama's boys or whatever the coach calls them."[47] One year later, a letter from the uncle of a boy who had had to be hospitalized after not reporting a concussion, for fear of being "called sissy," provoked Brady's blanket condemnation of the culture of the sport: "This boy's fear of being called a sissy if he doesn't submit to whatever the town sports' coach requires . . . is the ruling spirit of high school football."[48] (These were the only two columns in which Brady specifically mentioned head injuries; the following chapters will put those in a much broader context.)

Some of Brady's fellow health columnists shared his concern about the physical dangers of high school football;[49] others did not.[50] On consecutive days in December 1949, Hearst's International News Service published pro- and anti- viewpoints from two "prominent physicians" on the issue, with William Brady opposing the schoolboy game and the distinguished medical scientist Morris Fishbein defending it. (Fishbein, who had recently stepped down after twenty-five years as editor of the *Journal of the American Medical Association*, had written a scathing editorial in 1937 about Dr. Brady's syndicated column.)[51] Brady repeated his long-standing insistence that football was "a grown man's game," and high school boys risked serious heart damage.[52] Fishbein responded the next day that football was dangerous only on sandlots, "where the boys play without headgears and without other equipment." Reversing the position he had taken in his 1932 *JAMA* editorial, which had mocked defenders of the lethal sport and criticized physicians insufficiently concerned about "the sanctity of the healthy body," Fishbein now proposed that the platoon system (playing on just the offense or the defense) had made high school football less strenuous than even basketball, and he insisted that the "steadily improved" helmet—no longer "actually a weapon" but a "protective device"—had made it safer, too. (It would soon become impossible to make such a claim, as will be discussed in chapter 6.) Fishbein conceded that injuries still occurred at all age levels, mostly to knees, but "certainly not heart damage." Take that, Dr. Brady![53]

Anxious parents, looking for guidance from these "medical experts" on the risks of football for their sons, found no more consensus than had the public in the 1890s as they were discovering the new college game.

SHOULD YOUR BOY PLAY FOOTBALL? (AGAIN)

None of the other syndicated columnists shared Brady's preoccupation with boys playing football to avoid being called "sissies." But that the issue was more than a personal obsession for one cranky doctor, or existed only in obscure corners of the mainstream football culture, like pulp stories and school skits, is clear from major weekly and monthly magazines in the postwar years, particularly women's magazines again. "Should Your Boy Play Football?" was the title of no less than three of these articles,[54] and the answer was always yes, but . . . But *only* under proper conditions, such as those enumerated in Dr. Floyd Eastwood's ten-point "safety code," explained by the journalist Al Stump in his version of that article in *American Magazine* in October 1954. Soon after arriving to interview Eastwood, Stump claimed to have received "the biggest shock of my reporting life" when he learned that 518 football players had died since 1931, 158 of them on sandlots and 293 in high school games. (This was Bob Considine 's rhetorical strategy in *Good Housekeeping* in 1936: scare the bejeezus out of your readers before reassuring them at the end.)[55] But then Eastwood explained his ten-point code: the usual concerns about proper equipment, medical supervision, and strict officiating, plus demands that school programs manage travel and schedules judiciously, match like-sized boys, foster coach-family relations, and have a low-cost insurance plan. And he told Stump that he was letting his own son play junior high football under these conditions. By the end of the interview (and the article), Stump had decided that he and his wife would not let their son play on sandlots, "where there was no protection," but that he could play in high school—only "under Dr. Eastwood's safety code." The sportswriter Stump still believed that "the stand-on-your-own qualities and teamwork which football teaches will help make a man of him." But the father Stump "won't be up in the stands—yelling. I'll be close by the side lines—watching."[56]

Stump simply restated here the long-standing tension between *health* and *culture*, safety and man-making. Several other postwar writers also grappled with the game's entanglement with boys' psychological and emotional needs, distilled into that hyper-potent word "sissy." Of course, there was no consensus here, either. A November 1948 article in *Cosmopolitan*, titled "Who's Yellow?" and written for parents by an NFL coach, Jim Conzelman, debunked the idea that liking body-contact sports had anything to do with courage or that not liking them had anything to do with being "yellow." Boys should play football if they enjoy contact sports, Conzelman wrote, not "merely to quell a father's inferiority complex" (employing the psychoanalytic terminology that was becoming commonplace).[57] In a similar spirit, writers in *Redbook* in July 1958 and *Woman's Day* in November 1959 warned parents about their sons concealing potentially serious injuries "because they don't want to be called 'sissies.'"[58]

But other writers sympathized with boys' need to prove their non-sissy toughness, including a coach's wife, writing in *Parents' Magazine* in October 1946, who invoked that idea without the word itself when she dismissed mothers' objection to football's roughness by explaining why they should be eager for their sons to play. "Coaches often discover a lion's heart in a mouse of a boy," Mary Henry wrote. "Athletics gives such a boy a chance to prove himself and win the respect of his fellows."[59] Henry wrote this as a mother, not a "mom," the villain of choice in the postwar era for turning America into a nation of "sissies" by overprotecting her sons.[60] A distinguished psychiatrist, writing in the *Saturday Evening Post* in October 1946, described such a "mom," who "lured her son from football to tennis by being 'discovered' in tears when the boy returned from practice" and who later told him that "she lived in daily terror that he would be injured."[61] Another writer, in *Better Homes and Gardens* in September 1953, cited the declining fatalities in Floyd Eastwood's annual reports to plead for the benefits of athletics: "Excessively protective grownups, who turn a healthy boy into a weak sister, are obsessed with fears which are for the most part groundless. With proper precautions, all of the popular sports are reasonably safe."[62] In what was becoming another favorite cliché of the era, the writer added that football was safer for teenage boys than driving a car.[63]

The most passionate advocates for boys' football continued to value the game far beyond being merely safe enough, of course. In September 1954, writing in a syndicated Sunday newspaper magazine, Columbia University football coach Lou Little explained in great detail how youth football could be made fully safe, as if that was everyone's primary concern, and then added, as if an afterthought, "I think it's dangerous for a boy *not* to play football. Nowadays, particularly, when so much courage, moral and physical, is demanded of our sons."[64] (As always, the demands of the moment were not explained, just assumed.) A father, writing in *Redbook* in October 1955, described his eleven-year-old son's "having a loose baby tooth knocked out in his first junior-high football game" as the "proudest moment of his life" and the moment when "a little boy became a big boy." This was also the moment when the father learned "how a boy can be hurt more by self-doubt than by rough play on the football field."[65]

On the other hand . . . pushing a boy to play football could backfire. "If the Boy Turns Out to Be a Sissy," as an article in *Good Housekeeping* posed the dilemma in June 1959, what could a parent do? The writer interviewed specialists for their advice to parents of frankly sissy sons. They did not single out "mom" as the problem; in fact, mothers had to subtly manage their husbands, because "sissyhood is, at least subconsciously, an especially hard fact for the male parent." More generally, according to the experts, "parents do three major things that can cause a boy to become a sissy—overprotect him, neglect him, or set standards that confuse him because they are contradictory." Whereas fathers tended to think that a "real boy" was "ready with his fists or able to hurl himself at a hard-running tackler," the experts advised parents not to "force him to take boxing lessons or engage in the rougher contact sports," like football and hockey. "One of parents' common mistakes is feeling that these sports will toughen the boy, make him less afraid. The chances are that his fears will prevent him from having any success at them, and this will only deepen his sense of failure."[66] If success at football might cure sissyhood but failure could worsen the condition, what was a concerned parent to do?

These concerns about "sissy" boys, or boys risking serious injury to prove themselves not "sissies," recast the perennial conflict between health concerns and cultural imperatives in terms shaped by the popular discovery of child psychology in the postwar years, but also by anxiety about becoming a nation of "soft Americans," unfitted by prosperity for facing the postwar existential threat from the Soviet Union that required them to be *hard*.[67] The actual physical deficiencies of American children were quantified in 1955 in a comparative study of 7,000 European and American youths, ages six to sixteen, in which nearly 60 percent of the Americans failed one or more of six physical fitness tests, compared to less than 10 percent of the children from Italy, Austria, and Switzerland. The report reached all the way to the White House and prompted President Eisenhower to convene the conference that led to the President's Council on Physical Fitness in July 1956.[68] National magazines—*Newsweek*, *Sports Illustrated*, *American Magazine*, *Reader's Digest*, *U.S. News & World Report* (a twelve-page cover story)—published articles on the report's findings.[69] As schools around the country implemented the council's recommendations, push-ups and sit-ups became part of the grade school curriculum (along with those infamous duck-and-cover drills).

President Kennedy inherited Eisenhower's council and its concerns, as he laid them out in "The Soft American" in *Sports Illustrated* in December 1960, a month before taking office.[70] Other writers bemoaned the "Flabby American," the "Nation of Weaklings," or the "Generation of Marshmallows" or warned about a "muscle gap" with the Soviet Union as dangerous as the "missile gap."[71] The national call was for *fitness*, not for football and other contact sports. Fitness was essential for everyone, girls as well as boys; football (with its extreme physical demands and fundamental violence) was for a select few.[72] But the attraction for, or pressure on, boys to be among those few was the issue that troubled William Brady and some of the writers in women's magazines. Longtime concern about football's physical dangers confronted longtime but intensified concern about American "softness." Football's necessary and unnecessary roughness was more at issue in the 1950s than at any time since the 1920s, maybe even the 1890s.

FOOTBALL FOR BOYS

The postwar expansion of youth football occurred in this context. In 1956, the Pop Warner Conference, which since 1929 had fielded teams for all ages, shifted its focus to boys under seventeen, with particular emphasis on eight-to-thirteen-year-olds, for whom tackle football was unavailable in most public schools for reasons of safety or expense.[73] That year, the *New York Times* estimated that 90,000 children were currently playing on "midget" teams, and "midget" or "peewee" football took off from there.[74] One year after Pop Warner reoriented itself to youth football, the American Academy of Pediatrics issued a policy statement urging no tackle football for boys through age twelve, only to be widely ignored. As Kathleen Bachynski has put it, "Strikingly, the recommendations of professional societies such as the AAP against football among elementary and middle school aged children went largely unheeded. That pro-football arguments overshadowed the exceptional degree of cultural authority American physicians had attained at mid-twentieth century underscores the growing social power of competitive youth sports during the period."[75] By November 1959, according to a professor of education at New York University, "small-fry" football had been organized in more than 500 communities.[76] Culture trumped health, as always.

For high school football, participation recovered from wartime contraction and steadily grew through the 1950s, from perhaps 600,000 boys in 1950 to

760,000 in 1962.[77] With the tremendous growth in high school enrollment over the 1950s (from 3.6 million to 5.2 million), the percentage of boys playing football actually declined over the decade, from 16.8 percent to 12.6 percent, where it more or less stabilized.[78] While participation figures may not be wholly reliable for these years, with rates of participation well under 20 percent, the pertinent point is obvious: that playing high school football, whatever its actual benefits and harm, was always for a relatively small minority of American boys. (Dr. Brady's mention of the 75 percent of boys who did not play football was a low estimate.) Viewing football as essential for *national* interests, or for *American* manhood, made no more sense in the 1950s than it did in the 1890s or 1920s.

While most boys were *not* playing football (and never had been), more were playing than ever before, and the medical establishment responded. After a pause during the war and immediate postwar years, the *Journal of the American Medical Association* published a series of articles on football by physicians in the 1950s, including one by Allan Ryan, a founding member of the American College of Sports Medicine, and two by Augustus Thorndike, by this time recognized as a founding father of that new field. In November 1956, Ryan described physicians' "rising medical interest and action in athletic matters—particularly at the high school level . . . where sports participation is the greatest." Ryan explained that the American Medical Association's Bureau of Health Education, working with coaches and educators, was "pointing to the character-building advantages of football" but also to "the danger of young boys playing too many games"; to "the body-building potential of football," but also to "the body-destruction of ill-fitted uniforms and lack of preplay warm-up."[79] For Ryan, boys' *health* remained the primary concern, but *culture* ("character-building advantages") mattered, too. In that same issue, Thorndike called for "closer medical supervision of athletics" and was particularly concerned about "the problem of overtraining," which put athletes at greater risk of injury, including risk of concussion. ("Overtraining," of course, was "taking it," but from the perspective of physical health.) Thorndike repeated, more emphatically, the assertion from his textbook (in its fifth edition that year) that the "permitting of a player with cerebral concussion to continue play should not be tolerated." And he added this time, "Every follower of body-contact sports can recall having seen some player allowed to continue in a rugged contest without full capacity of his mental processes."[80] In March 1959, in the *Journal of the American Medical Association*'s lead article, Thorndike proposed an athlete's "Bill of Rights," which included good coaching, good equipment, and good medical care. In short, Thorndike insisted on the need to take concussions more seriously; he also believed that football was safe enough, if properly supervised and regulated.[81]

So did Robert Brashear, a physician in Knoxville, whose paper read before an American Medical Association meeting was published in the association's journal (*JAMA*) in November 1959 (presumably signaling editorial endorsement). It opened, "In recent years much has been said in the medical literature both for and against athletics in general and football in particular. Some authors extol football as a great builder of men, mentally, morally, and physically, while others condemn football, particularly because many of the injuries sustained playing football are carried over into later life. Football, however, must be accepted as an integral part of the American way of life, just as much as the automobile. Since we must accept athletics, it behooves us to find ways and means of preventing the most serious sports injuries."[82] In the conflict between health and culture, Dr. Brashear was calling for a truce.

"FOOTBALL IS VIOLENCE" IN HIGH SCHOOL, TOO

As did Tim Cohane, the sports editor of *Look*, in an article and pictorial on high school football in September 1962 that neatly captured the state of the schoolboy game at the end of the postwar, pre-sixties era.[83] Cohane's article recalled those written by the sportswriters Edwin Dooley, Dick Hyland, and Bob Considine in women's magazines in the 1930s, offering parents reassurance that high school football was safe enough, while laying out in more specific detail than ever the necessary conditions for making it safe. Cohane brought the issues from the 1930s up to date, with explanations of the latest developments in helmet design and the current controversies over hard-shell plastic helmets with face guards (much more on that later), along with an overriding new caveat that "in a sudden forced stop, as in a head-on tackle, no helmet will ever keep the brain from being brought into contact with the skull." Regarding players who had suffered a previous head injury, Cohane added a caution that had become increasingly confirmed by medical experts like Augustus Thorndike: "A record of one severe concussion or a number of mild ones also should disqualify a boy." Seemingly in response to the intensified anxiety about "sissies," Cohane also insisted that the first requirement for playing football had to be that the boy actually *wanted* to play. For a boy to "not enjoy the physical contact of the game . . . does not mean he is not manly." No boy should "be forced to play to prove that he is, or to gratify a father who wants his son to follow in his footsteps."[84]

Cohane's well-informed and sensible advice to parents was preceded by a short photo-essay that conveyed a quite different message. Its tagline ("In the high-school as well as the college and pro game . . .") led into a blunt title: "Football Is Violence." Four pages of photos showed rugged action and injured players from a game between two New York schools, the Chaminade High Flyers of Mineola and the Holy Cross Knights of Flushing. The caption to one photograph of a collision read, "Tackling confronts tackler and runner with the challenge of bodily risk and teaches them to meet it." Another caption described "an injured 'Knight'" who "grimaces in pain as the team doctor ministers to him on the bench." A third, for a downed player being helped by medical staff, read, "The 'Flyers' had their share of fallen in a game of typically bruising play." And the final, full-page photograph of a player being helped off the field, also grimacing, bore the caption, "Leg injuries are frequent, and the knee is exposed to the most punishment."

The first page of the brief accompanying text (unsigned but presumably approved, if not written, by Cohane as sports editor) cited Floyd Eastwood's annual reports, which confirmed that the "chances of a boy's getting killed on the gridiron are far less than for driving, swimming and other water activities, or handling firearms." Injuries, on the other hand, as suggested by the photos and captions, were nearly universal and inevitable. But that fact was among the game's virtues, not its shortcomings. A tagline on the second page, "Football's danger and pain are part of its value," introduced two brief paragraphs. The first read, "Football teaches a boy to cope with the risks of physical danger and pain, risks often inseparable from the act of living itself. The game also demonstrates the value of work, sacrifice, courage and perseverance. These lessons are especially salutary in our modern society with its delinquency problem, lack of discipline and physical softness." The second paragraph added this: "Football, nevertheless, is only for the boy who is physically qualified to play it and for the high school that conducts it properly. As a guide to help you answer the question of whether your boy should play football, see the following pages." This set up Cohane's signed piece, described above.

The sportswriter Cohane looked at football's roughness from a *health* perspective; the sports editor Cohane (longtime friend and admirer of famously tough coaches Red Blaik and Vince Lombardi) looked at it from a *cultural* perspective, for its "salutary" lessons.[85] The two were inextricably entangled and had been for decades. The sportswriter Cohane also insisted that high school football needed competent officials, who "live by the 'fast whistle'" and will not "tolerate unnecessary roughness and piling-on." And he pointed out that "spearing" (leading with the helmet in blocking or tackling) was potentially more dangerous for the blocker or tackler than for the well-padded target, contrary to the assumption of many critics of the tactic, and should be banned (much more on that later). Most telling, Cohane listed the fundamental requirements for high school football programs: that winning should be subordinated to other goals, that players "should not be drilled to the point of exhaustion," that coaches "should recognize that the conditioning time needed for hard contact varies with the individual," and that practices "should not be held in the heat of the day" (there had been three deaths from heatstroke the previous season). Finally, besides insisting, like commentators before him, that a doctor and a trainer should be present at all games, Cohane added, "and should be the sole judge of the fitness of the player to play or practice."

One might ask, apart from referees guilty of slow whistles, who was responsible for everything that increased football's inherent dangers—excessive contact drills, pursuit of winning at all costs, teaching spearing and piling on, driving players until they dropped, and sending injured players back into the game? In a word, *coaches*. Tim Cohane was writing about *high school* football here, not the high-pressure, big-time college (or professional) game. The fact that these seemingly commonsensical ideas needed saying at all points to extraordinary changes in college coaching in the 1950s that were filtering down to high schools, too.

Football's next crisis, its current one, would be a long time coming, but its seeds were sown in the 1950s.

CHAPTER 5

PAYING THE PRICE

On the last day of August 1954, newly hired Texas A&M coach Paul (Bear) Bryant loaded 111 players onto two buses for the ten-hour drive to the drought-stricken little town of Junction in the Texas Hill Country. After ten days of brutal two-a-day practices on dirt fields under a blazing sun, the team returned in a single bus with just 35 players, the remaining 76 having fled by then, most of them silently in the dark. Two years later, the remnant of those survivors, now seniors, won the Aggies' first conference championship in fifteen years and entered Texas football lore as the "Junction Boys."

So says the legend deeply embedded in both the history and mythology of college football, arguably the defining episode of the post–World War II era—also, inarguably, the quintessential tale of "taking it." College football and its underlying code of toughness were transformed in the 1950s and 1960s and, with them, youth and high school football, too. The epic tale of the Junction Boys was both a major event in that transformation and the ultimate mythologizing of it. The "Boys" were the young men who survived the most brutal preseason training regimen ever devised. But the actual hero of their story (and the beneficiary of their achievement) was their coach, Bear Bryant.

A COACHES' GAME

Coaches dominated college football in the postwar, Cold War era as never before, but football had been a coaches' game since nearly its beginning—as had resistance to coaches' control of what was supposed to be the *players'* game. With its system of "graduate advisors" (chiefly Walter Camp), Yale was the game's premier team in the 1880s, and a rule in 1891 (presumably pushed by Camp) decreed that "from the time that a team begins regular practice they should never be without a coach." This was a *should*, not a *must*, but it necessitated a new rule a year later that banned "coaching from the side lines."[1]

May the Best Coach Win

Figure 5.1. Cartoon, "May the Best Coach Win," in *Life*, October 19, 1928.

Coaches were useful, maybe even necessary, for preparing the players, but *the players* were to play the games themselves, "using their own muscle and their own brains," as the "Foot Ball Code" first inserted into the NCAA rule book in 1916 put it.[2]

As Princeton, Harvard, and other northeastern rivals adopted the Yale system, and their own graduates became the coaches who helped spread the game throughout the rest of the country, revisions or rewordings of the rules on sideline coaching (and substitution to enable it) in 1897, 1900, 1905, 1909, and 1910 suggest that they were as effective as the rules against offside play had been in the 1880s.[3] After limited substitution was first permitted in 1897, rule makers faced a particular challenge to prevent coaches from sending in instructions to their quarterbacks. The text of the rule on substitutes in 1919 is worth quoting in full for its almost comical effort to anticipate every possible stratagem by coaches to circumvent the ban on sideline coaching:

> A player may be substituted for another at any time, but, before engaging in play he must report to the Referee or Umpire. An incoming substitute shall not communicate in any way with any of the players upon the field until after the ball has been put in play. In case any change in the position of players is rendered necessary by the substitution, the substitute going in may give that information only through the Referee. In case the substitute sent in is to take the place of the man who had regularly been giving signals previous to his removal from the game, the man sent in may give the signal, but without consultation with the players until after the ball has been put in play. If the man who has been giving signals is not removed from the game when a new player comes in for the purpose of giving signals, the former must give the signal on the play following. A player who has been withdrawn from the game may return once, at the beginning of a subsequent period. A new player disqualified or suspended may not return to the game.[4]

Two more decades of coaches flouting the spirit of the rules and of critics complaining about the "coach-ridden" game would follow.

Then, in 1941, the NCAA simply turned the game over to coaches by adopting unlimited substitution as a matter of wartime expediency. Before 1941, in addition to the ban on a substitute speaking until after one play, a player who left the field for a substitute could not return until the following quarter. With freshmen suddenly eligible for varsity competition (to replace draftees and enlistees), the rules committee assumed that seventeen-year-olds filling rosters until they, too, were drafted would not be physically mature for sixty-minute football. With unlimited substitution, coaches could suddenly run players on and off the field at will, and the players could talk to anyone they liked. Strangely, the ban on sideline coaching, in place since 1892, remained in the *Official Rules* ("There shall be no coaching, either by substitutes or by any other person not participating in the game"[5]), as if open substitution had not turned control of the game over to coaches.

This concession to a desperate situation did not end with the war, however. As returning service veterans flooded campuses and football programs on the GI Bill, the rule on open substitution remained in place, leaving coaches with all the control during games that the NCAA had for so long tried to limit, now with bulging rosters of mature, war-toughened men. Michigan coach Fritz Crisler, in 1947, was the first to create separate offensive and defensive units to take full advantage of this wealth of material. Red Blaik at Army picked up the idea and named them "platoons," leading to what Notre Dame coach Frank Leahy would later call "the Two-Platoon era, from 1948 through 1952."[6] It ended as abruptly in 1953 as unlimited substitution had begun in 1941, when the NCAA Rules Committee startled everyone, including coaches who voted by a 4–1 margin to retain two platoons, by voting unanimously to restore one-platoon football by severely limiting substitutions again.[7] (In turn, the one-platoon era would end after the 1964 season, despite the reluctance of some on the rules committee, with the approval of 90 percent of head coaches.[8])

The decisions in both 1941 and 1953 were driven by external factors. The motive in 1953 was to cut costs by reducing squad sizes, after more than fifty colleges had dropped their football program following the war.[9] Abandoning two platoons was popular with those who had been upset by the disappearance of the "iron men" of the past who played both ways (simply because that was what the rules had required until 1941). In November 1949, Dan Parker, the iconoclastic sports columnist for the *New York Daily Mirror*, published a rant in *Cosmopolitan* against two-platoon football under the derisive title "Football Is for Sissies." Parker blamed coaches for what he termed "the game's emasculation." In Parker's words, "Football, the red-blooded sport, which called for physical prowess, teamwork, courage, and resourcefulness, has degenerated into a species of chess game, in which the rival coaches do all the thinking and use their players as pawns. The all-around football star has become extinct in this era of specialization and sissification."[10] It goes without saying that Parker welcomed the return of one-platoon football in 1953, as did his fellow sportswriters by a 5–1 margin in one informal poll (roughly inverting coaches'

4–1 preference in 1948 for the two-platoon system).[11] Sportswriters wanted iron men; coaches wanted control. (The NFL never abandoned two platoons.)

FOOTBALL AS WAR

As football's history attests, rules can have unintended consequences. When *Collier's* polled players and coaches on what to expect from the radical rule change for the 1953 season, all agreed that "two-way [one-platoon] football demands much better physical condition," and some foresaw a rougher game from an increase in "rugged man-to-man competition." One player predicted, "Guys who like contact will get a big bang out of the new rule."[12]

Whether "platoons" had anything to do with it, college football most certainly became more "rugged" during the one-platoon era (1953–64), which was dominated by a new generation of war-tested coaches, initially coaching war-toughened players. Whether the war shaped these coaches and the game that they taught is also uncertain. Of the fifteen men who coached AP national champions from 1946 through 1969, just two, Michigan's Bennie Oosterbaan (1948) and Michigan State's Biggie Munn (1952), did not see military service during World War II.[13] Of those who did, Robert Neyland (Tennessee), Jim Tatum (Maryland), Woody Hayes (Ohio State), Ben Schwartzwalder (Syracuse), and Bear Bryant (Alabama) were famously, or infamously, hard-driving coaches. Some of the coaches who served in the military saw combat; all of them witnessed basic training, where screaming drill sergeants drove recruits to be ready to march off to war. Who knows what lessons these football coaches might have absorbed?

Tough coaches were nothing new to college football. Among those who won postwar national championships, Neyland, Tatum, and Notre Dame's Frank Leahy all began their careers before the war, as did Wally Butts and Red Blaik (who titled his 1960 autobiography *You Have to Pay the Price*[14]). Before them there were Jock Sutherland, Biff Jones, and Frank Cavanaugh in the 1930s, Pop Warner and Bill Roper in the 1920s, and others going back all the way to some of the earliest postgrad Harvard, Yale, and Princeton in-season coaches, like Frank Butterworth, who tormented James Hopper and his teammates at Cal in the 1890s. Football fiction in popular magazines had two stereotypical coaches: fatherly "Pop" and tyrannical "Biff," with "Pop" always a good guy, "Biff" never.[15] In the same spirit, biopics of Knute Rockne (*Knute Rockne—All-American*, 1941) and Frank Cavanaugh (*The Iron Major*, 1943) transformed hard-driving coaches into celluloid "Pops." (The most famous actual "Pop"—Pop Warner—was no "Pop" at all.) Popular sentiment wanted coaches to be father figures. Sportswriters and football fans wanted coaches who *won*.

But if there had always been tough coaches, their toughness was relative, as was what was permissible in the pursuit of winning. By no means did all post–World War II coaches adopt the same methods, but some of them pushed toughness to unprecedented extremes in their treatment of both their own players and their opponents. For the toughest of the tough, football itself was less a game than a "100-yard war," as one writer titled his biography of Woody Hayes.[16]

Just as football itself was originally for the players, not the coaches, "taking it" had aways been understood to benefit *them*. In postwar football, "paying the price" (the more common term now) supposedly still served the players, but in magazine profiles and on the sports pages it was more closely associated with the coaches who demanded it in pursuit of victories and championships (plus the institutional power and financial rewards that followed). Its hallmarks were *conditioning* (through endless running and brutal contact drills) and *hitting* (through those same brutal drills, along with long and frequent full-contact scrimmages, followed by ferocity in games). Bear Bryant coined the term "kill or get killed" for his type of football at Texas A&M and Alabama.[17] Darrell Royal's Texas Longhorn teams played what he called "jaw-to-jaw" football ("every bit as terrific and punishing as Bear Bryant's," according to a sports columnist for the *Austin American*).[18] When Syracuse played Texas in the 1959 Cotton Bowl, *Life* called the game "A Brawling Battle of the Hard-Noses."[19] *Hard-nosed* belonged to no one coach or team but to a style of coaching and the kind of play taught by those coaches. Coaches and sportswriters concocted an elaborate glossary of toughness in the postwar era.

Reckless abandon, another term from that glossary, was used in 1950 to describe Oklahoma's "all-out brand of play" under Bud Wilkinson in trouncing LSU in the Sugar Bowl.[20] To play with reckless abandon meant nearly out of control and, more significantly, without regard for personal safety. Before 1950, the term had been occasionally used for basketball teams playing the era's modest version of what would come to be called "run-and-gun" offense, and sportswriters sometimes used it to describe moments in hockey matches or even baseball games when a player did something wildly aggressive. But football appropriated "reckless abandon" in the 1950s to describe players flying about the field, not on one crucial play but all the time. Both sportswriters and coaches increasingly used the term over the 1950s and 1960s, and by the 1970s they would be throwing the term itself about with reckless abandon.[21]

The outlier among these postwar hard-nosed coaches was Bud Wilkinson, whose forty-seven-game winning streak from 1953 to 1957, along with three national titles, made him *the* dominant coach of the 1950s. In addition to being gentlemanly, handsome, and cultured (with a master's degree in English literature)—a "Gridiron Galahad" and "The Golden Man of the Gridiron" in magazine profiles—Wilkinson was known to be no fan of "vicious hitting."[22] It is profoundly ironic, then, that it was Wilkinson, in 1947, his first season as head coach at Oklahoma, who devised the simple but brutally efficient drill that in varied forms became the quintessential test of "manhood" and "toughness" in football at all levels for decades afterward.[23]

The drill was indeed simple: a blocker and a tackler would face off in their stances between two tackling dummies, laid three yards apart on the ground, and on a coach's signal, a back would try to run between the dummies. Either the blocker would drive the tackler aside or the tackler would defeat the blocker and bring down the runner. Wilkinson created the drill for teaching the techniques needed for playing his 5–2 defense, in which three interior defensive linemen, lined up over the center and two offensive tackles, had to shed the blocker quickly (not overpower him) in order to stop a ball carrier to either side. If the linemen stopped inside runs, the linebackers could then cover more outside territory with their speed and athleticism (the hallmark of Wilkinson's teams rather than, say, ferocity).[24]

What Wilkinson devised for technical purposes, other coaches turned into a test of toughness and manhood. High schools, colleges, and at least one NFL team (the New York Giants in 1955) began in the 1950s adopting what Wilkinson simply called the "one-on-one" drill but that became known as "the Oklahoma drill" (for its origin) or "the Nutcracker" (for its new function).[25] In the 1960s, it became ubiquitous at all levels of football, most famously in the NFL, where Vince Lombardi in Green Bay[26] and Don Shula in Baltimore and Miami[27] made it an annual ritual to open training camp. In Pittsburgh, during the Steelers' Super Bowl years under Chuck Noll in the 1970s,[28] it was announced in advance, attended by wildly cheering fans and covered by wildly enthusiastic sportswriters, one of whom in 1973 proposed that the Oklahoma drill had been "invented" by "The Marquis de Sade" and "perfected in a Siberian concentration camp."[29] Mike Webster's auspicious debut in the drill as a Steeler rookie the following year would provide the opening chapter ("The Nutcracker") of the Fainaru brothers' 2013 *League of Denial*, the symbolic moment when Webster began destroying his brain. "Future generations would look back and cringe at the ritual," the brothers wrote, "almost a form of human cockfighting, thinking about the inevitable toll, but at the time it was a staple for all teams at all levels, as much a sign that football was back as the turning of the leaves."[30] The Oklahoma drill would remain an annual ritual for dozens, perhaps hundreds, of teams at all levels into the 2010s,[31] until its too-obvious relationship to head trauma could not be ignored. (It would finally be banned by the NFL in May 2019 and by the NCAA two years later.)

WOODY AND THE BEAR

While his simple one-on-one drill had long-term consequences for the transformation of football that led to the concussion crisis, Bud Wilkinson was an anomaly among the postwar coaches who led that transformation, most notably Woody Hayes and Bear Bryant. According to his initial profiles in national magazines (*Sports Illustrated* and the *Saturday Evening Post*) following his national championship in 1954, Hayes drove his first team at Dennison in 1946, after returning from the war, "so hard that authorities told him to ease up—or else." After three seasons at Dennison and then two at Miami of Ohio (where the "team pastime" was "hating Woody Hayes"), he arrived at Ohio State in 1951 with a promise to boosters to give them "the fightingest team you've ever seen" and "the best-conditioned." The writer for *Sports Illustrated* added, "That last was an understatement."[32] He described the "gamers" for conditioning that concluded Hayes's spring practices: "six or more laps at the end of each grueling practice session," which left players sprawled on the field from heat exhaustion. What Hayes called "gamers," some coaches called "gassers," while others used wind sprints, instead of laps, for the same purpose, as Hayes himself did later in his career.[33]

What was most significant in such profiles was their *celebration* of coaching brutality, despite some apparent ambivalence, when it led, in due course, to a national championship. "In 1951, Woody's first year at Ohio State, his players came close to mutiny," the *Post*'s Jack Clowser wrote. They held "grievance meetings" and went so far as to lock him out of the locker room before one game.[34] Success did not mellow Hayes. According to a 1962 profile by Roy Terrell in *Sports Illustrated* ("You Love Woody or Hate Him"), he was still "driv[ing] his players with a ferocity that would make a Marine Corps drill instructor look like Mary playing with her lamb." Hayes himself told Terrell, "I hope I work my teams harder than anyone else. . . . I try hard enough." Terrell added, "How the players feel about this, he doesn't know. 'Frankly,' he says, 'I don't give a damn.'" But Hayes claimed to do it for the players' sake. "There's a lot of silly talk about building character in college football," he told Terrell, "—and I happen to believe in it. In our society there aren't too many tough things that a boy can do anymore. Football is one of the few. He has to whip that guy across from him and he has to do it as a member of a team, playing within the rules. But a coach doesn't go out to build character, he goes out to win. The character will take care of itself."[35]

Over his nearly three-decade career at Ohio State, Hayes became known as much for his temper tantrums as for his teams' hard-nosed, three-yards-and-a-cloud-of-dust football—his violent outbursts indiscriminately directed at his own players, game officials, intrusive photographers, and unfriendly reporters—even at himself at practices (sometimes calculated for their effect on his players, according to one biographer).[36] His career would eventually implode in one of these tantrums on the field in front of a national TV audience, but that would not happen until 1978. Along the way, he would win thirteen Big Ten titles and five national championships with his brand of football. In the 1960s, Woody Hayes was the dominant college football coach in the country—next to Bear Bryant, that is.

Woody Hayes and Bear Bryant may have been the first coaches since Knute Rockne whose teams were identified more with *them* than with their star players—nothing remarkable from today's perspective, but a radical transformation of what began as emphatically a *students'* game. More than any other postwar coach, Bryant changed both how football was played and the public's tolerance for its violence. Bryant himself was as tough as they came. He earned his nickname as a large but "immature and belligerent" thirteen-year-old in tiny Fordyce, Arkansas, when for a dollar he agreed to wrestle a muzzled bear that bit his ear when its muzzle came off. (The bear's owner skipped town without paying Paul his dollar.)[37] At Alabama, playing against Tennessee in 1935 with a broken femur earned him immortality of sorts in a Ripley's "Believe It or Not" syndicated cartoon.[38] As a coach, Bryant basically expected his players to be as tough as he was, or he would run them off.

Like Woody Hayes, he had a clear purpose: not to build character but to *win*, which he described in the introductory chapter of his 1960 coaching manual as "the number one way of American life."[39] This sounds like routine Cold War jingoism, reflecting the unprecedented sense of American might that emerged from the Second World War, which put, in Winston Churchill's words, the United States at the "summit of the world" and made it, in Harry Truman's, "the most powerful nation, perhaps, in all history."[40] But it was a striking claim within the context of college football traditions, by which "winning at all costs" had long violated the sport's essential values ("it matters not if you win or lose . . ."). In a 1957 profile in the *Saturday Evening Post*, University of

North Carolina coach Jim Tatum made the statement later attributed to Vince Lombardi (and apparently originating with UCLA coach Red Sanders), "I don't think winning is the most important thing. I think it is the only thing."[41] Like Woody Hayes, Bear Bryant agreed, and he built his football programs on that principle. What was new in the 1950s was not that winning was actually the objective but that it was so openly acknowledged.

For Bryant as for Hayes, superior conditioning and violent hitting were the twin pillars of his formula for winning football, from the day that he took over Kentucky's program in 1946, following one season at Maryland after his discharge from the service (coaching men he brought with him from his US Navy preflight team). He shared these priorities not just with Hayes but also with many of the era's other coaches, but he pushed them to extremes beyond where most would go. At Kentucky, Bryant put in place the system that he would replicate at Texas A&M and Alabama. He arrived in Lexington in January 1946, too late for serious recruiting, leaving him to start spring practice in March with just 65 players. Through recruiting over the summer—returning servicemen and new freshmen still eligible under wartime rules—by the beginning of preseason practices in August he had 115 candidates, the most in school history, at which point the serious winnowing that would become a hallmark of his system began. Rosters of SEC teams published in the *Knoxville Journal* in late September listed 40 names for Kentucky, out of that original 115.[42] The following year, Bryant's 123 in the spring became 88 when training camp opened in September and then 46 on the final roster (for a late-season game).[43] When the NCAA rescinded freshman eligibility in 1948, the number of candidates, and thus the need for radical winnowing, sharply declined.

When Bryant arrived at Kentucky in 1946, Wally Butts had been coaching at Georgia since 1939. In a profile of Butts in the *Saturday Evening Post* in 1949, a player from that 1939 team described the new coach's first preseason training camp, in which "the boys were weeded out from the men quickly. I bet half the original squad quit. They just wouldn't pay the price. That session darn near killed me, but, as trite or silly as it may sound now, it made a man out of me."[44] Bear Bryant, then, was not the first coach in the Southeastern Conference to run off players who would not "pay the price," but he perfected the model and implemented it in three different football programs.

Bryant took his players away from campus to a military academy twenty-five miles outside Lexington, where he could run them and batter them in private, as he would later do at Junction. "Hands-on teaching" was Bryant's style from the beginning. As Keith Dunnavant would wryly put it in his biography,

"Thirty-two and as strong as a horse when he arrived in Lexington, Bryant liked to teach with his forearms and elbows."[45] Kentucky's 7–3 record that first season was the school's best since 1912. After two more winning seasons capped by Kentucky's first-ever bowl appearances, *Collier's* in September 1950 profiled Bryant as "Dixie's No. 1 Gridnaper" for his recruiting prowess. The next year, following the Wildcats' first-ever SEC conference title and an upset of #1-ranked Oklahoma in the Sugar Bowl, the *Saturday Evening Post* saluted him as "Football's Jittery Genius." *Collier's* sports editor Bill Fay noted that Bryant had "concentrated on toughening the players physically" when he took over the Kentucky program. Tom Siler, the sports editor of the *Knoxville News-Sentinel*, told *Post* readers that Bryant countered the "riotous hospitality showered on the athletes by the horsey set" in Lexington with a "tough-guy approach" that was "the first step in breaking down Kentucky's losing tradition."[46] Neither writer offered any details, and their bland language did not even hint at what that "toughening" or "tough-guy approach" entailed. But college football insiders, including the administrators who would hire him at Texas A&M in 1954 and then at Alabama in 1958, would have had a pretty clear idea.

After eight seasons at Kentucky, Bryant abruptly left for Texas A&M, just weeks after signing a twelve-year extension for a hefty raise. Bryant was the hot young coach who had transformed an SEC doormat into a national championship contender, but he labored in the shadow of basketball-mad Kentucky's already legendary coach, Adolph Rupp. After signing his own extension, Bryant read in the local paper that Kentucky had signed Rupp to a long-term extension as well, after the university president had promised him that "the Baron" would be retiring soon. Bryant exploded in rage and immediately quit, "triggering a bitter public fight," in which his friend the governor had to intervene on his behalf in breaking his contract. This was in February, when the only coaching vacancy was at Texas A&M, a pretty clear indication of how unattractive the Aggies' position was in 1954.[47]

The rest, as they say, is history—or in this case, myth.

BECOMING "JUNCTION BOYS"

The legend of the "Junction Boys" says that Bryant took 111 players on two buses to Junction, Texas, and returned ten days later with just 35 players on a single bus. Numerous versions of this story took their final form in a 1999 book-length account by Texas sportswriter Jim Dent and a TV movie made from it by ESPN in 2002.[48] Contemporary newspapers offer quite different basic facts, and what actually took place on those dusty fields in the Texas Hill Country remains elusive.

On March 8, 1954, barely a month after Bryant arrived in College Station, 104 prospective Aggie players, according to the Associated Press, took the field for his first spring practice.[49] Two weeks later, just 50 of them remained, and Bryant announced that future sessions would be held behind locked gates (away from reporters' prying eyes).[50] Not even the local *Bryan Daily Eagle* wrote anything about the departed 54 or why they had left the team. Another half dozen or so quit before the bus ride to Junction on August 31, when the *Daily Eagle* announced that "43 Texas Aggies, including three junior college transfers, left for Junction Tuesday," with Bryant expecting to return in two weeks.[51] (Other accounts, including the AP's, put the initial squad size at 45.)[52] Five more players, now identified by name (by the AP), left the team on the third day of practice, including two lettermen, one of whom, Joe Boring, had been an all-conference safety in 1952 (when two-platoon football still allowed for defensive specialists).[53] On September 8, the United Press identified 1953's all-conference center Fred Broussard as the sixth Aggie player to quit, while also noting that Bryant had decided to return to College Station the following day (not on September 13, as originally planned), because some of the boys were "getting a little homesick" and Bryant needed facilities to make movies of their practice sessions.[54] The next day, the *Houston Post*'s man on the Texas sportswriters' preseason tour of Southwest Conference training camps called Broussard the seventh to leave, not the sixth, reducing the squad from the original 45 to 38.[55] The Aggie football roster published in the *Austin Statesman* on September 10 had 38 names; the one in the *Fort Worth Star-Telegram* on the same day had 40.[56] The game program for the season opener with Texas Tech listed 32; for the November 13 game with Rice, 35.[57] Routine injuries would have reduced the number of active players for some games over the course of the season, perhaps below 30 at some point, as Bryant and others would later claim.

Why belabor this? Because the "Junction Boys" became college football's singular epic tale of what can be achieved by players willing to "pay the price." The Junction Boys had two lives: the one they survived in September 1954 in the Texas Hill Country and the one they lived afterward in their legend. Both lives were defined by *toughness*, but the legend amplified it. And the hero of the legend as it unfolded was really not the "Boys" but their coach, Bear Bryant.

The legend said that 111 started out at Junction; the Associated Press said 45, much less suitable for a legend. For perspective on that 45, the wire services reported a range between 45 and 66 on Southwest Conference preseason rosters (with Arkansas also at 45), from 60 to 72 in the Big Ten, and from 46 to 70 in the Southeastern Conference.[58] In this era of one-platoon football, 50 or 60 players were more than enough to build a team. In casting Bryant's Aggies as the ultimate Southwest Conference underdogs, Jim Dent claimed that the University of Texas had 120 varsity players in 1954—nearly twice the 66 reported by the *Austin Statesman* on the first day of preseason practice.[59] Dent also described Bryant preparing to face Texas Tech in the season opener with just 24 healthy players, against the Red Raiders' 80, only to be told by one of his assistants that they would actually have 100. The *Lubbock Evening Journal* reported 48 when preseason practice opened.[60] The Junction Boys, in other words, were never a uniquely tiny band of survivors but a somewhat smaller team of that era.

Dent's inflated figures could have been due to the absence of reliable sources, but they also served the epic dimensions of the tale he was telling.[61] Dent's narrative was also full of novelistic touches—conversations and even private thoughts reconstructed nearly fifty years after the fact—to bring his story to life. The rigors at Junction in 1954 were quite likely no greater than at Kentucky in 1946 or would be at Alabama in 1958, when Bryant took over that struggling football program; but the Junction Boys came to be both the ultimate symbol of Bear Bryant football and *the* epic story of what is possible in football for those who pay the price.

How that legend grew is an intriguing puzzle. In November 1956, as the Aggies closed in on a conference title, the Junction Boys were named in an Associated Press story that was carried widely in Texas and across the South, but the name seems not to have immediately taken hold.[62] A profile of Bryant in *Sport* magazine in 1958 did not even mention Junction in describing how Bryant became the "Great Rehabilitator" at Kentucky and Texas A&M by recruiting the best players (and paying them as needed, to keep up with the competition), not by brutally driving them.[63] Bryant himself may have laid the foundation for the legend in 1960, in the final chapter of his book, *Building a Championship Football Team,* written for the textbook publisher Prentice-Hall in its series of coaching manuals by prominent college coaches.

Written with the help of Gene Stallings (one of the Junction Boys in 1956 and an assistant at Alabama in 1960), Bryant's book had typical chapters on offensive and defensive tactics and techniques (more on those later), on the kicking game and practice drills, on building a coaching staff and developing a quarterback. But it also had the opening chapter on Byant's philosophy, noted earlier, and a final chapter, titled "Those Who Stay Will Be Champions," in which Bryant singled out winning the 1956 Southwest Conference title as the "thrill in particular" that he cherished from his first fourteen years in coaching. He had won that title, he wrote, with eight seniors left from the 1954 team who went to Junction and had not "dropped by the wayside" along with all of those others who did "not want to pay the price to be a winner." The thrill, Bryant explained, was not in beating Texas for the title but in "watching those boys work, grow, develop, and rise . . . to become champions." Those eight seniors in 1956 "were champs then, and they will always be champions, because they know, understand, and are willing to do what they must do to be successful."[64] This was the payoff that Bryant promised his players and implicitly promised other coaches who would adopt the "course" laid out in his book.

Bryant did not mention how many players had quit at Junction, and he did not call those eight seniors "Junction Boys," but in a review of the book an Associated Press sportswriter who covered Texas football singled out Bryant's comments on "the Junction boys" as one of the book's highlights, calling them "that hardy little corps that went through probably the toughest preseason training regimen in football history" so that their coach could "see just who wanted to play."[65] When Texas A&M hired Gene Stallings in December 1964, following seven losing seasons after Bryant left, the twenty-nine-year-old coach was welcomed as one of the "famed 'Junction Boys.'"[66] (Jack Pardee was the other player routinely identified as a "Junction Boy" over his long career as a player and coach in the NFL.) Stallings nurtured that connection, telling tales of the Junction Boys at offseason banquets during his tenure at A&M, including the detail about going out to Junction in two buses and returning in one.[67]

The "Junction Boys" were initially a local Aggie story. Bryant made them *his* story in his autobiographies—initially, in 1966, a five-part series in *Sports Illustrated* (written with John Underwood), which he expanded into a book (again with Underwood) in 1974. In the second installment of the *Sports Illustrated* series, Bryan added a few details about Junction that seem to have become the foundation for later versions of the story, when he marveled at losing "about 100 boys" and keeping "only 27." And he immediately added, "I have to believe I wouldn't lose that many today, because I'm not the driver I was and I probably don't demand as much, but let me tell you that was the beginning of a change in attitude at A&M."[68] In his expanded 1974 autobiography, Bryant repeated that formulation—the supposed excesses of a young coach that turned the program around—with slightly altered numbers. He also added the bit about the buses, mentioning that the team drove to Junction with "two full busloads" and returned "with less than half a load. Twenty-nine boys."[69]

The outline of the story was in place by the early 1970s, then, but the numbers attached to it remained in flux for another couple of decades. As Bryant and Alabama prepared for the 1980 Sugar Bowl, the syndicated columnist Joan Ryan wrote, "Some say it was 80 players, others claim it was more like 100."[70] In one of the many tributes following Bryant's shocking death in January 1983, less than a month after he retired, a writer for the Gannett News Service offered, "Of the 96 original 'Junction Boys,' only 27 were left after 10 days of workouts."[71] It was then left to biographers to settle the details—if they could. In 1987, Mickey Herskowitz, the one sportswriter on site at Junction, who could have witnessed the events, did not specify how many came and left, but he claimed that "over half the players who made the long bus ride from College Station dropped out." And he added, "As more names were released each day, coaches and writers around the country, and possibly a few parents, began to wonder what was going on in the Texas hill country."[72] (Those seven players identified in Herskowitz's *Houston Post*, or in the *Fort Worth Star-Telegram*, *Austin American* and *Statesman*, *Dallas Morning News*, and *Bryan Daily Eagle*, after quitting over the course of the first week at Junction did not quite add up to "over half" of the initial squad of forty-five reported in the press.) Keith Dunnavant, in 1996, put the count of players who arrived in Junction "somewhere between 90 and 115."[73] Jim Dent's instantly definitive account in 1999 fixed the number at 111. Six years later, perhaps doubting Dent's evidence, Allen Barra went with Dunnavant's "anywhere between 90 and 115."[74]

Gene Stallings appears to have been Dent's primary source for the details about Junction. After identifying himself with the legendary "Junction Boys," as he advanced through the coaching profession, Stallings was an assistant coach for the Dallas Cowboys (1972–85) when he met Jim Dent as a beat writer covering the team in training camp. Stallings later wrote the book's foreword, and in his own "Author's Note" Dent attributed his inspiration in writing *The Junction Boys* to "Stalling's passion for Junction" in their numerous conversations.[75] It would seem that Gene Stallings not only inspired Dent but provided much of the story as an eyewitness.

None of the biographers' numbers matched the contemporary reporting, but all of them were considerably more appropriate for building a legend. Dent himself seems to have recognized a problem with his 111: finding room for all of those players on two buses, which he described elsewhere in the book as holding 50 passengers each.[76] He came up with a creative explanation. In describing the players' return to College Station at the end of training camp and not even filling a single bus now, Dent noted, "On the way out boys had been crammed like sardines into the aisles and others had stretched out and slept in the overhead baggage compartment."[77] Really? For ten hours? (In his 2005 biography, Barra added a third bus, perhaps to address this bizarre scenario.)[78] If the press in 1954 can be trusted over the later legend, 104 Aggies turned out for spring practice, and 38 returned on the bus from Junction—in which case Bear Bryant *did* run off over 60 percent of his squad through brutal conditioning and hitting drills. But he did it mostly in what was for him a typical spring practice after taking over a new program, not in one uniquely hellish week in Junction, Texas, that made for superior drama and a grander legend.

INSIDE THE LEGEND

The power of the legend of the Junction Boys lies in the brutality that the "Boys" endured—their unparalleled capacity to *take it*, to *pay the price*. The more brutal the details, the more powerful the legend. Dent's book includes two scenes of truly shocking brutality. In the first, Bryant watched a junior tackle named Henry Clark being manhandled in a blocking drill. Dent described Bryant's reaction:

> The man with the leather exterior had rehearsed in his mind this little theater that would teach all of the boys a lesson in toughness. He ripped Henry's helmet from his head and grabbed the back of the boy's head with two meaty hands. "Now I'm gonna show you how to do this goddamn drill." Bryant then butted Henry in the nose with his forehead. He yanked his head forward again and again, bashing his skull into Henry's nose, lips, and eyes. Blood poured down Henry's neck and began to soak his white jersey. Even from forty yards away, players could hear the sickening thud as Bryant's forehead slammed into the boy's face. Finally, Henry fell like a sack of potatoes onto the hard ground. Stumbling forward, blood smeared across his forehead, Bryant breathed heavily as he turned toward the team. "Trainers! Get your butts over here and fix this boy's broken nose." The coach had three cuts on his forehead.

Moments later, out of earshot of the other players, Bryant told one of the student trainers, "Billy, fix his nose and tape him up. Give him a little break. But I want him back on the field before this practice is over."[79]

In Dent's second scene, a sophomore end named Billy Schroeder "toppled face-first into the crusty field" during a punting drill—the "conditioning phase of practice," running downfield to cover punts, over and over, with no water breaks allowed. (Bryant shared the common belief among football coaches of the time that being deprived of water made players tougher. Deaths from heatstroke were not identified in the annual report on fatalities until 1955; they would reach a record eight in 1970.)[80] Bryant yelled, "Get this goddamn big ox off the field and out of my sight," and then "marched toward the fallen boy and swung a right shoe into a motionless left leg. The hard smack could be heard more than fifty yards away." With Billy's face turning blue and his pulse "somewhere between 250 and 300" (who measured that?), a teammate muttered, "This boy's gonna die if we don't get him to the infirmary." The teammate took control of driving Billy there, where nurses packed him in ice and a doctor saved his life.[81]

Mickey Herskowitz, the sole sportswriter on site, was a twenty-one-year-old reporter for the *Houston Post* at the time (nineteen according to Dent, but twenty-one by the birthdate on his Wikipedia page). The *Post* in 1954 had become the first major Texas newspaper to assign any beat writer at all to the lowly Aggies, the land-grant all-male military state college near tiny Bryan, Texas, dwarfed in importance by the state's flagship university in Austin. As the kid, Herskowitz was relegated to the Aggie beat, while his veteran colleagues could stay home to cover Houston and Rice or get the plum assignment to UT in Austin. According to Herskowitz (responding to the movie version rather than to Dent's book), neither of those grotesque events happened, or happened in that way.[82] (Henry Clark also refuted Dent's version in an interview for a 2001 TV documentary on Bryant.)[83] At the time, Herskowitz's veteran colleague at the *Post*, Jack Gallagher, alluded to both incidents in his preseason preview of the Aggies. In assessing the leading candidates at each position, Gallagher noted that the team had two good ends in Billy Schroeder and team captain Benny Sinclair. "Lack of salt in his system [a quaint euphemism for heatstroke] kept Schroeder out of early workouts," Gallagher noted, but Billy was now fully recovered.[84] In his regular column on the same day, Gallagher did not name Henry Clark, but he was presumably the "well-padded guard 20 years his junior" against whom Bryant got "down on his hands and knees" to demonstrate a blocking stance and "then walked away 30 minutes later, his face streaked with blood."[85] The blood, in Gallagher's telling, was Bryant's, and Gallagher's point was that the coach was as tough as he demanded that his players be. (It should be noted that the 220-pound Bryant outweighed Clark by 15 pounds.) Going one-on-one with fully padded linemen would become a signature element of Bryant's coaching intensity in his early years at Alabama, too. Something happened to both Clark and Schroeder at Junction, but exactly what and how brutal remains unclear.

What Herskowitz saw, or did not see, over the eight days at Junction is unfortunately also not clear from his 1987 biography of Bryant. In a passage later adapted by Dent, Herskowitz recounted sending his first dispatch from Junction to his editors at the *Post*, following the Aggies' initial practice, which had included a scrimmage in full pads on a day when other conference teams were posing for photographs "or filling out forms or touching their toes," as Herskowitz put it. But the young reporter happened to call in his story from a phone booth outside a meeting room, where Bryant and his assistants could overhear him. Herskowitz recalled the scene: "I dictated a story that included some descriptive phrases about the crunch of bodies coming together, and the constant thunk of helmets crashing. . . . By the time I hung up the phone, a student manager was standing there. 'Coach Bryant would like to see you,' he said, coughing slightly." An awkward meeting followed, at which Bryant "convinced me that I was wrong, that I had not seen a full-scale scrimmage, and that a lot of mamas and papas would be upset if they thought he was up there in the hills, grinding their sons into the unforgiving earth. With great difficulty, I phoned the office back and edited (softened) my story."[86]

Here is what the *Post* published under Mickey Herskowitz's byline on September 2: "Only a handful of visitors looked on as 45 [!] Cadets . . . hit the practice field" and "embarked on Bryant's six-year plan" for returning A&M to greatness. Promptly at 6:15 a.m., with Bryant's "Let's get at it," the squad limbered up and then split into eight groups for twenty-minute timing drills and pass defense for the backs, "circle drills and contact work" for the linemen. (Those blandly named "circle drills" were better known as "bull in the ring": one player in the center ringed by several teammates who, on a coach's signal, charged him, one or two or more at a time. How violent the drill was depended less on the players than on the coaches screaming or not screaming at them. "Contact work" might have been an Oklahoma drill.) The morning session ended at 8:00. The afternoon practice that started at 4:30 ("behind locked gates") was "a bruising session that lasted until dark," in which the players "formed four squads . . . and spent over two hours on offense, including some light contact." A "bruising session" included "some light contact"? Afterward, the coaches declared themselves to be " 'satisfied' with the squad's first workout. No injuries occurred, though several players suffered first day sickness" (another quaint euphemism, this one presumably for puking after endless wind sprints).[87] The briefer Associated Press account in A&M's hometown paper, the *Bryan Daily Eagle*, used some of the same language.[88] From the beginning, the saga of the "Junction Boys" was spun by unreliable narrators.

The contemporary reporting from Junction, including Herskowitz's, confirms that Bryant's training camp was indeed brutal, though perhaps not so spectacularly vicious as Dent portrayed it a half century later. The fact that it was genuinely brutal is important for understanding Bear Bryant football, which would set the standard for much of the country by the end of the 1960s. The fact that exaggerating the brutality enhanced the legend is also important for understanding the popular fascination with, and acceptance of, football violence. Whether this was driven by forces of the historical moment or by something instinctual in human nature or simply by football fans' belief that winning justified anything is a mystery with no simple explanation.

One week in, at the Aggies' press day with Texas sportswriters, Bryant expressed frustration with their making a big deal of the players he was losing from the squad (just six or seven named so far). "Boys quit teams all the time," he reminded them. "Everybody has boys quit—Rice, Texas, Kentucky and everybody else. I get down here and everybody seems to think it's big news."[89] It was not the number but the losses of Joe Boring and particularly Fred Broussard, a former star in one case, the team's expected best player in the other, that were most shocking to the press. (Broussard would be taken in the fourth round of the 1955 NFL draft and have a brief pro career.) The next day, a reporter for the *Fort Worth Star-Telegram* responded to Bryant's comment: "Boys may quit teams, all right, but it is seldom when players of known ability such as Broussard and Boring leave after reporting for the fall practice."[90] A writer for the United Press openly wondered whether there was "'Civil War' at Texas A&M" where "Coach Paul (Bear) Bryant, the hard taskmaster Texas A&M College hired away from Kentucky for $90,000 and a 'free hand,' lost his eighth [*sic*] football player by secession today a week after his first fall practice session." The writer also noted, "None of those involved would admit any disharmony," but "there were several signs indicating that all was not well as Bryant's regime got away to a rugged start." According to the writer, none of the players contacted at their homes "would say that Bryant was driving the players too hard in workouts, nor had they any unkind things to say about the coach who pulled Maryland and Kentucky football fortunes out of the doldrums similar to the one which has affected Texas A&M in recent years."[91] Thirty years later, Mickey Herskowitz would account for the players' silence when he wrote, "The one thing everyone in that camp seemed to have in common that summer was fear. Fear of Bryant."[92]

Among the newspapers in which the UP story about a "Civil War" appeared were the *Philadelphia Inquirer*, *Detroit Free Press*, *Louisville Courier-Journal*, *Hartford Courant*, *Cincinnati Enquirer*, *Daily Oklahoman*, and *Salt Lake Tribune*, but not one of the Texas papers archived in Newspapers.com. Sportswriters in the 1950s supported the local coach, at least until he was fired, and his shortcomings could be acknowledged retrospectively. Texas sportswriters outside College Station who covered Southwest Conference football did hint at trouble in Junction. Broussard's quitting was the major incident: his walking off the field and then trying to return but being refused by Bryant, because "it wouldn't be fair to the rest of the squad." As the UP writer said, none of the players who either quit or stayed would talk to the press, except to say that Bryant told them not to talk to the press. Gene Gregston of the *Fort Worth Star-Telegram* was perhaps the most critical among the Texas writers.[93] Under a headline, "Bryant Liked Junction, but Maybe Players Didn't," Gregston on September 10 described an exchange with one of Broussard's teammates. "One of the players, who were told by Bryant not to talk too much to visiting writers, was asked by a scribe: 'I understand you lost another boy yesterday.' 'Boy, heck,' the player replied, 'we lost a man!' The player then quickly added, 'But don't say I said that.'" Gregston himself then added, "It is generally known around the league and in the press corps that Bryant had been conducting very rugged workouts at Junction. This was believed to be a major factor in the boys' quitting."[94]

The *Houston Post* was among the papers that published a page on each Southwest Conference team following its press day at training camp. Most of the *Post*'s preseason preview of the Aggies' season was written by Jack Gallagher, who hinted at brutality in Junction only to defuse it and ultimately to endorse Bryant's methods. His benign spin on the incident involving Henry Clark appeared in a story with a pointed title, "The Junction Training Routine Separated Men from the Boys." "Seven players quit in seven days," Gallagher wrote, "a development rather new to the Southwest Conference scene but hardly headline news in Bryant's Kentucky regime. Ten freshmen turned in their uniforms in the first week in Lexington last year." The Aggies' thirty-eight remaining players were "a hard core of toughened troopers," according to Gallagher. "The conditions under which Bryant conducted opening maneuvers were rather primitive, and he found out quickly who could take his regimen." Gallagher let Bryant himself summarize the team's readiness for the season: "I think we've got a good squad, although I've done a poor job of getting them ready."[95]

That "I've done a poor job" was already a signature Bryant line.[96] However disingenuous, it reflected an assumption that the team's success or failure depended on *him*, not on his players. To Bill Rives, the sports editor of the *Dallas Morning News* (whose preseason report on the Aggies was entirely positive), Bryant conceded that his team was "thin and small, but I hope and pray that I can give them the kind of leadership which will get them to do their best."[97] Again, the team's fortunes rested on *him*. College football, after all, was a *coaches'* game.

The legend of the "Junction Boys" is a tale of extreme personal sacrifice for the sake of becoming part of a championship team. But the matter of who qualified as a "Junction Boy" is another part of the puzzle. Was it just the eight seniors in 1956 who won a Southwest Conference title, or the entire thirty-eight who stuck it out at Junction in 1954? Of the eighteen sophomores who came back on that one bus, nine were gone in 1955, then one more in 1956, leaving the remaining eight to be christened. All eighteen went through the same hell, but how many of them qualified as "Junction Boys"? Of the eleven juniors on the 1954 roster who withstood the hardships, seven remained on the team in 1955,[98] normal attrition in a football program, but meaning that, of the thirty-eight who endured Junction to play in 1954, fourteen later left the program before they were seniors. Were the lives of only the remaining twenty-four heroically transformed by paying the price at Junction?

In that final chapter of *Building a Championship Football Team*, Bryant declared, "Those Who Stay Will Be Champions." Well, maybe. Of the thirty-eight players who returned from Junction, just eight won a Southwest Conference championship two years later (and then were not allowed to play in the Cotton Bowl, due to a two-year bowl ban for Bryant's recruiting violations in rounding up more talented players to replace them). Bryant also won that conference title, and a year later it propelled him to Alabama, where he would win three national championships in his first eight seasons (then three more in the 1970s after the integration of the SEC). At Alabama, *none* of the players on his initial squad in 1958 were around in 1961 for the team's first conference title since 1953 and first national championship since 1934. Players' careers were short, but coaches could play the long game.

ROLL, TIDE!

At the beginning of the 1957 season, *Life* published a photo-essay on Bryant's practice sessions at Texas A&M, "where the painful toughening-up process is made even tougher by the shuddering contact drills of its hard-bitten coach, Paul ('Bear') Bryant." The rest of the opening paragraph read: "A fanatic on defense, Bryant pits man against man in rugged personal tests of power and stamina. Players spend hours battering down each other's defenses. They learn to smash the ball with their heads to provoke fumbles. If a player feels he is superior to the man ahead of him, he can challenge him to a bitter blocking-tackling duel. 'A boy's got to want to play awful bad to play here,' says Bryant." The brief text concluded, "And he has gradually changed the football emphasis in the Southwest from high-gaited offense to leather-tough defense."[99]

Bryant would similarly transform the Southeastern Conference after taking over at Alabama a year later. Having turned around programs at Kentucky and Texas A&M, Bryant arrived in Tuscaloosa in January 1958 knowing exactly how to do it again. (Both the Wildcats and the Aggies immediately reverted to their losing ways after he left.) In contrast to Woody Hayes, Bryant, in Jim Dent's apt phrase (but my emphasis), was not *impulsively* but "*systematically* brutal."[100] Among other tactics, he liked to pick out an unlikely candidate for special abuse, perhaps a star player (like Fred Broussard), to send a message to the rest of the team. More generally, he believed that brutality in April and September won games in October and November, and he organized his offseason conditioning, spring practices, and September training camps accordingly. Offseason workouts and spring practice were for winnowing the freshmen down to those willing to pay the price (and talented enough) and for running off sophomores and juniors who could not help the team. Preseason training in September prepared those who survived for the long grind of the season.

That first season at Alabama, "voluntary" offseason conditioning sessions—one-hour, nonstop—began on January 10 and ended on March 19, when spring practice started.[101] For this, as Bryant related in his 1974 autobiography, "we didn't pussyfoot trying to find out who could play and who couldn't among the holdovers, the ones we'd have to go with that first season. We started right in with about as hard a series of spring practices as I could dream up." At the conclusion of the practice sessions allowed by the NCAA, Bryant named twenty-four players to a One-Hundred Percent Club, "based entirely on effort, not on a player's ability," while assigning the rest to a "voluntary" group for more wind sprints and drills.[102]

"And we didn't slack up in the fall, either," Bryant continued. Of the ninety-five who turned out for spring practice in March 1958, sixty-six showed up on September 1. "My plan was to bleed 'em and gut 'em," Bryant wrote in 1974, "because I didn't want any well-wishers hanging around."[103] That pungent image came from a colorful talker who grew up in the backwoods of Arkansas, but it also captured Bryant's attitude when he took over a new program and inherited the previous coach's players, the "holdovers." Whoever survived would be his team that season, and he did not much care who they were. After the second day of fall practice, Bryant told a writer for the Associated Press, "The riff-raff are fast eliminating themselves and we had two real good scrimmages."[104] The next day, the sports columnist for the *Montgomery Advertiser* attributed the line about "riff-raff" to "a coach," rather than to Bryant himself, and noted, "The same situation prevailed at every school that Bryant has undertaken a rebuilding job. He cleaned out Maryland, Kentucky and Texas A&M, his three previous assignments."[105] The writer was not being critical but simply telling his readers, in effect, to sit back and let Bryant discard the "riff-riff" and enjoy the results when he delivered championships.

Sportswriters in Texas had questioned the departure of players like Joe Boring and Fred Broussard. In Alabama, they left Bryant to do what he had to do, but elsewhere around the SEC there was more ambivalence. Commenting on Bryant's talk of "riff-raff," a columnist for the *Knoxville Journal* grouped Bryant with Frank Leahy and Jim Tatum as "realists" who "have done a lot to move college football out of the sports or game category into that of big business with not a conscience in a carload."[106] But Bryant also had his defenders outside Tuscaloosa. In his preview of the SEC season, the sports editor of the *Atlanta Constitution*, Jesse Outlar, excused "riff-raff" as a term used in "an unthinking moment," while offering nothing but praise for the previous results of Bryant's winnowing process. "Those who stay will butt you," Outlar wrote. "They'll play Bryant's type of hard-nosed football, which has produced successful results in the standings at Maryland, Kentucky, and Texas A&M." Noting that Bryant had a canvas fence around his practice field, to keep out prying eyes, Outlar declared, "Behind it are perhaps the hardest working kids in the SEC. All are tough physically, and many have acquired the mental toughness the Bear likes to talk about."[107] Whatever hell he put them through was justified by the results.

What exactly took place behind that canvas fence would come out only years later, most fully in Tom Stoddard's book on Bryant's "turnaround" season at Alabama, based on interviews with former players who described conditions much like at Junction.[108] Without going into details, Bryant himself confessed (boasted?) in his autobiography about his past coaching methods: "So I've laid it on the line to a lot of boys. I've grabbed 'em, shook 'em, kicked 'em, and embarrassed them in front of the squad. I've got down in the dirt with them, and if they didn't give as well as they took I'd tell them they were insults to their upbringing, and I've cleaned out their lockers for them and piled their clothes out in the hall." He did all of this because he wanted to "make them prove what they had in their veins, blood or spit, one way or the other, and praying that they would come through."[109]

That last phrase, whether genuine or self-promotional, asked readers to believe that, like Woody Hayes, whatever Bryant did to them was ultimately for his boys. True or not, there is no need to belabor the obvious point: that both the nature of Bryant's brand of toughness and his manner of instilling it in his players had profoundly changed from previous eras. A sport born in the elite enclaves of Harvard, Yale, and Princeton had been transformed into a battleground for those willing to fight for everything they got. This was more "democratic" but also more brutal. And it was embraced by ordinary fans. What had come to matter most in college football now, to turn Grantland Rice's famous lines on their head, was not how you played the game but whether you won or lost. The all-importance of winning had been blasphemy for college football's first half century or so, but it was becoming more or less indisputable in college football in the 1950s and 1960s (as it had always been in the pro game).

It is a truism in sport that one must pay the price to become a champion. It is also a hard fact of sport that many more pay the price than ever do become champion. For them, the price must not be too high and paying it must have value in itself, or it is not worth it. The conclusion of the 2002 movie of *The Junction Boys* hinged on the guilt that Bryant supposedly harbored for years over his brutal treatment of his players. When he finally meets up with them for a twenty-five-year reunion, he finds no hard feelings, only love and respect. The players all seem like winners in life; paying the price served them well.

The mythologizing of the Junction Boys evaded the obvious question: When was the price simply too high? The revelation of the secret in Mike Webster's brain just three years after the ESPN telecast would finally force a reckoning with that question.

CHAPTER 6

DISHING IT OUT

At the end of the 1953 season, *Look* sports editor Tim Cohane addressed "Gridiron Muckerism" as a newly urgent problem, with a tagline, "Football can maim or kill, even when played cleanly. Played any other way, it is indefensible." *Muckerism,* Cohane wrote, was a Victorian term that, in football, "denotes the knee in the groin, the covert slug to the head, the sneak 90-degree twist of the leg at the ankle or knee, the surreptitious kick in the head, the deliberate downfield clip." A true mucker did not act "in a sudden flare of anger or as a gesture of retaliation" but had "a deliberate plan to intimidate the opposition by illegal violence." Cohane pointed to the "deplorable yet interesting fact, which most coaches will readily admit, off the record, that a spirit of sadism, or even a spirit of murder, is a definite asset in a football game, when nothing else is considered except the final score."[1] Character-building, anyone? And Tim Cohane was a huge fan of college football.

Whether the play on the field had truly become dirtier, or popular magazines finally called more attention to it (rather than the usual feel-good profiles of coaches and the season's top teams), the public became accustomed to a higher level of football violence in the 1950s, which transformed the game's

Figure 6.1. Fred Ludekens illustration for Booton Herndon, “The Dirtiest Game of the Year,” *Saturday Evening Post*, October 18, 1952.

underlying cult of toughness in three distinct ways. Postwar football was emphatically not for everyone (as in Knute Rockne's fantasy of mandatory football for all) but for the select few who could meet its extraordinary demands, while coaches ran off the rest. "Taking it" still mattered, but more openly for the sake of winning, not for any pretense to building character. And "dishing it out" mattered more, as in prizefighting, which had long been disparaged for having violence as its primary purpose.

Cohane's was but one in a series of articles in *Look*, *Life*, *Collier's*, and the *Saturday Evening Post* over the 1950s that addressed the perennial conflict between necessary and unnecessary roughness at an increasingly blurred boundary between "aggressive" and "dirty" play. Among the games that Cohane singled out for particular shame were Cal–USC and Drake–Oklahoma A&M in 1951. In seven pages of vivid photographs, *Life* had captured "the most brutally spectacular game" of a "zany" season, when #1 Cal was upset by a USC team "impersonating Murder, Inc." and led by their "human gorilla, Pat Cannamela," who put Cal's star running back, John Olszewski, out of the game the second time he carried the ball. Photos of "several California stars retired by injuries" graced the brief text.[2] A week later, on the first play of the contest between Drake and Oklahoma A&M (Oklahoma State), a defensive end named Wilbanks Smith delivered a forearm to the face of Drake's Johnny Bright that broke his jaw, after Bright had handed off the ball and was several yards away from the action. A photographer for the *Des Moines Register* captured the incident in a sequence of seven photographs, which were published two weeks later in *Life* (along with one of a Texas A&M player slugging Bright in the face in Drake's previous game). The slugging became a particular scandal because of the racial dimension—Bright was Black and Oklahoma A&M (like Texas A&M) still all-white—but Bright was also leading the NCAA in total offense, and, as *Life* wrote, "Nobody could say for sure that Wilbanks Smith intended to break Bright's jaw or that he was under a coach's orders. But for A&M the best way to win that football game was to get Bright out of it."[3]

Notwithstanding the claims for football's building of character, going after the other team's best player had been a more or less open strategy since the game's beginnings—including, on several occasions, to justify an all-white team's targeting the other team's lone Black star. The slugging of Bright was just the latest in a series of such ugly racial incidents dating back to the turn of the century.[4] But it also contributed to what Cohane, two years later, would decry as a new era of "muckerism" (and may have inspired the 1952 story whose illustration heads this chapter).[5]

In condemning football "muckerism," Cohane defended what he called "legitimate violence" (as he would do in his article on high school football discussed at the end of chapter 4), making the age-old distinction for a new rougher game. He also claimed that "the big majority of those closest to the boys who have been killed or maimed by the game believe firmly that it is worth the price." Really? How could the sports editor of *Look* magazine have known that? In 1953 alone, thirteen players died from "direct" injuries (six high schoolers, three collegians, two non-NFL professionals, and two sandlot players) and another four "indirectly."[6] And what about 1952? 1951? 1950? A "big majority" of those players' families agreed it was "worth the price"? Cohane simply expressed what had become a football truism, an article of unexamined faith in his world. Cohane went on: "This is a tribute to the good things in football, *particularly its character-building role no cynic ever has succeeded in sneering out of existence*" (my emphasis). Cohane himself had previously defended Red Blaik and Army following the 1949 season for playing "aggressive," not "dirty," football.[7] Magazine profiles of Michigan's Ron Kramer in 1956 and USC's McKeever twins, Mike and Marlin, in 1959 and 1960 made the same distinction, including an explicit "Case for Rough Football" in defense of Kramer.[8]

Bear Bryant was the most controversial coach in this decade of controversies over "aggressive" and "dirty" play, becoming a lightning rod for those issues after his arrival at Alabama. Already in 1953, according to Cohane, "no section plays consistently rougher football than the South." That would have been Bryant's final season at Kentucky before leaving for Texas A&M in 1954 and then Alabama in 1958, to push the SEC further in that direction. In 1960, Edwin Pope, the sports columnist for the *Miami Herald*, called Bryant "more unpopular among fellow coaches than anyone I have ever known."[9] In November 1961, as Bryant was closing in on his first national championship at Alabama, *Time* called him "a relentlessly brutal taskmaster" who "lives, eats and breathes football with an angry fervor that few rival coaches can pretend to understand."[10] A month later, after Alabama won that title, Roy Terrell in *Sports Illustrated* (admiringly) described Byant's defensive unit as eleven relatively small players, without "a real standout prospect [for the NFL] in the lot," who hit "again and again and again with the viciousness of a pack of sharks until someone goes down."[11]

Then in 1962, the roof caved in over Bryant's head. *Sports Illustrated* titled its preview of the 1962 football season in the SEC "A Turn to Toughness" and singled out Bryant as the principal cause. As Auburn coach Shug Jordan told *Sports Illustrated*'s writer, "It's a hell-for-leather, helmet-bursting, gang-tackling game we play now in the Southeastern Conference. . . . Since Bear Bryant came back to Alabama it's the only game that can win."[12] A month later, the *Saturday Evening Post* laid bare Bryant's kind of football in a piece written by Furman Bisher, the sports editor of the *Atlanta Journal* (and friend of Georgia Tech coach Bobby Dodd, Bryant's temperamental and philosophical opposite). Titled "College Football Is Going Berserk," Bisher's article had a tagline, "A game ruled by brute force needs a housecleaning," and it offered Bryant as the #1 despoiler of the game. Bisher's chief case in point was a punt return in the previous season's Alabama–Georgia Tech game, in which an Alabama linebacker named Darwin Holt "struck halfback Chick Graning of Georgia Tech such a devastating blow to the face that for days afterward Graning looked like Joe Louis after his knockout by Rocky Marciano." Sprinting downfield to cover the punt, Graning had slowed when the 'Bama return man called for a fair catch. As Bisher described the play, Holt "veered from his apparent course to the Alabama bench and delivered a sudden forearm blow under the face bar of Graning's helmet as Graning eased up." (Graning was hospitalized for four weeks with a broken nose, cheek, and other facial bones, plus five teeth knocked out and a concussion—details surprisingly not mentioned by Bisher.)[13] Holt had denied it was intentional, and his coach had backed him up, but Bisher had visited an Alabama practice that week, where Bryant noted that Holt was in sweats rather than pads, because "he's so tough we don't let him scrimmage during the week. He's liable to hurt somebody."[14] If Bryant was joking, he badly misread his audience in Furman Bisher. That "somebody" proved to be Chick Graning.

"To be sure, football is a game of toughness," Bisher wrote, echoing Tim Cohane and countless others before him. "The ability to take and deliver a jarring blow in a legal manner is *admirable as well as necessary* [my emphasis]. But the coach who encourages or even tolerates a player who violates the spirit of the rules is placing the future of football in jeopardy." For Bisher, Bryant epitomized a much broader problem in the college game. The "illegally thrown forearm" and "the 'bull block' of a plastic-helmeted head," which were becoming common, were matters of "coaching intent" and not just at Alabama. Besides Bryant, Bisher mentioned Woody Hayes, Jim Tatum, and Iowa's Forest Evashevski as coaches who "taught hard-nosed football and demanded Marine Corps conditioning." At the same time, game officials had become "less vigilant" and alumni more enamored of "hardfisted, driving, demanding commandants of campus installations run on military lines." If Bisher was right, there was much complicity in brutalizing an already rough game, but coaches were the primary agents of change.

Bryant not only was outraged by Bisher's attack but also sued the *Post* for libel.[15] Of course, he was fiercely supported (and Bisher vilified) in Alabama, and he also had less partisan defenders, like the AP's Will Grimsley, speaking to the Montgomery Quarterback Club a few days after the piece in the *Post* came out. "What is wrong with the hard-nosed, hard-hitting football?" Grimsley asked rhetorically. "It's a mystery that a coach could teach anything but hard-tackling." According to Grimsley, the country was "getting too pussy-footed anyhow. . . . If we're getting soft then we need coaches of Bryant's ilk. . . . Personally I hope we have more hard-nosed football and more hard-nosed men among our politicians and military leaders."[16] A simplistic Cold War mentality found a champion in Bear Bryant.

HEADS OR SHOULDERS?

Bisher insisted that the game's brutality was neither accidental nor attributable to rogue players but was taught by coaches—a matter of "coaching intent." He pointed out that the NCAA's committee on injuries had recently reported that "many coaches instruct players to use their hard plastic helmets as weapons in making blocks and tackles" and that "tacklers seem to be under instruction to maim the ball carrier rather than merely bring him down." Worst of all, "These same players were becoming high-school coaches" and teaching the same techniques to adolescent boys (while using drills like "bull in the ring," to toughen them up, he could have added).[17]

Bisher was, in fact, describing techniques that Bear Bryant openly promoted in *Building a Championship Football Team*, his coaching manual, published two years earlier. In chapter 2 ("The Theory of Winning Football"), Bryant included a section titled "*You Must Beat Your Opponent Physically*" (his italics), in which he wrote that "teams that win consistently are the ones in the best physical condition" who also "out-mean" their opponents "by hard blocking and tackling."[18] In that term *out-mean*, Bryant announced the transformation of college football. Try to imagine Professor Eugene Richards or sportswriter Grantland Rice or even Army coach Red Blaik using that term.

In chapter 4 ("Our Kind of Football"), Bryant explained his defensive philosophy, singling out the importance of "gang tackling," which typically meant the entire defense swarming to the ball carrier. Many coaches promoted gang-tackling for instilling "desire" in their players and emphasizing "pursuit" while potentially causing fumbles.[19] Bryant expressed a different purpose. "Frankly we want the first man to the ball carrier merely to hold him up," he wrote, "and not let him get away, so we can unload on him. You can punish a ball carrier when one man has him 'dangling,' and the others gang tackle him hard." Bryant immediately added, "I am not implying we want our boys to pile on and play dirty football merely to get a ball carrier out of the game."[20] Of course not.

Out-mean the opponent. *Punish* him. With no fanfare, Bear Bryant was announcing a football revolution here. In other chapters, he described the proper techniques for offensive and defensive linemen playing this new kind of football. Offensive line blocking had three precise steps: First, "strike a jarring blow with the forehead"; second, "bring the head up as contact is made"; and third, "drive . . . forward, then upward." For a two-on-one (double-team) block, the "post man" should "aim the nose guard at the middle of the target" and "strike a good blow with the forehead," while the "drive man" struck "a jarring blow with the forehead below the armpit." For defensive linemen, depending on the position, the first move was to "play the center's head with a quick hand shiver," or "play either the guard or tackle with a quick flipper or shiver," or "deliver a hand or forearm shiver to the head of the offensive end," and so on, for each player in every possible alignment.[21] That innocuous-sounding "flipper" would become more commonly known as the "head-slap," most notoriously wielded to devastating effect by the Los Angeles Rams' "Deacon" Jones. (The NFL would ban it in 1977, but not the NCAA.)

To appreciate just how remarkable Bryant's manual for fellow and future coaches was in 1960, it can be set alongside the preceding ones in Prentice-Hall's series written by Texas's Dana Bible (1947), Notre Dame's Frank Leahy (1949 and 1951), Missouri's Don Faurot (1950), Oklahoma's Bud Wilkinson (1952 and 1957), Michigan State's Biggie Munn (1953), and Georgia Tech's Bobby Dodd (1954). To a man, they taught techniques for properly executing *shoulder* blocks and *shoulder* tackles, as if there were no other kind. Wilkinson's explanation of the basic one-on-one block was typical. The lineman was to drive his head at the opponent's belt buckle, adjusting to the direction of his charge until, "an inch or two from contact," he would slide his head right or left, in order to move his man in the desired direction by making contact with "the proper shoulder."[22] On defense, a lineman was to ward off blockers with either a "forearm or hand shiver," targeted "just below the numerals on the man's jersey." A tackler was to aim his head at the ball; since it would be carried in one arm or the other, "the head will just clear the ball carrier's body when it is aimed at the ball. This will insure a solid shoulder instead of an arm tackle" (easy to break free of).[23] Wilkinson's coauthor on his 1957 book on defensive football, his line coach Gomer Jones, wrote a third coaching manual on Oklahoma football (*Offensive and Defensive Line Play*) for Prentice-Hall in

1961 (*after* Bryant's, that is), in which the techniques for blocking, tackling, and delivering a forearm shiver were unchanged.[24]

Blocking and tackling with the *shoulder*; targeting the opponent's *body*, not his head, with a forearm: That's what every one of these other coaching manuals taught.[25] For all of these coaches in all of these books, there were just two kinds of blocks—the ubiquitous *shoulder block* and the infrequently used *cross-body block* in the open field—and two kinds of tackles, one of them correct (the *shoulder tackle*) and the other wrong (the *arm tackle*, which risked losing the ball carrier). In both blocking and tackling, the head was a *guide*; the shoulder made *contact*. And the target was the opponent's torso, never his head. For coaches who taught it, a defensive lineman's "forearm shiver" was delivered with the heel of the hand and a straight, stiff arm to the opponent's shoulder, in order to straighten him up and toss him aside, not to smash his head with a looping swing.[26] At the far extreme, Georgia Tech's Bobby Dodd was the anti-Bryant among these prominent coaches. His basic philosophy began with the principles that "football is a game" and that even practices should be *fun*.[27]

Bear Bryant's philosophy began with *punishing* opponents, with the head as both principal weapon and target. Whether or not Bear Bryant was the first coach to teach blocking and tackling with the hard-shell-plastic-helmeted head (more on that shortly), what was unprecedented in 1960 was his frankly expressed philosophy of defeating opponents by *punishing* them. Rival coaches testified that Byant changed Southwest Conference and Southeastern Conference football. At the same time, his philosophy and tactics offered coaches elsewhere, including high school coaches, a new winning method with proven success. *Building a Championship Football Team* openly made college and schoolboy football a game of *dishing it out*, as professional football had always been.

THE BRYANT IDEA

Bryant's methods spread most directly through his assistants who went on to be head coaches elsewhere, including Jim Owens, Jerry Claiborne, and Phil Cutchin from his staff at Junction. Owens (who also coached under Bryant at Kentucky for three years before following him to Texas A&M) took over at the University of Washington in 1957, straight from A&M's Southwest Conference championship. He immediately instituted Bryant's program of "punishing practices," epitomized in what became locally legendary as the "Death March" on September 10, 1957: fifteen-yard wind sprints up and down two football fields, repeated perhaps fifteen times, until players "staggered and fell" and then "crawled" and "babbled and cried like babies as the assistants lined down the field and urged them on." According to the boosterish chronicler of this event, "Some had their spirits broken. Others lost respect for the coaches and didn't wat to pay the price required and left the program. Some resolved to stay the course and embrace the principles of the program."[28] Owens also brought Bryant's "challenge drills . . . conditioning drills, scrimmages, punting drills, and hitting with the helmet" to the Pacific Northwest. Upset wins over Wisconsin and Minnesota in the 1960 and 1961 Rose Bowls, while establishing UW among the football elite and Owens as a major college coach, introduced Bryant techniques to the Midwest, too. One of Owens's assistants, Bert Clark, tried exporting his tactics to Washington State in 1964, without much success, and the return of two-platoon football in 1965 took away Owens's own advantage in having hyper-conditioned, punishing players. He won his last conference title in 1963 but had changed the game on the West Coast.

Jerry Claiborne and Phil Cutchin coached under Bryant at Kentucky and Alabama as well as at Texas A&M before becoming head coaches at Virginia Tech in 1961 (Claiborne) and Oklahoma State in 1963 (Cutchin). Like Owens, they tried to follow their leader. Inheriting what he judged a group of slow and undersized players at Virginia Tech, Claiborne told the sports columnist for the *Roanoke World-News* during his initial spring football program that he was at least "hoping he can get what boys he does have to enjoy 'hitting.'" He apparently did and went on to a long, mostly successful twenty-eight-year coaching career at Virginia Tech, Maryland, and Kentucky. Cutchin introduced the "Bear Bryant System" of "fierce hitting" and "spartan-conditioning" at Oklahoma State in 1963, but he never won more than four games in any of his six seasons there.[29] Overall, the Bryant coaching legacy from his early, most hard-driving coaching years was mixed.

That legacy played out most painfully at Kentucky, where Charlie Bradshaw, a former player for Bryant at Kentucky and one of his assistants at Alabama, had the distinct misfortune to implement the Bryant system under the scrutiny of a national publication on the lookout for sports scandals. Bradshaw took over Kentucky's losing program in 1962, after the firing of Blanton Collier, who had succeeded Bryant in 1954.[30] In Bradshaw's initial season, several days before "College Football Is Going Berserk" appeared in the *Saturday Evening Post*, *Sports Illustrated* published "The New Rage to Win," by Morton Sharnik and Robert Creamer, about the early returns on Bradshaw's attempt to bring "Bryant's football philosophy" to Kentucky. Bradshaw had arrived in Lexington the previous January with a public vow "to develop players who are 'loose, reckless and mean,'" coached by a staff of "Christians with integrity"(!).[31] Nine months later, Sharnik and Creamer described how that was working out.

"The Bryant idea is harsh and simple," they wrote: "Get tough, aggressive players; impress upon them that the only thing that matters is victory, no matter what it costs, train them and train them and train them to an absolute peak of condition; teach them to hit—hit the opponent hard and keep on hitting him until inevitably he falters and makes a mistake; capitalize on that mistake."[32] This was the Bryant system that Bradshaw immediately began implementing on his arrival in January with a brutal offseason conditioning program. The drills included wrestling matches that *Sports Illustrated*'s writers called "more like brawling." Two players would "brawl" until one dropped, who would then have to "brawl" with the next one and the next one until he finally won, while coaches screamed at them nonstop the whole time. (The *Sports Illustrated* piece led the NCAA to punish Kentucky, not for abusing athletes but for having coaches present for offseason conditioning sessions.) Four players quit after the first week, a total of fifteen by the end of the offseason program.

When spring practice arrived, Kentucky fans were excited by the second coming of Bear Bryant. "The name of the game is knock," one of them explained to Sharnik; "old Charlie reminds me of the Bear." Bradshaw, a little man, could not physically dominate his players, like Bryant did; instead, as Sharnik and Creamer wrote, he "punishes players who aren't aggressive enough in practice by running them back and forth until they are exhausted." Like Bryant, Bradshaw coached his players to tackle helmet-first, and when a player missed a tackle, an assistant coach would yell, "Butt him, damn you." Coaches would "bang players in the head with a forearm to make a lesson clear." One player who quit did not mind the coaches' hitting him—he considered that "part of football"—but he despised their hypocrisy when they denied it. One assistant, who smacked a player in the mouth with his fist and broke a tooth, insisted to Sharnik, "I was demonstrating the proper execution and I guess my forearm must have caught him in the mouth" (instead of the head, I guess). The assistant explained that a boy cannot be taught toughness but must learn it by the coaches' example. He also added, out of the blue but apparently as the ultimate justification, "We teach the word of Christ."[33]

Twenty-three more players quit during spring practice, including at least one "devout Baptist" because of the coaches' hypocrisy. "Christ taught love," he told *Sports Illustrated*. "Charlie Bradshaw teaches us to punish, to destroy the other man." Another player who quit, according to his mother, had "too much character to want to get out and kill," and a third did not "believe winning is worth the price." A fourth felt that football should be fun as well as rough; a fifth, that football was a sport, not a business. By September, Bradshaw's initial squad of eighty-eight in January was down to thirty-two for the season opener.[34] The *Sports Illustrated* writers had seen something "a bit totalitarian" in Bradshaw's system of turning players into "automaton[s] . . . wholly dominated by the coach and wholly dedicated to football. It is Total Football. And it pays off—perhaps not so much for the player as it does for the school and the coach." It turned out that it paid off for no one this time.

Lexington sportswriters and editors denounced the *Sports Illustrated* piece as a "hatchet job" and fully supported Bradshaw's tactics. From the beginning of spring practice, they viewed the massive loss of players who were "unwilling to pay the price" as the necessary condition to replicate the revered Bear Bryant's success at Texas A&M.[35] A headline in the *Lexington Herald* on September 13 reminded readers, "Bryant's First Texas A&M Squad Got Down to Only 26 Survivors; Two Years Later They Won Crown." Sports editor and columnist Ed Ashford believed that Bradshaw might do even better: "Like Bryant, Bradshaw has found many of the players he inherited from his predecessor are not willing to 'pay the price.' But Bradshaw still has a rugged and determined 32, plus an ailing trio, going into his first season at UK. Bradshaw won't win the SEC title this year, but he'll do better than 1–9, and then . . . next year, well, maybe Charlie's championship express will come a year earlier than Bryant's!"[36]

Even the Wildcats' team doctors supported Bradshaw while denigrating the players who quit. Two days before the season opener against Florida State, three of them organized a panel at a meeting of the Kentucky State Medical Association to mount a defense of Bradshaw, based on their analysis of practice films and their own interactions with players. As a writer for the *Courier-Journal* reported, "All three doctors defended the rough, all-out type of football played on most college teams in the Southeastern Conference and recently instituted at the U.K. by new coach Bradshaw." According to one of the doctors, "Football is a hard, tough sport that requires hard, tough conditioning. The boys who quit football at Kentucky this year probably shouldn't have been there in the first place." (The doctors did, however, recommend that the players be allowed to drink water during practices.)[37]

On the day of the Florida State game, a writer for the *Courier-Journal* christened Bradshaw's survivors the "Thin Thirty," undoubtedly anticipating future glory that would set them alongside the "Junction Boys" among football's legendary survivors.[38] Instead, after an embarrassing scoreless tie with Florida State, the Wildcats finished the season 3–5–2; followed by 3–6–1, 5–5, 6–4, 3–6–1, 2–8, and 3–7 (while, on the credit side, becoming the first SEC school to field an integrated football team, in 1967). The Bryant idea did not work out so well for Charlie Bradshaw.

CHAPTER 6

HITTERS AND QUITTERS

Quitters were as essential as *hitters* in the Bryant system that Bradshaw replicated. They elevated the distinction of those who paid the price to be a winner. How Bryant himself felt about those who quit, he summed up rather pithily, when he told his players at Kentucky before one practice that "today we're gonna separate the champions from the turds."[39] In his first season at Alabama, when one player quit after a brutal practice, Bryant cleaned out his locker and threw his clothes into the street. As *Time* reported, "I wanted the others to learn that it doesn't pay to be a quitter."[40] Bryant also told his players that those who paid the price would be winners at life, too. Quitters would always be losers.

Actually, no. Shannon Ragland's account of Kentucky's "Thin Thirty" includes brief biographical sketches of sixty-eight players he had tracked down (out of the eighty-eight reported in the Lexington papers) who were on the roster when Charlie Bradshaw took over the program in January 1962.[41] The thirty-eight who quit at some point between conditioning drills in January and the opening of the season in September included six future lawyers and one prosecutor, four physicians, two engineers (one of them also a physician), a school superintendent, a university administrator, a university professor, an architect, a sportswriter, and various businessmen, salesmen, managers, career military officers, and civil servants. The thirty who stuck it out went on to a similar range of careers, though with fewer professionals (two physicians and one lawyer) and a higher proportion of coaches and teachers (a common career path for football players majoring in physical education in this era). Neither group more conspicuously "won" or "lost" in life. Some would argue that the "quitters," with more professionals, were disproportionately the "winners" by conventional standards.[42]

Players quit the brutal football programs of the 1950s and 1960s for many sound reasons: contempt for their coaches, respect for themselves, understanding that injuries could be serious, academic priorities, a sense that the benefit did not justify the cost. Sharnik and Creamer cited several examples in their October 1962 *Sports Illustrated* article. Ten of the so-called quitters at Kentucky in 1962 did not quit football at all, just Bradshaw football, going on to play after transferring to other schools. (Three went on to play professionally, one for nine seasons in the NFL.)[43] The Lexington papers in 1962 would not even print the names of the players who quit, because, as the sports editor of the *Lexington Herald* put it during Charlie Bradshaw's first spring practice, quitters should not "be given a lot of publicity."[44] A quitter forfeited his right to respect as a person. But outside Lexington, hometown papers were interested in knowing why their local boys, recent high school stars, had walked away from a chance to play college football at the state's flagship university. A player from Murfreesboro, "obviously trying to avoid comment that would put either the university or coach Charlie Bradshaw in a worse light than they already are in," finally told the local writer, "There just ceased to be any fun in the game."[45] A player from Nashville, also reluctant to talk, only said, "I just didn't want to play football like it's being played there," and then added, "There are a lot more important things than playing football."[46] A third player, the projected starting center from Paducah, was more forthright. "I quit the team," he told the local sports editor, "because of the physical and verbal abuse to me and especially to my teammates which I couldn't stomach. . . . I took everything this spring and I could take it this fall, but I just don't feel it's right . . . and when 50 boys quit since last spring, it speaks for itself."[47]

That player was John Mutchler, and Shannon Ragland provided a fuller account of his decision. In a tackling drill in spring practice, whose purpose was "to run off a little used quarterback" by having "the entire defense pounding the boy," Mutchler refused to hit him when his turn came. An enraged assistant coach rushed Mutchler, who "snatched [him] by the collar and held him close," to keep him from throwing punches. Bradshaw himself then charged Mutchler, cursing him, but when he tried to throw a "forearm shiver to the head," Mutchler grabbed it in mid-swing and growled, "If you touch me again, I'll kill you." A startled Bradshaw backed off. Mutchler had no problem with "taking it," but he balked at "dishing it out" to an already brutalized teammate, as was demanded in many of the drills contrived by the Bryant–Bradshaw school. Mutchler, as Ragland put it, "didn't have the heart to hurt a helpless man." He was also shocked by his own murderous rage toward Bradshaw. Mutchler did not quit immediately after the incident but was among those who did not return in the fall.[48] Instead, he transferred to Western Kentucky, where he was a second-team Little All-American in 1963 (after sitting out the 1962 season because of transfer rules).

John Mutchler's story is particularly impressive for the character it shows, but it also reflects on "quitters" and "toughness" more broadly. Bear Bryant wrote about his players who stuck it out at Junction in 1954 having nowhere to go if they quit, as he himself, the eleventh of twelve children, growing up impoverished in rural Arkansas in the 1910s and 1920s, had had nowhere to go if he failed at football at Alabama. For Bryant, as for many of his players at A&M, playing football in college offered escape from poverty or, more positively, access to a middle-class life. At Alabama in 1958, according to

Tom Stoddard, most of the players were first-generation college students, as Bryant had been.[49] Those who grew up with little did not have to prove their toughness because they had been "taking it" their whole lives.

What John Mutchler did required "toughness" of a different sort from what mattered to his coaches. Quitting was never easy, and so-called quitters often made painful choices. To quit meant to be cut off from the brotherhood of teammates and the bond of a shared code, and possibly to be haunted by doubts about self-worth. For *Meat on the Hoof*, Gary Shaw's 1972 exposé of playing football at Texas under Darrell Royal in the early 1960s, Shaw interviewed former teammates who had quit. "Still to this day," one of them told him, "I feel you and the others who stuck it out all the way have something inside of you that I don't have." Another teammate told Shaw, "Quitting was the hardest thing I ever did"—harder than sticking it out would have been.[50]

John Mutchler balked at beating up a teammate, but some players thrived on it. One of Bryant's players at Alabama told Stoddard, "Coach Bryant didn't run anybody off. . . . Those of us that stayed eliminated those others. . . . Had I not done what was necessary . . . somebody would have eliminated me."[51] In any blocking or tackling drill, one player wins and the other loses, but the competition need not reach the level of *kill or be killed.* At Kentucky, according to Keith Dunnavant, "Often, at the end of practice, Bryant would call out for the players to pair off and go one-on-one in blocking and tackling drills until one partner dropped from sheer exhaustion."[52] At Texas A&M and Alabama, Bryant's players could challenge for starting positions: the backup facing off against the starter, with the winner to claim the coveted spot. (Jim Owens took Bryant's "challenge" drill to the University of Washington.) Two-on-one, three-on-one, many-on-one drills (like "bull in the ring") challenged the toughness of the *one* but also of the two or three or many: Were they "tough" enough to punish their teammate? All football players must compete with each other for places on the team, for playing time, for starting positions. Brutal drills at Alabama or Kentucky required that they *punish* each other as well. Dishing it out, not taking it, was the name of the game. What sort of character would *that* toughness build? one might ask. What sort of character did John Mutchler show in saying no?

THE HELMET AS WEAPON AND LEGISLATING BRUTALITY

The helmeted head and the forearm were the weapons of choice for "dishing it out," both of them made possible by the development of the hard-shell plastic helmet (with attached face guard), arguably the most far-reaching and consequential development in postwar football—and in the entire history of football in relation to head trauma. With leather helmets, blocking or tackling with the shoulder had been a simple matter of self-preservation, and a forearm to an unprotected face would have been an act of overt viciousness and invited retaliation (as well as disqualification by rule since 1932).[53] Introduced in 1939 by the John T. Riddell Company, the plastic helmet did not transform the game overnight, because its plastic was initially too brittle, prone to shatter on impact. (The National Football League banned it for one season in 1948.)[54] Not until the early 1950s was a model durable enough to be widely adopted. The single-bar facemask began appearing on plastic helmets (as evident in photographs and illustrations) around 1955–56. Players in earlier eras (like those mentioned by Bill Cunningham and Frank Scully) had suffered brain injuries, but such injuries would not become epidemic until the head became the primary weapon in blocking and tackling. That required the development of the hard-shell plastic helmet. It also required coaches to teach using it as a target and weapon.

Concern that helmets might be used as a weapon were nearly as old as the first primitive leather versions in the 1910s, and the plastic helmet was quickly recognized by some as "more a weapon of offense than defense."[55] When the Associated Press polled sportswriters and broadcasters after the 1952 season for their ten recommendations for the NCAA Rules Committee to consider at its upcoming meeting, #5 on their list was to "eliminate the dangerous 'helmet block,'" which occurred "when a blocker lowers his head and rams his hard plastic helmet into a would-be tackler's face."[56] No action by the rules committee followed.

The plastic helmet also prompted attention from the medical community, where initial concern focused on the attached face mask rather than on the helmet itself. Writing in the *Journal of the American Medical Association* in August 1961, Dr. Richard C. Schneider, a professor of neurosurgery at the University of Michigan (with coauthors who included the football coach and athletic director at Michigan), warned that a hand or forearm to the plastic face mask could shove it upward as a lever, driving the back of the helmet down on the cervical spine with catastrophic consequences.[57] ("Grasping" the face mask became a personal foul in 1957, although shoving it remained legal.)[58] Three months later, *Sports Illustrated* introduced the broader public to Schneider's research after eighteen players had died in just the first half of the 1961 season, three-fourths of them from injuries to the head or neck.[59] In January 1962, the Associated Press reported on a survey of 7,500 school athletic officials in which a third "thought face masks contributed to injuries to the wearer."[60]

Such controversy did not prevent blocking and tackling with the head from becoming the norm. As noted earlier, Jim Owens brought helmet-first hitting from Texas A&M to the University of Washington in 1957, as an "innovation" on the West Coast that he also introduced to the Big Ten, when Minnesota players in 1960 were surprised by the ridges of scabs on UW players' foreheads. Owens's chief assistant, Tom Tipps, recalled for the historian of those Husky teams, "Opposing coaches made a big deal about our use of the helmet and that our players were punishing their players. I suspect we were."[61] A possible timeline for adopting the helmet as a primary weapon would seem to start with Bryant in the Southwest in the mid-1950s (after helmet construction improved sufficiently), then was exported to the West Coast by Jim Owens and brought to the Southeast by Bryant in the late 1950s, coming last to the Midwest in the 1960s. Bryant's coaching manual from 1960 also spread the gospel of punishing opponents with the helmet everywhere it was read or its ideas were embraced, regardless of geography. However it came about, by the end of the 1960s, leading with the helmet had become the standard blocking and tackling technique throughout college (and professional) football and had trickled down to high schools, too. The seeds of today's concussion crisis were planted here.

And where was the NCAA and its rules committees while all of this was happening? The "forearm shiver" that Bryant taught had been illegal in some form or other virtually since football's beginnings—essentially a variation on the "slugging" that plagued the early game. As noted in chapter 3, among the rules adopted in 1932, following Cadet Sheridan's death, was a ban on any use of the hands by the defense to strike an opponent's head, neck, or face. Over time, penalties ranged from fifteen yards to half the distance to the goal line to disqualification (or some combination of these). In 1960, when Bryant described it as a basic technique for his defensive linemen, the ban was covered by Rule 9 (Conduct of Players), Section 1 (Suspension Fouls), Article 2: "No player shall meet an opponent with the knee, strike any part of an opponent's person with locked hands, forearm, elbow or upper arm, or strike an opponent's head, neck or face with the heel, back or side of his hand during the game or between the periods." That would seem to be pretty comprehensive. The penalty was fifteen yards and mandatory suspension.[62] In January 1962, Allan Ryan, representing the American Medical Association's committee on sports at a meeting of football organizations in St. Louis, could have been reviewing Bryant's book when he described an increase in injuries due to techniques "being introduced by certain coaches who like to see the play a little more rugged." As reported by the Associated Press, Ryan singled out "spearing," "gang tackling," and the growing use of the elbow as "a formidable offensive weapon" as the game's current major problems.[63]

Spearing meant leading with the helmet in tackling. Ryan did not mention *butting*, an alternative term that came to mean leading with the helmet in blocking. The rules committee first addressed "butting" in 1964, when it added a new contact foul to Rule 9: "No player shall deliberately and maliciously use his helmet or head to butt or ram an opponent's head, neck or face."[64] This would have continued to allow striking a defensive player's torso (hitting him "in the numbers") with the helmet, but for 1965 the rule was broadened to include any part of the opponent's body, though still only if done *deliberately and maliciously*.[65] "Spearing" did not appear in an NCAA rules publication until 1970, when its distinction from "butting" was explained: "'Spearing' is not to be confused with 'Butt Blocking.' 'Spearing' is the deliberate and malicious use of the head and helmet in an attempt to punish a ball carrier after his momentum has stopped. 'Spearing' is a vicious act committed by a defensive player. 'Butt Blocking,' (Stick Blocking, Head Blocking), is an offensive technique involving initial and sustained contact with the head as the primary blocking surface either in close line play or in the open field."[66] *Spearing* was a foul; *butt blocking* was a permissible technique. Moreover, the words "deliberately and maliciously" in the 1964 rule that banned butting or ramming penalized *intentions*, rather than the actions themselves, and thus all but guaranteed that officials would call few fouls. By the committee's more detailed definition of spearing in 1970, ball carriers still moving were open targets—until 1976, when the words "after his momentum has stopped" were dropped from the official definition. (The National Federation of High School Associations also finally banned spearing in 1976.)[67] The NCAA's definition also narrowed spearing to "intentionally strik[ing] a runner with the crown or the top of the helmet."[68] The act no longer needed to be judged *malicious*, but it still had to be *intentional*, and hitting with the *front* of the helmet, rather than the top, was still permitted. However numbing these details, the verbal technicalities are important for illustrating how successive NCAA Rules Committees danced around the brutal transformation of football in the 1950s and 1960s, seemingly with some uneasiness but also insufficient desire or will to fully address it.

The delay in taking serious action against using the helmet as a weapon would seem to reflect the power of coaches to preserve their preferred techniques rather than, say, medical uncertainty about its potential risks for players. When Dr. Ryan in 1962 decried the use of the helmet and forearm as dangerous weapons, he had asserted that the solution had to come from "sportsmanship," not rules alone.[69] For the NCAA, *sportsmanship* had been enshrined in its nonbinding Football Code, which since 1916 had preceded the enumerated rules in the NCAA's annual publication. In 1938, a paragraph on "Coaching Ethics" was added to the code, and in 1953 a new statement was tacked on to the end: "The football helmet is for the protection of the player and is not to be used as a weapon."[70] This was only a principle of "coaching ethics," however, not an enforceable rule.

In 1969, following Ohio State's national championship the previous season, Woody Hayes self-published his second coaching manual, *Hot Line to Victory*. In the earlier one, *Football at Ohio State* in 1957 (also self-published), he had described the same blocking and tackling techniques as Wilkinson, Dodd, and the rest of the Prentice-Hall coaches/authors.[71] (Hayes sold these books at coaching clinics, by mail order, and on the OSU campus, rather than through a publisher.) When he brought out *Hot Line to Victory*, he sent a copy to Bear Bryant with the inscription, "To Bear Bryant, The Greatest College Coach in America."[72]

The book appeared amid the ongoing controversies over spearing and butting. In chapter 2, among straightforward descriptions of eight "Basic Running Plays" in the Ohio State offense, Hayes inserted a section titled "An Explanation of the Spear Block," which he described as a technique "as essential to our offense as gasoline is to an automobile." He then immediately added, "Perhaps the word 'spear' is a misnomer, for the blocker is NOT, repeat NOT, trying to butt the defender with his head. On the contrary, 'spear' means to us to step DIRECTLY at the defender, and to aim at the defender's middle with the blocker's axis of his body so that he will have weight on both feet as he drives through the defender. In doing this the blocker can take the defender whichever way the defender moves." His rationale was technically sound: By aiming the head at a defender charging to one side or the other, "our so called spear block ends up in a shoulder block; but if the blocker had aimed with a shoulder block, he would have completely missed the defender." Hayes further explained that "the blocker's head must always be Up, Up, Up, as far as it will go, for about ninety percent of the impact is taken on the chest."[73] There was nothing *malicious* about Ohio State's "spear block," as Hayes defined it, and contact with the front of the helmet, not the top, technically met the NCAA requirement. But no less than the technique that Bear Bryant taught, it used the helmet as the primary weapon in blocking.

The head was also involved in Hayes's techniques for defensive linemen in warding off blockers. A middle guard lined up over the center should "deliver a blow, destroy the block of the center by *meeting his head gear with yours*" (my emphasis). For a defensive tackle lined up on the offensive tackle and slanting toward the guard: "Drive your forearm across tackle's head."[74] Remarkably, Hayes had nothing at all to say about tackling techniques—perhaps too controversial by this time.

In 1976, the American Football Coaches Association attached its own statement to the paragraph on "Coaching Ethics" in the Football Code. Two of its three points addressed using the helmet as a weapon: First, "the helmet shall not be used as primary point of contact in the teaching of blocking and tackling," and second, "greater emphasis by players, coaches and officials should be placed on eliminating spearing." (The third one, unrelated, banned the use of self-propelled blocking and tackling machines.)[75] The first point rejected the techniques that coaches like Bear Bryant and Woody Hayes had long been teaching and that had been adopted throughout the football world. The second point basically conceded that the official ban on "spearing" for the past five years had been ignored. NCAA rules had about as much effect on the use of the helmet as a weapon as they had had on offside play in the 1880s and sideline coaching for many decades afterward.

The development of a durable hard-shell plastic helmet with face mask made leading with the helmet in both blocking and tackling possible, perhaps inevitable. Using it as a weapon, to punish opponents, also became possible, but *not* inevitable. That required coaches with a certain mindset and the complicity, whether enthusiastic or reluctant, of rules committees and sports organizations. The hard-shell plastic helmet made football immediately more violent. Turning it into a weapon made it potentially devastating in ways no one could imagine at the time.

FOR WHOM THE BELLS TOLL

The disconnect of the rules from their professed spirit in the Football Code, and from the techniques actually taught by coaches, can seem particularly perverse in light of recent revelations about the possible long-term consequences from even routine head blows. If viewed in the context of the medical understanding of non-catastrophic head injuries at the time, it makes at least a bit more sense. From 1933 to 1962, Dr. Augustus Thorndike had repeatedly called for awareness of the seriousness of concussions, while at the same time advising that returning to play was safe once symptoms disappeared. Over the 1960s, Dr. Richard Schneider led the crusade for safer helmets and safer football, through presentations at conferences, medical meetings, and American Football Coaches Association conventions.[76] His campaign culminated in 1973 in a book, *Head and Neck Injuries in Football*, whose subtitle, *Mechanisms,*

Treatment, and Prevention, conveyed the range of topics and issues that it addressed. Among the "mechanisms of injury" to heads and spinal cords, Schneider singled out "spearing" and "stick blocking," which he declared "*the single most devastating technique to arise as a result of the protection afforded by the plastic helmet and its face guard*" (the italics are his). Schneider's primary concern was for the rare catastrophic head or spinal injury. Regarding more routine concussions, he followed Mal Stevens and Augustus Thorndike in classifying three degrees by their symptoms (unsteadiness, mental confusion, memory loss, tinnitus, dizziness, loss of consciousness) and by recovery times: first degree, for no loss of consciousness and "mild" symptoms; second degree, for loss of consciousness no longer than three to four minutes and "moderate" symptoms; and third degree, for loss of consciousness longer than five minutes and "severe" or prolonged symptoms. He also concurred with his predecessors that most concussions were not very serious, and in all cases the absence of symptoms indicated full recovery.[77]

With the wide adoption of the hard-shell plastic helmet and its use as the contact point in both blocking and tackling, "getting your bell rung" became a routine part of the game. That expression (describing what Schneider would have classified as a first-degree concussion) seems to have entered the football glossary around 1959, when Darrell Royal told reporters after the Texas–Oklahoma game that his quarterback, Bobby Lackey, had come out of the game in the opening quarter because he "got his bell rung" on the Longhorns' first possession. Lackey remained on the bench until late in the half, when he returned to the field in time to engineer a crucial scoring drive before time expired. The writers covering the game celebrated Lackey as a gutsy hero (the term was long gone, but he showed "grit"). And they reported with seeming amusement that he remembered nothing afterward.[78]

The phrase "getting your bell rung," not what it described, seems to have been a novelty to the sportswriters covering the game. The sports editor of the *Austin American* devoted an entire column to Lackey's injury, complemented by a cartoon of a helmeted head under a bell chiming, "Bong!" The account of Lackey's temporary mental confusion in the *Fort Worth Star-Telegram* was headlined "Lackey Flunked 1-2-3 Test When 'Bell Rung'" and was accompanied by two photos of Lackey in the first half, sitting dazed on the bench with the team trainer.[79] Whether Royal coined the phrase or just introduced it to a wider public, it began popping up sporadically on sports pages in the 1960s and became ubiquitous in the 1970s (more or less in tandem with "reckless abandon"). It often resulted from a forearm shiver to the head, a key weapon in players' new basic arsenal, whose purpose was to ring the other guy's bell: to stun him momentarily or, perhaps, with a more severe blow, force him to the sidelines. In either case, getting your bell rung was assumed to be temporary and ultimately inconsequential.[80] And with each rung bell, mild head trauma became a little more normalized and sanitized.

Serious head and neck injuries *were* taken seriously. Fatal head injuries, in fact, peaked in the 1960s (driving the research of Richard Schneider and others), specifically in 1968, when thirty-two players (at all levels) died. From the 1940s through the 1960s, as plastic helmets gradually replaced leather ones, the percentage of football fatalities from head and neck injuries actually *increased* in relative terms: from 62 percent of all fatalities in the 1940s (46 percent head, 16 percent neck), to 80 percent in the 1950s (64 and 16), to 90 percent in the 1960s (72 and 18).[81] Players nonetheless undoubtedly *felt* safer as helmets improved, even as coaches were increasingly teaching them to block and tackle with those helmets. Rather than try to fix the rules, football leaders turned their focus to the safety of helmets for a solution. In April 1970, representatives of college, junior college, and high school sports federations met with representatives of the five major helmet manufacturers to create the National Operating Committee on Standards for Athletic Equipment, for the purpose of establishing helmet safety standards. The committee's initial standard in 1973 became mandatory for NCAA members in 1978 and for high schools in 1980.[82]

Whatever the major shortcomings of the research and testing, the NOCSAE standards instantly made helmets *seem* safer. And fatalities did dramatically decline after the 1960s: from 175 "direct" fatalities due to head injuries in the 1960s to 89 in the '70s, 51 in the '80s, 37 in the '90s, and 32 in the '00s. Less noticed, catastrophic brain *injuries*—permanent damage resulting from a single traumatic blow—increased as fatalities declined: from twenty-nine for the years from 1984 (when tabulations began) through 1990, to fifty-three for 1991–2000, to seventy-one for 2001–10.[83] These were the numbers compiled by Floyd Eastwood's successors at the University of North Carolina. The National Football Head and Neck Injury Registry, established in 1971, issued a report in 1979 on 176 cases of permanent quadriplegia from 1971 through 1978 and attributed them to "the development of a protective helmet–face mask system that has effectively protected the head, and by so doing has allowed it to be used as a battering ram in tackling and blocking techniques, thus placing the cervical spine at risk."[84] (The registry got the effect on spinal cords right, but not the "effectively protected" head.) The hard-shell plastic helmet made football seem safer to the public and *feel* safer to the players, but it put players at greater risk than ever before, as no one yet had a clue just how much it endangered the brain.

END OF AN ERA

College football's era of extreme brutal coaching effectively ended around 1969 (at least temporarily) in a series of player rebellions in major football programs around the country. The rebelling players were overwhelmingly African American, and their issues were racial—discriminatory treatment by white coaches and trainers, "stacking" (restriction to certain positions), lack of Black assistant coaches—but their complaints more broadly challenged the absolute authority of the Man in charge. Uprisings by players against their coaches had broken out at the University of Nebraska after the 1953 season (over Bryant-like brutal treatment by the coach, Bill Glassford)[85] and at the University of Washington two years later (over unrelated issues),[86] but these were isolated incidents. The rebellions in 1969 seemed like a mass movement.

They began at Maryland and Oregon State on the same day, February 25, with the latter a harbinger of the ones that would soon follow. A coach's suspension of a Black player at Oregon State, for growing an offseason mustache contrary to team rules, sparked a walkout by the overwhelming majority of Black players on the team. In April, after sixteen Black players at Iowa boycotted the first day of spring practice and issued a set of demands, they were suspended by their coach. In response to these and several lesser disruptions, John Underwood wrote a three-part series for *Sports Illustrated* in August–September on "The Desperate Coach," in which he cast the beleaguered coach as a victim of self-indulgent players and craven administrators.[87] Within weeks, walkouts by Black players at Wyoming, then at Washington, and then at Indiana rocked the college football world with a new series of tremors. (A final major aftershock hit Syracuse and Ben Schwartzwalder in September 1970.)[88]

The rebellion at Maryland, the only one by white players, was also the only one directed specifically at the coaching tactics of the hard-nosed school. Bob Ward was considered Maryland's greatest all-time player, an undersized lineman known for his toughness when he played from 1948 to 1951 under Jim Tatum. Returning to Maryland as head coach in 1967, Ward coached like Tatum and Bear Bryant, but like Charlie Bradshaw he won too few games, just two in two seasons. After Ward slapped a player at an offseason workout on February 25, nearly the entire team signed a petition charging him with physical and mental abuse (as well as incompetence) and called for his dismissal.

Back in 1953 and 1955, the local press had supported the coaches at Nebraska and Washington, as it had supported Bryant in 1946, 1954, and 1958 and Bradshaw in 1962, when they took over programs and instituted brutal methods. But this was 1969, a different world on and off the football field, and Baltimore sportswriters (as well as university administrators) took the players' charges seriously. At one public hearing, as the *Baltimore Evening Sun* reported, player after player "told of being 'struck,' and 'cussed out,' and threatened with the loss of their scholarships." One player stated, "I've never hated anyone in my whole life the way I hate that man."[89] After such a public thrashing, Ward had no choice but to "resign" on March 5. The next day, an editorial in the *Evening Sun* described "The Bob Ward Story" as a melodrama with "a happy beginning and a dismal ending," whose final meaning, perhaps, was "simply the truism that when a team loses and loses, heads roll." But among other possible explanations, the writer suggested that "tough-guyness and verbal and physical brutality may not be the psychology best suited for dealing with the squad at a major eastern university in the late 1960s."[90]

That fall, Melvin Durslag of the *Los Angeles Examiner* drew a similar lesson after watching the University of Washington, without its protesting Black players, lose to a UCLA team at full strength. Durslag observed that a new "age of sophistication" and rising expectations called for a "sharp readjustment" by the coach, who must "relinquish . . . the iron-handed discipline he used to wield."[91] (Interestingly, there was no talk of "taking it" or "paying the price" as a cherished value under assault, even from John Underwood, whose chief concern in "The Desperate Coach" was with the defiance of coaches' *authority*.) The football rebellions of 1969–70, of course, were part of the broader political and countercultural rejection of entrenched authority in the late '60s and of the broader athletic revolution, indelibly captured by the clenched fists of Tommie Smith and John Carlos at the 1968 Mexico City Olympics.[92] But from a different perspective, the players willing to defy their coaches were also part of a postwar generation with expanded economic opportunities and expectations. The players that Bear Bryant inherited on his arrival at Kentucky, Texas A&M, and Alabama may have had nowhere else to go. College players born after 1945, who grew up amid 1950s and '60s prosperity, may have been increasingly less inclined to pay the price, because they had options.

If they were white, that is. Early in his 1974 autobiography, Bryant made a striking claim that, on his current Alabama teams, "The ones who will consistently suck up their guts and stick by you are the blacks, because they don't have anything to go back to." (Alabama had had an integrated varsity team only since 1971, four years after Kentucky integrated the SEC.)[93] Bryant recalled Michigan coach Bo Schembechler telling him, "A black won't ever quit you, and I got to thinking the way it had been for me, and he was right. Because I didn't have any place to go, either."[94]

Bryant's comment may have been intended as a mea culpa for the all-white teams that had brought him scorn outside the South in the 1960s (and cost him a national championship in 1966). Intended or not, it also refuted the racist stereotype noted in chapter 2 that Black players were *not* tough. But Bryant's statement also provokes one to consider how integration might have contributed to the end of the era of brutal coaching. A coach smacking or screaming at white players was like a stern father with a wayward son or a rock-jawed drill sergeant with a bumbling recruit. A white coach doing that to Black players enacted the much more disturbing symbolic drama of master and slaves. The Southwest Conference and Southeastern Conference, where Bryant-style football first took hold, did not begin integrating until the late 1960s.

Brutal "hands-on" coaching was not quite dead by 1970, but it was mortally wounded. Ohio State's firing of Woody Hayes, after he punched a Clemson player at the end of the nationally televised Gator Bowl in December 1978, was either the last dying throe or a twitch of the corpse. (For those who missed the game on television, *Life* published a remarkable double-page close-up photo in February of Hayes's less-famous second blow to the jaw of one of his own players, who had tried to intervene.)[95] The *final* twitch came the following October, when Arizona State fired Frank Kush after a former player filed a $1.1 million lawsuit for slugging him after a bad game the previous season.[96]

Unlike Woody Hayes, Bear Bryant had mellowed by the 1970s, on his way to becoming college football's Grand Old Man. In 1966, Bryant had used his serialized memoir in *Sports Illustrated* as an opportunity to repair his battered public image (while settling scores with some SEC coaching rivals). In the third installment, "Hit 'em Harder: The Only Game That Can Win," Bryant described arriving at Alabama in 1958 with an undeserved reputation for brutality, which then really blew up on him in the Holt–Graning incident three years later. Bryant insisted that he had *never* been as brutal toward his players as some people seemed to think, but when he *had* been, it was for the players' own good. He attributed those excesses to the misjudgments of an ambitious young coach, and he claimed to regret them now. He also assured readers he was no longer that same brutal "driver," while at the same time declaring that the "helmet-cracking" style of his Alabama teams was still the only way to win. These competing claims captured the contradictions not just in Bear Bryant but in the era's entire cult of extreme toughness.

Early in part 3 of his *Sports Illustrated* memoir, Bryant contemptuously dismissed a story that some "silly people" still believed: that he had had a "pit" at Texas A&M and "used to put two boys in at a time, and the one who crawled out was a starter." (A boy could hear that story growing up even in far-off Spokane, Washington.) "The truth is that if you really taught brutality and treated people as badly as people say I did you'd never be able to get a good football player on your team." Bryant admitted that in the past he had kicked players, but only to test them: "And if a boy lets me kick him and slam him around and he doesn't kick back I've said I didn't want him." In any case, it was good for the boy: "If hard-nosed football, 'brutal' football, is getting a boy to discipline himself, to get him in such keen physical condition that he will make fewer mistakes than the guy who isn't, that's what I'm for. If it took a pit to do that, I'd have a pit."[97] What Bryant now regretted was not clear.

In the appropriately titled final installment, "Mellow—and Still Fighting," Bryant noted that he did not even use the "circle drill" and "challenge system" much anymore and then went on to describe both of them as pretty harmless anyway. The circle drill ("bull in the ring," that is) forced the player in the circle "to be alert and quick or he'll get run over." The challenge drill, pitting a backup against the starter, while the coaches and other players "yell and everybody gets a big kick out of it," was good for "morale." He abandoned it only because it took up too much practice time.[98]

For all of the self-contradictions in his memoir, Bryant's mellowing toward his players was apparently real. In 1972, according to one of his biographers, when he hired a former player as a new assistant coach, Bryant told him, "You can't coach these boys today like I coached you." Another of his assistants around this time recalled his boss telling them, "Don't put your hands on them any more, because if you do, I'm going to be on the players' side."[99] By 1974, in his book-length revised autobiography, Bryant had even disavowed his once-fierce belief that "every boy who quits football is a quitter." He had come to realize that "for some it's just a matter of finding other interests, just like switching courses."[100] Well, maybe.

As a "new breed" of players arrived at college and coaches adapted or fell by the wayside, sportswriters also changed. A new generation emerged in the 1970s in cities beyond New York (last and least in small college towns) who aspired to be more than boosters for the home team and its coach. The writer for the *Baltimore Evening Sun* was sympathetic to the players in their rebellion against Bob Ward in 1969. Another revolt of football players a few weeks later, against a brutal pre-spring conditioning program at Florida State, was ignored in the local press at the time and went nowhere. Four years later, a similar revolt of twenty-eight players at FSU warranted a three-day, multi-article series in the *St. Petersburg Times*[101] (followed by multiple irate defenses of coach Larry Jones and his program by the sports editor of the *Tallahassee Democrat*, still a hometown loyalist).[102] Sports journalism underwent no uniform transformation over the 1970s and 1980s, but a canvas fence around a practice field became less likely to keep local reporters from trying to find out what was going on behind it.

But if the brutal extremes of the Bryant school became mostly a relic of the past by the 1970s,[103] its techniques for blocking and tackling with the helmet as a primary weapon were now firmly entrenched in the game. In 1978, *Sports Illustrated* published another three-part jeremiad on the ills of college football by John Underwood, this one titled "Brutality: The Crisis in Football." Responding to what he called an epidemic of injuries the previous season—1 million players at 20,000 high schools and 70,000 college players at 900 schools, along with a 100 percent injury rate in the NFL—Underwood in part 1 raised football's age-old question: In a game in which physical risk was inescapable, how much was acceptable? "Apparently a lot," he concluded. The most serious injuries, as Underwood reported, including 80 percent of fatalities, were due to the "modern hard-shell football helmet," described by the team doctor at Oklahoma State as "the damndest, meanest tool on the face of the earth." Underwood summed up what had happened when coaches discovered that it could be "an effective weapon": "Techniques known as butt-blocking and butt-tackling became prevalent. Players rammed headfirst into pileups, into defenders, into hapless quarterbacks and into immobile running backs to put the finishing touch on tackles. The helmet became the game's principal instrument of intimidation, and terms like 'spearing,' 'spiking' and 'sticking' became part of the argot."[104]

Underwood charged that the 1976 rule that banned striking "a runner with the crown or the top of the helmet" was "only sporadically enforced. And face-to-numbers blocking and tackling (the front of the helmet or the face guard making initial contact) is still legal, and it is estimated that eight out of 10 coaches teach it." (Regarding "spearing" and "stick blocking," Dr. Richard Schneider in his 1973 book had mentioned coaches who contended that it was "impossible to play football without applying those techniques.")[105] The defender of "The Desperate Coach" back in 1969 and Bear Bryant's collaborator on his autobiographies in 1966 and 1974 had concluded that *coaches* were the chief obstacle to making football safe enough to play.

By 1978, "crises" had long been part of the rhythm of football seasons, and this one came and went without generating enough outrage to drive major change. In 1981, as the sport historian Ronald Smith has pointed out, the first new *Sports Medicine Handbook*, published by the NCAA since 1933, "failed to address the concussion issue at all." (The organization would not include concussion guidelines in its *Handbook* until 1994).[106] The potential *long-term* damage from football was assumed to be to joints (knees in particular), and that risk was still regarded as an acceptable price to pay for the benefits of playing football. Over time, "crack-back blocks" and "chop blocks" would join "spearing" and "butting" on the list of proscribed techniques, but players would continue to block and tackle with their heads, getting their bells rung and resuming play as soon as the ringing stopped. Technical improvements to helmets would make them more comfortable and feel even safer, so that it would become increasingly possible for the most aggressive players to feel invulnerable as they flew around with "reckless abandon" and launched themselves like missiles at their opponents.

In his case against brutality, Underwood offered seven suggestions for making football safer, three of which involved limiting the use of the helmet in blocking and tackling: "Make all deliberate initial-contact helmet hits, by any part of the helmet, illegal"; "make all deliberate hits above the shoulders illegal"; "make any flagrant foul involving the head punishable by immediate ejection of the offending player."[107] These would be in football's future, but it would take three more decades and a finally unignorable crisis to get there. No one yet had a clue to the secret that would be found in Mike Webster's brain.

Figure 7.1. Cover of *Life*, October 14, 1966. Licensed from Curtis Licensing.

CHAPTER 7

FOOTBALL VIOLENCE AS SPECTACLE

In October 1955, *Life* published a photo-essay on professional football titled "Savagery on Sunday." As always with *Life*, the story was in the photographs: of Philadelphia Eagles linebacker Wayne Robinson, with arm cocked and fist clenched, putting "something extra into it as he pounces on the Cleveland ball carrier"; of the Eagles' Frank Kilroy landing knee-first on a fallen New York Giants quarterback; of a pair of Cleveland defensive ends pummeling an Eagles passer; of a helmetless LA Rams guard clutching his face after being slugged by a Baltimore Colt.[1] *Life* made its case so effectively that Robinson and Kilroy sued for defamation.[2]

Four years later, the journalist Thomas Morgan in an essay in *Esquire* accounted for the sudden popularity of pro football by its providing "an escape from or a substitute for the boredom of work, the dullness of reality." For the crowd watching the game, living "its daily life in a tightly-civilized, humdrum community . . . pro football is, in contrast, a kind of sanctioned savagery."[3]

Pro football was still "savagery" in 1959, but "*sanctioned* savagery" now, which satisfied a deep public need for escape from an unfulfilling existence. Into the 1950s, professional football had been no more respectable than prizefighting, in part for sharing a primary purpose of inflicting pain on the opponent, while college football had long valued its violence for building character through "grit" and self-restraint. The NCAA's initial "Foot Ball Code," printed as a preamble to the *Official Rules* in 1916, indirectly touched on the fundamental obstacle facing any form of *professional* football from the outset: "Both in play and by tradition foot ball is a distinctively academic game—the game of the schools and the colleges. The friends of the game must accordingly rely on the schools and colleges for the preservation of its past traditions and the maintenance of the high standards of sportsmanship in its play, which are to be expected in a distinctively academic game."[4]

Irrespective of colleges' failures to maintain their own "high standards of sportsmanship," football's origins as "the game of the schools and the colleges" shaped the public's response to the violence of professional football from the beginning. Football's elemental roughness, within the rules, built character in schoolboys fighting for Alma Mater but was merely brutal and mercenary for grown men playing for pay. The first actual professionals (as opposed to subsidized players on the school teams) were former collegians playing for metropolitan athletic clubs in the 1890s. The first fully professional teams were formed among factory workers in small towns in Ohio in the early 1900s, basically for the purpose of betting by local "sports." Current college stars competing under assumed names were highly valued by professional teams and the "sports" who laid wagers on them—and a blight on the college game if they were found out. In the most scandalous early episode, the exposure of ringers from Notre Dame and the University of Illinois in a high-stakes game between rival Illinois towns in 1921 prompted the Big Ten to ban anyone associated with professional football from ever coaching, refereeing, or having any other role in college football. In a football world dominated by the professed values of the (elitist) amateur collegiate game, professional football represented degradation, corruption, and the temptation of virtuous collegians.[5]

The organization that became the National Football League was founded in 1919 with clubs representing cities like Akron, Canton, Racine, and Rochester, as well as Chicago, Cleveland, and Detroit. Teams came and went through the 1920s and early 1930s, depending on precarious finances, as pro football was mostly ignored by the rest of the country. Red Grange's turning pro in 1925, immediately after his last college game, thus shocked the collegiate world and briefly brought unprecedented attention to the pro game. More significantly, it opened the door for other college stars to play pro football after leaving school (if they had no prospects for better-paying and more permanent employment). Reorganization of the NFL in 1933 into what quickly became a big-city league (except for Green Bay) set the stage for the pros to begin attracting working-class fans in cities like Chicago and New York that had no major public university with a football team. But daily newspapers outside NFL cities continued to cover pro football with nothing more than brief wire-service summaries of Sunday's games on Monday.[6]

After World War II, the NFL's four-year rivalry with the All-America Football Conference (1946–49) exposed fans in more cities to professional football, but to reach deeply into the middle class and beyond the relatively few cities with franchises, pro football needed television, which arrived in the 1950s at the same time that the new cult of toughness was transforming the college game. Professional football players entered the 1950s with a negative dual image as mercenary brutes and grown men playing what was fundamentally a boys' game, postponing the personal and financial responsibilities of adulthood.[7] By the end of the decade they were larger-than-life sports heroes. Their "savagery" had become "sanctioned."

DIRTY FOOTBALL

As pro football was gaining fans in Chicago and New York, popular magazines with their national readerships continued well into the 1950s to portray the pros as either thugs or overgrown rowdy boys, sometimes both, as in the profile of Chicago Bears defensive end Ed Sprinkle as "The Meanest Man in Football" in *Collier's* in 1950. Sports editor Bill Fay breezily described Sprinkle as a connoisseur of illegal tactics ("tripping," "chucking," "spinning") that were "virtually undetectable" by officials (and unthinkable to celebrate as the behavior of a college player). Fay made it all sound like roughhouse fun, despite the ugly brawl that Sprinkle provoked with LA Rams players and the "mayhem" he inflicted on the New York Giants in the 1946 playoffs, which produced a separated shoulder, a "brain concussion," and two broken noses. One of the accompanying photos showed Sprinkle "testing Cardinal back Charley Trippi's Adam's apple" with his elbow on a sideline tackle. Sprinkle might have been "the most feared and universally disliked player in pro football," but Fay's jokey writing made his actions no big deal—pro football, after all, was not to be taken seriously.[8]

Sprinkle's rival, or successor, as "dirtiest player in the league," according to *Time* in 1954, was the LA Rams' "rib-cracking linebacker" Don Paul (one of the players caught by *Life*'s photographer in "Savagery on Sunday" the following year). "Pro Football being what it is," Paul accepted that reputation "for what it is meant to be—sheer flattery." Those comments were just a sidebar in a profile of the reigning two-time champion Detroit Lions and their good-ol'-boy quarterback, Bobby Layne. In its first-ever cover story about professional football, *Time* described the pro game as "better and more complex" than the college game, but also "rougher. 'We play rough and we teach rough' says Lions coach Buddy Parker. 'And when I say rough I don't mean poking a guy in the eye. I mean gang tackling—right close to piling on.'" (College coaches did not have to invent gang-tackling in the 1950s.) *Time*'s writer added, "If mugging goes on, it obviously goes best at the bottom of a pile up. Ball carriers who join the pros fresh from the unskilled slugfests of collegiate football learn fast how to fall with knees doubled and cleats in the air—a practice nicely calculated to scare off any unnecessary tackler. A runner who doesn't throw his arm in front of his face the moment he is brought down is either foolhardy or unconscious."[9]

As pointed out in the previous chapter, magazine stories about rough play in college football in the 1950s either justified the player's "aggressiveness" or condemned his "muckerism." Stories about dirty pro players made no distinction, because no principles were at stake. According to *Time*, "the scars of battle are inevitable" in professional football, but the pros would not have it any other way. "No matter how rough or tricky the game, pro players never seem to lose the happy-go-lucky attitude of men who like the way they earn their living." Like Bill Fay's, the breezy style made pro football violence seem no more consequential than Wile E. Coyote's getting crushed by another boulder, as the Road Runner speeds away—unthinkable for a story about brutality in college football, where players were expected to be "aggressive" but also play by the rules and where damage to players could not be dismissed as a joke.

Professional football at midcentury did not yet stand alongside baseball and college football as a truly national sport. And while women had an important place in the college football world (to cheer and to admire the football hero, of course, not to be that hero), pro football still belonged to a masculine subculture, not unlike bare-knuckle prizefighting in the nineteenth century.[10] In the NFL's early years, pro teams had been widely assumed to play inferior football to the kind played by top college teams, held back by their lack of a serious commitment and their purely mercenary motives. In the 1940s, victories over the collegians in the annual College All-Star Game began changing that assumption, and by the 1950s, as the pros continued playing two-platoon football, while the colleges switched back to one, the pros' more-rested specialists played "better, more exciting football" than ever, according to a writer in *Sports Illustrated* in 1955. "Yet hanging like a pall over the otherwise brilliant play are two nasty words: 'dirty football.'"[11]

Accusations of dirty play in the 1950s came from *within* the NFL, too (not everyone accepted it as jolly fun), most damningly from one of its greatest stars, the Cleveland Browns' all-pro quarterback Otto Graham. First in *Sports Illustrated*, six weeks before that *Time* cover story on Bobby Layne in 1954, then in remarks made to the Quarterback Club in Atlanta the following year that were picked up by the wire services, and finally in the *Saturday Evening Post* in 1956, while confirming his retirement at the end of that season, Graham voiced concerns that were hard to dismiss. Graham's *Sports Illustrated* piece was titled "Football Is Getting Too Vicious," and it identified the chief problem as an overemphasis on winning, which put a premium on getting the opponent's best players out of the game. (The fact that this was a practice in college football, too, makes that particular charge against pro football rather ironic.) Graham confirmed the point made by *Time* in its cover story on Layne when he wrote that, because of the "growing use of fists, arms and elbows, mostly aimed at the face," a tackled runner covering his face with his free arm as he went down had "become almost a classic gesture in pro football in recent years."[12] For Graham, it was no joke. Two years later in the *Post*, he tried to depart the NFL gracefully by insisting that the league "as a whole is a clean one" but had "some dirty players, just as there are in college and high-school football." He did, however, object to Commissioner Bert Bell's "position that no player in the league is ever deliberately dirty. I know this is not true because I have seen it happen."[13]

SANCTIONING SAVAGERY

Life's "Savagery on Sunday" appeared in that context in 1955. Four years later, with the New York Giants headed for a second straight championship game against the Baltimore Colts, *Life* published a very different photo-essay on NFL "savagery." Titled "Greetings to Our Victims in Play-off," and subtitled "Rough Trio Leads Giants' Savage, Successful Defense," it celebrated the team's strong-side, weak-side, and middle linebackers, known in football jargon as "Sara," "Wanda," and "Meg." The incongruous feminine nicknames suited *Life*'s penchant for jokiness, but they also accentuated, by contrast, the ruggedness of the Giants' three linebackers, who were obviously football-made *men*. The subject itself was most significant: *defensive* players, rather than a quarterback or running back, celebrated as the heart of the team and the embodiment of the thrilling game they played. Sticking with two-platoon football had created opportunities not just for quarterbacks and running backs who were weak on defense but also for defensive specialists, who would not just be marking time until they got the ball back. But it was the *appeal* of defensive football that was truly new. Two weeks earlier, *Time* had published its second pro football cover story, this one titled "A Man's Game," with Sam Huff, the Giants middle linebacker ("Meg," that is), on the cover. Two weeks before that, the *Saturday Evening Post* had profiled the more typical star quarterback, except the quarterback was no glamour boy but potbellied, hard-partying Bobby Layne again, and the story was titled "This Is No Game for Kids."[14]

Either something had happened to the public's tolerance for pro football violence between 1955 and 1959, or the media had finally caught up with how the public actually felt about it. The indictment of pro football for an overemphasis on winning, for putting opponents' best players out of the game, and for overall brutality, even as college football was embracing those same values, would suggest that opposition to the pro game might not have been very strong by this time, or would not have lasted in any case. What most dramatically happened in pro football between 1955 and 1959 was the 1958 title game between the New York Giants and Baltimore Colts, decided in sudden-death overtime, with 30 million watching the NFL's first national telecast after several years on regional networks. *Sports Illustrated* titled its account "The Best Football Game Ever Played," and it has subsequently become widely taken to mark the birth of "the modern NFL."[15] Pro football needed television to reach a national audience, but what held that audience and kept it coming back had to be the game on the field—the *violent* game on the field. Those stories in *Life* and *Time* in the season following that game confirmed pro football's appeal without explaining it. For that explanation, nothing can surpass Thomas Morgan's essay in *Esquire*, "The Wham in Pro Football."

Morgan elaborated on an idea from a 1957 essay in the liberal intellectual quarterly *Dissent* by Dan Wakefield, who claimed that, contrary to intellectuals' typical scorn, "bigtime athletics" provided rituals through which men "graft an element of glory onto the deadly drudgery of everyday life." Wakefield found it ironic that the same intellectuals who dismissed spectator sports also "rant against the menace of conformity, the lack of individualism, the dulling results of 'canned' entertainment, the lifelessness of men who are more interested in retirement plans and Rotary meetings than in trying to lead a life of personal fulfillment at the risk of losing security and approval." Those pedantic scolds clearly could not see that professional football (like Major League Baseball, too) provided "one of the few ways of livelihood in our society that is filled with risk, devoid of security, and dependent solely on individual skill for success."[16]

Wakefield did not distinguish football from baseball in this regard. Morgan's essay was announced on *Esquire*'s cover as "Pro Football: The Cult of Violence." According to Morgan, what made pro football—not baseball, and not just any football but *pro* football—"the best game played in America today" was its *violence*. After a long discussion of the pros' superior talent to collegians' (a sign of the times that this still had to be argued, not assumed) and their rising social status ("pro football is still legalized brutality, but the players are not regarded as brutes any more"), Morgan turned to the motivations that drew people to *this* game rather than to another. Morgan acknowledged that fans came to the stadium for many reasons: to gamble, to relax, "to watch the panorama," "to show football as it should be played to their children," to feel "pride in the fact that their town fields a good team." But that would be true for baseball, too (or college football for that matter), so the question remained: Why "*pro football*—and why now?"[17]

Morgan's answer was in his essay's tagline: "With the decline of exuberance in daily life, Americans want their sports harder, faster, and meaner." *Meaner* is what Dan Wakefield had left out. "All crowds have sadistic streaks," Morgan wrote, "and pro games let them show this. The crowd gasps when two giants collide, but, as the *Ole*! of the bullfight, the sound is delicious. . . . For fans unfulfilled in their daily lives, to see an end smashed in mid-air by a pass defender—that's pleasure!" Morgan's comments on spectators' need to escape the dullness of their lives echoed not only Wakefield but also the era's leading sociologists—David Riesman, William Whyte, C. Wright Mills—who were diagnosing the crushing weight of conformity in 1950s America, the meaninglessness of work (whether "white collar" or "blue denim," in Wakefield's terms), the grinding "rat race" of trying to make a living, the uncertainties of men confronted by shifting gender roles. Morgan observed that women attended pro football games but were outnumbered 4 to 1—"tolerated . . . but neither encouraged nor welcomed"—a masculine subculture in transition. (The NFL in the 1970s would begin working mightily to expand that female audience.)

After more than a half century of mostly irrelevance, professional football had found its time. Pro football was still "savagery" on Sunday but "sanctioned" now, to satisfy a public need. The sanctioning, as always, would be confirmed and enhanced by the media, but it had to come ultimately from the fans, whose experience, according to Morgan, was "not only vicarious" but also participatory, "a mutual exaltation of some necessary virtues." Thrilling to pro football's "sanctioned savagery" was to *experience* that savagery, not just witness it (in the same way that appreciating art was to experience art). In what Morgan called the "strange (for America) equilibrium of the Eisenhower era . . . it is possible that the new popularity of the game is, in part, a response—a violent response to dullness."

Thomas Morgan alone articulated the case fully, but he spoke for an emerging consensus in the mass media. *Esquire* published "The Wham in Pro Football" just after *Time* and *Life* published their stories on the New York Giants' linebackers, players known for their violence, not for artistry or finesse. Over the next few years, virtually all of the major weekly magazines published photo-essays celebrating the violence of pro football that, just a few years earlier, had marked it as second-class. *Sports Illustrated,* in October 1960, offered a cover and seven pages of photos of "The Violent Face of Pro Football." The *Saturday Evening Post,* in November 1962, devoted six pages to "Sunday's Gladiators." *Look's* "Madness Is a Game on Sunday" (in nine pages of photos) in December 1963 and "War on Sunday" (in seven) in November 1968 increased the ante. *Life* topped them all with "Controlled Violence of the Pros," in October 1966, from a pull-out cover (see figure 7.1) to sixteen pages of photographs.[18] Two television specials, *The Violent World of Sam Huff* (narrated by Walter Cronkite) in 1960 and *Mayhem on a Sunday Afternoon* (directed by William Friedkin) in 1965, celebrated pro football on the same terms. In *The Violent World,* Huff told Cronkite, "We try to hurt everybody."[19] As *punishing* as Bear Bryant's brand of football at Alabama was in these years, it would have been unthinkable for Bryant or one of his players to say that in an interview.

All of these magazines put pro football's "sanctioned savagery" or "controlled violence" at the center of a game that from the beginning had been rooted in a fundamental tension between violence and artistry. Even the dull violence of mass play in the 1880s and 1890s was countered by ingenuity in the modes of attack. Opening up the game led to thrilling running backs, from Jim Thorpe to Red Grange to Tom Harmon to Jim Brown. Loosening the restrictions on the forward pass led to Benny Friedman, to Sammy Baugh and Sid Luckman, to Otto Graham and Johnny Unitas. As pro football ratcheted up the violence, the artistry kept pace. *Look* captured that tension in describing players as "agile mastodons" who "charge like sprinters and block like tanks," and who "transform an atavistic spectacle into sudden ballets by the running, feinting, weaving, leaping of plays that surpass belief."[20] *Life* described players "fight[ing] with a delicate violence, using skills as precise as they are brutal and blunt." Violence was transformed by artistry, rather than artistry enhanced by violence. Photos needed no text to be eloquent on the primacy of violence: no long passes snared by balletic receivers in these pictorials but the bare head and shoulders of a Steelers player lying on the turf next to his helmet after it has been ripped off (*Saturday Evening Post*); Giants and Browns players brawling in the mud (*Look*, 1963); the Kansas City Chiefs' six-foot-seven defensive tackle Buck Buchanan closing in on the New York Jets' Joe Namath with arms spread like a pterodactyl, or Angel of Death, filling two pages (*Look*, 1968). No surprise, *Life* had more than its share of the most powerful photos, from the 1966 fold-out cover of muddied Packers and Browns colliding in a scrimmage to the four Browns linemen in an interior image, covered in mud, standing as if grim sentinels awaiting a fearsome assault.

Pungent captions reinforced the stories told by the photos. "In the ruck of the line the huge men fight their most savage (and least noticed) wars. The rules are their own, and almost the only law the linemen know is survival" (*Sports Illustrated*). "Orthodox tactics [for pass-rushers] call for pinning the quarterback's arm, but Buck Buchanan of the Kansas City Chiefs prefers head-hunting. 'I like to club him around the head. You try to ring his bell'" (*Look*, 1968). Some captions were whimsical, like the comment on the Pittsburgh player looking lifeless on the ground—"Helmet ripped loose by a bruising play, Steelers' guard Mike Sandusky finds a moment of peace" (*Saturday Evening Post*)—or a Cleveland player's observation that "it gets less friendly as the game goes on" (*Life*). The jokes did not minimize the violence but reinforced the players' stoicism, which marked them as a superior breed of men.

As violence was central to pro football, so was the pain that inevitably followed—simply "part of the game," as *Sports Illustrated* noted. "There is no question but that pro football is the ultimate test of a man's strength and endurance and of his willingness to endure pain and risk serious injury," Harry T. Paxton wrote in the *Post*'s "Sunday's Gladiators." "The pros accept the fact that bruises, cuts, sprains and fractures are normal hazards of their trade," *Life* added. "The good ones give no thought to this." For them, the excitement of the game "serves as an anesthetic" that wears off afterward, with the pain lingering into Tuesday or Wednesday, or later in the week as successive seasons marched on. As the Giants' thirty-nine-year-old quarterback, Charlie Conerly, told *Life*, starting a Sunday still in pain from the previous week's game signaled it was time to retire.

Well beyond "taking it" for a higher purpose, at the heart of college (amateur) football since its beginnings, pain and injury were essential elements of pro football's heroic grandeur, glamorized for their own sake in the 1960s as never before. Thomas Morgan made this point most emphatically in a second essay for *Esquire*, "The American War Game," in October 1965. From its cover photograph of a lineman kneeling on the field, arms folded in prayer, below a caption, "Heaven help him—he's going to play 60 minutes of pro ball," to the double-page illustration of "The 15 Dirtiest Plays," to the single page of eight headshots of pro football's "Tough Guys" (four "Givers" and four "Receivers," with a tagline, "Some dish it out, some take it—but all know it is better to give than to receive"), and finally to the double-page illustration of a player in undershorts, standing next to the thirteen pieces of protective equipment that he will put on ("This Stuff Is to Keep Him from Getting Hurt . . . It Doesn't Always Work"), *Esquire* put pain and injury at the center of the experience of playing professional football.

Alongside these whimsical illustrations and captions, Morgan explored that idea in great detail and all seriousness. Morgan took the idea that pro football was a "war game" beyond the superficial jargon of blitzes and bombs, because it "not only sanctions physical violence but requires it on every play." "Even the fundamental strategy of pro football is a function of pain, violently inflicted," Morgan noted in a particularly pithy phrase: the administering of pain over the course of the game, to wear down the opponent for the advantage it might eventually yield. (This was Bear Bryant's strategy, too.) Offensive linemen pounded their opponents "with the knowledge that persistent torture may pay dividends at any time, most likely in the final period." Defensive players used pain as "a strategic weapon against backs, too. Tackled again and again, twisted, stomped, gouged and repeatedly buried under a half ton of flesh, even the best may be discouraged by the fourth quarter."

Morgan described the notorious case of the Steelers' bruising fullback John Henry Johnson, who "once hit the Cardinals' Charley Trippi with a blindside block that fractured Trippi's skull and broke his nose." On other occasions he broke a teammate's jaw in practice and an opponent's jaw in a game. When four of the man's teammates attacked him, he clubbed them with a steel sideline marker that he had pulled from the ground, until a referee finally stopped him. (Johnson would be among those later diagnosed with CTE.) All of this sounds like an indictment of pro football in the spirit of *Life* magazine's "Savagery on Sunday" in 1955. But time and context had radically changed. "The corollary of such violence," Morgan continued, "is the stoicism of the players as they suffer it. The Giants' aging quarterback, Charlie Conerly, who had been knocked out in his first two games as a pro, who suffered lost teeth, a cheek fracture, and countless spinal concussions, and who became known as the most beat-up man in football, once told me, 'It only hurts when you lose.' But this is poetry. Pro football hurts, win or lose."

Many of these and other acts that Morgan described were easily as egregious as Darwin Holt's forearm to Chick Graning's face in the Alabama–Georgia Tech game in 1961, which unleashed a firestorm of condemnation. If the boundary in college football in the 1950s and 1960s between "aggressive" and "dirty" play was sometimes blurred, in professional football it was virtually erased. "You get penalties when you get caught," one coach told *Time* in 1959, "and touchdowns when you don't."[21] Instead of dismay or moral outrage, the accounts by Thomas Morgan and other writers evoked a sense of wonder that the players could withstand such brutality and come back for more. According to Morgan, fans not only tolerated but gloried in pro football's brutality for a simple but powerful reason: "It is our own taste for violence that is ecstatically fulfilled down on the field."

This was the pro football world that would have to be utterly reenvisioned after the discovery of chronic traumatic encephalopathy in Mike Webster's brain.

SELLING SAVAGERY

Life continued celebrating pro football's sanctioned savagery into the 1970s, with cover stories on "Suicide Squads" in December 1971 ("The Wedge Meets the Headhunters") and on "Rough, Tough Pros" in October 1972 (bare-chested, snarling Bob Lilly on the cover, with beefcake studio portraits of Dick Butkus, Larry Csonka, Alan Page, Willie Lanier, Charlie Sanders, and Lilly inside).[22] Three months later, *Life* suspended publication, the last of the major weekly magazines to be displaced by television, whose sounds and moving images would take the spectacle of pro football violence to entirely new levels.[23] Popular magazines may have helped establish pro football in the 1960s, but television was its lifeblood. Fans could have no real idea how violent pro football was, or could be, until the coming of television, and not just television itself but the technical advances (telephoto lenses, slow-motion cameras, instant replay) that brought NFL violence up close to the viewer and made it personal.

Those sounds and images legally belonged to the National Football League, which, after struggling into the 1950s against a reputation for savagery, wholeheartedly embraced its image as *sanctioned* savagery in the 1960s. The modern NFL, quite simply, built itself on the game's violence, and it would sell itself as controlled violence to its hugely expanding television audience over the rest of the century and into the next.

In 1969, to commemorate the fiftieth anniversary of its founding, the NFL produced a coffee-table book, *The First Fifty Years*, which reads like a compilation of the photographs and articles in popular magazines over the past decade. The opening chapter, "A Game for Our Time," could have been written by Thomas Morgan, from the opening paragraph that described the football field as "an area for war, with rules and unwritten ethics of classic warring places"; to the second paragraph that set the pro football player alongside "the gladiator in the arena, the knight at the joust," in the West's long tradition of "symbolic wars"; to the third paragraph that called pro football "basically a physical assault by one team upon another in a desperate fight for land" and "a game of physical dominance," in which "the weak are punished unmercifully and the unskilled are run off the field." For players, the gridiron was a stage for "performing with a courage and skill raised above savagery only by the meaningful purpose and inner discipline of civilized man." Both "atavistic spectacle" and "thrilling art," pro football embodied "the powerful grace of modern dance put to a purpose against a background of impending pain." Savagery sanctioned by artistry.[24]

Other chapters more prosaically traced pro football history, tactical developments, and the evolution of equipment and uniforms, alongside profiles of the greatest players of the NFL's first half century. The heart of the book was a photo-essay that recreated a typical NFL game day as "The Planned Collision," moving from the players' physical and mental preparation in the locker room for "*the most violent collisions that man, in his long combative history, has ever invented*" (italics in original) to the playing out of the game itself. The text and particularly the photos invited readers inside the world of professional football, to see and feel what the players experienced: a world of violent collisions, in which only the strong survived.

With *The First Fifty Years*, the NFL unreservedly embraced its popular image as sanctioned savagery. The book was followed, in 1973, by *The Pro Football Experience*, an even larger coffee-table book (weighing over six pounds) with even more stunning photographs, divided into sections, preceded by brief texts. The introduction by the sportswriter Roger Kahn (better known for elegiac books on baseball) was titled "The Lure of the Game" and described football, among other things, as "a ritual for coming of age" for American boys and as a sport that, "with its excitement, violence, danger, courage, pain, touches the maleness of things." Beyond "the spectacle, the color, the deft television," Kahn concluded, "that, I think is the secret source of its success."[25]

The maleness of things. Defined by violence and pain. This was NFL football as it became America's Game (as opposed to the "American Way of Life," represented by college and high school football in the 1940s and 1950s). NFL Films, the league's in-house video production company, began assembling compilations of violent collisions in the late 1960s, with titles like *Bellringers* (1967) and *The Nutcracker Suite* (1968), which led in time to the storied "crunch" series of the 1980s—*Crunch Course* (1985), *In the Crunch* (1987), *Crunch Course II* (1988), *Crunch Masters* (1989)—along with *Merchants of Menace* (1989), *Strike Force* (1989), *Big Blocks and King Size Hits* (1989), *Thunder and Destruction* (1992), *NFL's Greatest Tackles* (1995), *Total Impact* (1996), and so on. In 2011, when former players first sued the NFL over concussions, their lawsuit would include a section titled "The NFL Markets and Glorifies Football's Violence through NFL Films," which cited these videos as evidence of the league's "agenda to promote the most violent aspects of NFL football and to urge players at every level of the game to disregard the results of violent head impacts."[26]

The NFL branded itself with Big Hits. The television networks (with the league's approval) branded their telecasts of NFL football with Big Hits. When *Monday Night Football* introduced halftime highlights in 1970, narrated by Howard Cosell, they instantly became their own TV phenomenon (apart from the novelty of a football game televised in prime time). After *SportsCenter* debuted on ESPN in 1979, it made highlight films the primary source of football video for most viewers. Studio shows before and after network broadcasts of Sunday NFL games showed highlight films; the NFL created its own network in 2003 with the full NFL Films archive at its disposal; *Sunday Night Football* debuted on NBC in 2006, preceded by *Football Night in America* with highlights of the day's games. Highlights and replays were everywhere, with Big Hits featured as prominently as touchdown passes.

Video gamers could create their own highlight-worthy hits at home on EA Sports' *Madden NFL*, which from its debut in 1988 replicated the collisions in NFL games. The 2005 edition introduced a "Hit Stick," to ratchet up defensive players' blows, followed in 2006 by a "Truck Stick," for the offense to do the same. EA Sports was an independent business, but as its partner the NFL held "creative control over the final product." As Tim Layden reported in *Sports Illustrated* in 2007, league officials were "wary of *Madden*'s accentuating violence," but they "signed off on all editions of the game in circulation."[27]

In September 2003, ESPN debuted a new segment on its *Monday Night Countdown* pregame show that aired before the game itself on ABC. (This was before ABC acquired ESPN, and they were still rivals.) Hosted by Chris Berman, the program included three segments with highlight films from the previous day's games, narrated by former NFL players in the studio. Ron Jaworski, an ex-quarterback, presented "Sunday Drive," a key scoring drive in one of the big games. Michael Irvin, a former receiver, offered "Playmaker," someone who had an outsized impact on the outcome of his game. And Tom Jackson, a former hard-hitting linebacker for the Denver Broncos, narrated "Jacked Up!," the five biggest hits from Sunday's games. After each replayed hit, Jackson would call out, "He got . . . ," and the rest of the crew would holler, "Jacked up!"

The plays were first shown at normal speed and then in slow motion. Each hit, even when appearing one after another, happened with startling suddenness, a body moving in one direction jolted in the opposite direction or dropped to the turf, instantly, without warning. The hits were like a really cool high school physics experiment illustrating Newton's Third Law of Motion (the one about actions and equal, opposite reactions), or like combat scenes in a superhero movie or video game, only *real.* It was always astonishing that the jacked-up player bounced back up—and he *always* bounced up, because ESPN (or the NFL) banned showing plays that resulted in injuries (or penalties). Many of the hits would now warrant disqualification for "targeting," but in 2003 there was no such rule, and for viewers the hits were an uncomplicated shot of adrenaline.[28]

"Jacked Up!" became so popular—"appointment television" for fans and "required viewing around the league"—that by 2006 the five hits had increased to six, three of them still in the pregame show but the top three, in ascending order, shown at halftime, to lure viewers from the game telecast on ABC.[29] In 2005, to compete with ESPN's "Jacked Up!," CBS's game-day studio show *The NFL Today* introduced the "Pounder Index" (playing off economists' "Quarter-Pounder Index" for measuring relative costs of living),[30] which assigned a numerical score on a ten-point scale to the week's biggest hits. As sports columnist Bob Raissman derisively described it in the *New York Daily News*, studio host Greg Gumbel, "in an authoritative tone (he's actually probably choking back laughter), will explain through some kind of hocus-pocus how each hard hit or tackle we're about to see has been assigned a rating. . . . And as some player's head is about to explode, bet the ranch one of the cast members, most likely Shannon Sharpe, will laugh, finding this fully sponsored gratuitous violence hysterical."[31]

Highlight hits were pure spectacle: Big Hits with No Consequences. (Any concussions that resulted were managed on the sidelines, off-screen.) If these hits had any relation to the "injury plagues" periodically reported in *Sports Illustrated* cover stories, or to the studies of former NFL players' long-term disabilities in recent years, no one was saying. But the "Pounder Index" lasted just that 2005 season, and a year later "Jacked Up!" disappeared, too. Something had changed.

THE CORE OF A PERSON

Over the years while the NFL was branding itself as "sanctioned savagery," Big Hits *did* have consequences, sometimes instantly. In 1977, Oakland Raiders defensive back George ("Hit Man") Atkinson *twice* knocked Pittsburgh Steelers wide receiver Lynn Swann out of games with concussions, leading the Steelers' coach, Chuck Noll to charge Atkinson with being part of a "criminal element" in the NFL, leading in turn to Atkinson's suing Noll for defamation and producing a serious, though brief, image problem for the league.[32] In 1978, Atkinson's teammate, safety Jack Tatum, leveled New England Patriots receiver Darryl Stingley with a vicious but fully legal hit that left him unconscious on the field and, after recovery, a quadriplegic. (Tatum not only expressed no remorse but titled his autobiography the following year *They Call Me Assassin*.) Viewers of *Monday Night Football* on November 18, 1985, saw Giants linebacker Lawrence Taylor snap Washington quarterback Joe Theismann's tibia and fibula—shown over and over in slow-motion replay—with a clean and legal tackle. In 1991 and 1992, first Mike Utley and then Dennis Byrd were paralyzed not from Big Hits but from routine head blows: in Utley's case, from an ordinary collision; in Byrd's, by simply hitting his head on the turf when he fell. Most hits were not catastrophic, of course. Following John Underwood's three-part investigation of football brutality in 1978 (discussed in the previous chapter), *Sports Illustrated* tracked the NFL's routine injures with cover stories in November 1986 (Paul Zimmerman's "The Agony Must End," announced on the cover as "How to Stop the Injury Plague in the NFL") and December 1992 (Peter King's "The Carnage Continues"), when the toll for that season, as the tagline to King's story put it, was "staggering—but typical."[33] Concussions were not singled out as a major problem in these stories, which focused more on crippling leg injuries that cut seasons and careers short and led to long-term disabilities.

Concussions did not emerge as the most troubling injury in the NFL until the 1990s. Over the 1970s and 1980s, while NFL players were routinely getting their bells rung and returning to play in the same game, medical researchers were slowly learning more about concussions and their prolonged dangers, publishing their results in scientific and professional journals with little impact on public understanding or team medical practices. As early as 1974, researchers at Purdue and Northwestern were measuring the G-force of head impacts and discovering, as a group at Northwestern reported in 1974, that "a concussion need not be the result of a single blow but may be the cumulative effect of a series of blows."[34] In 1981, researchers measured cognitive and neurological dysfunction that lasted months after the original concussion.[35]

The particular dangers of repeat concussions, described in 1973 by Richard Schneider, were termed "second impact" by two researchers in 1984 in the *Journal of the American Medical Association.*[36]

As the founding editor of *The Physician and Sportsmedicine* in 1973, Allan Ryan in particular took up Schneider's campaign for vigilance regarding head injuries. In an editorial in 1974, Ryan challenged Schneider's belief that head protection was the key to minimizing head injuries (sandlot players, with the poorest protection, had the lowest fatality rates). Rather, it was the technique taught by coaches: "The physician must continue to focus on diagnosis and treatment and hope that preventive measures will come. But as all physicians know, the coach is much harder to treat than the athlete."[37] In another editorial, in 1979, he followed Schneider in asserting that "cessation of headache is probably the most reliable marker" of recovery, and he concluded that "the risk of lasting brain damage from concussions does not justify entirely eliminating contact and combative sports."[38] By 1987, however, Ryan was calling for "serious efforts to determine whether athletes who have sustained concussions may be susceptible to further, more serious brain injury, and whether they should continue to play football."[39] In 1986, the neurosurgeon Robert Cantu (who would become part of the group with Ann McKee at Boston University that would take the lead in identifying CTE in former NFL players when the concussion crisis erupted) recommended treatments for three grades of concussions that followed Richard Schneider's from 1973 but with more caution about recovery.[40]

While researchers were beginning to question whether the disappearance of symptoms always indicated full recovery, tragedies from repeat concussions remained rare. A team at the University of Virginia, led by the neuropsychologist Jeffrey T. Barth, reported in 1989 on a four-year study of 2,350 players at ten universities—the first study to use baseline testing for measuring the consequences of head impacts—which concluded that 10 percent of college football players would experience a mild head injury each season and that 40 percent would have at least one such injury in either high school or college; but also that "significant neuropsychological recovery will often take place in this healthy, young population within 10 days of their injury."[41] A 1991 study published in the *Journal of the American Medical Association* by researchers led by the neurologist James P. Kelly reported a 20 percent rate of concussions among high school football players each season, some with more than one, and warned that "repeated concussion can lead to brain atrophy and cumulative neuro-psychological deficits." Yet his team's proposed new concussion guidelines only increased recommended recovery times when there was no loss of consciousness.[42] The basic paradigm had not really shifted since the 1970s, or even the 1930s: The absence of symptoms, however long that took, indicated recovery. But the possibility of prolonged effects from even mild concussions and the particular dangers of repeated concussions were beginning to emerge.

This was roughly the state of knowledge in the medical and scientific communities in 1994, when *Sports Illustrated* brought unprecedented public attention to concussions as a serious NFL problem. New York Jets wide receiver Al Toon had retired after the 1992 season, at twenty-nine, still in his prime, but struggling with the lingering symptoms of repeated concussions. Two years later, Chicago Bears running back Merril Hoge, also twenty-nine, retired for the same reason in midseason. In December, triggered by Hoge's sudden retirement and a rash of concussions that had so far sidelined more than a third of the NFL's twenty-eight starting quarterbacks, a single issue of *Sports Illustrated* published a special section on head injuries.[43] The first of the three articles was Peter King's open letter to Commissioner Paul Tagliabue, "Halt the Head-Hunting." "During the '90s an unprecedented viciousness has pervaded the game," King wrote, "an "epidemic of brutal hits." Sounding like Tim Cohane in 1953 when distinguishing "muckerism" from legitimate aggressiveness, King acknowledged that "football is all about hard hitting—smart, clean hitting" and that "it would be idiotic to legislate against it." And concussions would occur regardless of equipment and rules. But the rampant "head-hunting"—helmet-to-helmet hits launched by flying defensive players—was decimating the ranks of quarterbacks, the players on whom the NFL most depended for drawing fans.

The third of the three articles, "A Bell Is Rung," was King's account of one of those quarterbacks, the LA Rams' Chris Miller, struggling to function after repeated concussions that season. Between King's two stories, Michael Farber's "The Worst Case" brought something genuinely new to a familiar discussion: the emerging science of concussions, explained for ordinary fans. This included the "post-concussion syndrome" tormenting Al Toon and former New York Giants linebacker Harry Carson and the "second-impact syndrome" that could kill rather than merely torment. Farber explained the current definitions of concussions' three grades and the "silent epidemic" of concussions in football, including the 250,000 each season among the 1.5 million high school players (one out of every six boys who played). "Concussions are underreported at all levels of football," Farber cautioned, due both to difficulties in diagnosing mild concussions and to players' not admitting them. Case in point: A spokesman for the NFL told Farber that "data supplied by the 28 teams" between 1989 and 1993 consistently showed "about four concussions per weekend." That would, astonishingly, add up to just 64 over a sixteen-game season, among 1,200 players, fewer than 3 per team, per season. Underreporting indeed.

Farber described the research of Jeffrey Barth, Robert Cantu, James Kelly, and other concussion experts. As Kelly told Farber, "It isn't just cataclysmic injury or death from brain injuries that should concern people. The core of a person can change from repeated blows to the head." That nebulous term, *core of a person*, described a condition not yet clinically confirmed but occasionally reported anecdotally, at least since Bill Cunningham wrote about punch-drunk football players in the 1930s.

The *Sports Illustrated* articles appeared in December 1994, the same month that NFL commissioner Paul Tagliabue appointed a Committee on Mild Traumatic Brain Injury. One would expect that the first task of such a committee would have been a thorough review of the existing research on its subject, beginning perhaps with the studies cited by Farber. Instead, the NFL committee looked at the data reported by the twenty-eight clubs (on those four concussions per weekend), on which it would base all its future published "research." The MTBI Committee's task, it turned out, was to protect the NFL brand, not the players.

THE WRECKING YARD

For members of the MTBI Committee, Tagliabue appointed just one neurologist, one neurosurgeon, and a biomechanical engineer, along with several team doctors, two trainers, and an equipment manager, with a rheumatologist for the chair, the New York Jets' team doctor Elliot Pellman (who had "treated" Al Toon's concussions).[44] Pellman was the NFL doctor who told Michael Farber that concussions were just "part of the profession, an occupational risk . . . like a steelworker who goes up 100 stories, or a soldier." On players' recovery from mild concussions and returning in the same game, Pellman told Farber, "Veterans clear more quickly than rookies. . . . They can unscramble their brains a little faster, maybe cause they're not afraid after being dinged." Cutting-edge brain science there. Tagliabue himself dropped a clue as to what the MTBI Committee's charge would be, when in December he dismissed concussions as "a pack journalism issue."[45]

In 1994, as the MTBI Committee was coming together, the NFL celebrated its seventy-fifth anniversary with another coffee-table commemorative book, this one strikingly different from the one in 1970 in muting the emphasis on violence in pro football without altogether disavowing it. Near the beginning of the book, on facing pages, were what had become the two iconic football photographs of the modern NFL's early years: New York Giants quarterback Y. A. Tittle, in 1964, kneeling in the end zone, helmetless, with blood steaking down his balding head after being sacked; and Giants running back Frank Gifford, in 1960, lying unconscious on the turf, as Philadelphia Eagles middle linebacker Chuck Bednarik danced over him in celebration. (The Gifford/ Bednarik photo would become a grotesque icon of NFL football when CTE was found in Gifford's brain tissue following his death in 2015 after several years of dementia.) The book's introduction by Dick Butkus, the NFL's most vicious hitter (and notoriously dirty player) of the late 1960s, also faintly echoed the celebration of violence in the fiftieth anniversary volume. "Of course, I wanted to put someone on his back every time I lined up," Butkus wrote in describing his love for the NFL.[46] But that was it. The chapters that followed were entirely historical, with none of the reflections on gladiators and warring armies, "courage and skill raised above savagery only by the meaningful purpose and inner discipline of civilized man," and all the rest in the 1969 volume. In part, the NFL no longer needed to proclaim what the book's readers absorbed weekly by watching pro football on television. In part, the NFL's association with violence was becoming more troubled and troubling.

Even as concern about concussions increased over the 1990s, pro football's long-term damage to joints remained popularly understood as players' primary health problem. In 1988, a survey of 440 former players by the *Los Angeles Times* had found that 78 percent suffered from some sort of disability. Studies conducted by researchers at Ball State University in 1990 and Harvard in 1997, plus surveys by *Newsday* in 1997, the *Los Angeles Times* in 2000, and the *Arizona Republic* in 2003, consistently found over 60 percent of NFL retirees dealing with permanent injuries, many of them utterly dependent on medications to mask the pain.[47]

These were the players who ended up in what a graphic 2001 cover story in *Sports Illustrated* called the NFL's "Wrecking Yard." The piece featured seven cases, including legendary quarterback Johnny Unitas, pictured on the cover clutching a football with his now-useless right hand (to play golf, he attached it to his club with Velcro). Hall of Fame running back Earl Campbell could barely walk; former Oakland Raiders offensive lineman Curt Marsh had a stump where his right foot had been amputated after misdiagnosis and botched treatment. "Paying the price" no longer meant "taking it" in endless, brutal practices or playing through pain but living with pain and disabilities from those injuries for the rest of one's life. Campbell was just forty-six; Chris Washington, the youngest, was thirty-nine.[48]

Among these seven men, only Campbell admitted that, had he known what the game would do to him, he might not have played it. He was a rarity. Crippled former NFL players surveyed in the 1990s and into the next decade overwhelmingly expressed no regrets about having played, and they insisted that they would unhesitatingly do it again. Their pain was an acceptable cost for the game's benefits, the chief of which seemed to be the addictive thrill of playing NFL football itself. Their complaints were limited to their clubs' mistreatment of their injuries (such as Curt Marsh's) and particularly to the Kafkaesque obstacles to getting disability payments from the fund jointly administered by the NFL and the Players Association. But then, just over a year later, after his own long residence in the NFL's "Wrecking Yard," Mike Webster died at age fifty, and Bennet Omalu conducted the autopsy. It would take a few more years, but fundamental assumptions about football's costs and benefits were about to be turned on their head.

THE SECRET IN MIKE WEBSTER'S BRAIN

This part of the story will be familiar, in both general outline and many of the particulars, thanks to brothers Mark Fainaru-Wada and Steve Fainaru's devastating indictment of the NFL in *League of Denial*, but it needs repeating here for the sake of future readers and because its absence would leave a huge gap in the story. In 2003, members of the NFL's MTBI Committee began publishing research papers from the data on concussions collected from the league's twenty-eight clubs in the journal *Neurosurgery*, edited by a distinguished neurosurgeon at the University of Southern California who also happened to be a consultant to the New York Giants. These papers repeated the claim that the NFL saw one concussion every three or four games; that concussed players recovered quickly and could safely return to play in the same game; that repeat concussions were rare and not particularly dangerous—all of this in ignorance, or defiance, of research emerging since the 1970s and despite the objections of peer reviewers.

The *New York Times* would later report that the NFL's MTBI Committee ignored "more than 100 diagnosed concussions" (including Steve Young's and Troy Aikman's, the ones most highly publicized when they forced early retirements),[49] but the more egregious problem was to take those 3–4 diagnosed concussions each weekend as all there were, rather than as the small portion that were actually diagnosed by team physicians. As for concussed players safely returning to play, committee members took their return to play as itself evidence of recovery. Pellman and fellow committee members Ira Casson and David Viano tried (unsuccessfully) to block publication of Omalu's paper on Mike Webster in *Neurosurgery*, and they also disparaged other new studies as they came out. In 2005, for example, researchers led by Kevin Guskiewicz at the Center for the Study of Retired Athletes at the University of North Carolina published (in *Neurosurgery*) results from a survey of 2,552 former college football players, which found that those who had had concussions were three times as likely to be suffering from depression.[50] A second major paper out of Guskiewicz's research at UNC, published in the official journal of the American College of Sports Medicine in 2007, found players who had had three or more concussions were five times as likely to be diagnosed with early-onset dementia.[51] Both papers would become widely cited as the concussion crisis would play out, but MTBI Committee members dismissed them because they were based on self-reporting. They challenged Omalu's paper for lacking *proof* that football caused his condition, as if such proof was even possible. NFL responses to the concussion crisis followed the tactics of Big Tobacco—produce bogus science while creating doubt around the real science—and were a foretaste of the attacks on the science of climate change and vaccinations that were coming.

Committee members' motive was simply to protect the interests of the National Football League, but their actions and inactions also reflected interestingly on the continuing tension between health concerns and cultural values. In 1986, the editor of the *Journal of the American Medical Association*, George Lundberg, in the midst of waging his own crusade against boxing in a series of three papers, noted in passing in the third one, "There may be a substantial prevalence of chronic brain damage in football players, but at this time no one seems to know." He echoed here the rumors of punch-drunkenness in football players reported by Augustus Thorndike and John Carroll in the 1930s, still unsubstantiated fifty years later. Lundberg then added, "One senses that the football enthusiasts, including the sports medicine establishment, may not want to know."[52] Physicians who were football fans could embody the tension between health and culture most personally. For physicians who were also employed by NFL clubs and who sent obviously damaged players—whether mildly concussed or with knees shot up with Novocain—back into games, contrary to how they would treat their own patients, that tension could become a full-blown conflict of interest.[53]

The bedrock assumption that Webster's autopsy exploded was the belief that the disappearance of symptoms meant full recovery from brain trauma.

As recently as 1999, the *Journal of the American Medical Association* had published an issue with an editorial and five articles on traumatic brain injury, one of which linked concussion to cognitive decline in college football players. In his accompanying editorial, James Kelly reiterated the long-prevailing assumption that "the effects of concussion usually resolve spontaneously and fully," but he also cautioned that "some individuals have persistent cognitive deficits."[54] Mike Webster's experience of devastating symptoms years after he stopped playing suddenly opened up new and frightening possibilities.

Webster's was a single case, until June 2005 (a month before Omalu's paper appeared in *Neurosurgery*), when another ex-Steeler lineman, forty-five-year-old Terry Long, killed himself by drinking antifreeze. Long's body and damaged brain showed up by happenstance in Omalu's lab, as Webster's had. This time, knowing the circumstances of Long's death and the depression that preceded it, Omalu suspected CTE and found it again. Again, he submitted his findings to *Neurology*, where it was published in November 2006 (again, over the objections of MTBI Committee members).

Two cases now, but the general public was not yet aware of them. Omalu's third case came about more intentionally, and it was not reported in a medical journal this time but on the front page of the *New York Times*. As would later come out, the suicide of forty-five-year-old former Philadelphia Eagles cornerback Andre Waters in November 2006 caught the attention of a former Harvard football player and professional wrestler named Chris Nowinski, who had been forced to retire from World Wrestling Entertainment after multiple concussions.[55] When the neurosurgeon Robert Cantu, now at Boston University, explained that he was suffering the consequences of his multiple concussions, Nowinski embarked on a campaign to warn the public. Suspecting that Waters might have CTE, Nowinski contacted Omalu, as the sudden expert on the disease, and then contacted Waters's family to request the brain for autopsy. After Omalu indeed found CTE, Nowinski next contacted Alan Schwarz, a freelance baseball writer and contributor to the *New York Times*, whom Nowinski had met around the publication of his own book, *Head Games: Football's Concussion Crisis from the NFL to Youth Leagues*, in October.[56] (Schwarz could take on the story because, unlike the full-time football reporters, he had no fear of jeopardizing his "access" to NFL sources.) Schwarz pitched a human-interest story about Nowinski and his crusade to Tom Jolly, the sports editor at the *Times*, but Jolly recognized something very different: a third case of CTE in a former professional football player who died young under disturbing circumstances. The *Times* ran Schwarz's "Expert Ties Ex-Player's Suicide to Brain Damage" on the front page on January 18, 2007.

Not just neuroscientists and sports medicine professionals but sportswriters, journalists, and increasingly the general public were beginning to discover Mike Webster's secret.

Over the next four years, Schwarz would write well over a hundred more stories for the *Times* on every aspect of what would quickly become a "concussion crisis." Alan Schwarz and the *New York Times* made CTE a mainstream public health story, not just a medical science or football story, and what the public knew about CTE, until the story exploded in the media in the fall of 2009, came mostly from Schwarz's reporting in the *Times*. Schwarz's stories, as they appeared day to day, week to week, month to month, became themselves the public discovery of concussions' true dangers, as well as a documentary record of it for future generations, from January 2007 until June 2011 (when Schwarz moved to the *Times*' National Desk, to cover public health more broadly).

Following his front-page story on Andre Waters and CTE in January, Schwarz over the next five months wrote about former Patriots linebacker Ted Johnson, already suffering at the age of thirty-four, just two years into retirement, from symptoms indicating early-onset Alzheimer's disease; about a thoroughly discredited Elliot Pellman's stepping down as chair of the NFL's MTBI Committee; about the wives of former players coping with their husbands' dementia; about the research coming out of the University of North Carolina on the long-term damage from concussions; about MTBI Committee coauthors repudiating their own papers' altered assertions; about Justin Strzelczyk, a third former Steeler lineman, who had died in a fiery car crash almost three years earlier and whose body was exhumed on the suspicion that his behavior pointed toward CTE, to become Bennet Omalu's fourth case.[57]

At this point, Webster, Long, Waters, and Strzelczyk were four cases of a grotesque disease without *proof* that football head trauma caused it, but instead of taking them as a siren call to broaden and deepen their investigation, MTBI Committee members doubled down on their denials. On June 19, the NFL convened a one-day Concussion Summit in Chicago, to which it invited presentations by oppositional researchers (conspicuously excluding Bennet Omalu), but only to dispute their claims, and held it behind closed doors, to exclude the media from reporting firsthand. (Schwarz hung around in the hallway to catch the participants as they left their sessions.)[58] A week later, a subcommittee of the US House of Representatives met in Washington to hear testimony from former players who were struggling with mental and physical disabilities and threatened legislative action if the NFL and the Players Association did not do something about their unnavigable process for getting financial assistance. Alan Schwarz was there, too.[59]

Schwarz's story about wives focused on Eleanor Perfetto, married to Ralph Wenzel, a former lineman for the Steelers and San Diego Chargers, and Sylvia Mackey, married to John Mackey, the Hall of Fame former tight end of the Baltimore Colts. Both men had played in the late 1960s and early '70s and were now living in the same care facility in a fog of dementia, unable even to remember that they had once been teammates. (Both would be diagnosed with CTE after their deaths.) An impassioned letter from Sylvia Mackey to Commissioner Tagliabue a year earlier had led to the "88 Plan" (named for Mackey's jersey number), which would provide up to $88,000 a year to former players diagnosed with dementia. The NFL and the Players Association formally launched the plan in February 2007 with letters sent to twenty-two former players known to be eligible.

For Schwarz's front-page story on the wives in mid-March, Sylvia Mackey had told Alan Schwarz that she had been "approached many times by lawyers who wanted to use me in a lawsuit" against the NFL, but she pursued the 88 Plan with Tagliabue instead, because it would also benefit other players and their families, not just her own.[60] The NFL cast their agreement rather differently. A league spokesman told the Associated Press that the 88 Plan was intended "to provide resources to former players and their families for care and treatment of a debilitating disease that affects many elderly people" (not just football players, that is). For the NFL, it was an act of pure benevolence toward aging retirees, unrelated to their football injuries. "No one involved with the program claims Mackey or any other ex-NFL player with dementia or Alzheimer's is in such a condition because of hits sustained while playing," the AP writer explained.[61]

DAMAGE CONTROL

The NFL's transparent strategy for fending off disability claims and lawsuits from former players and their families, while accepting no liability for the long-term consequences of their injuries, minimizing payouts, and maintaining a positive public image, was inherited by Roger Goodell when he succeeded Tagliabue as commissioner in September 2006. In addition to taking on the 88 Plan, Goodell in his first year replaced Pellman as chair of the MTBI Committee and convened the Concussion Summit, which aired the issues without confronting them. At the end of July, *Sports Illustrated* published a cover story, "The Big Hit," whose long tagline neatly summed up a dilemma that Goodell now faced: "Players live for it, fans love it, media celebrate it—and all bemoan its devastating consequences. The brutal collision of bodies is football's lifeblood, and the NFL's biggest concern."[62] That fall, "Jacked Up!" quietly disappeared from *Monday Night Countdown* on ABC. And in August, still without admitting any connection between concussions and later brain damage, the NFL announced that concussed players should not return to the practice or game in which they were injured.[63]

This was the NFL's first tentative pivot away from total denial toward acknowledgment that concussions posed a serious problem.[64] Potential long-term brain damage to players was a threat to football, but *brand damage* from NFL indifference to that threat could be more dangerous. In September, the league distributed a pamphlet to players that warned them about concussions while still denying the extent of the potential damage that researchers were increasingly discovering (italics in the original): "*Current research with professional athletes has not shown that having more than one or two concussions leads to permanent problems if each injury is managed properly. It is important to understand that there is no magic number for how many concussions is too many. Research is currently underway to determine if there are any long-term effects of concussions in NFL athletes.*"[65]

The NFL would not complete its pivot for two more years. The following months were relatively uneventful, but in September 2008, Alan Schwarz reported that former Houston Oilers linebacker John Grimsley, dead at forty-five from an accidental self-inflicted gunshot, was the NFL's fifth confirmed case of CTE and the first for the recently created Center for the Study of Traumatic Encephalopathy at Boston University and for neuropathologist Ann McKee.[66] McKee and Chris Nowinski, along with Robert Cantu and Robert Stern, had founded the CSTE in June, after Nowinski fell out with Omalu and ended their brief collaboration.[67] In January 2009, at a press conference a week before the Super Bowl in Tampa, McKee announced that Tom McHale, a forty-five-year-old former Tampa Bay lineman, who had died from an accidental overdose of the drugs with which he was trying to control the chaos in his head, had become the NFL's sixth case.[68] This was the public event that identified CTE with McKee, Nowinski, and the CSTE, rather than with Bennet Omalu, now working with his own team. Over the coming months and years, McKee would become the face of CTE research, and her lab at the CSTE would become the final destination for most of the brains of former players who died young and violently, or old and demented, whose families wanted to know whether football was the cause.

Each announcement in the press of another player found with CTE was a new shock, but the number of confirmed cases remained small, and members of the MTBI Committee were still hammering on the absence of any *clinical proof* that football had caused these players' brain damage. Then, on September 30, 2009, the front page of the *New York Times* (Alan Schwarz again) and wire-service stories in newspapers everywhere reported on a survey of 1,063 former NFL players conducted by researchers at the University of Michigan and commissioned by the NFL itself, in which the players or their families reported rates of dementia nineteen times greater than the norm for men between the ages of thirty and fifty and six times greater for men over fifty.[69] The customary denials by the NFL, this time attacking its own commissioned study for being based on survey responses rather than on clinical data (what had it expected when it commissioned the study?), seemed increasingly desperate as well as indifferent to the well-being of the men who had built the league.

A month later, Jeanne Marie Laskas's "Game Brain" in the monthly magazine *GQ* detailed the full story of Mike Webster, Bennet Omalu, the discovery of CTE, and the struggle for recognition of the disease in the face of NFL deniers, even as Omalu was finding it in the brains of Terry Long, Andre Waters, and Justin Strzelczyk, too. (The 2015 film *Concussion*, starring Will Smith as Omalu, would be based on Laskas's article, which she would also turn into a book with the same title that year.) Laskas also recounted the NFL committee's dismissal of Kevin Guskiewicz's two major papers from his surveys of former players that tied depression and "mild cognitive impairment" to repeated concussions. The broader public was now becoming aware of the research that the MTBI Committee had been debunking or ignoring.[70]

Malcolm Gladwell's "Offensive Play" in the *New Yorker*, later in October, completed a triptych of explosive national stories within less than a month. Gladwell recounted the discovery of CTE by Bennet Omalu and particularly the clinical work of Ann McKee, the passionate Green Bay Packers fan struggling to come to terms with the terrible things she was finding in the brains of fourteen former players of all ages, from sixty-six-year-old ex-Minnesota Viking Wally Hilgenberg to an eighteen-year-old whom she could not name. (The names of most of the players had not been made public.) Gladwell also described Kyle Turley, just two years into retirement but already suffering symptoms indicating CTE. Like most of those players in the NFL's "wrecking yard," Turley "loved playing football so much that he would do it all again," he told Gladwell. In ranging over the emerging research and researchers, Gladwell's most troubling news for football's future was about the studies currently being conducted by Guskiewicz at the University of North Carolina, which used sensors in players' helmets to record the force of every head impact they received in practices and games—more than a thousand of varying force for a single player over the course of a season, an accumulation of *sub*concussive hits possibly more damaging long-term than outright concussions. (Big Hits were violent spectacle, seemingly without consequences; subconcussive hits were no spectacle, all consequence.) "At the core of the C.T.E. research," Gladwell wrote at one point, "is a critical question: is the kind of injury being uncovered by McKee and Omalu incidental to the game of football or inherent?" This was the question now confronting the public, as the NFL's "concussion problem" would become a full-blown public health issue.[71]

Congress weighed in again, this time more forcefully. At a hearing in late October, after the report on the Michigan study and the articles by Laskas and Gladwell had appeared, members of the House Judiciary Committee lambasted Goodell for adopting Big Tobacco's game plan of denial in the face of overwhelming evidence.[72] Gay Culverhouse, the daughter of the Tampa Bay Buccaneers' former owner, testified that the members of the Judiciary Committee needed "to understand very clearly that the team doctor is hired by the coach and paid by the front office. This team doctor is not a medical advocate for the players. The team doctor's role is to get that player back on the field."[73]

With continuing defiance now a greater risk than admission, the NFL completed the pivot that Goodell had begun more tentatively in 2007. In November, Pellman's replacements as cochairs, Ira Casson and David Viano, "resigned" from the MTBI Committee, and the NFL announced new protocols for concussion management.[74] Then in December, with no fanfare, an NFL spokesman, while explaining a $1 million donation to the CSTE at Boston University (more NFL benevolence), told Alan Schwarz, "It's quite obvious from the medical research that's been done that concussions can lead to long-term problems."[75]

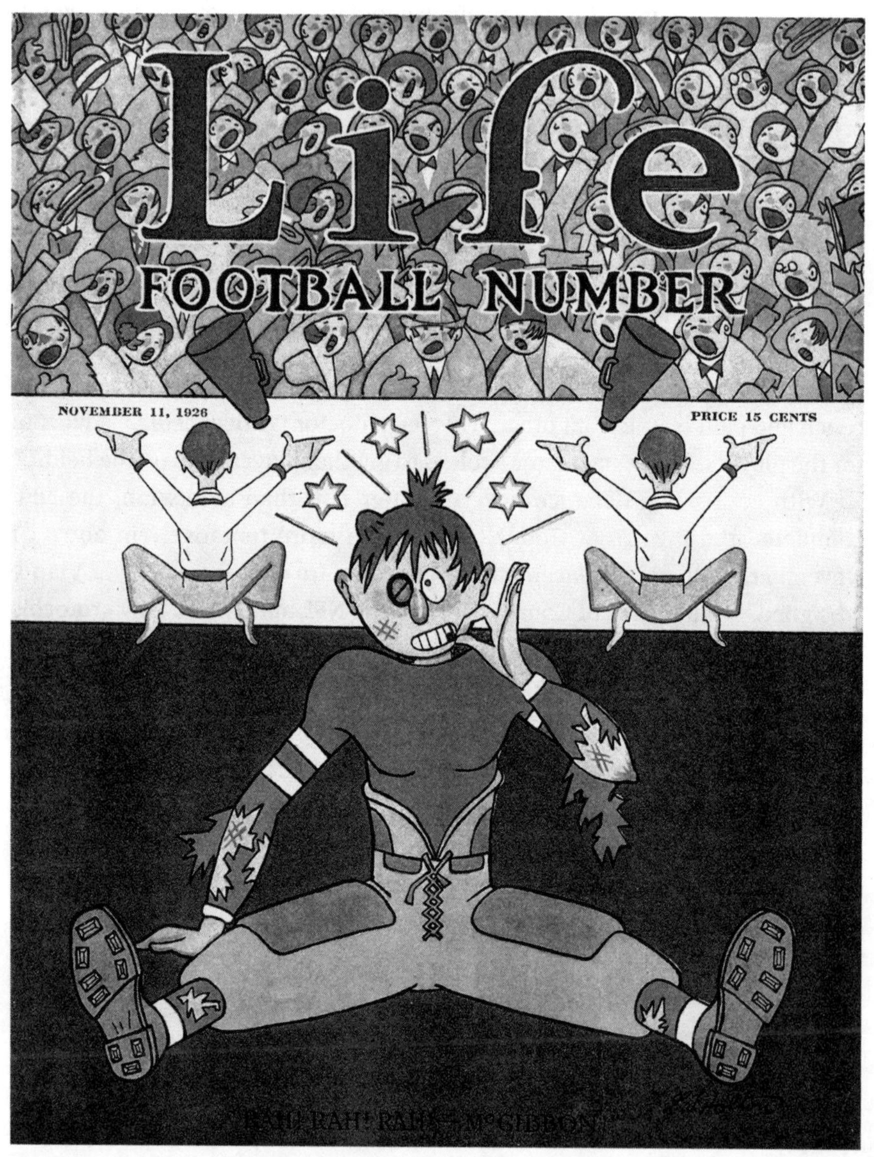

Figure 8.1. L. T. Holton's cover for *Life*, November 11, 1926.

CHAPTER 8

THE END OF SANCTIONED SAVAGERY

Getting your bell rung was no longer a joke, as it had been for much of football's history, all the way back to 1906, as reported at the time by Harvard's team doctors. CTE upended every aspect of the "sanctioned savagery" that had fueled the NFL's rise to preeminence since the 1960s and that had trickled down even to high schools and youth leagues, along with the taunting and end zone celebrations and other superficial elements of NFL spectacle that kids everywhere took up. "Taking it" and "paying the price" now meant putting not just one's body but one's mental capacity and "core of identity" at risk. "Dishing it out," with helmet-first blocking or tackling, now more than ever meant endangering oneself more than the opponent. "Taking it" could be suicidal; "dishing it out" could be suicidal *and* murderous. As for football's *necessary* roughness, fundamental since the game's beginnings and amplified enormously in the 1950s and 1960s, how much "roughness" could now be tolerable, let alone necessary? And a new question now loomed: How safe could football be and still be football?[1]

The NFL had no choice but to start doing more to protect its players. It also had to convince fans that it was committed to doing so and assure parents that football was safe enough for their sons (the NFL's future players) to play. In his October 2009 *New Yorker* piece, Malcolm Gladwell described Ann McKee showing him the CTE-riddled brain of an unnamed eighteen-year-old. In April 2010, a twenty-one-year-old offensive lineman from Penn named Owen Thomas, who had hanged himself in his apartment, became McKee's first college football player diagnosed with CTE.[2] If neither played pro football, and one never played beyond high school, who was safe? At the congressional hearing in October 2009, representatives had pointed to the "trickle-down effects on high school and college players" that, in the case of returning to play with concussions, "are very real and can be fatal."[3] In January 2010, Alan Schwarz reported that Washington and Oregon were taking the lead among the states with laws mandating concussion education for youth football coaches and team doctors and for establishing return-to-play guidelines for concussed players (for managing concussions, that is, not preventing them). Washington's so-called Lystedt Law was named for a thirteen-year-old middle schooler, Zackery Lystedt, who in 2006 had been permanently brain-damaged by a second concussion suffered just two plays after the first one. The Lystedt Law began as a local matter that would expand into a national movement reaching all fifty states.[4]

In March 2010, Roger Goodell appointed two distinguished neurosurgeons with no ties to the NFL (one of whom helped pass the Lystedt Law in Washington) to replace Ira Casson and David Viano on the renamed and repurposed NFL Head, Neck and Spine Committee.[5] That summer, Goodell charged the new committee chairs with producing a poster for NFL locker rooms, which effectively announced a break with the pamphlet sent to players three years earlier that denied any scientific proof of a link between head trauma and later brain damage.[6] The new poster, headed "CONCUSSION—A Must Read for NFL Players . . . Let's Take Brain Injuries Out of Play," issued an unambiguous warning: "Repetitive brain injury, when not treated promptly and properly, may cause permanent damage to your brain."[7] The league also addressed its marketing of violence again. For the 2010 season, *Monday Night Football* (on ESPN now, instead of ABC) opened for the first time since 1986 without the image of two helmets crashing and exploding into fragments—at the request of the NFL "out of concern that it glorified violent hits to the head."[8] "Sanctioned savagery" was officially dead.

DOES FOOTBALL HAVE A FUTURE?

What followed the NFL's pivot in 2009–10 was a period of disorientation and uncertainty throughout the football world, as officials began penalizing the kind of Big Hits that used to make the highlight shows and parents struggled to know whether their sons were at serious risk of brain damage. Following the 2010 season, just before the Super Bowl, an article in the *New Yorker* by Ben McGrath posed the question, "Does Football Have a Future?" and captured the uncertainties and confusion of this moment. McGrath reviewed football's long history of violence, with its well-understood orthopedic risks, and how that suddenly changed with the discovery of CTE in the brains of Mike Webster, Terry Long, Andre Waters, and Justin Strzelczyk, along with so much else subsequently learned from Alan Schwarz's reporting. "What we now know from reading Schwarz," McGrath wrote, "is that retired N.F.L. players are five to nineteen times as likely as the general population to have received a dementia-related diagnosis; that the helmet manufacturing industry is overseen by a volunteer consortium funded largely by helmet manufacturers; and that Lou Gehrig may not actually have had the disease that bears his name but suffered from concussion-related trauma instead." Since 1960, NFL players had been diagnosed with amyotrophic lateral sclerosis (ALS) at seven times the rate one "would expect from a random population sample."[9] (Gehrig might have suffered his head trauma while playing football at Columbia before his baseball career with the Yankees.)

For a sense of the current state of NFL football, McGrath attended the Pittsburgh Steelers–Cleveland Browns game on October 17, 2010, a day on which eleven players around the league were knocked out of games with concussions from ferocious hits, earning one sportswriter's designation as "Black and Blue Sunday." The league imposed $175,000 in total fines "on three hard hitters" from those games and warned of future suspensions. The Steelers' James Harrison, who was fined $75,00 and "vilified in the press" for two of those hits, admittedly played by Sam Huff's honored dictum, "I try to hurt people." But that potential "hurt" was exponentially greater now. The rules regarding "defenseless" players had not changed; "the league just seemed to want them enforced differently," McGrath wrote, "and with an eye toward outcome and appearance as much as technique." An NFL spokesman's talk of eliminating "devastating hits" on "defenseless" players led McGrath to wonder, "Was this really football?" Steelers owner Art Rooney was sympathetic to his players' being asked "to do something different from what they've been trained to do over the years." They were "not sure what they can do at this point."

Rooney also told McGrath that Steelers fans were sending Harrison ("a man who earned several million dollars a year for his toughness") donations toward paying his fines. "I think our fans want to see our players continue to play football the way they understand football should be played," Rooney said. And apparently so did sportswriters, as McGrath discovered. "Up in the press box, I'd notice a casual disdain for the initial efforts to sanitize the game as the referees tossed yellow flag after yellow flag." To McGrath's surprise, among the players he talked to, the Steelers' free safety Troy Polamalu, who played the game at a level of reckless abandon (McGrath called it "brilliant abandon") beyond anyone else in the league, actually welcomed referees' efforts to make the game safer. Having already had "at least seven concussions," Polamalu told McGrath that "'this game's on the verge of getting out of hand,' and he defended the refs who were 'just trying to protect it.'"

Elsewhere around the league, players and fans were also struggling with the newly rigorous enforcement of rules against unnecessary roughness. In *Concussion*, Jeanne Marie Laskas transcribed an exchange among studio commentators at ESPN following a *Monday Night Football* game in 2010 that echoed what McGrath heard in the press box at Pittsburgh. Among the ex-players in the studio, only Steve Young, who had a very personal understanding of the seriousness of concussions after having to retire because of them, approved the league's new penalties and suspensions. Former Detroit linebacker Matt Millen complained, "You can't take the competition and the toughness and all that stuff that go into making the game great—you can't take it out of the game." Trent Dilfer, another former quarterback, sided with Millen instead of Young, calling it an "absolute joke" that the league was going to "rob" fans of their pleasure in a "gladiatorial" game played by men "sacrificing their bodies and laying it all on the line." (The recycling of "toughness" and "gladiatorial" combat from earlier decades suggests just how deeply embedded those ideas were in the football culture.) When Young insisted that defenses would have to ease up on defenseless players, Millen countered, "You can't!" Stuart Scott, the studio host (who had never played a down in the NFL), declared, "*That's not football!*"[10]

But could rule changes actually make the game safe *enough*? Ben McGrath wondered. Would football come to be played only by lower-class, mostly minority kids with no better life prospects? Was NFL football so dependent on its "savagery" that "the game will be nothing" if that was taken away? After surveying the proposals and views of leading experts on CTE, like Chris Nowinski and Ann McKee, McGrath offered his own tentative conclusion: "I'm not so convinced that violence fully explains football's popularity as a spectator sport." For evidence, he cited "the most exciting moment in this football season" that he had himself witnessed: a sixty-five-yard punt return by the Philadelphia Eagles' 175-pound DeSean Jackson, to beat the New York Giants in a December game. After making one Giant "gunner" after another miss him in a spectacular run, Jackson suddenly slowed down as he approached the end zone and began running parallel to the goal line, so that time would expire before he scored, leaving the Giants no chance to get the ball back. The play was both thrilling and brilliant and utterly absent of violence. "Averted danger is the essence of football," McGrath decided—then immediately added in his final lines, "But what if he'd been clobbered? And what if some of those blocked tacklers whom we laugh at are hearing bells and are too ashamed to admit it?" Danger might be momentarily averted, but it always loomed.

Just a few days after McGrath's January article appeared, ex–Chicago Bear Dave Duerson shot himself in the chest, expressly to save his brain for the autopsy that he was convinced would reveal CTE. Duerson's calculation was more stunning than the suicide itself, the clearest indication yet that CTE now *haunted* football. The story went viral in the mainstream media. Alan Schwarz wrote not one but three pieces on Duerson's suicide in February, plus a fourth in May, when the results of Ann McKee's autopsy confirmed Duerson's self-diagnosis. Duerson's suicide was grimly ironic as well as tragic, because he happened to have served as one of the Players Association's three representatives on the joint committee with the NFL that consistently denied ex-players' appeals for disability compensation.[11]

Later in February, still 2011, Ollie Matson, the great halfback for the Chicago Cardinals and LA Rams in the 1950s, died with dementia at eighty. Two months after that, ex-49er Joe Perry, the NFL's dominant fullback in the 1950s before the arrival of Jim Brown, died at eighty-four, also with dementia. And in June, John Henry Johnson, the pile-driving fullback for the Steelers and other teams in the '50s and early '60s, joined them, at eighty-one. Within five months, three of the giants from the 1950s and early 1960s (Sam Huff's era) had died, and all were later found to have CTE. Popular understanding of football's violence was undergoing a radical transformation, not all at once but fitfully, one postmortem diagnosis at a time.

Dave Meggyesy, the 1960s rebel whose *Out of Their League* in 1970 had indicted the NFL for its dehumanizing violence and racism, told Ben McGrath that he did not think that football's future would be "driven by public opinion, but by lawyers and insurance companies." Terry Bradshaw, the ex-Steeler, now a fixture in the studio on Fox football broadcasts, warned after James Harrison's run-in with the league, "There's a potential lawsuit out there that's devasting." That lawsuit happened, or rather began to happen, in July 2011, when seventy-five former players filed it against the NFL in Los Angeles Superior Court for "willful concealment of evidence of the long-term effects of head injuries" that had "led to the players' current brain damage."[12]

(Jumping ahead for a moment: Dozens more lawsuits would follow that would eventually be consolidated into a single class-action suit representing 4,500 former players, initially settled in September 2013 for $765 million but not finally approved until April 2016.[13] By settling with its players, the NFL would avoid having the sorry history of its shabby treatment of players and systematic ignoring of expert medical guidance exposed in court. By settling with the NFL, former players would receive relief *now*. Or so they thought. It would turn out, as the *Washington Post* would report in a series of investigative pieces, that over the first seven years of players' claims under the settlement, while nearly $1.3 billion had been awarded to 1,700 players, another 1,300 players had been denied benefits because they failed to meet criteria that defined dementia more stringently than the medical norm, requiring multiple symptoms to confirm it, not just one or two. The league also had guaranteed "state-of-the-art" testing for dementia—as well as for Alzheimer's, Parkinson's, and ALS (though not CTE)—but would not pay for MRI brain scans when technical improvements after the agreement was signed made them essential for such tests.[14] When it came to its players, the NFL giveth when it had to and taketh away, or at least withholdeth, when it could.)

In 2010, the NCAA had finally mandated that every Division I school have a concussion management policy, but, as sport historian Ronald Smith noted, it "never enforced the requirement."[15] By 2011, the entire sports world was deeply unsettled by a cascade of reports on the dangers of head trauma.[16] In September 2011, two health writers published a book, *The Concussion Crisis*, filled with painful stories about athletes of both genders in multiple sports whose lives had been derailed in a "silent epidemic" of brain injuries.[17] In November, three former college football players and a soccer player filed a class-action suit against the NCAA, the first of what would become several hundred lawsuits against the organization and its conferences and schools.[18] For the 2012 season, Pop Warner limited contact at practices, eliminated kickoffs and three-point stances for the youngest players, and banned head-on tackling and blocking drills.[19] That same season, USA Football, the youth football organization founded in 2002 with funding from the NFL and the NFL Players Association, launched "Heads Up Football" with training for coaches on how to teach blocking and tackling with the head up and to the side, as those college coaches in the 1950s had taught. (Within a few years, the program's apparent success in reducing concussions would be undermined when analysis by the *New York Times* determined that the reported data were faulty. The seeming salvation of youth football would instead become a flashpoint for more controversy.)[20] High school associations began requiring medical staff on the sidelines and implementing new protocols for concussion management.

Amid all of this, the exposure in March 2012 of "Bountygate," the New Orleans Saints' team-wide system of paying bounties to players for putting opponents out of the game, which could have been a scandal at any time, in any year, was a sharp reminder that in some neighborhoods of the NFL nothing had changed.[21] Going after the other team's best player was old news; paying blood money was the novelty. And then, in May, Junior Seau's suicide at just forty-three, less than three years after retiring, with the memory of his joyful "reckless abandon" still fresh in the memories of football fans everywhere (followed by the inevitable diagnosis of CTE in December), was the most shocking case yet. (Behind the scenes, Seau's death also marked the most ghoulish scramble for a cadaver among rival CTE research groups.)[22] In November, researchers reported that 3,439 NFL players with at least five credited seasons between 1959 and 1988 had a mortality rate comparable to the public at large but a *neurodegenerative* mortality rate three times higher.[23] Ben McGrath could not have been the only one wondering if football had a future.

The NFL was doing what it could to project an image of committed concern. In September 2012, the league announced a donation of $30 million to the National Institutes of Health for research on concussions, with no strings and a promise of no interference in awarding grants. (Again looking ahead: Even that gesture, and the very real financial substance behind it, would later be tarnished when a congressional committee in 2016 found that the chair of the reconstituted NFL Head, Neck and Spine Committee had submitted his own proposal for the NIH's major $16 million grant from the NFL funds, trying to steer them away from the group at Boston University, which the NFL considered its nemesis in controlling the concussion narrative.[24] Four months later, to repair the damage, the NFL would announce that it would spend another $100 million on new technology and research on head trauma.)[25]

Whether to protect its players or its brand, the NFL seemed to be doing what it could, but how much would be enough?

CHAPTER 8

THE WAR ON FOOTBALL

And how were football fans reacting to all of this? In August 2013, two months before the PBS series *Frontline* aired the documentary version of Mark Fainaru-Wada and Steve Fainaru's *League of Denial*, a conservative journalist named Daniel J. Flynn published a book decrying what his title called *The War on Football. League of Denial* and *The War on Football* framed the NFL's "concussion crisis" in ways as radically different as could be imagined. While the Fainaru brothers laid bare the NFL's "war on science" through its Mild Traumatic Brain Injury Committee, Flynn imagined a "war on football" being waged by self-interested researchers and liberal elites who were overstating the dangers of concussions and CTE for their own benefit, putting a game at risk that was essential to the nation's well-being.[26] In addition to exposing the various individuals and institutions cashing in on what he called "Concussions, Inc.," Flynn targeted "highbrains" like Malcolm Gladwell, who had recently denounced football at a symposium at the University of Maryland as "a dumb and violent nineteenth-century game that serves no educational function," and even President Barack Obama, for his comments reported in the *New Republic* the previous January:

> I'm a big football fan, but I have to tell you if I had a son, I'd have to think long and hard before I let him play football. . . . And I think that those of us who love the sport are going to have to wrestle with the fact that it will probably change gradually to try to reduce some of the violence. In some cases, that may make it a little bit less exciting, but it will be a whole lot better for the players, and those of us who are fans maybe won't have to examine our consciences quite as much.[27]

This was waging *war* on football?! It would be hard to find a more reasonable and nuanced response than Obama's in speaking as both a fan and a parent (albeit of daughters, not a son) at a time of great uncertainty about the game's safety. (In May 2014, President Obama would host a Healthy Kids and Safe Sports Concussion Summit in the East Room of the White House.[28]) And he sounded like Ann McKee, the passionate lifelong Green Bay Packers fan struggling with the significance of what she was finding in former players' brains. Or like the journalist Steve Almond, who would publish his own "reluctant manifesto," *Against Football*, in 2014.[29]

Flynn was particularly concerned about the dire threat to American *boyhood* in the current efforts to "emasculate" a game that he defended with a litany of the arguments for football's necessary roughness since the 1890s. American boys today, he wrote—"overfed, overmedicated, and, to coin a term, underfathered" (a dog whistle to white conservatives)—needed football more than ever. He quoted Walter Camp on the boy who would become a "real man" as one who has "bred in the very marrow of his bones the desire for personal physical combat with boys of his own age on the athletic field." Without naming him, he recast Knute Rockne's rants from the 1920s about lounge lizards and rumble-seat cowboys when he mocked "such superficial trends as chest waxing, perfumed body sprays, skinny jeans, and beta-male sit-com characters" while also worrying more earnestly that "levels of testosterone in American males have been falling rapidly for several decades."[30] The antidote was football, a "game of grit and glory," a "post-industrial passage rite," a "game of the soul" more than the body. Following Camp, Rockne, and innumerable others, Flynn declared, "Football hasn't grown especially hard. Society . . . has grown soft."[31]

In making his case, Flynn at one point defended a controversial Pop Warner coach in Southbridge, Massachusetts, whose website featured the team slogan, "Are you tough enough?" and whose players had left one opposing team with five concussions after a particularly one-sided game. In response to the subsequent uproar, the coach had lambasted his critics for their "further pussification of America."[32] Flynn was a big fan of the coach. Flynn did not so much address the concussion crisis from a different perspective from the Fainaru brothers'; he nearly ignored it altogether. "Concussions can mess with our brains," he acknowledged on the very first page, only to spend the rest of the book avoiding that uncomfortable fact while returning over and over to the decline in football fatalities, or the above-average life expectancy of NFL players, or some other measure of the game's health benefits. He cited a 1994 study by the National Institute for Occupational Safety and Health that found lower rates of various life-threatening ailments among former NFL players, as if those canceled out whatever concussions might be doing. "Football is good for you," he stated bluntly.[33] (Singling out Frank Gifford as an example of a former player's long, happy life, unaware that Gifford was already struggling with dementia, turned out to be grotesquely ironic.) Flynn finally mentioned CTE on page 111, only to dismiss it in four pages as an excuse for the reckless, self-destructive off-field behavior of players like Junior Seau. Flynn here followed in the long tradition of not taking boxers' punch-drunkenness seriously, because they supposedly abused their bodies outside the ring (and, unstated, for being lower-class and usually ethnic or racial outsiders).[34]

Within the long tradition of competing views on football violence, Flynn paid lip service to health (those 1994 NIOSH statistics on lower rates of certain illnesses) but stood staunchly on the side of culture, while the Fainaru brothers focused entirely on damage to health. Flynn's chief concern was *boys'* need for football. "Boyhood isn't a disease to be medicated away," he raged at the beginning of the book. "Boyhood is the age that makes men. Boys need activity and exercise, not Ritalin and Adderall. They need competition and camaraderie. They need direction and discipline. They need male role models. They need fun. They find all this on a football field."[35] Flynn's was just one more voice, though a particularly strident and defensive one, in the long tradition of proclaiming football a necessary tonic for American boys and for American manhood more generally. The figures on boys' football participation cited in chapter 4 can be updated to provide a context here. In 2013, when *The War on Football* was published, 3.6 percent of kids aged six to twelve played organized youth football, and roughly 13 percent (1.09 million of the 8.4 million boys enrolled) played on high school football teams.[36] That was the *American boyhood* imperiled by the loss of football—and a reminder that claims about football's benefits to the nation's manhood always involved a small minority of the country's boys and young men.

On the face of it, it would seem bizarre to politicize head trauma in football, as if the concerns were a liberal conspiracy or conservatives were indifferent to the well-being of their own sons. But this was well into the Bush–Obama era, when Americans were already becoming entrenched in red and blue tribes that dictated much of the "culture" around football. Liberals were *soft*—they wanted to relieve all pain and suffering everywhere, for everyone, at whatever cost. Conservatives were *hard*—they insisted on personal responsibility everywhere, for everyone, at whatever cost. The "war on football" became a trope in conservative media and among conservative commentators. ESPN radio commentator Danny Kanell, a former New York Giants quarterback, "sparked a brush fire" in December 2015, as Nancy Armour put it in *USA Today*, when he posted on Twitter, "The war on football is real. Not sure source but concussion alarmists are loving it. Liberal media loves it." Kanell was apparently responding to an op-ed in the *New York Times* by Bennet Omalu, warning parents to not let their boys play football, or perhaps to the trailers for the film *Concussion* currently playing in theaters.[37] On their radio program, Kanell's ESPN colleague Dan Le Batard reminded him, "The liberal media did not write those suicide notes" left by Dave Duerson and Junior Seau. "Kids are dying." Armour and Justin Tasch of the *New York Daily News* blasted Kanell in their columns.[38]

A month later, Republican presidential candidate Donald Trump told supporters at a rally in Reno that "football has become soft like our country has become soft," and he fumed, "Who wants to watch these crummy games?" now that the NFL had banned "what used to be considered a great tackle, head-on and violent," by the likes of Ray Nitschke, Dick Butkus, and Lawrence Taylor. Trump had stopped watching NFL games, he told the crowd.[39] (His own "war" against the NFL, dating from the 1980s, when owners first denied him a franchise, played out during his presidency chiefly to stir up his base over the league's allowing Black players to kneel during the national anthem and demonstrate for social justice.)[40] In May, Breitbart News called CTE research "'junk science' portending a war on football."[41] In October, at another Trump rally, when a woman returned to the event after fainting, Trump compared her to current NFL players: "See, we don't go by these new, and very much softer, NFL rules. Concussions—'Uh oh, got a little ding on the head? No, no, you can't play for the rest of the season'—our people are tough."[42] As president, Trump ranted again that the NFL was "ruining the game" by making it safer just one day after the announcement that former Patriots tight end Aaron Hernandez had severe CTE when he hanged himself in prison while serving time for murder.[43]

The "war on football" was no more real than the "war on Christmas" being combated by righteous folk at Fox News, but it would continue to fuel conservative outrage against efforts to make football less violent. By 2017, according to the political reporter Mark Leibovich, "to much of the American heartland, in football hotbeds like Pennsylvania, Alabama, and Texas, the game represents a way of life under attack. Fans, coaches, and many players resent the boutique coastal sensibilities that they believe exaggerate the risk of brain injuries."[44] Speakers at USA Football's annual pre–Super Bowl conventions in Orlando in 2017 and 2018 echoed Daniel Flynn's rhetoric about an embattled American institution. Addressing the convention in January 2017, as USA Football was considering "a drastically altered youth football game in response to declining participation and increasing public belief that the game is not safe for children to play," ESPN commentator and former coach Jon Gruden railed against the "geniuses that are trying to damage the game, and ruin the game."[45] At the 2018 convention, "fearful that football could turn into boxing, a once-popular sport that fell off the media map," as Ken Belson reported in the *New York Times*, "USA Football and the N.F.L. are now pushing flag football as a safe way to get children to play some version of the game." The president of the Pro Football Hall of Fame told the coaches in attendance, "If we lose football, we lose a lot in America. . . . I don't know if America can survive." The CEO of the Green Bay Packers added, "I don't want to sound like President Trump, but the liberal media has got football in its cross hairs."[46] These conservative commentators and convention speakers had become a proxy army for an NFL that could not afford their belligerence. And as a public health issue hijacked by ideology (*culture* with a passionate political agenda), CTE anticipated COVID.

Insofar as there was an actual war on football, it was being waged in courtrooms, not in research laboratories or the "liberal media," and not on the game itself but on the organizations and corporations that ran it and profited from it at the expense of the players. In February 2015, as the NFL and NCAA lawsuits were playing out elsewhere, a mother sued the Pop Warner organization three years after her twenty-five-year-old son had committed suicide and was found to have CTE. Joseph Chernach had played Pop Warner from age eleven to fourteen but went on to play in high school, too, which would compromise the culpability of Pop Warner alone. "The case," as the *New York Times* noted when the suit was filed, "has the potential to upend the economics of youth football leagues."[47] Three months later, a player filed a class-action lawsuit against the Illinois High School Association, the first against a state organization, three years after being airlifted to a hospital, unconscious from his second concussion in the same practice scrimmage. In dismissing that case in October, the judge signaled what was at stake, ruling that "football players assume the risk of playing contact sports and that increased liability could harm high school football, potentially even causing it to be abandoned."[48] (Culture trumped health in this judge's courtroom.) Pop Warner settled with the Chernach family in March 2016 for an undisclosed amount,[49] two months after settling a separate suit, originally filed in November 2013 by fifteen-year-old Donnovan Hill, who was left paralyzed from the chest down after a head-first tackle in 2011, and his mother. (Hill died in May 2016 from complications after additional surgery.)[50] Those anonymous fatalities on sandlots in the 1930s had some names and faces in the 2010s.

None of these cases became major national stories, but concern among parents was growing through social media. And the number of NFL players with CTE continued to rise, including Hall of Famers Bubba Smith, Ken Stabler, and Frank Gifford, plus one after another of what would become (as of this writing) six members of the Miami Dolphins' 1972 undefeated team.[51] NFL players still in their prime began retiring early, a dozen or so in 2014–15 alone, including stars like Calvin Johnson, Marshawn Lynch, and Patrick Willis, none yet thirty years old and all relatively injury-free.[52] San Francisco 49ers linebacker Chris Borland sparked the greatest media reaction when he retired in 2015, at the age of twenty-four, after a single breakout rookie season, forgoing the NFL riches that came only with free agency after four years in the league.[53] In 2017, Baltimore Ravens offensive lineman John Urschel retired after three seasons, expressly to save his brain for his PhD program in math at MIT and the long career that would follow.[54] The public could only wonder, When and how will it all end?

By July 2016, 85 percent of the 1,000 adults polled by the UMass Lowell Center for Public Opinion had accepted the scientific proof of a link between CTE and playing football, and 87 percent believed that "CTE is a serious public health issue."[55] In August, as part of *Sports Illustrated*'s annual NFL preview, Austin Murphy envisioned the possible "end of football" and speculated that, should this transpire, future historians would point to 2016 as the watershed year. On March 9, Pop Warner settled its first lawsuit; on March 24, the *New York Times* reported on the MTBI Committee's undercounting of concussions; on June 12, AIG stopped selling insurance for head injuries in both youth football and the NFL; on July 20, the NFL announced Elliot Pellman's departure from "the league's oxymoronic Mild Traumatic Brain Injury Committee"; and on July 27, the *New York Times* reported on the false claims for reducing concussions through Heads Up Football.[56]

And this one disruptive year still had five months to go. Following the *Sports Illustrated* story, on September 1, two more mothers of sons who played Pop Warner football as children and died violently in their twenties with CTE in their brains launched "the broadest challenge yet to youth football," a class-action lawsuit against Pop Warner, USA Football, and the National Operating Committee on Standards for Athletic Equipment (for "certifying helmets that were not designed to properly protect younger players").[57] Kimberly Archie, whose son Paul died at twenty-four in a reckless motorcycle accident, and Jo Cornell, whose son Tyler at twenty-five died by suicide, were not interested in a financial settlement but were on a crusade to end tackle football for boys too young to play it safely.[58] In December, a month before the trial was to begin, a federal judge dismissed their suit on the grounds that they "failed to prove that their sons' deaths were directly linked to head trauma sustained a decade earlier as young players."[59] It was turning out that, among football organizations, only the NFL was at serious risk of legal liability over brain damage from head trauma suffered before, say, 2009, due to the preceding years of denial and misuse of data by its MTBI Committee. But the NFL had settled its players' lawsuit without having to admit culpability.

In July 2017, Ann McKee reported in a study published in the *Journal of the American Medical Association* that she had so far found CTE in the brains of 3 men (out of the 14 she examined) who had not played football beyond high school, in 48 out of 53 who had not played beyond college, and in 110 of 111 former NFL players.[60] McKee was frank about the "tremendous selection bias" in studies limited to individuals whose behavior led their families to request autopsies. But researchers at NYU and Emory University calculated that those 110 cases represented 9.6 percent of all former NFL players who died between February 2008 and May 2016, the time frame of McKee's study. Because others could have died with undiagnosed CTE, 10 percent would be the *minimum* percentage that died with CTE.[61] (Again looking ahead: By February 2023, McKee's tally of former NFL players with CTE would stand at 345, out of 376 autopsied.[62] In September 2024, a Harvard study of 2,000 former NFL players would report that 34 percent of them believed that they had CTE.[63] And the previous December, on the eve of awarding the Heisman Trophy, the *Washington Post* would report that four previous Heisman winners—Howard "Hopalong" Cassady and Paul Hornung from the 1950s and Pat Sullivan and Charles White from the 1970s—had been diagnosed with CTE so far, and others were suspected to have it, joining the many Pro Football Hall of Famers.)[64]

As evidence of the toll on players from the past just kept coming, the great question became whether efforts to make football safer were actually protecting current players. Year-to-year rule changes, beginning in 2009, incrementally made NFL football less violent while still looking very much like football. One set of new rules increased protection for "defenseless players," not just quarterbacks, kickers, and receivers but also long snappers and, eventually, any player who might be blindsided. Another set made kickoffs safer by reducing the number of runbacks (kicking off from the thirty-five-yard line instead of the thirty; moving the ball after a touchback out to the twenty-five instead of the twenty) and by eliminating the "bunch" formation for the kicking team and the "wedge" for the receiving team (the last vestiges of permissible "mass-momentum" football), all of this culminating (for now) in 2024's so-called Dynamic Kickoff, with rules too complicated for summary here. A third set progressively limited the use of the helmet as a weapon and eventually banned "initiating contact with the helmet" altogether.[65]

The NFL (in bargaining with the Players Association) also limited the number and duration of full-contact drills and scrimmages, both in training camps and during the season (while adding a seventeenth game to the schedule, a clear signal of the owners' relative commitment to player health and profits). As noted in chapter 5, in May 2019, the NFL banned the Oklahoma drill, a training camp ritual for many NFL clubs and college teams alike for more than a half century.[66] A writer at ESPN, in 2015, had described the Oklahoma drill as "one part time-honored tradition, one part skill-building exercise, one part utterly insane, head-on car crash." He observed that, "in the post-concussion era, the Oklahoma encapsulates the psychological push and pull of the game—a secretly thrilling and at times sickening three-second snapshot of everything we love and now fear about football."[67] The risk of injuries had already, by 2015, made the Oklahoma drill "cost-prohibitive" for NFL teams (although Jacksonville, Tennessee, and Cincinnati still used it occasionally), but it remained "popular as ever in college" (the writer mentioned Ohio State, LSU, Michigan, and Tennessee), and it was "still a mainstay among high school and peewee players, who are most vulnerable to brain injuries."[68] The NCAA would ban the Oklahoma drill in May 2021, two years after the NFL.[69]

In 2022, the NFL mandated the wearing of padding on the outside of helmets ("Guardian caps") for practices. (The Kansas City Chiefs' Willie Lanier had done this on his own after nearly dying from a subdural hemorrhage as a rookie in 1967.) Two years later, padded caps were permitted in games for those who chose to wear them. With the 2024 season having just concluded, it appeared that just a handful of players wore them, with minimal comment in the press.[70] At the same time, the commissioner and owners continued pushing for an eighteenth regular season game, against the players union's safety concerns, doubling down on their commitment to profits at the risk of player health.[71]

At the college level, in another holdover from the 1950s and 1960s, what the head trainer at the University of Oklahoma in 2018 called "Junction Boy Syndrome" continued in programs where "coaches use offseason workouts as a tool for developing mental and emotional toughness—as a way to inflict physical pain and suffering, the better to push the limits of what their players are willing and able to endure." The trainer, Scott Anderson, had tabulated thirty-three college football deaths from 2000 to 2016, of which just six were from traumatic collisions and twenty-six of the other twenty-seven occurred in the offseason. The death of a player at the University of Maryland in June 2018, after a spring workout, following the hospitalization of three University of Oregon players in January after an offseason session, led to charges of a "toxic culture" at Maryland and an investigation by the university.[72] The intense scrutiny that comes with 24/7 media had made Bear Bryant methods virtually impossible to conduct in secrecy.

By the end of the 2010s, no broadcaster of an NFL game was complaining that referees should just "let the players play." The NFL and Players Association were limiting contact and trying to protect players. Everyone was accepting the reality that football had to be made as safe as possible, particularly regarding head blows. The question had become a simple one: Could the game be safe *enough*?

WHO'S PLAYING TACKLE FOOTBALL NOW?

Because the concussion crisis was playing out not just in the press and partisan media but also on the field and in broadcast booths during NFL games, and even in a feature film, *Concussion*, starring megastar Will Smith as Bennet Omalu in 2015, the public was well aware of the basic issues at least by July 2016, as that UMass poll indicated. A second UMass poll (in partnership with the *Washington Post*), in August 2017, had similar findings: 80 percent believed that repeated brain trauma caused CTE, and 83 percent agreed that football's causing brain injuries was "settled science." That same poll also found that 57 percent of American adults believed football to be safe in high school, while 53 percent felt it unsafe before then. Forty-two percent opposed tackling before age fourteen, 42 percent approved it, and 8 percent opposed it at any age.[73] There was less consensus when the questions became more specific.

Participation in both youth and high school football declined over the 2010s, though not as dramatically as some claimed. According to the Aspen Institute's annual reports on the "State of Play" in the United States, the number of children aged six to twelve playing tackle football fell from 1.045 million in 2010 (3.8 percent of all children in that age group, already a tiny minority) to 1.007 million in 2013 (3.5 percent). After continuing decline and then bumps in 2022 and 2023 following the pandemic, just 758,485 boys were playing, a drop of 27 percent from 2010.[74] But from data reported annually by the National Federation of High School Associations, that 27 percent translated only to a 6.9 percent decline in the number of boys playing eleven-man high school football over the same years (from 1,108,441 in 2010 to 1,031,508 in 2023, after dipping below 1 million in 2021, the first year following two pandemic seasons, for which no data were collected).[75]

Twenty-seven percent is a dramatic falloff; 6.9 percent, over fourteen years, not so much. (The small percentage of all kids playing tackle football, whether in 2023 or in 2010, also lessens the suggestion of a national crisis.) The greater decline in youth football was likely driven by an emerging consensus among researchers that boys should not play tackle football before the age of fourteen, or even twelve. But also, the cultural stakes were higher in the high school sport for parents and communities as well as for the boys playing. Given the supposed *liberal* "war on football" and its defense by conservatives, noting where the declining participation in high school football was sharpest should confirm that divide. The four most populous states in 2022 included blue California (39 million), red Texas (30.6 million), red Florida (22.6 million), and blue New York (19.6 million). Of the four, all but New York were college football recruiting "hotbeds," the top three of which for 2024, according to one website, were the southeastern United States (particularly Florida, Georgia, and Alabama), Texas, and California.[76] For comparison, then, adding red Georgia (#8 in population at 11 million) and, for balance, blue Illinois (#6 at 12.6 million) would create broader samples.

Collectively, total participation in the three blue states declined 20.2 percent from 2009 to 2023: a drop of 14 percent in California, 25.7 percent in Illinois, and 30 percent in New York. Over the same period, it *increased* 4.6 percent overall in the three red states, with a gain of 10,000 boys playing football in Texas (and about 950 in Georgia and 250 in Florida). In 2019, the *New York Times* used data adjusted for population growth in reporting that both Texas and California saw a 10 percent decline in high school football participation from 2009 to 2018.[77] But the 171,246 boys playing in Texas in 2023, up from 161,210 in 2009, compared to 89,667 in California, down from 104,224, seem more meaningful. Comparing participation figures to state populations produces a particularly dramatic measure of high school football's relative thriving in red and blue states. The combined population of the three blue states in 2022 was 71.2 million, of whom 153,359 participated in high school football. Total population of the three red states was 64.2 million, and 242,800 played on high school teams.

Comparing California and Texas as alternate universes has become a parlor game for political commentators in recent years. California had just sixty-nine fewer high schools than Texas reporting participation data to the National Federation of High School Associations in 2023, with a little over half as many boys playing football (89,667 to 171,246). California has had its share of national football powerhouses over the years, but high school football has mattered more in Texas than in California since long before the concussion crisis and long before states became so openly entrenched as red or blue. In 2000, for example, before CTE had been discovered in football players, Texas (population 20.9 million) had 158,321 boys playing high school football, while California (33.9 million) had 97,236; and such numbers barely hint at Texans' legendary obsession with the schoolboy game as a source of community pride and a rite of passage for young boys. In recent years, while countless parents elsewhere were agonizing over football's risks to their young sons, teams in the Texas Youth Football Association were banging heads for four seasons of *Friday Night Tykes* (2014–17) on cable television.

California, on the other hand, first attempted to ban tackle football for kids under twelve in 2018, without getting the bill out of committee. In December 2023, a committee of the state assembly passed such a ban on a 5–2 vote, moving it on to consideration by the full assembly and the senate sometime in the new year. Only in a blue state could such a ban be seriously considered. But even in a blue state, such a ban could be in jeopardy if the governor had national political aspirations. Gavin Newsom almost immediately promised to veto the bill, should it pass.[78]

Red-staters today notoriously reject the science of climate change and COVID vaccines, and the wisdom of "experts" more generally, but skepticism about the science of CTE may be less significant in Texas than what is at stake in high school football there. Thanks to Ken Belson of the *New York Times*, Marshall, Texas, a typical Texas town crazy about its high school football team, offers an instructive case study of the tension between health and cultural values where the football culture is hugely important. In May 2014, after an impassioned presentation about the dangers of CTE by a local retired physician, the school board in Marshall, the county seat of bright-red Harrison County (71 percent for Trump in 2016, 75 percent in 2024), voted unanimously to drop tackle football in the seventh grade, the earliest year it had been available through the public schools. Pop Warner and the Boys and Girls Club in Marshall had been offering tackle football to younger kids, but the Boys and Girls Club had felt the need to add a flag football program the previous year for "parents who aren't comfortable with their child competing in tackle football due to various personal reasons." As Belson recognized when he arrived in Marshall, here was the dilemma facing parents, schools, and communities everywhere, playing out in this East Texas town of 24,000.[79]

It turned out that the local high school coach supported the move, because he felt that the seventh graders were not being properly coached before they got to him. But Marshall was "a one high school town where football is everything," and, as Belson quickly realized, "because it is happening in Texas, an otherwise small move to end a seventh-grade tackle program reflects how the issue of brain trauma has begun to affect the football landscape." Belson's initial story was titled "Football's Risks Sink In, Even in Heart of Texas." But other concerns soon came into play, and two and a half years later, when Belson returned for a follow-up story, his title this time was "Tackle Football Makes a Comeback in the Heart of Texas." Both Pop Warner and the Boys and Girls Club had dropped tackle football altogether since his first visit, for "lack of players" or "potential liabilities." But local parents and coaches in 2016 had created two new tackle football organizations for five-to-twelve-year-olds, each with four teams, picking up the seventh graders who had lost tackle football in the public schools.

What Belson also discovered was that race and economic opportunity were critical factors in saving tackle football in Marshall. "Most of the players on the new tackle teams are African-American," Belson reported, in a town that was 40 percent Black and where Black families' median income was nearly 40 percent lower than whites'. For Black players, "the sport is more often seen as a pathway to eventual prosperity," and football was believed to offer "the best way to toughen youngsters and potentially earn them a college education." Their coaches, nearly all Black, too, encouraged the kids to dream of the NFL, telling them, "The ball there on the ground will take you around the world. It's your ticket." Parents concerned about head trauma were pleased that many of the coaches had taken USA Football's Heads Up course (likely unaware that claims for its safety had been distorted). Here were all of the hopes (and illusions) that kept parents from abandoning the game.[80]

Belson returned to Marshall one last time, three years later, to report that the school board had voted unanimously to bring back seventh-grade football, because fathers had worried that if their sons did not *hit* until eighth grade, they would not be ready for high school. After a flirtation with health concerns, in other words, *culture* (along with economic opportunity) was back in control. As Belson also reported, "In Marshall, residents extol what they see as football's virtues: the discipline and hard work of players who start practicing in the stifling summer heat. They also appreciate the way coaches, through tough love, teach accountability." Black parents and community leaders felt this most strongly. A local Baptist preacher told Belson, "Football has saved a lot of kids. . . . Some people don't want to say that, but that's just the way it is. They become a good football player, they don't want to fail. Football is their way out."[81]

The UMass poll from 2016, which found widespread awareness of CTE in football, also found that 43 percent of whites and Latinos, but just 28 percent of Blacks, were less likely to let their sons play. In the 2017 poll, half of Latinos and Blacks approved of tackling before high school, compared with 38 percent of whites. In December 2023, the *Washington Post* published "The Divided States of Football" series with five articles on youth and high school football in communities in Texas, California, Ohio, and Mississippi that confirmed how participation in youth and high school tackle football has been tied to politics, race, class, and geography.[82] The lead story reported on the paper's latest poll, in April–May 2023, which found that overall approval of football had "barely budged" from a similar poll in 2012 (a decline from 67 to 64 percent).

However, 75 percent of self-identified conservatives would now recommend youth or high school football, but just 44 percent of liberals would—compared to 70 and 63 percent in 2012. The overall participation rate for high school football in states that voted for Donald Trump in 2020 was 1.5 times the rate for states that went for Joe Biden.[83]

Youth football was surviving by turning to flag football (with the full support of the NFL and USA Football). More kids have been playing flag than tackle since 2017; by 2023, the difference was about 1.1 million to 758,485. Those kids playing flag were more likely to live in relatively prosperous white suburbs than in poorer Black urban cores.[84] Whether in Sacramento, Abilene (Texas), Dayton (Ohio), or rural Mississippi, Black kids, poor kids, and kids in traditional "football hotbeds" were disproportionately still committed to playing youth and high school *tackle* football. Whatever the locale, the *Washington Post* writers also consistently found an uneven distribution, tied to realities of race and class, of the financial resources that could make the game safer to play. A brutal irony emerged in the competing realities that poor Black kids needed football more, for access to college and a decent life, while better-off white kids had the well-funded and well-supervised (safer) football programs. Football's future was becoming dependent on boys and young men who had "nowhere else to go."

EPILOGUE

Football's Future

For its 100th anniversary in 2019, the NFL's commemorative volume was again a decade-by-decade history of the league, its most memorable games, and its greatest players, but this time with a foreword by Peyton Manning, a rather different spokesman from Dick Butkus in 1994. Manning described NFL football, for all of its technological advances and increasing sophistication, as "still a battle of wills and a battle of wits," as if it had never been anything like a war.[1] The iconic photograph of Chuck Bednarik celebrating over Frank Gifford reappeared (with a caption absolving him of any foul play), and bruisers from Joe Schmidt, Ray Nitschke, and Dick Butkus to Lawrence Taylor and Ray Lewis were among the featured players, but with no comments on their ferocity. Many of the photographs of football action spoke for themselves—football without *some* violence would not have been football, after all—but the text never dwelled on that fundamental reality.

The NFL took a financial hit during the pandemic but rebounded spectacularly, with $111 billion in new TV rights deals signed in 2021 that extend through 2032–33.[2] If TV viewership is the measure, NFL football has barely been affected by the concussion crisis. In 2010, an average of 17.9 million viewers watched each weekly game. After dips and spikes, falling as low as 14.9 million in 2017 (still far above any other sport), the league averaged that same 17.9 million viewers in 2023, the highest since 2015. A slight decline in 2024, to 17.5 million, was still the second-highest since that year. [3] Viewership did not keep up with the population growth of 30.1 million over these years, but the NFL was holding its own in an increasingly crowded media landscape and continued to eclipse all other programming. Of the top 100 TV broadcasts in the United States in 2023, 93 were NFL games, up from 82 in 2022, 75 in 2021, and 72 in 2020.[4] That number returned to 72 in 2024, another election year, with presidential and vice-presidential debates, along with election-night returns, claiming four of the top eight highest-rated programs.[5]

With 123.7 million viewers, the 2024 Super Bowl was the most-watched ever (with an assist from the pop star Taylor Swift, without whom the game would still have easily topped the previous high of 115.1 million in 2023)—the most-watched *television program*, not just a Super Bowl, ever.[6] For the 2025 Super Bowl the Kelce-Swift romance was old news, and the game, which began as Kansas City's quest for a historic "three-peat," turned into a Philadelphia blowout, with all drama gone by the beginning of the fourth quarter; yet it *still* averaged 127.7 million viewers, a new all-time high.[7] In 2023, *Sunday Night Football* was the highest-rated TV series for the nineteenth consecutive year (since its debut in 2006); *Monday Night Football* was second, and *Thursday Night Football* (on the streaming service Amazon) third.[8] Not everyone follows NFL football today, but with close to half the total population watching some part of the Super Bowl each year, it remains the closest thing to a genuine "mass" culture left in America.

Despite the relative calm off the field that has settled in, an underlying uncertainty about football's future remains. The game's previous crises all passed, but the concussion crisis has been different from the moment that long-term *brain* health was known to be at stake, potentially turning football's long-standing cost-benefit analysis on its head. By now players, parents, and fans can know from research that

- cognitive impairment can result from head blows even without concussion;[9]
- a "second impact" (repeated head blow) is more dangerous than the first one;

- repetitive subconcussive blows can be more dangerous than concussions, and long-term brain damage can result from their accumulation;[10]
- the earlier an NFL player starts playing football, the greater are his chances of later cognitive impairment and CTE;[11]
- the collective force of head hits, not just their cumulative number, increases the odds of developing CTE.[12]

Presumably most unnerving of all, boys and young men who do not play beyond college, or even high school, can develop CTE.[13]

What remains unknown, even to researchers, the journalist Patrick Hruby summed up neatly, though not exhaustively, in the *Washington Post Magazine* in September 2020: "Researchers don't know why some people who suffer repeated head hits develop CTE while others do not. They don't know how many hits are too many. They don't know exactly how the disease first arises, or how and why it spreads across the brain over time. They don't know why individuals develop different symptoms with different levels of severity. They don't know how common CTE is, nor how risky football and other contact sports truly are."[14] To cut to the heart of the matter, researchers do not yet know how many football players at all levels will develop CTE as the game is now played, or whether anything can prevent it, short of not playing. That was in 2020. Researchers have been learning more, but these fundamental questions have not yet been answered.

Consider the uncertainty surrounding the death in December 2021 (from an unrelated cause) of thirty-three-year-old four-time Pro Bowl wide receiver Demaryius Thomas, who was found to have Stage 2 CTE.[15] Or the suicide eight months earlier, after murdering six people, of Phillip Adams, also thirty-three, also found to have Stage 2 CTE.[16] Both Thomas and Adams entered the NFL in 2010, as the league was beginning to institute rules to reduce head impacts. Thomas played ten NFL seasons; Adams, six. One could only wonder whether they had already damaged their brains in their pre-NFL years, or whether, in Adams's case, six NFL seasons on special teams (including two documented concussions) were all that it took to wreak havoc in his brain within six years of leaving the game. Thomas was already demonstrating CTE symptoms barely two years after retiring. Did the new rules not matter? Did they arrive too late?

The most ambitious current research project, designated "Diagnose CTE" and funded by the National Institutes of Health (the $16 million project that the NFL had tried to steer away from researchers at Boston University in 2015),[17] is an "8-year multi-site research project," as the project website describes it, with Boston University's Robert Stern as the lead investigator, and 120 former NFL players, 60 former college players, and 60 healthy controls as the subjects. The website lists six objectives:

- To collect and analyze neuroimaging and fluid biomarkers for the detection of CTE during life.
- To characterize the clinical presentation of CTE.
- To examine the progression of CTE over a three-year period.
- To refine and validate diagnostic criteria for the clinical diagnosis of CTE.
- To investigate genetic and head impact exposure risk factors for CTE.
- To share project data with researchers across the country and abroad in order to expedite growth in our understanding and treatment of this disease.[18]

That initial objective, to find a biomarker for diagnosing CTE in living brain tissue, is what everyone involved or interested in football at any level is waiting for, whether they know it or not. Only then can the extent of the risk of long-term brain damage begin to come into clearer focus. As early as December 2010, Alan Schwarz had reported from the annual meeting of the Radiological Society of North America that a team from Brigham and Women's Hospital in Boston had used MRI scans to detect signs of CTE in five athletes, including three retired NFL players.[19] But that promise of a definitive test proved premature. Periodic reports out of Boston University (in 2017, 2019, and 2021) announced progress by Stern's group,[20] and in November 2022, Ken Belson reported in the *New York Times* that a biomarker "that can be seen in samples of blood, saliva, or spinal fluid or by using brain imaging scans" could be available "in as few as two years."[21] In February 2024, spokespersons for the BU group announced, "Researchers Are One Step Closer to Diagnosing CTE During Life, Rather Than After Death." The researchers' measured "the amount of p-tau pathology across 11 different brain regions in 364 brains with autopsy-confirmed CTE" from BU's brain bank.[22] More research was still needed, but this could be a crucial step toward developing a test that would not instantly solve the mysteries of who develops CTE and how, and how the disease progresses, but would make pursuit of those answers possible. And on those answers could hang football's future.

"Sanctioned savagery" is dead, but NFL football still thrives. With its new TV contracts and the Washington Commanders franchise selling for $6 billion in April 2023, league business has continued as if its future is not in jeopardy. The game's appeal is undiminished. NFL football is still plenty rough but does not depend so much on *spectacular* violence, on Big Hits. A new generation of talented young quarterbacks is filling the air with stunning touchdown passes, aided in part by rules that protect them from most contact and their receivers from at least the most brutal hits. Receivers catching those long pinpoint passes, with one hand or two and feet tapping down just within the sideline, continue to astonish despite how common they have become. The NFL has consciously shifted football's fundamental tension between violence and artistry more toward artistry but without eliminating the essential violence altogether. Under the new concussion protocols and expanded rules on *un*necessary roughness, the best defensive players are no longer the conspicuously toughest but the most skilled (some of them the same players). The NFL's best linebackers today are not like the "headhunters" of yore but large, mobile athletes, fast enough to cover a tight end or running back on long passes, while also strong and quick enough to shed blockers, stop outside running plays, and sack quarterbacks. The best cornerbacks are not intimidators in the Dick "Night Train" Lane/Jack Tatum mold but "lock-down corners" who use their speed, quickness, and intelligence to knock the ball away instead of the receiver's head off. The game that they are playing today is no less thrilling, no less an escape from "the dullness of reality" (or from pandemic-induced inertia or a toxic political and cultural climate), than the one with the periodic explosions of concussive violence. *More* thrilling often, as the transcendent skills of quarterbacks and receivers, cornerbacks and edge rushers can seem more astounding than ever. In the near term, with Donald Trump's return to the White House on a wave of resentment and contempt for "experts," the clamor for resurrecting a "warrior culture" of Big Hits could grow louder, but "America's Game" requires blue as well as red fans (and their disposable income). Football may matter more to conservatives, but it matters to a lot of liberals, too. And the NFL needs both.

Since 2020 or so, college football has been consumed with its own turmoil and mad pursuit of revenues, as if the game's survival were no longer in question: first the expansion of the SEC and Big Ten and then the disappearance of the Pac-12 and the corollary expansion of the Big Twelve, the Atlantic Coast

Conference, and Big Ten again, along with the expansion of the postseason playoffs; plus an agreement to pay athletes in order to avoid a more devastating lawsuit amid the total chaos of players' unlimited free agency through the transfer portal and their right to sell their names, images, and likenesses in an unregulated market. College football faces an uncertain future, to say the least, irrespective of CTE. High school football today languishes or thrives, as dictated by race, economics, politics, and geography. Youth football is surviving on similar terms and by embracing flag football.

But with all the rules and regulations to make it safer, is tackle football now or will it ever be safe enough? Testing for CTE in current high school, college, and NFL players would be instantly revealing, but finding a reliable biomarker would only begin to solve the mysteries of CTE. Longitudinal studies of players at all ages and levels would have to be conducted. Will evidence of CTE appear immediately with head trauma, or be delayed? If delayed, for how long? Once CTE is present, will debilitating symptoms appear immediately, or be delayed? Will the disease always progress, even in the absence of additional head trauma? Beyond numbers of seasons played and head blows absorbed, who will be more vulnerable, and why? Answers to these questions will be probabilities, not certainties; pertaining to groups, not individuals; regarding symptoms that might not appear for many years. In short, they will depend on *science*. A large number of Americans have given up cigarettes because of smokers' greater likelihood of contracting lung cancer. Others have not. Those who give up smoking are likely to be better off financially, to have more to live for, than those who do not. Trust in or distrust of science, along with the more recent scorn of "experts" of all kinds, could also affect decisions about CTE, as could the presence or absence of life opportunities.

Among those who would absolutely trust science would be insurance companies, who might be the ones to determine football's future at all levels below the NFL. But if players and parents would have a say, what will it be? How much risk will they be willing to take, if/when the risks are more clearly but not completely known? I became accustomed to thinking, as CTE was being discovered in the brains of more and more former players, that we now know that football is riskier, in more insidious ways, than we ever knew before—though just how risky to how many, we do not know—and I have wondered, When we know more, how will we respond? But in recent years, I have become acutely aware that the "we" in those sentences is a fiction, implying a consensus that does not exist (and never did) and that ignores our racial, class, gender, geographic, and personal diversity, further complicated by a corrosive red/blue political divide.

Football's concussion crisis has become a full-blown public health issue, due not just to the risk for so many boys and young men but also to the financial burden it places on the health system. At the same time, football continues to have its cultural power for players, parents, and fans. Football survived its earlier crises but with less at stake. Whether it will survive this one remains uncertain for now. As researchers begin answering fundamental questions about CTE, parents will weigh their new information against their families' continuing needs and values. Schools and sports organizations (if insurers have not decided for them) might have to weigh ethics against economics. Since the NFL's business is to make money, not raise children or educate them, it could survive as long as there were enough large and skilled athletes to play the game (most likely attracting predominantly poor and minority kids with "nowhere else to go") and fans to keep it profitable. Reassuring themselves that NFL players are well paid and "know what they're getting into" (as one often hears today), could fans keep watching what they know to be literally, not metaphorically, a gladiatorial game?

When the *New Yorker*'s Ben McGrath interviewed Chris Nowinski in 2011, after estimating that at least 20 percent of the NFL's current players would develop CTE, Nowinski wondered aloud, "What number is going to be the tipping point" for fans when the actual figure is known? "They may look sideways at ten per cent," Nowinski ventured. "Maybe it needs to be fifty percent."[23] In September 2014, as part of the legal proceedings in the players' lawsuit against the NFL, the league submitted findings from its own commissioned actuarial study, which, as the Associated Press reported, projected that 28 percent of "former players will develop debilitating brain conditions, and that they will be stricken earlier and at least twice as often as the general population."[24] That was before the NFL dramatically changed the rules on helmet contact. If scientists ever reach a point where they can calculate the risks for high schoolers, for collegians, for professionals, what number will "we" accept?

NOTES

ABBREVIATIONS

AP	Associated Press
BG	*Boston Globe*
FWST	*Fort Worth Star-Telegram*
JAMA	*Journal of the American Medical Association*
LH	*Lexington Herald*
NYDN	*New York Daily News*
NYT	*New York Times* (*New York* was hyphenated until December 1894, after the newspaper had been purchased by Adolph Ochs.)
NYW	*New York World*
PM	*Parents' Magazine*
SEP	*Saturday Evening Post*
SS	*Sport Story*
WP	*Washington Post*

INTRODUCTION

1. Frank Litsky, "Mike Webster, 50, Dies; Troubled Football Hall of Famer," *NYT*, September 9, 2002.

2. For a very different approach, see the sport sociologist Dominic Malcolm's overview of the scholarship on the concussion crisis in the English-speaking world, *The Concussion Crisis in Sport* (London: Routledge, 2020).

3. Drew Gilpin Faust, "The Men Who Started the Civil War," *Atlantic*, December 2023. Faust was writing about the morally necessary violence of John Brown's raid on Harpers Ferry in contrast to the violent terrorism unleashed on Black Americans after the collapse of Reconstruction.

CHAPTER 1

1. “Mighty Savage Football,” *New York Sun*, November 28, 1884. Quotes in the next few paragraphs are from this source.

2. Parke H. Davis, *Football: The American Intercollegiate Game* (New York: Scribner’s, 1911), 467.

3. For the details here from the early conventions, see the appendix to Davis’s *Football*, 461–505 (the citations are from 467, 468, 470, 472, 473, 474–75, and 475). Camp also printed the rules from the 1876 convention (along with subsequent revisions and the complete rules for the 1887 season) in “The Game and Laws of American Football,” *Outing*, October 1887, 76–85.

4. Davis, *Football*, 469, 470, 471.

5. Davis, *Football*, 84.

6. Davis, *Football*, 87.

7. Davis, *Football*, 87.

8. “Intercollegiate Slugging,” *BG*, November 26, 1884 (editorial).

9. Eugene L. Richards Jr., “Foot-ball in America,” *Outing*, April 1885.

10. “Fighting at Football,” *NYW*, November 25, 1883.

11. See John Sayle Watterson, *College Football: History, Spectacle, Controversy* (Baltimore: Johns Hopkins University Press, 2000), 23–38. Eliot’s comments on football in his annual reports to Harvard’s Board of Overseers were often picked up by newspapers and repeatedly condemned the element of “violent personal collision” in football as a factor that disqualified it as a proper intercollegiate sport. See, for example, “President Eliot’s Report,” *BG*, February 25, 1885; “Athletics at Harvard,” *BG*, January 25, 1888; and “President Eliot on Sports,” *Baltimore Sun*, February 21, 1894.

12. “Fighting at Football,” *NYT*, November 29, 1884.

13. “Yale Outplays Princeton,” *NYT*, November 28, 1886. This was a subhead.

14. “Wesleyan’s Football Sluggers,” *NYT*, November 20, 1887; “Making It a Game for Gentlemen,” *NYT*, November 27, 1887.

15. “Rough Play at Football,” *NYT*, October 23, 1890; “Fighting Football Players,” *NYT*, October 18, 1891; “Rough Play Won the Game,” *NYT*, November 27, 1891.

16. “Yale Wins a Glorious Day,” *New York Sun*, November 25, 1887 (“A Minimum of Slugging”); “Victory for Yale,” *New York Sun*, November 26, 1893 (“Captain Hinkey Did No Slugging but Kept Wrangling with the Officials”); “What the Players Say,” *NYT*, December 1, 1893 (noting “the absence of slugging and unmanly interference”); “Will Not Be a ‘Slugging’ Game,” *NYT*, November 29, 1894 (the vow of Harvard’s players preparing for Penn; just “one exhibition of slugging” occurred, “and that a mild one”); “Yale, 24, Princeton, 0,” *NYT*, December 3, 1894 (“A Contest Free from ‘Slugging’”); “Not a Brutal Game,” *NYT*, December 3, 1894 (a minister’s judgment of the same contest); “Old Eli’s Waterloo,” *New York Sun*, November 22, 1896 (“No Signs of Slugging and Only Four Men Slightly Injured”).

17. *New York Evening World*, November 19, 1889, and November 28, 1891.

18. *NYT*, November 28, 1891.

19. Quoted in Dave Revsine, *The Opening Kickoff: The Tumultuous Birth of Football Nation* (Guilford, CT: Lyons Press, 2014), 97. Revsine’s source is Amos Alonzo Stagg’s 1927 autobiography.

20. See, for example, D. B. St. John Roosa's and I. G. Schurman's contributions to "Are Foot-Ball Games Educative or Brutalizing?," *The Forum*, January 1894; Caspar Whitney, "Amateur Sport," *Harper's Weekly*, December 12, 1896 ("the sensation-mongers of the 'new journalism'"); Charles F. Thwing, "Football: Is the Game Worth Saving?," *The Independent*, May 15, 1902; and Edwin G. Dexter, "Newspaper Football," *Popular Science Monthly*, March 1906.

21. Davis, *Football*, 84.

22. Davis, *Football*, 84.

23. Revsine, *Opening Kickoff*, 39.

24. "Proud Blue," *BG*, November 20, 1892.

25. "Rah! Rah! Rah! Yale!," *NYT*, November 20, 1892.

26. Davis, *Football*, 96–97.

27. For several examples, see "To Yale Belong the Flags," *NYW*, November 25, 1887; "Yale's Blue Kickers Win," *New York Sun*, November 28, 1890; "Yale Feels Better Now," *NYW*, November 28, 1890; "Princeton Tigers Beaten 19 to 0, but They Did Fight Splendidly," *NYW*, November 27, 1891; "Harvard's Football Team Beaten Six to Nothing," *NYW*, November 20, 1892; "Is It Harvard or Yale?," *New York Sun*, November 25, 1893; Edgar Saltus, "Rome Brought Up to Date" ("Gladiators Battling in an Arena before Patricians and Plebians"), *New York Journal*, November 22, 1896; "Yale-Princeton Gossip," *New York Tribune*, November 29, 1896; "Death on the Football Field," *New York Herald*, November 13, 1897; Langdon Smith, "Grand Though Indecisive Struggle between Harvard and Yale," *New York Journal and Advertiser*, November 14, 1897; "Gladiators Ready," *New York Herald*, November 19, 1897; "Two Great Football Battles Will Be Fought This Afternoon on College Fields," *NYW*, November 20, 1897; "Quakers Claim Championship," *NYW*, November 21, 1897. The most over-the-top ones were the *World*'s from November 27, 1891, and the ones for the Hearst papers by Edgar Saltus in 1896 and Langdon Smith in 1897.

28. Godkin's editorials in the *New York Evening Post* were reprinted in the *Post*'s weekly magazine, *The Nation*. See, from *The Nation*, "The Glorification of Athletics," December 1, 1892; "Football Again," November 30, 1893; "The Athletic Craze," December 7, 1893; "The New Football," November 29, 1894; "Athletics and Health," December 20, 1894; and "Football and Manners," December 27, 1894. Eliot's attacks on football, in his annual addresses to Harvard's Board of Overseers, were reprinted in the *Harvard Graduates' Magazine* and excerpted in the Boston press (sometimes picked up by other papers). On Eliot as "Football's First Big-Time Critic," see Watterson, *College Football*, 27–29.

29. Philip Poindexter, "A First Glimpse at Foot-Ball," *Frank Leslie's Illustrated Newspaper*, December 8, 1892.

30. Theodore Roosevelt, "The Value of an Athletic Training," *Harper's Weekly*, December 23, 1893.

31. See, for example, "Are Foot-Ball Games Educative or Brutalizing?," *The Forum*, January 1894; and J. William White and Horatio C. Wood, "Intercollegiate Football," *North American Review*, January 1894.

32. Eugene Lamb Richards, "The Football Situation," *Popular Science Monthly*, October 1894.

33. "President Eliot on Sports," *Baltimore Sun*, February 21, 1894. The report was published in its entirety in the *Harvard Graduates' Magazine*, March 1894.

34. Richards, "Football Situation."

35. "Athletics and Health," *The Nation*, December 20, 1894. Editorials were unsigned.

36. Davis, *Football*, 487.

37. Walter Camp, *Football Facts and Figures* (New York: Harper Brothers, 1894), 59. For discussions of Camp's book, see Ronald A. Smith, *Sports and Freedom: The Rise of Big-Time College Athletics* (New York: Oxford University Press, 1988), 92–93; Watterson, *College Football*, 33–35; and Roger R. Tamte, *Walter Camp and the Creation of American Football* (Urbana: University of Illinois Press, 2018), 178–80.

38. See Camp, *Football Facts and Figures*, 90, 180, and 204.

39. Smith, *Sports and Freedom*, 92–93. Following Smith, as the concussion crisis was unfolding, the public health historian Emily Harrison described a letter in Camp's papers in which he had "crossed out in crayon" a description of a head injury that did not appear in the published book, leaving only the player's effusions about "one of the grandest" of games. Emily A. Harrison, "The First Concussion Crisis: Head Injury and Evidence in Early American Football," *American Journal of Public Health*, May 2014, 824–25.

40. Caspar Whitney, Amateur Sport (column), *Harper's Weekly*, December 1, 1894.

41. See his attack on E. L. Godkin in Camp's *Facts and Figures*, 29–31, reprinted from his column.

42. Caspar Whitney, Amateur Sport (column), *Harper's Weekly*, November 4, 1893.

43. See, for example, "Yale Again Triumphant," *NYT*, November 25, 1894 ; "Yale 12, Harvard 4" ("Game at Times Was Rough, and Many Men Were Injured, Murphy of Yale Seriously"), *BG*, November 25, 1894; "A Gentle and Joyous Game," *NYT*, December 1, 1894; "The Crisis in Football," *Christian Advocate* (New York), December 6, 1894; "Encouraging Athletics," *New York Observer*, December 13, 1894.

44. Caspar Whitney, Amateur Sport (column), *Harper's Weekly*, December 8, 1894.

45. Lodge's remarks were transcribed in "Commencement.—The Alumni Dinner," *Harvard Graduates' Magazine*, September 1896, 67.

46. W. Cameron Forbes, "The Football Coach's Relation to the Players," *Outing*, December 1900.

47. The best-known of the earliest Black players are William Henry Lewis at Amherst and Harvard, George Jewett at Michigan, George Flippin at Nebraska, Matthew Bullock at Dartmouth, and William Clarence Matthews at Harvard, but a few others who played in the Midwest have been identified in recent years. See Jordan James, "First Black Player in History of Major College Football Programs," *247 Sports*, February 13, 2018, https://247sports.com/gallery/black-history-month-first-black-player-for-major-college-football-programs-115102938/.

48. Richard Henry Pratt, *Battlefield and Classroom: Four Decades with the American Indian, 1867–1904*, ed. Robert M. Utley (New Haven, CT: Yale University Press, 1964), 317–19. See Matthew Bentley, "Playing White Men: American Football and Manhood at the Carlisle Indian School, 1893–1904," *Journal of the History of Childhood and Youth* 32 (2010): 188–209; and my *Reading Football: How the Popular Press Created an American Spectacle* (Chapel Hill: University of North Carolina Press, 1993), 235–47.

49. *NYW*, November 29, 1895.

50. The short, spectacular history of the football teams from the Carlisle Indian Industrial School has been thoroughly chronicled. See also John Bloom, *What an Indian Can Do: Sports at Native American Boarding Schools* (Minneapolis: University of Minnesota Press, 2000); Sally Jenkins, *The Real All-Americans: The Team That Changed a Game, a People, a Nation* (New York: Doubleday, 2007); and Matthew Bentley and John Bloom, *The Imperial Gridiron: Manhood, Civilization, and Football at the Carlisle Indian Industrial School* (Lincoln: University of Nebraska Press, 2022), which was Bentley's PhD dissertation, accepted for publication, and then completed by Bloom after Bentley's death in 2018.

51. For an early example, see the cover of *Puck* by CJT (Charles J. Taylor), November 30, 1892.

52. Davis, *Football*, 92.

53. Spalding first advertised "Morrill's Nose Mask" in its 1891 *Spalding's Official Football Guide* (New York: A. G. Spalding & Bros., 1891); the annual publication was "revised" each year by Walter Camp. (The Poe cited in the ad was the second of six brothers, distant cousins of the famous author, who played for Princeton from 1882 through 1901.) The ad in the 1893 edition credited Harvard captain Arthur Cummock for conceiving it and John Morrill of Boston for patenting it. The ads continued to appear through the 1921 edition.

54. See *Spalding's Official Foot Ball Guide*, 1891; *Spalding's Official Foot Ball Guide*, revised by Walter Camp (New York: American Sports Publishing, 1892).

55. See Chris Hornung, "Who Invented the Football Helmet," January 15, 2017, AntiqueFootball.com, www.antiquefootball.com/who_invented_football_helmet.htm, which has photographs of both Naismith and Reeves in their head gear. The photo of Reeves is cropped from a team photo that can be seen on NCAA.com, in which Reeves cradles a ball marked "'94" (www.ncaa.com/news/football/article/2022-12-10/army-navy-football-memorable-moments-all-time-history). Rather than discrediting the 1893 date, 1894 would have been Reeves's senior year at the academy and could have been his second season of wearing the padded cap.

56. See *Spalding's Official Foot Ball Guides* for 1895–99, "edited" now (not "revised") by Camp and all published by American Sports Publishing in New York. The 1908 *Guide* advertised five different models: three skullcaps, two with straps; two of the caps were made from "soft black leather" and one from "firm tanned black leather, molded to shape." The strap style disappeared after 1917. Many thanks go to Gregory Bond, curator of the Joyce Sports Research Collection at the Hesburgh Libraries, University of Notre Dame, for tracking down many of these helmet ads for me.

57. Harry Beecher, "Football Player of '97 Armored Like a Knight of Old," *NYW*, October 17, 1897.

58. "Open" and "mass" play might seem analogous to "boxing" and "slugging" in prizefighting, except that mass play delivered no decisive blow, and open play required less fine-tuned practice than mass play and involved hard tackles. "Sanctioned savagery" manifested itself differently in the two sports.

59. "The Injured Players—None of Them Will Die," *New York Evening World*, October 23, 1897.

60. "Death on the Football Field," *New York Herald*, November 13, 1897. Also from the *Herald*: "Is Football under the Ban?," November 8, 1897; "Blow to Football," November 9, 1897; "Football's Future," November 10, 1897; "Death Caused by Football," November 11, 1897; "Another May Die; Game Goes On," November 12, 1897.

61. "Fierce Struggle Ends in a Tie," *New York Herald*, November 14, 1897.

62. "James J. Corbett Declares That Football Is More Brutal and Dangerous Than Prize-Fighting," *NYW*, November 14, 1897.

63. "'Cruel,' Says a Bull-Fighter," *NYW*, November 21, 1897.

64. *New York Evening World*, November 10, 1897.

65. "The Hero of the Hour," *New York Herald*, November 13, 1897.

66. Christopher C. Meyers, "'Unrelenting War on Football': The Death of Richard Von Gammon and the Attempt to Ban Football in Georgia," *Georgia Historical Quarterly* 93 (Winter 2009): 388–407.

67. David M. Nelson, *Anatomy of a Game: Football, the Rules, and the Men Who Made the Game* (Cranberry, NJ: Associate University Presses, 1994), 484–85 and 439 for the helmets and padding.

68. Editorial (untitled), *New York Tribune*, November 10, 1900, 8.

69. Charles F. Thwing, "The Ethical Functions of Foot-Ball," *North American Review*, November 1901, 627–31.

70. Caspar Whitney, "The Sportsman's View-Point," *Outing*, January 1902, January 1903, and January 1904. In January 1905, Whitney returned to his complaints about "battering ram" football, not because it was more dangerous than open play but because "it tends to lessen individual knowledge and skill and therefore to retard the development of the game and to make it less interesting."

71. Roosevelt's best-known and most-quoted speeches and essays include "The Strenuous Life," originally a speech in 1899 and then published in 1900 in a collection of his speeches and writings under the same title, and "The American Boy" in the juvenile magazine *St. Nicholas*, March 1900. Roosevelt's role in the 1905 football crisis has been often retold, most fully in John L. Miller's *The Big Scrum: How Teddy Roosevelt Saved Football* (New York: Harper Collins, 2011), whose subtitle points to his overstating of Roosevelt's role, a claim that became dogma for football's conservative defenders in the face of a "war on football" waged by the liberal elites, to be discussed in chapter 8. Casting Roosevelt as an enemy of the "elites" of his day (his own class, whose interests football was meant to serve, in his view), in order to make him a proper conservative for 2011, unfortunately undermines a well-researched book.

72. Theodore Roosevelt, "The Harvard Spirit," *Harvard Graduates' Magazine*, September 1905.

73. "Professor" Mike Donovan was a former prizefighter who became a boxing instructor at the New York Athletic Club and taught Roosevelt to box. He sparred with Roosevelt as both governor of New York and president. After Roosevelt left the White House, Donovan published a book on their relationship, *The Roosevelt That I Know* (New York: B. W. Dodge, 1909).

74. See Watterson, *College Football*, 166–68. The author of the *McClure's* articles (June and July 1905), Henry Beach Needham, was a friend of Roosevelt's.

75. "Hears Football Men," *WP*, October 10, 1905.

76. "Fair Football," *BG*, October 12, 1905.

77. "Can a Gentleman Play Football?," *NYW*, magazine section, November 5, 1905.

78. "Coach Reid on Football," *BG*, November 9, 1905. And see Revsine, *Opening Kickoff*, 191–92. Reid's statement was published in papers around the country.

79. These were the accounts on the *front* page of the *New York Evening World* and *New York Tribune* (the *New York Herald* relegated it to sports but with a photograph of Junior conferring with his coaches). A subhead in the *Evening World* declared, "Though Light in Weight He Proved Spirit in Yale-Harvard Contest." The *Tribune* noted that "Roosevelt weighed only 145 pounds and was lighter than any man on the Yale team."

80. "Roosevelt, Jr., Knocked Out in Hot Game," *New York Evening World*, November 18, 1905; "Yale Downs Roosevelt," *New York Tribune*, November 19, 1905; "Teddy, Jr., in Strenuous Game," *New York Herald*, November 19, 1905; "President's Son as Sample 'Victim' of Football Game," *NYW*, November 20, 1905. The *Tribune* had separate stories on the game and on Ted Jr., both on the front page.

81. *BG*, November 26, 1905.

82. "Sound Knell of Brutal Football," *Chicago Daily Tribune*, November 27, 1905.

83. "Favor Revision of Rules," *NYT*, November 27, 1905; "Football Reform by Abolition," *The Nation*, November 30, 1905; "Football Reform by Abolition," *Literary Digest*, December 9, 1905. *The Nation* in this period was a weekly literary supplement to the *New York Evening Post* and had been regularly calling for the abolition of football since the early 1890s. The *Literary Digest* aggregated stories on timely topics from newspapers around the country, in this case from the *Evening Post*. The reprintings of Matthews's statement appeared in a slightly different form from the *Tribune*'s, presumably as it was drafted by the *Tribune* for syndication. The comments on virility, courage, and war were in the reprintings.

84. The Big Game became a rugby match through 1914, along with contests with club teams in British Columbia and the Bay Area and visits from the Australian Waratahs in 1912 and the New Zealand All Blacks in 1913. See Robert J. Park, "From Football to Rugby—and Back, 1906–1919: The University of California–Stanford University Response to the 'Football Crisis of 1905,'" *Journal of Sport History* 11 (Winter 1984): 5–40.

85. "Move to Oust Camp," *New York Tribune*, November 27, 1905. On January 9, 1906, as the committee that would revise the rules was struggling into being, the *NYT* reported why the new committee had agreed not to abolish unanimous consent: "The trouble is again of Yale's making. It is a statement that Walter Camp is determined not to abandon the one-man veto rule, which in operating in the past meant one-man domination, with Walter Camp in the position of dictator. It is a well-known fact that football men at Yale, in spite of Camp's professions to the contrary, do not want to see any changes in the rules that will alter the present style of the game, and Harvard's practical threat to abandon the game if there be no changes has not scared Yale." See "Changes in Football Promise a Dead-Lock," *NYT*, January 9, 1906. The committee, in fact, would soon drop the requirement.

86. The fourteen members represented Harvard, Yale, Princeton, and Penn but also Army, Navy, Cornell, Dartmouth, and Haverford in the East; Nebraska, Chicago, Minnesota, and Oberlin in the "West" (as the Midwest was regarded at the time); and the University of Texas, designated to represent southern colleges. This is how the

committee was presented in Walter Camp, ed., *Spalding's Official Football Guide 1906* (New York: American Sports Publishing, 1906).

87. The new committee elected a chairman from Camp's old committee and a secretary (Camp's long-entrenched position) from Haverford, who immediately resigned and named Reid to replace him. When the group then agreed that legislation would be passed by a two-thirds majority, in a stroke Camp became just another member of the committee. See "Football Coalition Is Finally Secured," *NYT*, January 13, 1906. For the maneuverings of the new and old rules committees and Harvard's threat to go it alone, see Tamte, *Walter Camp*, chaps. 44 and 45.

88. From the *NYT*: "New Football Game Shaped by Committee," January 28, 1906; "New Football Game Not Yet Completed," February 11, 1906; "Football Reform Code Has Been Completed," March 4, 1906; "Football Committee Announces New Rules," April 1, 1906; "New Football Rules Phrased and Codified," April 15, 1906.

89. *Spalding's Official Football Guide 1906*, 121–22.

90. *Spalding's Official Football Guide 1906*, 93-96.

91. "New Football Rules Phrased and Codified"; *Spalding's Official Football Guide 1906*, 105, 94.

92. *Spalding's Official Football Guide 1906*, 138–39.

93. "Timely Sporting Topics," *New York Tribune*, April 30, 1906. The *Tribune* reported that the goal of the committee, according to W. T. Reid, was "to so legislate that mass plays of the old hammer and tongs variety would be unprofitable and an open game possible. . . . Fortunately the tactical beauties of the game, which by the way are its strongest features, have been retained and the football general will still be quite as essential as speed and courage and brawn."

94. Caspar Whitney, "Football for 1906," *Outing*, September 1906.

CHAPTER 2

1. Ronald A. Smith, "The NCAA Concussions, and the Lack of Concern for Athletes," *Journal of Sport History* 51, no. 2 (Summer 2024): 16.

2. Edward H. Nichols and Homer B. Smith, "The Physical Aspect of American Football," *Boston Medical and Surgical Journal*, January 4, 1906; "Injuries in Football at Harvard," *BG*, January 5, 1906.

3. "Surgical Aspects of Football," *JAMA*, January 13, 1906, 122–23. The author was presumably George Simmons, *JAMA*'s editor at the time.

4. See Stephen T. Casper, "Punch-Drunk Slugnuts: Violence and the Vernacular History of Disease," *Isis*, June 1922, 266–88; Emily A. Harrison, "The First Concussion Crisis: Head Injury and Evidence in Early American Football," *American Journal of Public Health*, May 2014, 822–33; and particularly Kathleen Bachynski, *No Game for Boys to Play: The History of Youth Football and the Origins of a Public Health Crisis* (Chapel Hill: University of North Carolina Press, 2019). Harrison discusses the medical establishment's response to the 1905 crisis.

5. On Camp experimenting with the forward pass at Yale, see Roger R. Tamte, *Walter Camp and the Creation of American Football* (Urbana: University of Illinois Press, 2018), 254–55.

6. After the season, Walter Camp recruited Cochems to write the chapter "The Forward Pass and On-Side Kick" for the 1907 edition of *Spalding's How to Play Football*, with photographs of Robinson to illustrate the possible passing techniques—the overhand spiral (Cochems's preference) or the underhand toss (either end-over-end or with fingers on the laces). Even with the overhand spiral, the photographs show a ball more cradled than gripped. Tight spirals and pinpoint accuracy were decades away. See *Spalding's How to Play Football*, ed. Walter Camp (New York: American Sports Publishing, 1907), 43–52; and Tamte, *Walter Camp*, 250–56.

7. John Sayle Watterson, *College Football: History, Spectacle, Controversy* (Baltimore: Johns Hopkins University Press, 2000), 401 (a table of fatalities from 1905 to 1916).

8. Caspar Whitney, "The View-Point," *Outing*, January 1907 and January 1908. For 1908, Whitney turned the review over to Glenn "Pop" Warner, the coach of the Carlisle Indians, who limited himself to the tactical advances and challenges of the season; see "The View-Point," *Outing*, January 1909. Whitney left *Outing* shortly after.

9. "Football Mortality among Boys," *JAMA*, December 21, 1907, 2088. (*JAMA*'s fatality figures were slightly different from the ones that Watterson summed up.) Bachynski took her title, *No Game for Boys to Play*, from this editorial. *JAMA* also published editorials on football fatalities and injuries in 1902 ("The Football Mortality," December 6); 1904 ("The Football Fatalities and Injuries of 1903," January 30); 1905 ("Brutality of Football," October 21; and "Football and Its Dangers," November 25); 1906 ("Surgical Aspects of Football," January 13; "Football Fatalities," October 6; "Improvement in Football Pathology," December 8); and 1908 ("Football Casualties," December 19), but then no more until 1931 (following Cadet Sheridan's death).

10. "The Deadly Mass Play," *NYT*, November 2, 1909.

11. "A National Menace," *Washington Evening Star*, November 1, 1909.

12. *BG*, November 14, 1909.

13. See, for example, "University Player Crushed in Game Dies from Injuries," *Washington Herald*, November 14, 1909.

14. "The World of Sport," *Outing*, January 1910. (Camp's preceding piece was "Football in 1909.")

15. "Football Pivot Is Forward Pass," *NYT*, February 7, 1910.

16. "Forward Pass Is Left in Football," *NYT*, May 14, 1910; "Alterations in Rules for 1910," in *Spalding's Official Foot Ball Guide for 1910*, ed. Walter Camp (New York: American Sports Publishing, 1910), 142–43.

17. "Alterations in Rules for 1912," in *Spalding's Official Foot Ball Guide*, ed. Walter Camp (New York: American Sports Publishing, 1912), 89.

18. In 1915, a pass out of bounds became a loss of down, not a loss of ball. In 1938, incompletions in the end zone no longer meant loss of the ball. In 1945, passing from anywhere behind the line of scrimmage (rather than at least five yards behind it) became legal. Also, in 1934, the circumference of the ball was reduced to make accurate passing easier. See David M. Nelson, *Anatomy of a Game: Football, the Rules, and the Men Who Made the Game* (Cranberry, NJ: Associated University Presses, 1994), 448–49.

19. "Football in 1911," *Outing*, January 1912.

20. The first novel known to have a description of a true football game was Mark Sibley Severance's *Hammersmith: His Harvard Days* (Boston: Houghton, Osgood, 1878),

but before that William T. Washburn's *Fair Harvard: A Story of American College Life* (New York: G. P. Putnam & Sons, 1869) had an opening chapter with a series of three frosh-soph (presumably "Bloody Monday") "foot-ball" matches, and George Henry Tripp's *Student-Life at Harvard* (Boston: Lockwood, Brooks, 1876) had a chapter on "Bloody Monday," the annual freshman initiation ritual with the two sides with indeterminate numbers trying to kick a ball over the other's goal. This was the last vestige of the harum-scarum sport, dating back to medieval Britain, that became organized into football in the nineteenth century in England and then the United States. The point of "Bloody Monday," or the similar ritual with other names at other colleges, was for the freshmen to prove themselves against the sophomores at the beginning of the school year, or for the sophomores to establish their superiority. College novels in the 1890s and early 1900s invariably continued to have a chapter on the frosh initiation ritual or an actual intercollegiate football game. See John Seymour Wood, *College Days, or Harry's Career at Yale* (New York: Outing, 1894); James Barnes, *A Princetonian: A Story of Undergraduate Life at the College of New Jersey* (New York: G. P. Putnam's Sons, 1896); Jesse Lynch Williams, *The Adventures of a Freshman* (New York: C. Scribner's Sons, 1899); Richard Holbrook, *Boys and Men: A Story of Life at Yale* (New York: C. Scribner's Sons, 1900); Reginald Wright Kauffman, *Jarvis of Harvard* (Boston: L. C. Page, 1901); and Joy Lichtenstein, *For the Blue and Gold: A Tale of Life at the University of California* (San Francisco: A. M. Robertson, 1901), a story about James Hopper's alma mater. Football had a significant place in college life and thus in the fiction about college life from early on.

21. Football stories for boys also appeared in 1894: A. T. Dudley, "The Generous Side," *St. Nicholas*, November 1894; and Jesse Lynch Williams, "The Scrub Quarterback," *Harper's Young People*, November 23, 1894.

22. Frank Norris, "Travis Hallett's Half-Back," *Overland Monthly*, January 1894.

23. See, for example, Edwin Oviatt, "'89—2—5,'" *Frank Leslie's Popular Monthly*, December 1902; and Edward Felton Wheaton, "Celebrity Baldwin: A Football Story of the Cardinal and Blue and Gold," *Sunset*, November 1903.

24. James Hopper, "The Strength of the Weak: The Story of the Full-Back Who Got Used to It," *SEP*, October 22, 1904. Quotes in the next few paragraphs are from this story.

25. The football player as "knight," consecrating himself to Alma Mater before the big game, was a motif in several of Hopper's football stories. See "The Passing of the Vet," *McClure's*, November 1904; "The Idealist," *SEP*, October 14, 1905; and "The Freshman," *SEP*, September 9–30, 1911 (a three-part serial). He also wrote about this sense of holy duty to Alma Mater in a nonfiction account, "The Last Grind for the Big Game" (*Everybody's Magazine*, November 1911), in which, at the team's retreat, "the boy" who has made the team feels "like the novice of the Middle Ages about to be knighted . . . consecrating himself" on his cot in his room.

26. See, for example, William Almon Wolff, "Time Enough, Damn You," *Leslie's Weekly*, November 6, 1920; and stories by Lawrence Perry ("Man to Man," *SEP*, November 20, 1920; "Bull Pup and Tiger Cub," *Collier's*, October 31, 1925; "Straight-Arm Stuff," *Collier's*, November 5, 1927) and Jonathan Brooks ("Brothers under the Pigskin," *Collier's*, November 22, 1924).

27. "Our Greatest Popular Spectacle," *Literary Digest*, December 2, 1922.

28. Grantland Rice, "The Stuff Men Are Made Of," *Collier's*, October 24, 1925.

29. The overview of football in the 1920s in these paragraphs comes from my *King Football: Sport and Spectacle in the Golden Age of Radio and Newsreels, Movies and Magazines, the Weekly and the Daily Press* (Chapel Hill: University of North Carolina Press, 2001).

30. "Rockne Finds What He Dubs as Third Sex," *Detroit Free Press*, September 28, 1922. See also, for example, "Knute Rockne Guest at Marion Banquet," *Muncie Morning Star*, March 6, 1923; "Cake-Eaters to Put Football on Society Editor's Beat—Rockne," *Chicago Tribune*, January 5, 1925; "Famous Football Coach in Talk Here Urges Youths to Be Men Not 'Pastry Cutters,'" *Huntington (IN) Press*, April 10, 1925; "Ed Hughes' Column," *Tucson Citizen*, May 7, 1925; and "Real Men," *Cincinnati Enquirer*, October 3, 1927. For a discussion of these banquet speeches, see Murray Sperber, *Shake Down the Thunder: The Creation of Notre Dame Football* (New York: Henry Holt, 1993), 151–52.

31. In "The Life Story of Knute Rockne," published in twelve parts in many papers over the days immediately following Rockne's death in a plane crash in March 1931, Robert Barron of the *New York Evening Post* described the fantasy in great detail. See it, for example, as carried in the *Pittsburgh Post-Gazette*, April 14, 1931.

32. For the Cake Eaters vs. the Tea Hounds in 1922, see "Novel Entertainment by Notre Dame Coach," *BG*, October 24, 1922. In their "anecdotal history" of Notre Dame football, Michael Bonifer and L. G. Weaver describe the Notre Dame USC halftime game between the "Rough-necks" and the "Tiller Boys," "clad in assorted ballet tutus, lace gowns and frilly petticoats," prancing around the field, as an incomprehensible dud that Rockne's student assistant stopped "after a couple of minutes," as the spectators sat there, baffled. Bonifer and Weaver comment that "it sure didn't have the effect Rock had planned." Michael Bonifer and L. G. Weaver, *Out of Bounds: An Anecdotal History of Notre Dame Football* (Blue Earth, MN: Piper Press, 1978), 50–51. I have not found any contemporary newspaper accounts of the Notre Dame–USC halftime performance.

33. "Knute Rockne Don't Admire Sissy Boys," *Colton (CA) Daily Courier*, March 5, 1928.

34. "The Redemption of Fullback Jones" (*SEP*, October 26, 1912) reworked the plot of "The Strength of the Weak," with bucking over and over into an unmovable line as an alternative to punting in the face of a terrific rush.

35. "Effeminate Men," *Indianapolis News*, April 4, 1922; "Rockne Suggests That Football Be Made Compulsory," *Pittsburgh Press*, April 3, 1927; "Urges Compulsory Football for Boys," *BG*, April 5, 1929.

36. Knute K. Rockne, "Football . . . a Man's Game," *The Mentor*, November 1929.

37. William Roper, "Bill Roper on 'Soft Men,'" *New York Herald Tribune Sunday Magazine*, October 7, 1928. This article is the source of the quotes in the following paragraph as well.

38. George Owen Jr., "Football—Pleasure or Grind?," *The Independent*, November 7, 1925.

39. "Few Football Players Enjoy Game, Says Owen," *BG*, November 5, 1925. For the AP's story, see, for example, "Owen of Harvard Sees Gridders as Gladiator Slaves," *Chicago Tribune*, November 5, 1925.

40. George Trevor, "Owen Commended for Courage in Speaking Truth," *Brooklyn Daily Eagle*, November 11, 1925 (this was Trevor's column from the *New York Sun*). The book was *Football Days* (1916).

41. "Owen's Views on Football Disputed by Best Players," *BG*, November 16, 1925; David P. Reed, "Is College Football Doomed?," *The Outlook*, December 23, 1925.

42. Dr. Morton Prince, "Hand Back the Game to the Boys!," *The Forum*, December 1926.

43. "Demoting the Half Gods of College," *The Independent*, October 21, 1927; John R. Tunis, "The Great God Football," *Harper's Magazine*, November 1928.

44. Upton Sinclair, "Killers of Thought," *The Forum*, December 1926.

45. According to the NFHS website ("NFHS Centennial Celebration"), the organization was founded as the Mid-West Federation of State High School Athletic Associations, then renamed the National Federation of State High School Athletic Associations in 1923, and dropping "Athletic" in 1970.

46. For the most complete history of early high school football, see Robert Pruter, *The Rise of American High School Sports and the Search for Control, 1880–1930* (Syracuse: Syracuse University Press, 2013); and for a succinct overview, see my "Football Town under Friday Night Lights: High School Football and American Dreams," in *Rooting for the Home Team*, ed. Daniel Nathan (Champaign: University of Illinois Press, 2013), 68–79. See also Bachynski, *No Game for Boys to Play*, chap. 8.

47. "N.Y. Health Director Is Dinner Guest Here," *Peninsula Times Tribune* (Palo Alto, CA), December 16, 1929, 7. Rogers was on his way to address a teachers' convention.

48. Frederick Rand Rogers, *The Future of Interscholastic Athletics* (New York: Teachers College, Columbia University, 1929), 91, 129. Rogers's book is another source for which I am indebted to Bachynski's *No Game for Boys to Play*, 26.

49. Rogers, *Future of Interscholastic Athletics*, 35.

50. Rogers, *Future of Interscholastic Athletics*, 90.

51. Rogers, *Future of Interscholastic Athletics*, 129.

52. Paul Gallico, "Big Explosion! Pfft," *NYDN*, October 24, 1929.

53. The injury rate varied widely by institution, from 3.2 to 74 percent, for numbers of participants ranging from 44 to 345 (with an average of 135 per institution), all of which undermined the conclusions based on the data. Howard J. Savage et al., *American College Athletics*, Carnegie Foundation for the Advancement of Teaching, Bulletin Number 23 (New York: Carnegie Foundation, 1929), 141.

54. Savage, *American College Athletics*, 140.

55. Savage, *American College Athletics*, 140, 142–43.

56. Savage, *American College Athletics*, 144.

57. See Jaime Schultz, *Moments of Impact: Injury, Racialized Memory, and Reconciliation in College Football* (Lincoln: University of Nebraska Press, 2016), chap. 1. Schultz goes on to explore the events that led to the renaming of Cyclone Stadium at Iowa State as Jack Trice Field in 1997. I discuss Trice's death in *King Football*, in the context of other major incidents in the integrating of college football.

58. "Ames Player Dies; Injured on Gridiron," *Des Moines Register*, October 9, 1923.

59. "Ames Star, Hurt in Minnesota Game, Is Dead," *Minneapolis Tribune*, October 9, 1923.

60. "Ames Football Star Wrote Creed on Eve of Game That Ended Life," *Minneapolis Tribune*, October 10, 1923. The piece appeared in roughly three dozen papers archived in Newspapers.com, both metropolitan and small-town papers (though no *NYT*, *NYDN*, *Chicago Tribune*, or *LAT*).

61. Besides "The Strength of the Weak," see also "The Passing of the Vet," *McClure's*, November 1904; "The Idealist," *SEP*, October 14, 1905; "The Freshman," *SEP*, September 9–30, 1911 (three-part serial), and "The Last Grind for the Big Game."

62. "The Observer's Column," *Minneapolis Daily Star*, October 13, 1923.

63. Elmer D. Mitchell, "Racial Traits in Athletics," *American Physical Education Review*, April 1923, 151–52. The other articles were published in March and May.

64. Researchers have recently claimed to have found racial disparities in the treatment of pain, based on an assumption that Blacks feel less pain than whites, which would suggest that the old stereotype has not died. See James N. Druckman et al., "Racial Bias in Sport Medical Staff's Perceptions of Others' Pain," *Journal of Social Psychology* 158, no. 6 (2018): 721–29.

65. See, for example, the coverage in the *NYDN* for October 25–27. Sheridan's death was headline news everywhere on October 27.

66. Grantland Rice, "The Sportlight," *Detroit Free Press*, October 26, 1931.

67. Paul Gallico, "It Happened to a Soldier," *NYDN*, October 26, 1931.

68. Ed Hughes, "Ed. Hughes' Column," *Brooklyn Daily Eagle*, October 26, 1931. Hughes's allusion was to Harte's "The Outcasts of Poker Flat," a classic story that Hughes could assume his readers would recognize.

69. Ralph McGill, "Break of the Day," *Atlanta Constitution*, October 27, 1931.

70. Westbrook Pegler, "Flaws Always Will Out, Even in Grid Rules," *Chicago Tribune*, October 30, 1931.

71. "Death of a Cadet," *NYT*, October 28, 1931.

CHAPTER 3

1. "40 Players Killed in Football Season," *NYT*, December 6, 1931.

2. As reported and compiled by the National Center for Catastrophic Sport Research at the University of North Carolina in its "Annual Survey of Football Injury Research" and collected into *Football Fatalities and Catastrophic Injuries, 1931–2008* by Frederick G. Mueller and Robert C. Cantu (Durham: Carolina Academic Press) in 2011, with a second edition (for 1931–2016) in 2019.

3. "40 Players Killed in Football Season."

4. "Football Deaths: What Shall We Do to End Them?," *Literary Digest*, December 26, 1931.

5. "The Spotlight on Sports," *Outlook and Independent*, December 30, 1931 (also cited in the next paragraph).

6. Herbert W. Barker, "Possible Grid Rules Changes Are Uncertain" (AP), *Lexington Leader*, January 1, 1932.

7. "Making Football Safe for the Men on the Gridiron," *Literary Digest*, March 5, 1932.

8. These are the claims of the longtime secretary of the rules committee and the principal chronicler of football's rules. See David M. Nelson, *Anatomy of a Game:*

Football, the Rules, and the Men Who Made the Game (Cranberry, NJ: Associated University Presses, 1994), 201.

9. "Reform of Football," *JAMA*, March 12, 1932, 51–52.

10. "At Least in One Department—Work Successfully Required," *Yale Daily News*, March 17, 1932; Zipp Newman, "Dusting 'em Off," *Birmingham News*, March 27, 1932.

11. "More about Football—Health," *JAMA*, September 3, 1932, 834. I identify Morris Fishbein as the author, because he was *JAMA*'s editor in 1932 (and will reappear in the following chapter). Following the editorial, *JAMA* published one more, on December 24 ("Football Fatalities of 1932," 2186–87), in which the writer (presumably Fishbein again) called for better regulation and medical supervision, particularly of sandlot, semipro, and club football. This would be *JAMA*'s last editorial on football injuries (as opposed to articles on the treatment of specific ones) until the 1990s.

12. Bill Cunningham, "A Doctor Watches Football," *Collier's*, October 22, 1932 (also cited in the following paragraph).

13. "Toll in Football to Date Totals 37," *NYT*, December 29, 1932.

14. See table 1.1 in Mueller and Cantu's *Football Fatalities*, 13.

15. "The Control of Football Injuries," *JAMA*, October 7, 1933, 1180.

16. Marvin Allen Stevens and Winthrop Morgan Phelps, *The Control of Football Injuries* (New York: A. S. Barnes, 1933), 60–61.

17. Edgar Fauver, Augustus Thorndike, and Joesph E. Raycroft, *National Collegiate Athletic Association Medical Handbook for Schools and Colleges* (Princeton, NJ: Princeton University Press, 1933), 31–32. For an overview of medical experts' views on concussions, see Sarah K. Fields and R. Dawn Comstock, "Concussions: Medical and Legal Controversies in Football," in *Touchdown: An American Obsession*, ed. Gerry Gems and Gertrude Pfister (Great Barrington, MA: Berkshire, 2019), 81–97.

18. Fauver et al., "*National Collegiate Athletic Association Medical Handbook for Schools and Colleges*," 35.

19. Fauver et al, "*National Collegiate Athletic Association Medical Handbook for Schools and Colleges*, 35.

20. Both boxing fiction and journalism are full of such usages.

21. In *League of Denial*, the Fainaru brothers describe concussion over "the long history of brain research" as "the neurological equivalent of a stubbed toe." See Mark Fainaru-Wada and Steve Fainaru, *League of Denial: The NFL, Concussions, and the Battle for the Truth* (New York: Crown Archetype, 2013), 32.

22. Augustus Thorndike, *Athletic Injuries: Prevention, Diagnosis and Treatment* (Philadelphia: Lea and Febiger, 1938), 93–95.

23. Thorndike, *Athletic Injuries*, 115–17. In an article reviewing the same five years of athletic injuries at Harvard, published in the *New England Journal of Medicine* shortly after his book appeared, Thorndike barely mentioned concussions (the 106 cases among 3,923 injuries recorded) and simply reiterated that "the patient must not resume athletic competition or exercise until recovery is complete." See Augustus Thorndike, *New England Journal of Medicine*, September 29, 1938, 464.

24. "Dr. Augustus Thorndike, 89, Sports Medicine Specialist," *NYT*, February 1, 1986.

25. N. P. Nelson, "The Nature, Frequency, and Age Incident of Injuries in Interscholastic Football," *Research Quarterly*, October 1933, 78–98; Joseph H. Burnett and Fred

J. O'Brien, "Survey of Football Injuries in the High Schools of Massachusetts," *Research Quarterly*, October 1933, 91–98; Thomas N. Horan, MD, "Analysis of Football Injuries," *JAMA*, August 4, 1934, 325–27. Burnett and O'Brien published an earlier study of the 1929–30 seasons, which they incorporated into their article for *Research Quarterly* (and whose results Stevens and Phelps included in their 1933 book, *Control of Football Injuries*). See Joseph H. Burnett and Fred J. A. O'Brien, "Survey of Football Injuries in the High Schools of Massachusetts," *Journal of Health and Physical Education*, October 1931, 32–33, 50. That article's concluding summary was repeated verbatim in the 1933 article. I calculated the rate of "serious" injuries in California from the authors' injury rate of 22.15 percent, of which 32 percent were "serious."

26. Kathleen Bachynski, *No Game for Boys to Play: The History of Youth Football and the Origins of a Public Health Crisis* (Chapel Hill: University of North Carolina Press, 2019), 87–93. The following discussion is deeply indebted to Bachynski's groundbreaking book and the sources it identified.

27. *Ladies' Home Journal* (edited by Edward Bok) published one editorial and three articles on football between 1895 and 1911, just one of them by a woman. See "Foot-Ball and Women," November 1895; Christine Terhune Herrick, "My Boy at School," April 1906; Henry Richards, "Frank Talks with Boys' Parents," part 5: "If You Want Your Boy to Be Strong," June 1910; and Morris Joseph Clurman, "Is It Not Time for Parents to Act?," September 1911.

28. Edwin F. Patton, "Which Sports for the Adolescent?," *PM*, August 1931.

29. The expanded *Woman's Day* began publication in 1937. In 1939, the combined circulation of the five magazines was 9,540,531. See *N. W. Ayer & Son's Directory of Newspapers and Periodicals* (Philadelphia: N. W. Ayer & Son, 1939), 1191.

30. The same title was used by Mary Stuhldreher in *McCall's*, November 1951; Al Stump in *American Magazine*, October 1954; and Andrew W. Grieve in *PM*, October 1956.

31. Maxine Davis, "Touchdown! And If Your Son Made It, It's a Thrill Worth Living for, Says Mrs. Knute Rockne," *Good Housekeeping*, October 1932.

32. The Hall of Fame of the National Football Foundation identifies Lea as Princeton's first "official" coach in 1901 (for one season). "Langdon 'Biffy' Lea," National Football Foundation Hall of Fame, accessed January 2, 2025, https://footballfoundation.org/hof_search.aspx?hof=2085.

33. Mrs. Langdon (Biffy) Lea, "Is He Hurt?," *Ladies' Home Journal*, November 1935.

34. Ellen Travers Beard, "Can He Take It?," *Ladies' Home Journal*, January 1938.

35. Jean E. Curtis, "We Must Let Them Go," *PM*, August 1939.

36. Arthur W. Wilson, "We All Play Touch Football," *PM*, November 1934; Stewart Schackne, "Sports I Want My Son to Enjoy," *PM*, November 1939.

37. "Is Football Worth While?," *Woman's Day*, October 7, 1937.

38. Edwin B. Dooley, "Making Football Safe," *Woman's Home Companion*, November 1932.

39. Bob Considine, "No Holiday for Death," *Good Housekeeping*, October 1937.

40. Dooley was the chairman who suspended Muhammad Ali's boxing license in 1967 for refusing to be drafted into the army.

41. Dooley, "Making Football Safe."

42. Edwin B. Dooley, "How Dangerous Is Football?," *PM*, October 1933.

43. Dick Hyland, "It's a Tough Game," *Good Housekeeping*, September 1934.

44. Bob Considine, "Death on the Gridiron," *Good Housekeeping*, September 1936.

45. Considine, "No Holiday for Death."

46. James V. Williams, "Can the Teens Take It?," *PM*, February 1939.

47. *Cosmopolitan* was combined with *Hearst's International* from 1925 to 1952, when it became the women's magazine known today. I will simply refer to *Cosmopolitan* in later notes.

48. Bill Cunningham, "Football—Not for *My* Son," *Cosmopolitan*, December 1939 (also cited in the next few paragraphs).

49. Edward J. Carroll Jr., "Punch-Drunk," *American Journal of the Medical Sciences*, May 1936, 709.

50. Frank Scully, "Stumble-Backs—Does Football Make Players Stupid?," *Liberty*, October 9, 1937.

51. Historian of science Stephen T. Casper argues that the mocking vernacular for punch-drunkenness undermined serious medical and scientific investigation of the disease. See his "Punch-Drunk Slugnuts: Violence and the Vernacular History of Disease," *Isis*, June 2022, 266–88.

52. James L. Knox, "This Bunk about Stumble-Backs," *Liberty*, December 4, 1937.

53. Art Cohn, "Cohn-ing Toward," *Oakland Tribune*, September 29, 1937.

54. Jimmy Powers, "The Powerhouse," *NYDN*, October 10, 1937.

55. "Is It Worth the Energy?," *Billings Gazette*, December 17, 1939.

56. Jimmy Jemail, "The Inquiring Fotographer," *NYDN*, December 10, 1939; Bernard Swanson, "Four Parents of Golden Gophers Have Answers for Cunningham's Outburst?," *Minneapolis Star-Journal*, December 7, 1939.

CHAPTER 4

1. Ellen Travers Beard, "Can He Take It?," *Ladies' Home Journal*, January 1938; James V. Williams, "Can the Teens Take It?," *PM*, February 1939.

2. Geoffrey Gorer, *The American People: A Study in National Character* (New York: W. W. Norton, 1948), 85. For reviews, see, for example, "What's Wrong With U.S.?—It's Female, Says Briton," *Baltimore Sun*, March 29, 1948; and James Farber, "Parade of Books," *San Francisco Examiner*, April 24, 1948. Taking off from Gorer, a writer in *Better Homes and Gardens* in December 1950 sounded an alarm for parents: "Are We Staking Our Future on a Crop of Sissies?" The author did not mention football as a potential antidote.

3. "Indian Scores 'Sissy' Football" (AP), *BG*, November 16, 1931. The short piece was widely syndicated.

4. HOP, "Sportdom's Highlights," *Austin American*, December 26, 1934. See also Chuck Welsh, "Sports Slant," *Somerset (PA) Daily Herald*, October 23, 1934, in which the sports editor insisted the local boys did not play "sissy football" simply because they "don't stoop to slugging."

5. "Coach Says Most Hurts Avoidable" (AP), *Hanover (PA) Evening Sun*, April 28, 1944.

6. *Tip Top Weekly* ran from 1896 to 1912 and *Top-Notch*, another juvenile magazine, from 1910 to 1937. *Popular Magazine* (1903–31) was written for older readers.

7. Issues from 1928 are missing from the microfilm and would likely include more of the stories that I discuss here.

8. W. B. M. Ferguson, "Runcie's Cowardice," *SS*, January 8, 1925. As a sign that little changed in football from its crisis years to its establishment as a truly national sport, "Runcie's Cowardice" was originally published in Street & Smith's *Popular Magazine* in January 1908.

9. Max Brand, "Thunderbolt," *SS*, October 25–November 10, 1932 (two parts). For more of this extreme sort, see Harold C. Burr, "The Wolf Man," *SS*, October 8, 1923; and John L. Swope, "The Inside of a Man," *SS*, October 22, 1924. "The Wolf Man," in *Sport Story*'s third issue, was seemingly a tongue-in-cheek send-up of the Darwinian argument about football's value in releasing the inner savage. A "meek" student named Enoch Sangler has "spells" of wolflike behavior on the football field, as when he sinks his teeth in an opponent's throat, until his roommate rushes out to tame him with a whip. Because satire and parody were not hallmarks of *Sport Story*, it's hard to know what to make of this story.

10. Jackson Scholz, "The Sixth Letter," *SS*, First January Number, 1930 (also cited in the next paragraph).

11. Roderick Jones, "Tiger Courage," *SS*, Second November, 1930.

12. From *SS*: Raoul F. Whitfield, "Angel Face," October 22, 1925; Paul Sand, "Graceful," November 22, 1926; Herbert L. McNary, "Half Pint," October 25, 1931; T. W. Ford, "Softy," December 10, 1931; Robert N. Bryan, "Nice Boy!," March 10, 1933; T. W. Ford, "China Doll," April 10, 1934; Garver Wheeler, "Aunty's Boy," December 1939.

13. From *SS*: William Elliot Carleton, "The End Run," September 8, 1924; Whitfield, "Angel Face"; Robert N. Bryan, "The Touchdown Apollo," Second November Number 1935; T. W. Ford, "Gridiron Goats," First December Number, 1935.

14. From *SS*: Carleton, "End Run"; William Elliot Carleton, "The Fiddler from Philly," October 25, 1933; Jackson V. Scholz, "Gridiron Dancer," December 25, 1934; T. W. Ford, "Profile Guy," First March Number, 1937.

15. Carleton, "End Run."

16. Scholz, "Gridiron Dancer."

17. Other stories from *SS* not mentioned here, in which accusations or concerns about being "yellow" are prominent, include William P. Livengood, "The Last of the Millers," September 8, 1925; T. W. Ford, "Pigskin Feud," October 15, 1931; T. W. Ford, "The Backfield Black Sheep," October 25, 1932; Dabney Horton, "The Drop-Kicker," November 25, 1932–January 10, 1933; Robert Harron, "The Yellow Jersey," December 10, 1932; T. W. Ford, "Pigskin Pins," December 25, 1932; Robert N. Bryan, "Little Firebrand," January 10, 1933; and Robert N. Bryan, "Pinch Passer," Second December Number, 1936.

18. From *SS*, see Herbert Reed, "The Anchored Back," Second September Number, 1930; Philip Scruggs, "The Way of Honor," Second November Number, 1929: Henry Soskin, "The Quitter," First August Number, 1930; Ford, "Pigskin Feud"; Ford, "Softy"; T. W. Ford, "Break That Line," November 10, 1932; Ford, "Pigskin Pins"; Bryan, "Nice Boy!"; David Garth, "Battling Sixteen," November 25, 1933–January 10, 1934; Eric Rober, "The Cheer Heeder," First January Number, 1937; and Ford, "Profile Guy."

19. Sarah K. Fields and R. Dawn Comstock, "Concussions: Medical and Legal Controversies in Football," in *Touchdown: An American Obsession*, ed. Gerry Gems and Gertrude Pfister (Great Barrington, MA: Berkshire, 2019), 83.

20. Edwin Dooley, "How Dangerous Is Football?," *PM*, October 1933.

21. "Leaders of the Morrow," *Cincinnati Enquirer*, November 18, 1928.

22. "Sissy Football," in *Successful Stunts: Fifty Short, Impromptu Dramatic Stunts for Social Occasions*, ed. Katherine Ferris Rohrbough (New York: Harper and Brothers, 1929), 49–53.

23. A search of "sissy football" in Newspapers.com turned up over 100 performances by 1939, continuing less frequently through the 1940s and into the 1950s, with the last one in 1962 (a total of sixteen more in these later years). Obviously, these are just the ones reported in the local press (and in newspapers in the database). It is not possible to know whether all of these performances followed the same script, but the basic joke would have always been the same.

24. "Girls Busy on Fall Dresses," *Ogden Standard-Examiner*, November 19, 1939.

25. For a very compressed overview of high school football's place in American culture, see my essay "Football Town under Friday Night Lights: High School Football and American Dream," in *Rooting for the Home Team*, ed. Daniel Nathan (Champaign: University of Illinois Press, 2013), 68–79. See also Bachynski, *No Game for Boys to Play*, 159–80.

26. On youth football, see Bachynski, *No Game for Boys to Play*, chap. 2, 28–47; and Jack W. Berryman, "From the Cradle to the Playing Field: America's Emphasis on Highly Organized Competitive Sports for Preadolescent Boys," *Journal of Sport History* 2, no. 2 (Winter 1975): 112–31.

27. "Life Goes to a Kids' Football Game," *Life*, November 21, 1938.

28. "Life Goes to a Kids' Football Game," *Life*, October 9, 1939. The issue is titled "Kids' Football."

29. "Kids' Football," *Life*, November 10, 1947.

30. "Boys Town Plays Cadets," *LAT*, November 26, 1938; Carl Blume, "Boys Town Trims Cadets, 20 to 12," *LAT*, November 27, 1938; Leo Adam Biga, "Boys Town: How Father Flanagan's Barnstorming Sports Teams Gained National Fame," *Nebraska Life* 11 (March–April 2007): 18–25.

31. Frank Tolbert, "Mighty Mites," *Collier's*, November 22, 1941.

32. "The Cradle of Pro Football Cheers for a Great High-School Team," *Life*, October 2, 1939.

33. In 2023, Washington High would win its twenty-fifth state championship but its first since 1970.

34. Walter Bingham, "Football from the Cradle," *SI*, November 13, 1961; Carl L. Biemiller, "Football Town," *Holiday*, November 1949.

35. "Look Goes to a High-School Football Week End," *Look*, November 18, 1941.

36. "Amarillo's Golden Sandies," *Look*, November 17, 1943.

37. "High School Football," *Look*, October 2, 1945.

38. Pete Martin and Ben Carroll, "The Whole Town Made the Team," *SEP*, November 22, 1947.

39. "Football-Crazy Town," *Life*, December 4, 1950.

40. Dr. William Brady, "Health," *Hartford Courant*, December 31, 1931.

41. See Brady's columns, which appeared as "Personal Health Service," by William Brady, MD, in the *LAT*, June 25 and July 25, 1932, and December 21, 1938; and in the *Madison State Journal*, April 27, 1944. Also as "Here's to Health," *LAT*, January 3, 1946; "Doctor William Brady," *LAT*, September 29, 1948; and "New Role Advised for School Football," *LAT*, October 6, 1948. See also the editorials in *JAMA* on the same theme: "The Dangers in College Athletics," April 11, 1903; "Athletics and Health," February 8, 1913; "Athletic Strenuosity," July 25, 1925.

42. William Brady, MD, "Personal Health Service," *Green Bay Press-Gazette*, December 22, 1948.

43. In addition to the ones cited below, in notes 44–48, see these by Dr. William Brady (or William Brady, MD): "Personal Health," *Hartford Courant*, December 5, 1949; "Personal Health," *Hartford Courant*, June 6, 1951; "Dr. Brady's Column," *Madison (WI) Capital Times*, July 5, 1951; "One More Boy's Life Charged to Football," *Indianapolis News*, January 9, 1952;, "Your Health," *LH*, February 2, 1954; and "Personal Health," *Hartford Courant*, October 26, 1955. After 1955, Dr. Brady's preoccupation with "sissies" hit a pause. In 1968, he reprinted his two 1952 columns regarding "sissies" (as if they were new), and in October 1971, just four months before he died, at ninety-one, he reprinted one of his July 1951 columns. See "Personal Health," *Hartford Courant*, September 3, 1968 (reprint of January 9, 1952, column); "Personal Health," *Hartford Courant*, August 21, 1970 (reprint of December 22, 1952, column); and "Your Health," *LH-Leader*, October 3, 1971 (reprint of July 11, 1951 column).

44. Dr. William Brady, "Here's to Health, *LAT*, February 8, 1948.

45. William Brady, MD, "Dr. Brady's Column," *Madison (WI) Capital Times*, July 5, 1951.

46. William Brady, MD, "Personal Health Service," *Green Bay Post-Gazette*, July 11, 1951.

47. William Brady, MD, "Personal Health," *Hartford Courant*, December 31, 1951.

48. Dr. William Brady, "Student Badly Hurt Avoiding 'Sissy' Title," *LAT*, December 11, 1952. Bachynski's citation of this line in *No Game for Boys to Play*, 28, sent me tracking Brady's columns.

49. See, for example, columns by Dr. Logan Clendening, MD: "Daily Talks on Diet and Health," *LH*, October 18, 1937; "Health Talks," *Richmond Times-Dispatch*, September 2, 1940; "Health Talk," *Chattanooga Times*, August 29, 1941; "Football Injuries," *St. Louis Post-Dispatch*, August 27, 1942; and "A Negative Vote on Football Question," *Jackson (MS) Clarion-Ledger*, December 21, 1944. Also, see two columns by Dr. Walter C. Alvarez of the Mayo Clinic: "Should Boys Play Football?," *Orlando Evening Star*, December 29, 1952; and "Football Dangerous to Juniors," *Indianapolis News*, February 25, 1959. In the 1952 column, Alvarez just "wondered" about parents encouraging their sons to play such a "rough sport" without really declaring a position.

50. See Dr. Theodore R. Van Dellen, "Football Injuries Highest among Younger Players," *NYDN*, November 29, 1950; George W. Crane, "Build Strong Heart," *Knoxville News-Sentinel*, September 10, 1958; and Peter J. Steincrohn, MD, "Medicine and Health," *Kansas City Times*, October 29, 1959. For an overview of the health columnists, see Richard Weiner, "The Doctors: An Historical Overview of Syndicated Columnists,

from Dr. William Brady to Dr. George Crane," *American Journalism* 14 (Summer–Fall 1997): 530–38.

51. Fishbein blasted Brady's column, which, "once conspicuous because of its educational efforts, has during recent years gradually departed from anything resembling accuracy or established medical science. It seems to strive constantly for sensational effects." See "The Misrepresentations of William Brady," *JAMA*, October 16, 1937, 1282–83. Again, I assume that Fishbein was the author of the unsigned editorial because he was the editor.

52. "Football Hurts Young Hearts, Should Be Outlawed in All High Schools, Doctor Contends" (INS), *St. Louis Star-Times*, December 19, 1949.

53. "Dr. Fishbein Defends Football in High Schools," *St. Louis Star-Times*, December 20, 1949; "More About Football—and Health," *JAMA*, September 3, 1932.

54. Mary Stuhldreher, "Should Your Boy Play Football?," *McCall's*, November 1951; Al Stump, "Should Your Boy Play Football?," *American Magazine*, October 1954; Andrew W. Grieve, "Should Your Boy Play Football?," *PM*, October 1956. Also see Stanley Frank, "Stop Maiming Athletes!," *Redbook*, November 1951; Jack Harrison Pollack, "Competitive Sports: Menace or Blessing," *PM*, June 1952; Mortimer H. Morris, "High School Football Can Be Made Safer," *PM*, September 1959; and George Weinstein, "Can Junior Football Hurt Your Boy?," *Good Housekeeping*, October 1960.

55. Bob Considine, "Death on the Gridiron," *Good Housekeeping*, September 1936.

56. Stump, "Should Your Boy Play Football?"

57. Jim Conzelman, "Who's Yellow?," *Cosmopolitan*, November 1948. Again, Gorer's *American People* could have provoked the article.

58. John Kord Lagemann, "How High-Pressure Sports Can Hurt Your Child," *Redbook*, July 1958; Dr. Charles A. Bucher, "Should Your Son Play Small-Fry Football?," *Woman's Day*, November 1959.

59. Stuhldreher, "Should Your Boy Play Football?"; Mary H. Henry, "Do You Fear Football?," *PM*, October 1946.

60. The attack on "mom" and coining of the term "momism" originated in a 1942 book (*A Generation of Vipers*) by Philip Wylie, a Princeton-educated writer of pulp fiction in the 1930s (and other books later, after his reputation was made by *Vipers*), but it was taken up by psychologists and sociologists, as well as by journalists, as numerous social historians have written about. See also Bachynski, *No Game for Boys to Play*, 39.

61. Dr. Edward A. Strecker, "What's Wrong with American Mothers?," *SEP*, October 26, 1946.

62. Frances Tennenbaum, "How Safe Are Home and School Athletics?," *Better Homes and Gardens*, September 1953.

63. See Bachynski, *No Game for Boys to Play*, 100–101.

64. Lou Little, "Teach Your Boy to Play It Safe," *Cincinnati Enquirer*, September 26, 1954. See Bachynski, *No Game for Boys to Play*, 40.

65. Henry Gregor Felsen, "Why I Want My Boy to Play Football," *Redbook*, October 1955.

66. Leonard Wallace Robinson, "If the Boy Turns Out to Be a Sissy," *Good Housekeeping*, June 1959.

67. See Lawrence R. Samuel, "The Blossoming of Child Psychology in Postwar America," *Psychology Today*, July 20, 2022, www.psychologytoday.com/us/blog/psychology-yesterday/202207/the-blossoming-child-psychology-in-postwar-america.

68. A millionaire Philadelphia contractor, John B. Kelly (father of the actress Grace), who had been an Olympic sculler in 1920 and 1924 and then a lifelong advocate for physical fitness, encountered the study and passed on its findings to the governor of Pennsylvania, who informed the president. This account comes from Robert H. Boyle, "The Report That Shocked the President," *SI*, August 15, 1955; and "Are We Becoming 'Soft'? Why the President Is Worried about Our Fitness," *Newsweek*, September 26, 1955.

69. "Are We Becoming 'Soft'?"; John B. Kelley, "Are We Becoming a Nation of Weaklings?," *American Magazine*, March 1956 (condensed in *Reader's Digest*, July 1956); "Is American Youth Physically Fit?," *U.S. News & World Report*, August 2, 1957.

70. John F. Kennedy, "The Soft American," *SI*, December 26, 1960.

71. Max Eastman, "Let's Close the Muscle Gap!," *Reader's Digest*, July 1961. See also Donald J. Mrozek, "The Cult and Ritual of Toughness in Cold War America," in *Rituals and Ceremonies in Popular Culture*, ed. Ray B. Browne (Bowling Green, OH: Bowling Green University Popular Press, 1980), 178–91; Robert L. Griswold, "The 'Flabby American,' the Body, and the Cold War," in *A Shared Experience: Men, Women, and the History of Gender*, ed. Laura McCall and Donald Yacavone (New York: New York University Press, 1998), 323–48; and Kurt Edward Kemper, *College Football and American Culture in the Cold War Era* (Urbana: University of Illinois Press, 2009).

72. John Kelley cited a high school football program in which 250 turned out but only 50 made the team as the wrong approach to young Americans' fitness. Kelley, "Are We Becoming a Nation of Weaklings?"

73. Bachynski, *No Game for Boys to Play*, 41–45.

74. Howard M. Tuckner, "Small Fry Football League on Long Island Still Growing," *NYT*, November 18, 1956. Cited in Bachynski, *No Game for Boys to Play*, 44.

75. Bachynski, *No Game for Boys to Play*, 82–84. I draw here on Bachynski's chap. 2, "We Are Not a Nation of Softies: Youth Football from the Great Depression to the Cold War."

76. Bucher, "Should Your Son Play Small-Fry Football?"

77. The National Federation of High School Associations did not begin collecting data on sports participation until 1969, when it reported that 853,537 boys played high school football that season. The sportswriter Bob Considine ("No Holiday for Death," *Good Housekeeping*, October 1937) claimed that 616,000 high school boys played in 1937, and Kathleen Bachynski cites an estimate of 600,000 by a National Federation of High School Associations secretary at a symposium in 1950 (*No Game for Boys to Play*, 33). In 1962, sportswriter Tim Cohane wrote that 760,000 high school boys were playing football that season ("Your Boy and High School Football," *Look*, August 28, 1962). How accurate these figures are is uncertain, but their suggestion of wartime contraction followed by recovery and growth makes sense. (In "Should Your Boy Play Football?" Al Stump wrote that 1,000,000 boys were playing at 16,000 high schools in 1954, but that figure seems hugely inflated in light of the documented 853,000 in 1969.)

78. Data on football participation of questionable reliability is set against published data on high school enrollments from the US Department of Education beginning in 1940. My enrollment figures are from *120 Years of American Education: A Statistical Portrait*, ed. Thomas D. Snyder (Washington, DC: US Department of Education, 1993), table 3, 15. If 600,000 boys played in 1940, that would have been 15.5 percent of the 3,870,000 fourteen-to-seventeen-year-old males attending high school. The same 600,000 in 1950 (after contraction, then recovery) would have been 16.8 percent of the 3,568,000 in 1950. And Cohane's 760,000 (see previous note) would have been 12.6 percent of the 6,032,000 in 1962. For 1969, the first year with both participation data from the National Federation of High School Associations and enrollment data from the Department of Education, the 853,537 boys playing football were 11.6 percent of the 7,374,000 male students. (For 1980, the figures worked out to 12.8 percent.)

79. A. J. Ryan, "The A.M.A. and Sports Injuries," *JAMA*, November 17, 1956, 1160–61.

80. Augustus Thorndike, "Prevention of Injury in Athletics," *JAMA*, November 17, 1956, 1126–32.

81. Augustus Thorndike, "Prevention of Injuries in College Athletics," *JAMA*, March 28, 1959, 1405–9.

82. Robert G. Brashear, "Basic Areas of Prevention of Athletic Injuries," *JAMA*, November 21, 1959, 1664–65. For a survey of twenty-six studies of concussion and American football published in medical journals from 1906 through 1959, see Gary Solomon and Allen Kent Sills, "A Retrospective View of Concussion in American Football: What Was Suggested Then We Now Know," *Physician and Sportsmedicine* 43, no. 3 (2015): 247–52.

83. "Football Is Violence," *Look*, August 28, 1962. This is the source of most of the quotes throughout this section.

84. Cohane, "Your Boy and High School Football."

85. For several years, Cohane spent idyllic all-male summer retreats at Bull Pond, near West Point, with Blaik, his assistants, and a few choice friends, and he later coauthored Blaik's autobiography, *You Have to Pay the Price*. Cohane's relationship with Lombardi began in their student days together at Fordham in the 1930s, was renewed at Bull Pond when Lombardi was one of Blaik's assistants, and continued when Lombardi became an NFL coach in New York in the 1950s and in Green Bay in the 1960s. For his reminiscences of the retreats at Bull Pond, see Tim Cohane, *Bypaths of Glory: A Sportswriter Looks Back* (New York: Harper and Row, 1963), chap. 15.

CHAPTER 5

1. *Spalding's Official Foot Ball Guide*, ed. Walter Camp (New York: A. G. Spalding and Bros., 1891), 7; Parke H. Davis, *Football: The American Intercollegiate Game* (New York: Charles Scribner's Son, 1911), 482.

2. *Spalding's Official Foot Ball Guide*, ed. Walter Camp (New York: American Sports Publishing, 1916), 125.

3. For the 1892, 1897, 1900, 1905, and 1910 rules, see Davis, *Football*, 482, 490, 491, 494, 503.

4. Rule III, "Players and Substitutes," published in *Spalding's Official 1919 Foot Ball Guide*, ed. Walter Camp (New York: American Sports Publishing, 1919), 6.

5. *The Official National Collegiate Athletic Association Football Guide 1941* (New York: A. S. Barnes, 1941), 277.

6. "Notre Dame's Frank Leahy vs. Oklahoma's Bud Wilkinson on the Return of One-Platoon Football," *Look*, October 6, 1953.

7. "Two Platoon System Safe from Change" (AP), *LAT*, January 10, 1953; Ben Funk, "NCAA Kills Two-Platoon Grid System" (AP), *LAT*, January 15, 1953.

8. "NCAA Committee Still Undecided on Sub Rule" (AP), *Cincinnati Enquirer*, January 16, 1965. Language in the rules banning "direct communication from the sideline with players on the field" would not disappear from the rules until 1967.

9. "Rules Committee in Exhaustive Discussion of Platoon Football" (AP), *LAT*, January 13, 1953. In a debate with Bud Wilkinson in *Look* magazine (October 6, 1953) over the return to one-platoon football, Frank Leahy put the number of eliminated football programs at fifty-seven. See "Notre Dame's Frank Leahy vs. Oklahoma's Bud Wilkinson."

10. Dan Parker, "Football Is for Sissies," *Cosmopolitan*, November 1949.

11. "If football had continued in the direction dictated by the two-platoon system, it was doomed," Parker wrote in the *New York Daily Mirror*. See "Writers Relieved by Ban of Two-Platoons" (AP), *FWST*, January 18, 1953 (which also includes the comments of other leading sportswriters who approved the new rule by 5–1).

12. Bill Fay, "Will the Fans Go for 'One-Platoon' Football This Fall?," *Collier's*, September 4, 1953.

13. Those who did see military service included Frank Leahy, Robert Neyland, Bud Wilkinson, Jim Tatum, Woody Hayes, Shug Jordan, Paul Dietzel, Bear Bryant, Ben Schwartzwalder, Murray Warmath, John McKay, Darrell Royal, and Ara Parseghian. For the players, coaches, and teams in service football in World War II and the Korean War, see John Daye, *Encyclopedia of Armed Forces Football: The Complete History of the Glory Years* (Haworth, NJ: St. Johann Press, 2014).

14. With Tim Cohane as his coauthor.

15. I discuss several of these stories in *King Football: Sport and Spectacle in the Golden Age of Radio and Newsreels, Movies and Magazines, the Weekly and the Daily Press* (Chapel Hill: University of North Carolina Press, 2001).

16. Jerry Brondfield, *Woody Hayes and the 100-Yard War* (New York: Random House, 1974).

17. At the end of Texas A&M's 1957 season, Bryant complained to a writer for the United Press, "We haven't played kill or get killed football in a single game this year" ("Auburn Looms as New National Champ, with Sooners, Aggies Beaten," *Nashville Banner*, November 18, 1957). The following year, Harry Mehre, the former Georgia and Ole Miss coach turned sports journalist, attributed Alabama's early success to Bryant's finding players who played his kind of football. "If you do not care for Bryant's war cry: 'Kill or be killed,'" Mehre wrote, "then you have no place on the Alabama football squad" (Harry Mehre, "Bear Bryant Wins Title for Re-Shuffling Success," *Miami News*, November 4, 1958). Two days later, the sports columnist for the *Louisville Clarion-Ledger*

predicted that "the 'Bama boys who have survived Bryant's excruciating elimination system—which calls for 'kill or get killed' football"—would be "too tough" for Tulane that week (Carl Walters, "Shavin's," *Louisville Courier-Journal*, November 6, 1958).

18. Fred Russell, "Pigskin Preview," *SEP*, September 6, 1958. Royal introduced the term in his first season at Texas (Bryant's last at Texas A&M) when, before the Oklahoma game, he told the local Longhorn Club in Austin that the only way to beat the Sooners would be "going out and fighting them jaw to jaw." Texas sportswriters immediately picked it up, and it became the Longhorns' brand under Royal and marked the Southwest Conference, as Bryant's marked the SEC. See, for example, Dick Moore, "'Jaw to Jaw' Game Needed," *FWST*, November 19, 1963 (for TCU against Rice).

19. "A Brawling Battle of the Hard-Noses," *Life*, January 11, 1960.

20. Charles Harbin Jr., "Oklahoma Smothers Louisiana State in Sugar Bowl Game," *Alabama Journal*, January 3, 1950.

21. A search for "'plays with reckless abandon' football" on Newspapers.com (on August 20, 2021) turned up 21 matches for 1951–60, 153 for 1961–70, 950 for 1971–80, 931 for 1981–90, 752 for 1991–2000, 519 for 2001–10, and 164 for 2011–20. Not every match was in relation to football, and many matches were the same story in multiple newspapers, but the relative numbers from decade to decade track the shift from one-platoon to two-platoon football in 1965, the explosion of the NFL's popularity beginning in the 1960s, and the beginning of broad public awareness of CTE in the 2010s.

22. Francis Wallace, "Gridiron Galahad," *Collier's*, October 14, 1950; Tim Cohane, "Bud Wilkinson: The Golden Man of the Gridiron," *Look*, November 13, 1956. Jim Dent makes the point about Wilkinson and "vicious hitting drills" in *The Undefeated: The Oklahoma Sooners and the Greatest Winning Streak in College Football* (New York: St. Martin's, 2001), 166–67.

23. John Scott, *Bud Wilkinson and the Rise of Oklahoma Football* (Norman: University of Oklahoma Press, 2021), 32–33.

24. David Fleming, "Is the Oklahoma Drill a Rite of Passage or Everything to Fear about Football?," *ESPN The Magazine*, August 18, 2015.

25. Press reports identified just a handful of the high schools and colleges that likely adopted the "Oklahoma drill" in the 1950s. For one high school, see Bob Ennis, "Tackle, Tackle, Who's Got the Tackle," *Fort Pierce (FL) News-Tribune*, September 21, 1955 (also "Weight's Up for Eagles," *News-Tribune*, September 2, 1959). Colleges included Georgia Tech under Bobby Dodd (Bill Allen, "Forris, Fulcher Join 'Hospital Corps' as Jackets Knock-Knock-Knock," *Atlanta Constitution*, September 6, 1955; Mickey Logue, "Punters Get High Priority on Dodd's 'Big Game' Hunt," *Atlanta Constitution*, March 26, 1957; "Coaches Smile after Tech Drill," *Atlanta Constitution*, October 8, 1958), the University of Tampa ("Spartans Run Hot-and-Cold in Drills," *Tampa Tribune*, September 7, 1956), the University of Wichita ("Shocks Have Fast Workout," *Wichita Eagle*, September 2, 1959), and Virginia Tech ("VPI Polishes Its Attack for Virginia," *Roanoke Times*, October 14, 1959). For the Giants, see "Howell Is Pleased with Giants Club," *Salem (OR) Capital Journal*, July 29, 1955. The Giants were holding training camp in Salem.

26. For Lombardi's use of "the Nutcracker" as his "test of manhood" in Green Bay in the early 1960s, see David Maraniss, *When Pride Still Mattered: A Life of Vince Lombardi* (New York: Simon and Schuster), 1999), 219. The *Green Bay Press-Gazette* reported on

Lombardi's training camp "Nutcracker" drills in 1964 (July 19, July 23, July 25, July 27, July 29), 1965 (July 25, July 27, July 29), and 1966 (July 17), several times with photos.

27. On Shula's Oklahoma drills at Baltimore in the 1960s, see the *Baltimore Sun* for August 1, 1963; July 24, 1964; July 30, 1965; July 18, 1966; July 18, 1967 (*Evening Sun*); July 19, 1968; and July 15, 1969. After Shula took over at Miami in 1970, he immediately instituted Oklahoma drills at the beginning of training camp (see *Miami News*, July 14, 1970; and *Miami Herald*, July 20, 1970). John Mackey (*Baltimore Sun*, July 30, 1965) and Bubba Smith in a syndicated column by Murray Olderman (see "Bringing Up Bubba Smith Is a Man-Size Job," *Lexington Leader*, August 23, 1967), future Hall of Famers—and victims of CTE—were singled out as stars of Oklahoma drills in Colts' training camps.

28. For reports on the Steelers' Nutcracker drills, see the *Pittsburgh Press* (July 20, 1972; July 18 and August 29, 1973; July 15, 1974 [Mike Webster's first Nutcracker]; July 30, 1975; July 9, 1976; July 13 and 23, 1976 [with great photo]; July 19 and 24, 1977; July 24, 1978; July 19 and 26, 1980).

29. Phil Musick, "Steeler Rookies Hit the Road," *Pittsburgh Press*, July 19, 1973. From the coverage in the *Pittsburgh Press* and *Pittsburgh Post-Gazette*—long stories rather than the typical paragraph or two in other NFL-city papers—the Nutcracker /Oklahoma drill was a particularly important part of the Steelers' culture in the 1970s, as they won four Super Bowls. See, for example, Glenn Sheeley, "The Nutcracker or Oklahoma Crude?," *Pittsburgh Press*, July 9, 1976; David Fink, "Steelers: Nutcracker Suite," *Pittsburgh Post-Gazette*, July 19, 1977; and Sheeley, "Steelers' Nutcracker Drill—Always Smashing Success," *Pittsburgh Press*, July 23, 1978.

30. Mark Fainaru-Wada and Steve Fainaru, *League of Denial: The NFL, Concussions, and the Battle for the Truth* (New York: Crown Archetype, 2014), 13. The brothers described how Webster, an undersized, not-very-fast fifth-round draft choice in 1974, proved to Chuck Noll and his new teammates in the Oklahoma drill that he was possibly the toughest guy on a Steelers team of tough guys that would win four Super Bowls over the next six years.

31. See Jake Trotter, "OU's Gift to Football," *Oklahoma City Daily Oklahoman*, August 22, 2010.

32. Jack Clowser, "Phooey on Popularity!," *SEP*, November 12, 1955; Robert Shaplen, "The Ohio State Story: Win or Else," *SI*, October 24, 1955. The statement about Miami was from Brondfield, *Woody Hayes and the 100-Yard War*, 20.

33. In his self-published football manual, Hayes described the "sixteen thirty-yard competitive sprints" that concluded his preseason practices, reduced to five or six once the season started. W. Woodrow Hayes, *Hot Line to Victory* (pub. by author, 1969), 198.

34. Clowser, "Phooey on Popularity."

35. Roy Terrell, "You Love Woody or Hate Him," *SI*, September 24, 1962.

36. John Lombardo, *A Fire to Win: The Life and Times of Woody Hayes* (New York: St. Martin's, 2005), 3.

37. Keith Dunnavant, *Coach: The Life of Paul "Bear" Bryant* (New York: Simon and Schuster, 1996), 15–25.

38. See, for example, "Believe It or Not by Ripley," *Knoxville Journal*, December 5, 1935, 5-B.

39. Paul W. "Bear" Bryant, *Building a Championship Football Team* (Englewood Cliffs, NJ: Prentice-Hall, 1960), 4.

40. Quoted in Daniel Immerwahr, *How to Hide an Empire: A History of the Greater United States* (New York: Farrar, Straus and Giroux, 2019), 226. In Immerwahr's own words, the United States at this historical moment "made more goods, had more oil, held more gold, and possessed more planes than all other countries combined," while wielding authority over 135 million people in addition to the 132 million in its own forty-eight states.

41. Mal Malette, "Jim Tatum of the Tarheels," *SEP*, November 2, 1957. The entry on "Winning isn't everything; it's the only thing" in Wikipedia (last edited August 6, 2024) identifies an article in the *Los Angeles Herald and Express* (December 7, 1953) and another in *Sports Illustrated* before the 1956 Rose Bowl (confirmed as December 26, 1955) that quote Red Sanders making the statement (as well as an unpublished memoir by the writer of the piece in the *Herald and Express* that says Sanders first said it after losing to USC in 1949).

42. Kyle Vance, "Bryant Disgusted, Calls Off Spring Football Drills," *LH*, March 9, 1946; Babe Kimbrough, "Largest Group in History Reports for Opening of UK Grid Practice," *LH*, August 20, 1946; "Data on Important SEC Grid Campaign," *Knoxville Journal*, September 29, 1946 (complete rosters of all SEC teams).

43. "Cats Open Spring Practice," *LH*, February 18, 1947; "88 Huskies on UK Lot as Bryant Ups Barrier," *LH*, September 2, 1947; game program for the Kentucky–Evansville contest, November 15, 1947 (courtesy of the University of Notre Dame, Joyce Sports Research Collection). (I have been unable to locate a roster for the opening game.) Dunnavant claimed that "high-school signees, tryouts, and ex-GIs swelled the Kentucky roster to more than two hundred players in the years immediately after the war," but that seems inflated, or perhaps was cumulative for two seasons. See, Dunnavant, *Coach*, 67.

44. Fred Russell and Guy Tiller, "Georgia Plays for Keeps," *SEP*, November 5, 1949.

45. Dunnavant, *Coach*, 68–69, 72.

46. Bill Fay, "Dixie's No. 1 Gridnaper," *Collier's*, September 23, 1950; Tom Siler, "Football's Jittery Genius," *SEP*, November 3, 1951.

47. Dunnavant, *Coach*, 90–92.

48. Jim Dent, *The Junction Boys: How Ten Days in Hell with Bear Bryant Forged a Championship Team* (New York: St. Martin's, 1999). The movie aired on ESPN on December 14, 2002, and remains available on DVD.

49. "Aggie Spring Drills Attract 104 Players" (AP), *FWST*, March 9, 1954.

50. "Aggies Will Work behind Locked Gates" (AP), *Lubbock Evening Journal*, March 23, 1954.

51. "Aggies Begin Workouts in Junction Wednesday," *Bryan (TX) Daily Eagle*, August 31, 1954.

52. See, for example, Mickey Herskowitz, "Scott Shines in Aggie Drill," *Houston Post*, September 2, 1954; "Three Position Changes Made as Ags Open Drills" (AP), *Fort World Star-Telegram*, September 2, 1954.

53. "No Discord, Say Aggies as 5 Quit" (AP), *FWST*, September 4, 1954.

54. "Aggies 'Go Home'" (UP), *Austin Statesman*, September 8, 1954.

55. Jack Gallagher, "Broussard's Exit Leaves 38 Aggies," *Houston Post*, September 9, 1954.

56. "1954 Texas A&M Football Roster," *Austin Statesman*, September 10, 1954; "Facts and Figures on A&M," *FWST*, September 10, 1954.

57. Game programs from the Joyce Sports Research Collection at the University of Notre Dame. I'm grateful to Patrick Milhoan, James Cachey, Debra Dochuk, and Gregory Bond for providing images of programs.

58. "SWC Schools Open Football Practice" (AP), *Corpus Christi Caller-Times*, September 1, 1954; "700 Report for Big Ten Squads" (AP), *Madison Capital Times*, September 1, 1954; "Maroons' Turnout Is Smallest" (AP), *Lexington Leader*, September 1, 1954.

59. Dent, *Junction Boys*, 107; Mark Batterson, "Longhorns Begin Season Training," *Austin Statesman*, September 1, 1954. Batterson wrote that "more than five dozen" turned out for the first practice.

60. Dent, *Junction Boys*, 146; "Red Raider Grid Squad Hits Drill Field," *Lubbock Evening Journal*, September 1, 1954. The game program for the Tech–Aggie game listed forty-nine Red Raiders (Notre Dame's Joyce Sports Research Collection).

61. Dent also got some fundamental things about 1950s football wrong. In setting the historical context, for example, he claimed that college football's public image in the early 1950s was "only a cut above pro wrestling" (true of pro football at the time but laughably wrong about the college game), and he explained Bryant's indifference to "spilt blood" at Junction as typical for coaches of the era because "most football powers brought in more than a hundred freshmen each year" (*Junction Boys*, 64). This became true for some teams in the Southwest Conference (and the SEC) after the return to two-platoon football in 1965 but not for one-platoon football in 1954.

62. "Coach Paul (Bear) Bryant speaks of his 'Junction Boys' with reverence," the AP reporter wrote. "It's the story of his success in rebuilding the football fortunes of Aggieland in three tempestuous years. . . . The work was tough and quite a few of the boys quit. But there was a hard core, that stuck it out and became football players." See "'Junction Boys Are Backbone of Champion Grid Squad" (AP), *Bryan Daily Eagle*, November 19, 1956.

63. Furman Bisher, "Bear Bryant: Football's Super-Salesman," *Sport*, May 1958. Bisher was the sports editor of the *Atlanta Journal* who would excoriate Bryant for coaching dirty football in a piece in the *SEP* in 1962.

64. Bryant, *Building a Championship Football Team*, 231–34.

65. Harold V. Ratliff, "Football Doctor," *Austin Statesman*, December 15, 1960.

66. "Stallings Hired by Aggies" (AP), *FWST*, December 8, 1964.

67. See, for example, "Local Quarterback Club Banquet Thursday Night," *Hearne (TX) Democrat*, January 27, 1966; "Stallings to Speak to Aggie Alumni," *Shreveport Journal*, May 29, 1967.

68. Paul Bryant with John Underwood, "A Run-In with Rupp, and Trouble Down in Texas," *SI*, August 22, 1966.

69. Paul W. Bryant and John Underwood, *Bear: The Hard Life and Good Times of Alabama's Coach Bryant* (Boston: Little Brown, 1974), 131, 139.

70. Joan Ryan, "The Junction Boys Remember," *Hartford Courant*, December 15, 1979.

71. Tom Weir, "'America's Greatest Football Coach' Dies" (Gannett News Service), *Iowa City Press-Citizen*, January 27, 1983.

72. Mickey Herskowitz, *The Legend of Bear Bryant* (New York: McGraw-Hill, 1987), 29.

73. Dunnavant, *Coach*, 100. Dunnavant apparently relied in part on an A&M student working at the bus station in Junction who "estimated that he sold bus tickets to as many as fifty Aggies" (104).

74. Allen Barra, *The Last Coach: A Life of Paul "Bear" Bryant* (New York: W. W. Norton, 2005), 169. A recent book about the 1968 Cotton Bowl, in which Gene Stallings coached Texas A&M to an upset victory over Bryant's Crimson Tide, mentions a grainy 8mm film shot by a local resident in August 1954 of the team's arrival in Junction in "two powder-blue-and-white buses" and of "players kicking up clouds of dust as they run across an open field during drills." The author does not mention how many players are seen on the film or anything about the film's location in an archive somewhere. He follows the accounts from the Bryant biographies and then reports, "Eyewitnesses [unidentified] generally estimate the total number to be around 100 players." No clarification here, despite the tantalizing discovery of the film. See Ron J. Jackson Jr., *Bebes and the Bear: Gene Stallings, Coach Bryant, and Their 1968 Cotton Bowl Showdown* (College Station: Texas A&M University Press, 2019), 51 and 64n16.

75. Dent, *Junction Boys*, ix.

76. In describing the buses on which the players had to flee, Dent explained that two different buses ran daily from Junction, the larger of which was a "fifty-seater." Dent, *Junction Boys*, 104.

77. Dent, *Junction Boys*, 145.

78. Barra, *Last Coach*, 169.

79. Dent, *Junction Boys*, 61.

80. Frederick O. Mueller and Robert C. Cantu, *Football Fatalities and Catastrophic Injuries, 1931–2016* (Durham: Carolina Academic Press, 2019), 84.

81. Mueller and Cantu, *Football Fatalities*, 119–22.

82. Stanley Awtrey, "'Junction Boys' Shines as Tale of Coach's Role," *Atlanta Journal-Constitution*, December 14, 2002.

83. Barra, *Last Coach*, 176.

84. Jack Gallagher, "Bryant's Unsettled Aggies Set at End," *Houston Post*, September 13, 1954.

85. Jack Gallagher, "The Junction Training Routine Separated Men From the Boys," *Houston Post*, September 13, 1954.

86. Herskowitz, *Legend of Bear Bryant*, 23–24.

87. Herskowitz, "Scott Shines in Aggie Drill."

88. "Bryan Broncs May Depend Heavily on Sophs," *Bryan Daily Eagle*, September 2, 1954 (the title refers to the local high school; the Aggie story was appended).

89. Jack Gallagher, "Broussard's Exit Leaves 38 Aggies," *Houston Post*, September 9, 1954.

90. Gene Gregston, "Difficult: Paul Faces Rough Job in First Year at A&M," *FWST*, September 10, 1954.

91. "'Civil War' at Texas A&M?" (UP), *Philadelphia Inquirer*, September 9, 1954.

92. Herskowitz, *Legend of Bear Bryant*, 25.

93. This notably excludes the *Dallas Morning News*, which is not archived on Newspapers.com.

94. Gene Gregston, "Bryant Liked Junction, but Maybe Players Didn't," *FWST*, September 10, 1954.

95. Gallagher, "Junction Training Routine Separated Men from the Boys."

96. Dunnavant, *Coach*, 74.

97. Bill Rives, "Miracle Man Bryant Will Need Magic Wand in Rebuilding Ags," *Dallas Morning News*, September 11, 1954.

98. Numbers taken from Aggie football rosters in the *Austin Statesman*, September 10, 1954; *Austin American*, September 12, 1955; and *FWST*, September 7, 1956.

99. "A Rugged Shakedown for a Tough Team," *Life*, September 23, 1957.

100. Dent, *Junction Boys*, 60.

101. Tom Stoddard, *Turnaround: The Untold Story of Bear Bryant's First Year as Head Coach at Alabama* (Montgomery: Black Belt Press, 1996), 86.

102. Bryant and Underwood, *Bear*, 165.

103. Bryant and Underwood, *Bear*, 165.

104. "Early Drill Sessions Please SEC Coaches" (AP), *Jackson (MS) Sun*, September 3, 1958.

105. Max Moseley, "The Grandstand," *Montgomery Advertiser*, September 4, 1958.

106. Tom Anderson, "From Up Close," *Knoxville Journal*, September 9, 1958.

107. Jesse Outlar, "What's behind the Green Door at Alabama?," *Atlanta Constitution*, September 11, 1958.

108. As at Junction with Billy Schroeder, one player had to be hospitalized with "sun-stroke" after running thirty fifty-yard wind sprints. Another player recalled continuing to run his wind sprints as he barfed over his shoulder, inspiring a cluster of assistant coaches to exclaim, "There's a man that wants to play." See Stoddard, *Turnaround*, 101.

109. Bryant and Underwood, *Bear*, 11.

CHAPTER 6

1. Tim Cohane, "Gridiron Muckerism," *Look*, December 29, 1953. In addition to the Cal–USC games described below, Cohane mentioned Army–Fordham in 1949 and Tulsa–Marquette, Toledo–Bradley, and Denver–Utah in 1951 as games marred by viciousness, along with major and minor teams from all parts of the country. Not even the Ivy League was immune, after Dartmouth in 1951 intentionally roughed up Princeton's Dick Kazmaier (the Heisman Trophy winner that year). Over a dozen players had been hurt in the 1952 season's four major bowl games, most of them "key men, at the All America level" and thus "proper targets for every legitimate violence an opponent could muster."

2. "Rough Day in Berkeley," *Life*, October 29, 1951.

3. "Bright's Jaw Broken, Drake Streak Ends, 27–14," *Des Moines Register*, October 21, 1951; "Caught by the Camera," *Life*, November 5, 1951.

4. The most notorious cases involved Dartmouth's Matthew Bullock against Princeton in 1903, Harvard's William Matthews against Yale in 1904, and Iowa's Oze Simmons

against Minnesota in 1935. Booton Herndon's "Time Out for Mayhem," *Esquire*, October 1953, discussed these and other incidents of racial mauling. On the Simmons incident, see Jaime Schultz, *Moments of Impact: Injury, Racialized Memory, and Reconciliation in College Football* (Lincoln: University of Nebraska Press, 2016), chap. 3. On the Bright incident, see Schultz's chap. 4 and also Lane Demas, *Integrating the Gridiron: Black Civil Rights and American College Football* (New Brunswick, NJ: Rutgers University Press, 2010), chap. 3. I also discuss these incidents in *King Football: Sport and Spectacle in the Golden Age of Radio and Newsreels, Movies and Magazines, the Weekly and the Daily Press* (Chapel Hill: University of North Carolina Press, 2001).

5. The story concerns the slugging of an opponent's Black star, who is the target of racist football fanaticism in the community, but otherwise has nothing in common with the Bright incident. See Booton Herndon, "Dirtiest Game of the Year," *SEP*, October 18, 1952. Herndon wrote another story about dirty football ("The Last Game," *Collier's*, January 8, 1949) and an article for *Esquire* ("Time Out for Mayhem") about incidents of dirty play in college, professional, and even service football. According to Herndon (in "Time Out for Mayhem"), the "dirtiest big-time football game ever played" was arguably the one between Navy Fleet City and the El Toro Marines for the 1945 service championship, in which Fleet City retaliated for the assaults on their diminutive Black star running back, Buddy Young, by going after El Toro's (white) quarterback, Paul Governali.

6. Frederick O. Mueller and Robert C. Cantu, *Football Fatalities and Catastrophic Injuries, 1931–2016* (Durham: Carolina Academic Press, 2019), 44–45.

7. Tim Cohane, "Why They Sling Mud at Army's Football Team," *Look*, January 17, 1950.

8. Bill Fay, "The Case for Rough Football," *Collier's*, November 23, 1956; "The Terror and His Twin," *Life*, November 16, 1959; Melvin Durslag, "Tough Twins at U.S.C.," *SEP*, October 22, 1960.

9. Edwin Pope, "Your Choice: Hall, Elliott, Royal, Bryant," *Miami Herald*, December 18, 1960. Among Bryant's most scathing critics was Jim Murray of the *LAT*, who traveled to Birmingham for the Alabama–Georgia Tech game in 1961, when Alabama was being considered as a possible opponent for UCLA in the Rose Bowl. (See Kurt Edward Kemper, *College Football and American Culture in the Cold War Era* [Chicago: University of Illinois Press, 2009].) Murray ripped Bryant and Alabama as suited only for "the white supremacy bowl" and also for being a "hard homicidal bunch" whose game with Georgia Tech "should have been called Multiple Contusion Bowl." See Jim Murray, "'Bama and Ol' Bear," *LAT*, November 19, 1961. This Alabama–Georgia Tech game was the one that Furman Bisher described the following year, as will be discussed below.

10. "A Bear at 'Bama," *Time*, November 17, 1961. Gene Stallings, now an assistant coach, described having "a lot of contact practices for holdovers" when Bryant took over at Alabama. "We wanted to find out who could run and who could hit—who wanted to play football. It was pretty rough."

11. Roy Terrell, "The Bear and Alabama Come Out on Top," *SI*, December 11, 1961.

12. Mervin Hyman, "A Turn to Toughness," *SI*, September 24, 1962.

13. Allen Barra, *The Last Coach: A Life of Paul "Bear" Bryant* (New York: W. W. Norton, 2005), 253.

14. Furman Bisher, "College Football Is Going Berserk," *SEP*, October 20, 1962 (also cited in the following paragraph). This was one of the regular guest editorials that the *Post* published as "Speaking Out."

15. Bryant sued for $500,000 and then settled for $360,000 for a second *Post* article accusing Bryant and Wally Butts of fixing an Alabama–Auburn game, without his own separate case coming to trial. See "Balm for a Gloomy Bear," *Time*, February 14, 1964. The journalists who most deeply researched the episode seem to agree that Butts did in fact pass on information to Bryant (which Bryant did not want or need) before the Auburn game. See James Kirby, *Fumble: Bear Bryant, Wally Butts, and the Great College Football Scandal* (New York: Dell, 1986); and Allen Barra's assessment of Kirby's evidence in *Last Coach*, 298–307. According to Bryant biographer Keith Dunnavant, had Bryant's own case gone to trial, Bryant would likely have won, but only after a character-destroying cross-examination that "could only have left him wounded." See Keith Dunnavant, *Coach: The Life of Paul "Bear" Bryant* (New York: Simon and Schuster, 1996), 176.

16. William Bobo, "Grimsley Defends Bryant, Hard Football," *Montgomery Advertiser*, October 23, 1962.

17. For photos of local high schools' bull-in-the-ring drills, see, for example, "Bull in the Ring," *Daily Iberian* (New Iberia, LA), August 26, 1960; "Bull in the Ring," *Orangeburg (SC) Times and Democrat*, September 14, 1960; and "Bull in the Ring," *Hanford (CA) Sentinel*, September 22, 1960. A couple of remarkable stories later in the 1960s went into considerable detail about the drill, with a breezy indifference to its impact on the boys subjected to it. See "Cavallaro Devises New 'Games' for Gridders," *Bayonne (NJ) Times*, September 5, 1963; and Randy Elliot, "Longest 2 Weeks Facing Prospects," *Tyler (TX) Courier-Times*, August 11, 1968.

18. Paul "Bear" Bryant, *Building a Championship Football Team* (Englewood Cliffs, NJ: Prentice-Hall, 1960), 13.

19. See, for example, Robert L. "Bobby" Dodd, *Bobby Dodd on Football* (New York: Prentice-Hall, 1954), 175. Dodd, as noted, was Bryant's philosophical and temperamental opposite.

20. Bryant, *Building a Championship Football Team*, 28.

21. Bryant, *Building a Championship Football Team*, 158–62, 35–41.

22. Charles (Bud) Wilkinson, *Oklahoma Split T Football* (New York: Prentice-Hall, 1952), 22, 27, 29.

23. Gomer Jones and Charles (Bud) Wilkinson, *Modern Defensive Football* (New York: Prentice-Hall, 1957), 24–25, 35.

24. Gomer Jones, *Offensive and Defensive Line Play* (Englewood Cliffs, NJ: Prentice-Hall, 1961), 32 (shoulder block), 115 (shoulder tackle), 119–20 (forearm shiver).

25. See Dana X. Bible, *Championship Football: A Guide for Player, Coach, and Fan* (New York: Prentice-Hall, 1947), chap. 2 ("Blocking") and chap. 8 ("Individual Defensive Play," section on tackling, 130–34); Frank Leahy, *Notre Dame Football: The T Formation* (Englewood Cliffs, NJ: Prentice-Hall, 1949), 158 (shoulder block), 197 (shoulder tackle); Frank Leahy, *Defensive Football* (Englewood Cliffs, NJ: Prentice-Hall, 1951), 126 (forearm shiver), 164 (shoulder tackle); Don Faurot, *Football Secrets of the "Split T" Formation* (Englewood Cliffs, NJ: Prentice-Hall, 1950), 139 (shoulder block), 221

(shoulder tackle); Clarence Munn, *Michigan State Multiple Offense* (Englewood Cliffs, NJ: Prentice-Hall, 1953), 158 (shoulder block); and Dodd, *Bobby Dodd on Football*, 40–41 (shoulder block), 171–74 (shoulder tackle).

26. See, Leahy, *Defensive Football*, 126; and Dodd, *Bobby Dodd on Football*, 182–83.

27. Dodd, *Bobby Dodd on Football*, chap. 2.

28. W. Thomas Porter, *A Football Band of Brothers: Forging the University of Washington's First National Championship* (Victoria, BC: Trafford Publishing, 2007), 48–49, 53. Porter cites the "Junction Boys" (Dent's version), and his account echoes Dent's in many particulars. But it also confirms the view of the contemporary press. After the Huskies' stunning upset of Wisconsin in the 1960 Rose Bowl, *Time* mentioned "rib-rattling practice sessions" as the key to the Huskies' turnaround ("Sport: Blacksmith-Type Boy," *Time*, October 3, 1960). For its preseason preview of the Huskies in 1967, *Sports Illustrated* looked back at that turnaround: "Attrition the first two years (still referred to by players of that time as the Death March) was frightful. But the hard core that remained learned to play the game 'from the heart'" ("Ten Years after the Death March, the Huskies Attack Again," *SI*, September 11, 1967). The "national championship" in Porter's title was awarded by the Helms Foundation following the Rose Bowl, at a time when the AP, UPI, and other major awards were announced before the bowl games.

29. Bob McLelland, "Sports Corner," *Roanoke World-News*, April 27, 1961; Bill Connors, "OSU Gets Winning System," *Tulsa World*, August 25, 1963.

30. Taking over from Bryant in 1954, Collier had transformed the team culture by treating his players decently and respectfully, but he won too few games. He left Kentucky for the Cleveland Browns, first as an assistant under Paul Brown in 1962 and then as head coach in 1963 after Brown was fired, winning an NFL championship in 1964 (with a bit of help from Jim Brown). Bradshaw inherited a group of players from a losing program accustomed to decent treatment.

31. Larry Boeck, "Bradshaw Goal to Win Games—with Decency," *Louisville Courier-Journal*, January 24, 1962; Ed Ashford, "It Says Here," *LH*, January 12, 1962.

32. Morton Sharnik and Robert Creamer, "The New Rage to Win," *SI*, October 8, 1962 (also cited in the next few paragraphs).

33. On the interpenetration of football and religion in the South, see Eric Bain-Selbo, *Game Day and God: Football, Faith, and Politics in the American South* (Macon, GA: Mercer University Press, 2009).

34. Shannon Ragland, *The Thin Thirty: The Untold Story of Brutality, Scandal and Redemption for Charlie Bradshaw's 1962 Kentucky Football Team* (Louisville: Set Shot Press, 2007).

35. See Ed Ashford, "It Says Here" ("UK Is Victim of 'Hatchet Job' in National Sports Magazine"), *LH*, October 4, 1962; Ed Ashford, "It Says Here" ("Bradshaw's Squad Is Dwindling, but That's What He Expected"), *LH*, April 24, 1962; Billy Thompson, "If Others Want to Quit, Let Them Quit Now—Hutch," *LH*, April 25, 1962; Billy Thompson, "Pressbox Pickups" ("Fans Pulling Even Harder For Bradshaw"), *LH*, April 29, 1962; Bill Neikirk, "Fore! UKat Gridders Likened to Bad Golfers," *Lexington Sunday Herald-Leader*, May 20, 1962.

36. Ed Ashford, "It Says Here," *LH*, September 13, 1962. Ellipsis in the original.

37. William Miller, "Doctors Okay U.K. Football, Say Films Back Up Coach," *Louisville Courier-Journal*, September 21, 1962.

38. Larry Boeck, "Bradshaw, 'Thin Thirty,' Debut Today," *Louisville Courier-Journal*, September 22, 1962.

39. Dunnavant, *Coach*, 69.

40. "Bear at 'Bama."

41. Ragland, *Thin Thirty*, 295–321.

42. When Bo Schembechler became head coach at Michigan in 1969, he hung a sign on a wall in the fieldhouse with Bryant's line from 1960: "Those Who Stay Will Be Champions." A player who quit that first year, after walking out of Schembechler's office, scrawled at the bottom of the sign with a Magic Marker: "And those who leave will be doctors, lawyers, engineers, architects, bishops, generals, statesmen and captains of industry." See Michael Rosenberg, *War as They Knew It: Woody Hayes, Bo Schembechler, and America in a Time of Unrest* (New York: Grand Central, 2008), 12.

43. That was Dale Lindsey, who, after transferring to Western Kentucky, played for the Cleveland Browns from 1965 to 1972, and then for the New Orleans Saints in 1973.

44. Ashford, "It Says Here" ("Bradshaw's Squad Is Dwindling, but That's What He Expected").

45. F. M. Williams, "Maples, Owen Join Exodus, Football No Longer Fun," *Nashville Tennessean*, September 8, 1962.

46. Tom Powell, "Respects Cat Coaches, Owen Says on Return," *Nashville Tennessean*, September 9, 1962.

47. Jim Elkins, "Sportalk" ("Mutchler Tells Why He Quit UK Grid Team"), *Paducah (KY) Sun-Democrat*, September 9, 1962.

48. Ragland, *Thin Thirty*, 149–50.

49. Tom Stoddard, *Turnaround: The Untold Story of Bear Bryant's First Year as Head Coach at Alabama* (Montgomery: Black Belt Press, 1996), 50.

50. Gary Shaw, *Meat on the Hoof: The Hidden World of Texas Football* (New York: St. Martin's Press, 1972), 38, 73. Shaw vividly described brutal offseason "Medina Sessions" and spring practice "Shit Drills." Medina Sessions, named for the team trainer who conducted them, were similar to the program that Ragland described at Kentucky. Before each "session" Medina would announce, "Some of you men will make it and some of you won't. We are here to separate the men from the boys" (78). Shit Drills, after spring football ended, were required for players below fourth string on the depth chart, with the undisguised purpose of running them off.

51. Stoddard, *Turnaround*, 95.

52. Dunnavant, *Coach*, 69.

53. "Striking with the first or elbows" or "locked hands" had warranted disqualification and loss of half the distance to the goal since 1906 (*Spalding's Official Football Guide for 1906*, ed. Walter Camp [New York: American Sports Publishing, 1906], 132–33.) In 1932, the "forearm" was explicitly added as a banned weapon and the "head, neck or face" as the forbidden target (*NCAA Official Intercollegiate Football Guide*, ed. E. K. Hall [New York: American Sports Publishing, 1932], 46).

54. Beau Riffenburgh, "Tools of the Trade," in *Total Football: The Official Encyclopedia of the National Football League*, ed. Bob Carroll et al. (New York: HarperCollins, 1997), 36–37.

55. Mort Weisinger, "They Don't Have to Get Hurt," *LAT*, November 27, 1949.

56. Hugh Fullerton Jr., "Ten Big Questions Face National Grid Rules Group" (AP), *Alabama Journal*, December 19, 1952.

57. Richard C. Schneider et al., "Serious and Fatal Football Injuries Involving the Head and Spinal Cord," *JAMA*, August 12, 1961. For the counterargument that the new helmets were safer, see Richard H. Alley Jr., "Head and Neck Injuries in High School Football," *JAMA*, May 4, 1964.

58. *The Official National Collegiate Athletic Association Football Rules* (Phoenix: College Athletics Publishing Service, 1957), 38.

59. George Walsh, "18 Football Deaths: Is It the Helmet?," *SI*, November 6, 1961.

60. "Rule Changes Won't Ease Injury Problem" (AP), *Indianapolis News*, January 4, 1962.

61. Porter, *Football Band of Brothers*, 55.

62. *The Official National Collegiate Athletic Association Football Rules* (Phoenix: College Athletics Publishing Service, 1960), 43. In 1946, the foul was covered by Rule 10 and penalized by half the distance and disqualification (*Official Football Rules of the National Collegiate Athletic Association* [New York: A. S. Barnes, 1946], 46). By 1950, it was in Rule 9 in restructured rules and was penalized by fifteen yards, with suspension for "flagrant" offenders (*The Official National Collegiate Athletic Association Football Rules* [Phoenix: College Athletics Publishing Service, 1950], 50). Beginning in 1952, suspension became mandatory again (*The Official National Collegiate Athletic Association Football Rules* [Phoenix: College Athletics Publishing Service, 1952], 34), and the rule remained unchanged at least through 1976 (after which I stopped checking).

63. "Rule Changes Won't Ease Injury Problem."

64. *The Official National Collegiate Athletic Association Football Rules* (Phoenix: College Athletics Publishing Service, 1964), 45. The following year, limiting the ban to the "head, neck or face" was dropped and the word "unnecessarily" added. (When would butting be *necessary*? one might ask.) See *The Official National Collegiate Athletic Association Football Rules* (Phoenix: College Athletics Publishing Service, 1965), 45.

65. *Official National Collegiate Athletic Association Football Rules*, 1965, 6.

66. *The Official National Collegiate Athletic Association Football Rules Interpretations* (Phoenix: College Athletics Publishing Service, 1970), 68. *Rules Interpretations* were volumes published in addition to the *Official Rules*.

67. Kathleen Bachynski, *No Game for Boys to Play: The History of Youth Football and the Origins of a Public Health Crisis* (Chapel Hill: University of North Carolina Press, 2019), 181.

68. *The Official National Collegiate Athletic Association Football Rules* (Phoenix: College Athletics Publishing Service, 1976), 28, 69. Definitions appeared in Rule 2.

69. "Rule Changes Won't Ease Injury Problem."

70. *The Official National Collegiate Athletic Association Football Handbook for Coaches and Officials* (New York: National Collegiate Athletic Bureau, 1953), 6; *The Official*

National Collegiate Athletic Association Football Rules (Phoenix: College Athletics Publishing Service, 1967), 10.

71. Hayes declared "the shoulder block" fundamentally "important . . . to our running game" (83) but with no explanation of it or of how it was taught. He also referred to "the moment of shoulder contact" (108) in a tackling drill, as if a shoulder tackle was assumed and need not be explained. Describing a defensive lineman delivering a blow to neutralize a blocker in one drill did prompt a brief moment of self-consciousness, when Hayes wrote, "The expression 'deliver a blow' is somewhat misleading for it may infer undue roughness. This is not the case, as the hands are aimed at the shoulder pads and never at the head." See W. Woodrow Hayes, *Football at Ohio State* (pub. by author, 1957), 83, 108, 111.

72. One of the wire services sent this out as a sports note that was picked up by at least a handful of sports columnists. See, for example, sports columns in the *Lexington Herald* (November 28), *Biloxi Sun Herald* (November 28), *Pensacola News* (December 2), *Amarillo Globe-Times* (December 9), and *Tennessee Democrat* (Nashville) (December 21).

73. W. Woodrow Hayes, *Hot Line to Victory* (pub. by author, 1969), 28.

74. Hayes, *Hot Line to Victory*, 211, 216.

75. *NCAA Official Football Rules and Interpretations 1976* (Shawnee Mission, KS: National Collegiate Athletic Association, 1976), FR 6–7.

76. See, for example, "Appeal for Changes in Helmets" (AP), *San Francisco Examiner*, May 4, 1961; "Surgeon Would Bar Hard Grid Helmets" (AP), *Sacramento Bee*, November 4, 1964; "New Helmets Scored by Physicians" (UPI), *Provo (UT) Daily Herald*, May 14, 1965; and Dick Collins, "First Time Around," *Austin Statesman*, November 1, 1967 (part of the column was on Schneider, "He Proposes Making Football Safer"). With Bartley E. Antine, Schneider also published the article "Visual-Field Impairment Related to Football Headgear and Face Guards" in *JAMA*, May 17, 1965.

77. Richard C. Schneider, *Head and Neck Injuries in Football: Mechanisms, Treatment, and Prevention* (Baltimore: Williams and Wilkins, 1973), 116, 165. Schneider described "stick blocking" as a tackling, not blocking, technique, little different from "spearing," but his overriding concern was for any use of the helmet as a weapon.

78. Lou Maysel, "Top o' Morn," *Austin American*, October 13, 1959.

79. "Lackey Flunked 1-2-3 Test When 'Bell Rung,'" *FWST*, October 13, 1959.

80. A search for "got his bell rung" on Newspapers.com (on October 12, 2021) turned up 3 matches in 1959 (confirmed in February 2025, and none before then), all of them the same quotation from Royal in Texas and Oklahoma papers, then 54 for 1960–69, 590 for 1970–79, 513 for 1980–89, 564 for 1990–99, 667 for 2000–2010, and 252 for 2011–20, many of these late ones rueful references to the old days when "getting your bell rung" seemed no big deal. It might have appeared earlier than 1959 in different wording, but the pointed attention that it received in the Austin and Fort Worth papers suggests that it was novel.

81. Mueller and Cantu, *Football Fatalities*, 37, 53, 78. I calculated the percentages from the authors' tables.

82. Mueller and Cantu, *Football Fatalities*, 311–18; Bachynski, *No Game for Boys to Play*, 139–45.

83. Mueller and Cantu, *Football Fatalities*, 68, 78, 89, 98, 124, 128, 150, 154, 180, 186. Mueller and Cantu succeeded Floyd Eastwood when his annual survey was taken over by the University of North Carolina on his retirement.

84. Joseph S. Torg et al., "The National Football Head and Neck Injury Registry: Report and Conclusions 1978," *JAMA*, April 6, 1979.

85. Known as the "baby-faced assassin" when he played guard for the "exacting taskmaster" Jock Sutherland at Pitt in the 1930s, Glassford had accomplished what looked like a miraculous Bear Bryant turnaround in 1950, his second season at Nebraska, with "a fearsome program designed 'to separate the men from the boys,'" which earned a profile in the *SEP* (Harry T. Paxton and B. F. Sylvester, "The Hungry Young Coach of Nebraska, December 27, 1951). But after ten wins over the next three seasons, forty-two players signed a statement in January 1954 demanding his removal for ridiculing, embarrassing, and threatening them with loss of their scholarships ("Players' Statement," *Lincoln Journal*, January 15, 1954). Glassford survived by invoking his ironclad contract, but after two more mediocre seasons (6–5, 5–5) he resigned and went into business.

86. In Seattle, the players' rebellion over vague and petty complaints appears to have been orchestrated by boosters who were paying them out of a slush fund, which UW coach John Cherberg exposed after losing his job. (See coverage in *Seattle Times*, *Seattle Post-Intelligencer*, and *Tacoma News-Tribune* for November–December 1955 and January–February 1956.) Cherberg's exposure of the slush fund triggered revelations of similar slush funds at USC, UCLA, and Cal, which led to the dissolution of the Pacific Coast Conference in 1959. Cherberg himself, popular with the press and with Husky fans (aside from those big-money boosters), was elected Washington's lieutenant governor in November 1956 and held that position for thirty-two years through eight election cycles. I discuss both of these episodes in *Bowled Over: Big-Time College Football from the Sixties to the BCS Era* (Chapel Hill: University of North Carolina Press, 2009).

87. John Underwood, "The Desperate Coach," *SI*, August 25, 1969; followed by "Shave Off That Thing," September 1, 1969; and "Concessions—and Lies," September 8, 1969.

88. I discuss these incidents at some length in my *Bowled Over*, with additional references to other discussions of the incidents.

89. Jim Hawkins, "Gridder Rebellion Seen Forcing Bob to Give Up Post," *Baltimore Evening Sun*, March 4, 1969.

90. "The Bob Ward Story," *Baltimore Evening Sun*, March 6, 1969.

91. Melvin Durslag, "Durslag Says: Days of Iron Hand Dead," *Seattle Post-Intelligencer*, November 7, 1969.

92. Harry Edwards and Jack Scott were the major leaders of the athletic revolution in college sports, with apostate players Dave Meggysey, Chip Oliver, and Gary Shaw contributing major texts.

93. On the integration of the Southeastern Conference, see Charles H. Martin, *Benching Jim Crow: The Rise and Fall of the Color Line in Southern College Football, 1890–1980* (Urbana: University of Illinois Press, 2010); and my *Bowled Over*.

94. Paul W. Bryant and John Underwood, *Bear: The Hard Life and Good Times of Alabama's Coach Bryant* (Boston: Little Brown, 1974), 17.

95. "Woody Finally Strikes Out," *Life*, February 2, 1979.

96. Ken Leiker, "Kush Removed as ASU Coach," *Arizona Republic* (Phoenix), October 14, 1979, 1. The lawsuit by punter Kevin Rutledge was thoroughly covered by the *Arizona Republic* over the previous ten days.

97. Paul Bryant and John Underwood, "Hit 'em Harder: The Only Game That Can Win," *SI*, August 29, 1966.

98. Paul Bryant and John Underwood, "Mellow—and Still Fighting," *SI*, September 12, 1966.

99. Stoddard, *Turnaround*, 216–17.

100. Bryant and Underwood, *Bear*, 11.

101. The series in the *St. Petersburg Times* by Fred Girard ("Ex-FSU Players Unveil Violations," June 10, 1973; "Players Charge FSU Reneged on Grants," June 11, 1973; "New Athletic Breed Demands Answers," June 12, 1973) was accompanied by numerous other stories by his *Times* colleagues. Girard's third article mentioned the 1969 incident, including complaints at the time over the "brutal and animalistic" offseason program.

102. From the *Tallahassee Democrat*: Bill McGrotha, "Sports Journalism at Its Worst," June 14, 1973; Bill McGrotha, "And the Unfavorable Reflections," June 13, 1973; "Under the Banner of Truth, the Times Rides Again," June 14, 1973; "Remarkable Declaration of Innocence," June 27, 1973. After 8–4 and 7–4 seasons in 1971 and 1972, FSU went 0–11 in 1973, and Jones was removed. Bill Peterson had been the coach in 1969.

103. In the past, maybe, but still alive in the memories and fantasies of at least some football fans. An astonishing cover story in *Sports Illustrated* in 1984 (April 30), titled "The Toughest Coach There Ever Was," memorialized a junior-college coach in rural Mississippi in the 1950s and 1960s named Bob Sullivan, known to all as "Bull," or "Cyclone," or sometimes "Bull Cyclone" for the full effect, who drove his players brutally and relentlessly in his quest for a "perfect" (undefeated) season but was kept from it by a petty college president. For one of Sullivan's legendary drills, to "spice up" practice and make his players as tough as he had had to be in surviving the horrors of Okinawa in 1945, he would wrap a mattress around an oak tree for his player to hit, to see if they could knock down an acorn. What was astonishing was less what Sullivan did to his players in the 1950s and 1960 (mostly out of the Bear Bryant playbook) than the fact that it was a cover story in *Sports Illustrated* in the 1980s and written by its star features writer, Frank Deford.

104. John Underwood, "An Unfolding Tragedy," *SI*, August 14, 1978.

105. Schneider, *Head and Neck Injuries in Football*, 123.

106. Ronald A. Smith, "The NCAA, Concussions, and the Lack of Concern for Athletes," *Journal of Sport History* 51, no. 2 (Summer 2024): 23, 25.

107. Underwood, "Unfolding Tragedy."

CHAPTER 7

1. "Savagery on Sunday," *Life*, October 24, 1955.

2. Samantha Barbas, *Newsworthy: The Supreme Court Battle over Privacy and Press Freedom* (Stanford, CA: Stanford University Press, 2016), 88. The players won.

3. Thomas Morgan, "The Wham in Pro Football," *Esquire*, November 1959.

4. *Spalding's Official Foot Ball Guide*, ed. Walter Camp (New York: American Sports Publishing, 1916), 126.

5. For a synthesis of the scholarship on early pro football, see Richard C. Crepeau, *NFL Football: A History of America's New National Pastime* (Urbana: University of Illinois Press, 2014), 3–19.

6. For media coverage of Grange and the NFL in the 1920s and 1930s, see my *King Football: Sport and Spectacle in the Golden Age of Radio and Newsreels, Movies and Magazines, the Weekly and the Daily Press* (Chapel Hill: University of North Carolina Press, 2001).

7. A writer named William Fay wrote ten pro football stories for the *SEP* and *Collier's* between 1938 and 1953 about aging stars, good-hearted but childlike, who needed good women to show them how to be grownups. I discuss these in *King Football*.

8. Bill Fay, "The Meanest Man in Football," *Collier's*, November 25, 1950.

9. "A Pride of Lions," *Time*, November 29, 1954 (also cited in the next paragraph).

10. See Elliott J. Gorn, *The Manly Art: Bare-Knuckle Prize Fighting in America* (Ithaca, NY: Cornell University Press, 1986).

11. Melvin Durslag, "Pro Football's Plenty Rough," *SI*, November 28, 1955, quoted by Michael MacCambridge in *America's Game: The Epic Story of How Pro Football Captured a Nation* (New York: Random House, 2004), 85.

12. Otto Graham, "Football Is Getting Too Vicious," *SI*, October 11, 1954.

13. Otto Graham, as told to Harry T. Paxton, "I'm Through With Football," *SEP*, October 6, 1956. For Graham's remarks to the Atlanta Quarterback Club and defensive responses by Commissioner Bell and Wellington Mara, the son of the owner of the New York Giants, see Larry Fox, "Graham Hits 'Vicious Play'; Vows '55 Last Season in Pros," *Atlanta Constitution*, November 8, 1955; "'Aggressive' Not Dirty, Bell Replies" (AP), *Atlanta Constitution*, November 9, 1955; and "Giants' Official Challenges Graham Rough Play Charge" (AP), *Atlanta Constitution*, November 10, 1955. Graham did not retire after the 1955 season, as he publicly announced, but returned in 1956 after promising his coach Paul Brown that he would not leave the team without a capable quarterback.

14. Bobby Layne, as told to Murray Olderman, "This Is No Game for Kids," *SEP*, November 14, 1959; "A Man's Game," *Time*, November 30, 1959; "Greetings to Our Victims in Play-Off," *Life*, December 14, 1959.

15. Tex Maule, "The Best Football Game Ever Played," *SI*, January 1, 1959.

16. Dan Wakefield, "In the Defense of the Fullback," *Dissent*, Summer 1957, 311, 313. Wakefield was a young journalist early in a career that began with sportswriting in his native Indianapolis and would soon include best-selling novels and Broadway screenplays.

17. Morgan, "Wham in Pro Football" (also cited in the next few paragraphs).

18. "The Violent Face of Pro Football," *SI*, October 24, 1960; "Sunday's Gladiators," *SEP*, November 24, 1962; "Madness Is a Game on Sunday," *Look*, December 3, 1963; "War on Sunday," *Look*, November 26, 1968; "Controlled Violence of the Pros," *Life*, October 14, 1966. These issues are cited in the next few paragraphs.

19. Quoted in Ben McGrath, "Does Football Have a Future?," *New Yorker*, January 31, 2011.

20. "Madness Is a Game on Sunday."

21. "A Man's Game."

22. "The Wedge Meets the Headhunter," *Life*, December 3, 1971; "Six Pros Tougher Than Tough," *Life*, October 6, 1972.

23. *Life* continued to publish special issues and resumed as a monthly in 1978, in time to capture Woody Hayes's career-ending punch in the Gator Bowl noted in the previous chapter.

24. *The First Fifty Years: A Celebration of the National Football League in Its Fiftieth Season* (New York: Ridge Press, 1969), 23–30 (also cited in the next paragraph). Jesse Berrett's *Pigskin Nation: How the NFL Remade American Politics* (Urbana: University of Illinois Press, 2018), 24–28, called my attention to this commemorative volume.

25. David Boss, ed., *The Pro Football Experience* (New York: Harry N. Abrams, 1973), 29. In *Pigskin Nation*, Berrett wrote that Boss "endorse[d] the idea that the NFL was absolutely worthy of serious intellectual consideration, then present[ed] so many possible interpretations that no single one could dominate" (28). Just so, and Boss described pro football as a game, not a war (224). Pain and violence were prominent in *The Pro Football Experience* among many other elements.

26. From the text of the lawsuit online, June 7, 2012, https://s3.amazonaws.com/s3.documentcloud.org/documents/367298/nfllitigationmastercomplaint.pdf, 12–13. On NFL Films, see Travis Vogan, *Keepers of the Flame: NFL Films and the Rise of Sports Media* (Urbana: University of Illinois Press, 2014); Berrett, *Pigskin Nation*, 40–52; and my *Brand NFL: Making and Selling America's Favorite Sport* (Chapel Hill: University of North Carolina Press, 2007), esp. 14–18.

27. Tim Layden, "The Big Hit," *SI*, July 30, 2007.

28. Layden, "Big Hit." A history of "Jacked Up!" was produced as a twenty-five-minute video by someone called JaguarGator9. See "The Complete, Controversial History of Jacked Up," YouTube, accessed January 2, 2025, www.youtube.com/watch?v=vDouUrig4m4.

29. Layden, "Big Hit."

30. The Quarter-Pounder Index was introduced with tongue slightly in cheek by *The Economist* in 1986 as a shorthand measure for cost-of-living comparisons, using the local price of the McDonald's quarter-pound hamburger in different cities. McDonald's sponsored the Quarter-Pounder Index segment on CBS.

31. Bob Raissman, "'Clown Prince,'" *NYDN*, November 13, 2005.

32. For a discussion of this episode, see Steven E. B. Lechner," A Swann's Song: The NFL's War on Violence and a Concussion Crisis Averted in the 1970s," *Journal of Sport History* 51, no. 2 (Summer 2024): 73–86.

33. Paul Zimmerman, "The Agony Must End," *SI*, November 10, 1986; Peter King, "The Unfortunate 500," *SI*, December 7, 1992 ("The Carnage Continues" was the headline on the cover).

34. S. E. Reid, H. M. Epstein, and M. W. Louis, "Brain Trauma inside a Football Helmet," *Physician and Sportsmedicine*, August 1974, 32–35, quoted in Jason P. Shurley and Janice S. Todd, "Boxing Lessons: An Historical Review of Chronic Head Trauma in Boxing and Football," *Kinesiology Review* 1 (2012): 175. For a survey of the literature on concussion, see Shurley and Todd (170–84) and Christopher Nowinski, *Head Games: Football's Concussion Crisis* (East Bridgewater, MA: Drummond, 2007).

35. Rebecca W. Rimel et al., "Disability Caused by Minor Head Injury," *Neurosurgery* 9, no. 3 (September 1981): 721–28.

36. Richard L. Saunders and Robert E. Harbaugh, "The Second Impact in Catastrophic Contact-Sports Head Trauma," *JAMA*, July 17, 1984, 538–39.

37. Alan J. Ryan, "Teaching Dangerous Techniques," *Physician and Sportsmedicine*, October 1974, 85.

38. Alan J. Ryan, "A Hit in the Head," *Physician and Sportsmedicine*, September 1979, 49-51.

39. Allan J. Ryan, "Brain Injuries in Football," *Physician and Sportsmedicine*, June 1987, 39.

40. Robert C. Cantu, "Guidelines for Return to Contact Sports after a Cerebral Concussion," *Physician and Sportsmedicine*, 1986. The 1973 book is Schneider's *Head and Neck Injuries in Football*, discussed earlier (see chap. 6, n. 77).

41. Jeffrey T. Barth et al., "Mild Head Injury in Sports: Neuropsychological Sequelae and Recovery of Function," in *Mild Head Injury*, ed. Harvey S. Levin, Howard M. Eisenberg, and Arthur L. Benton (New York: Oxford University Press, 1989), 272.

42. James P. Kelly et al., "Concussion in Sports: Guidelines for the Prevention of Catastrophic Outcome," *JAMA*, November 27, 1991, 2867–69, cited by Kathleen Bachynski, *No Game for Boys to Play: The History of Youth Football and the Origins of a Public Health Crisis* (Chapel Hill: University of North Carolina Press, 2019), 189.

43. Peter King, "Halt the Head-Hunting"; Michael Farber, "The Worst Case"; and King, "A Bell Is Rung"; all in "Head Injuries" section of *SI*, December 19, 1994. These articles are also cited in the next few paragraphs.

44. Mark Fainaru-Wada and Steve Fainaru, *League of Denial: The NFL, Concussions, and the Battle for Truth* (New York: Crown Archetype, 2013), 126.

45. For Tagliabue's comment, see Phil Anastasia, "Wishing upon a Star (or Two) This Holiday Season," *Camden (NJ) Courier-Post*, December 24, 1994. I have not been able to pin down a date on which Tagliabue formed the MTBI Committee, but in "The Worst Case," Farber described a meeting on December 9 between Tagliabue, Dr. Ira Casson (an original member of the MTBI Committee), and another team doctor "to discuss concussions and suggest ways to cut down on their frequency. No concrete proposals were adopted." That would seem to suggest that there was not yet a committee addressing the issue, but this meeting may have led to it.

46. Will McDonough et al., *75 Seasons: The Complete Story of the National Football League, 1920–1995* (Atlanta: Turner Publishing, 1994), 18.

47. Gene Wojchiechowski and Chris Dufresne, "Football Career Is Taking Its Toll on NFL's Players," *LAT*, June 26, 1988; Bob Glauber, "Special Report: Life after Football" (in ten parts), *Newsday*, January 12–16, 1997; Paul Gutierrez, "Pain Game" (part of a "Special Report on NFL Injuries"), *LAT*, January 25, 2000; Dan Bickley, "Modern-Day Gladiators" (three parts), *Arizona Republic* (Phoenix), January 16–18, 2003. Glauber reported on the Ball State study in "Cheering Stops, Trouble Starts," in *Newsday* on January 12, 1997; and Bickley reported on the Harvard study in "You Play, You Pay," on January 16, 2003, and in "Quality of Life, Early Deaths Haunt Linemen," on January 17, 2003, in his series in the *Arizona Republic*.

48. William Nack, "The Wrecking Yard," *SI*, May 7, 2001. In Mark Leibovich's *Big Game: The NFL in Dangerous Times* (New York: Penguin, 2018), 276, he quotes Campbell mocking the NFL's current game and players for not being as tough as in his day. See Josh Peters, "Campbell Says Game Not Played the Same," *Memphis Commercial Appeal*, January 31, 2017. Campbell here retracted the regret he expressed in *Sports Illustrated*'s "Wrecking Yard" in 2001.

49. Alan Schwarz, Walt Bogdanich, and Jacqueline Williams, "In N.F.L., Deeply Flawed Concussion Research and Ties to Big Tobacco," *NYT*, March 24, 2016.

50. Kevin M. Guskiewicz et al., "Association between Recurrent Concussion and Late-Life Cognitive Impairment in Retired Professional Football Players," *Neurosurgery* 57, no. 4 (October 2005): 719–26.

51. Kevin M. Guskiewicz et al., "Recurrent Concussion and Risk of Depression in Retired Professional Football Players," *Medicine and Science in Sports and Exercise*, June 2007, 903–9.

52. George D. Lundberg, "Boxing Should Be Banned in Civilized Countries—Round 3," *JAMA*, May 9, 1986, 2483–85.

53. Legal scholars made this case in the context of the players' lawsuits against the NFL over head trauma. See Christopher R. Deubert, I. Glenn Cohen, and Holly Fernandez Lynch, *Protecting and Promoting the Health of NFL Players: Legal and Ethical Analysis and Recommendations*, Petrie-Flom Center for Health Law Policy, Biotechnology, and Bioethics, Harvard Law School (commissioned by The Football Players Health Study at Harvard University), November 2016, Executive Summary, 13. The writers' number-one recommendation was to address this conflict by establishing "two distinct groups of medical professionals," one to represent the players' medical needs, the other to represent the clubs' financial interests. The idea was quixotic, but it addressed a fundamental challenge for team doctors.

54. James P. Kelly, "Traumatic Brain Injury and Concussion in Sports," and Michael W. Collins et al., "Relationship between Concussion and Neuropsychological Performance in College Football Players," both in *JAMA*, September 8, 1999, 964–70.

55. Ben McGrath first told this story in "Does Football Have a Future?," *New Yorker*, January 31, 2011; and then the Fainaru brothers did in *League of Denial*.

56. The Fainaru brothers described Nowinski seeking Schwarz's help to interest the *Times* (Fainaru-Wada and Fainaru, *League of Denial*, 203).

57. Alan Schwarz articles in the *NYT*: "Dark Days Follow Hard-Hitting Career in N.F.L.," February 3, 2007 (Johnson); "N.F.L. Doctor Quits amid Research Doubt," March 1, 2007; "Wives United by Husbands' Post-N.F.L. Trauma," March 15, 2007; "Concussions Tied to Depression in Ex-N.F.L. Players," June 1, 2007; "N.F.L. Study Authors Dispute Concussion Findings," June 10, 2007; "Lineman, Dead at 36, Exposes Brain Injuries," June 15, 2007 (Strzelczyk). In November 2006, Peter Keating wrote a devastating piece about Pellman as "Dr. Yes" in *ESPN The Magazine* (November 11, 2006), which the Fainaru brothers credit for beginning the exposure of the NFL's MTBI Committee. Pellman would be replaced by Ira Casson and David Viano as cochairs, the group's other lead attack dogs though with better credentials, who themselves would resign under pressure three years later.

58. Schwarz interviewed key participants afterward. See Alan Schwarz, "Player Silence on Concussions May Block N.F.L. Guidelines," *NYT*, June 20, 2007.

59. Alan Schwarz, "Congress Scolds N.F.L. and Union," *NYT*, June 27, 2007.

60. Schwarz, "Wives United by Husbands' Post-N.F.L. Trauma," front page.

61. "For Ailing NFL Players, a New Program" (AP), *LAT*, March 25, 2007.

62. Layden, "Big Hit."

63. Alan Schwarz, "New Advice by N.F.L. in Handling Concussions," *NYT*, August 21, 2007.

64. I follow Fainaru-Wada and Fainaru *League of Denial* here.

65. Fainaru-Wada and Fainaru, *League of Denial*, 227.

66. Alan Schwarz, "Players to Leave Brains to Concussion Study," *NYT*, September 24, 2008.

67. Jeanne Marie Laskas tells this story in "Game Brain," *GQ*, October 2009. The Fainaru brothers also tell the story fully in *League of Denial*.

68. Alan Schwarz, "New Sign of Brain Damage in N.F.L.," *NYT*, January 28, 2009.

69. Alan Schwarz, "Dementia Risk Seen in Players in N.F.L. Study," *NYT*, September 30, 2009.

70. Laskas, "Game Brain."

71. Malcolm Gladwell, "Offensive Play," *New Yorker*, October 19, 2009.

72. Alan Schwarz, "N.F.L. Scolded over Injuries to Its Players," *NYT*, October 29, 2009.

73. Quoted in Daniel Goldberg, "Mild Traumatic Brain Injury, the National Football League, and the Manufacture of Doubt: An Ethical, Legal, and Historical Analysis," *Journal of Legal Medicine*, April–June 2013, 157–91 (p. 11 in the online pdf version). On Culverhouse's concern for Tampa Bay's players, see also Alan Schwarz, "Ex-N.F.L. Executive Sounds Alarm on Head Injury," *NYT*, October 28, 2009.

74. Alan Schwarz, "N.F.L. to Shift in Its Handling of Concussions," *NYT*, November 22, 2009; Alan Schwarz, "N.F.L. Head Injury Study Leaders Quit," *NYT*, November 24, 2009.

75. Alan Schwarz, "N.F.L. Acknowledges Long-Term Concussion Effects," *NYT*, December 20, 2009. Congress held more hearings the following month in Detroit, where Casson continued to deny the connection of concussions to brain damage. See Alan Schwarz, "Congress Examines N.F.L. Concussions," *NYT*, January 5, 2010.

CHAPTER 8

1. For an account of the concussion crisis that covers some of the same ground as mine, see Kathleen Bachynski, *No Game for Boys to Play: The History of Youth Football and the Origins of a Public Health Crisis* (Chapel Hill: University of North Carolina Press, 2019), chap. 9 ("This Is Your Brain on Football").

2. Alan Schwarz, "Suicide Reveals Signs of a Disease Seen in N.F.L.," *NYT*, September 13, 2010.

3. Alan Schwarz, "N.F.L.'s Influence on Safety at Youth Levels Is Cited," *NYT*, October 29, 2009.

4. Alan Schwarz, "States Take the Lead Addressing Concussions," *NYT*, January 30, 2010; "The Lystedt Law: A Concussion Survivor's Journey," CDC online, March 12, 2010, www.cdc.gov/headsup/pdfs/stories/031210-zack-story.pdf.

5. Alan Schwarz, "N.F.L. Picks New Chairman for Panel on Concussions," *NYT*, March 17, 2010.

6. Alan Schwarz and Ken Belson set the two documents against each other in their article about the lawsuit filed by former players against the NFL in July 2011. See Ken Belson and Alan Schwarz, "Concussion Treatment Cited in Suit against N.F.L.," *NYT*, July 20, 2011.

7. Mark Fainaru-Wada and Steve Fainaru, *League of Denial: The NFL, Concussions and the Battle for the Truth* (New York: Crown Archetype, 2013), 290.

8. Katie Thomas, "N.F.L.'s Policy on Helmet-to-Helmet Hits Makes Highlights Distasteful," *NYT*, October 21, 2010.

9. Ben McGrath, "Does Football Have a Future?," *New Yorker*, January 31, 2011 (also the source for the next few paragraphs).

10. Jeanne Marie Laskas, *Concussion* (New York: Random House, 2015), 231.

11. Alan Schwarz in the *NYT*: "Before Suicide, Duerson Said He Wanted Brain Study," February 20, 2011; "N.F.L. Players Shaken by Duerson's Message," February 21, 2011; "A Suicide, a Last Request, a Family's Questions," February 23, 2011; "Duerson's Brain Trauma Diagnosed," May 3, 2011.

12. Belson and Schwarz, "Concussion Treatment Cited in Suit against N.F.L."

13. Fainaru-Wada and Fainaru, *League of Denial*, 309. The book ends with the settlement in 2013, which was not finally approved by an appellate judge until April 2016.

14. Will Hobson, "The Broken Promises of the NFL Concussion Settlement," *WP*, February 4, 2024; Will Hobson, "As Denials Pile Up, NFL Settlement Ignores 'Critical' Tests," *WP*, August 20, 2024. See also Will Hobson, "Scouring Social Media, a Firm Fights NFL Settlement Payouts," *WP*, December 31, 2024, on the firm that must approve players' claims but drags out the process, scours claimants' social media for evidence that they are fully functioning despite their diagnoses, denies claims approved by the settlement's certified doctors, and has lost 60 percent of those doctors since 2018 over their own frustrations. Previously, Hobson reported on the players' successful challenge to the practice of "race-norming" in evaluating their mental decline. See "NFL, Former Players Agree to Remove 'Race-Norming' from Concussion Settlement Evaluations," *WP*, October 20, 2021; and "Hundreds of Black Former NFL Players Get Awards After End of 'Race-Norming,'" *WP*, August 12, 2022.

15. Ronald A. Smith, "The NCAA Concussions, and the Lack of Concern for Athletes," *Journal of Sport History* 51, no. 2 (Summer 2024): 25. Smith's article was part of a special issue on "Concussion's Past." For a thorough indictment of the college football establishment, including its indifference to head injuries (based on interviews with former players), see Nathan Kalman-Lamb and Derek Silva, *The End of College Football: On the Human Cost of an All-American Game* (Chapel Hill: University of North Carolina Press, 2024).

16. For an overview of the medical and legal controversies of the concussion crisis, see Sarah K. Fields and R. Dawn Comstock, "Concussions: Medical and Legal

Controversies in Football," in *Touchdown: An American Obsession*, ed. Gerry Gems and Gertrude Pfister (Great Barrington, MA: Berkshire, 2019), 81–97.

17. Linda Carroll and David Rosner, *The Concussion Crisis: Anatomy of a Silent Epidemic* (New York: Simon and Schuster, 2011).

18. See George Vecsey, "College Athletes Move Concussions Into the Courtroom," *NYT*, November 30, 2011; Ben Strauss, "N.C.A.A. Deal Revamps Head-Injury Care," *NYT*, July 30, 2014; Strauss, "Former Player Opposes Settlement in N.C.A.A. Concussion Suit," *NYT*, June 9, 2015. A preliminary settlement of *Arrington v. NCAA* in July 2014 was rejected by the judge in December, who then approved the settlement in January 2016—over the continuing objections of the lead plaintiff, Adrian Arrington, due to the absence of compensation for players. See Ben Strauss, "Judge Approves Settlement in Head Injuries Suit Against N.C.A.A.," *NYT*, January 27, 2016. The players won just $75 million, for testing and medical monitoring, but the judge denied the NCAA immunity from future lawsuits, effectively unleashing a torrent of personal and class-action complaints against schools, conferences, and the NCAA. In February 2019, the Associated Press reported that the NCAA faced "more than 300 lawsuits from football players who claim their concussions were mistreated, leading to medical problems spanning from headaches to depression and, in some cases, early onset Parkinson's or Alzheimer's disease." See Ralph D. Russo, "Wave of Concussion Suits to Test NCAA" (AP), *Baltimore Sun*, February 8, 2019.

19. Anahad O'Connor, "Trying to Reduce Head Injuries, Youth Football Limits Practices," *NYT*, June 14, 2012; and see Pop Warner website.

20. In July 2015, USA Football released the results of a study of the program commissioned from an independent data analytics firm, which claimed a roughly 30 percent reduction in concussions—34 percent in games, 29 percent in practices—and 76 percent fewer injuries overall. A year later, Alan Schwarz reported that the analytics firm had misused the data and that there was "no demonstrable effect on concussions during the study, and significantly less effect on injuries overall." See Gary Milhoces, "Study Results Positive for Heads Up Football" (USA Today Sports), *Indianapolis Star*, February 17, 2015; and Alan Schwarz, "N.F.L.-Backed Youth Program Says It Reduced Concussions. The Data Disagrees," *NYT*, July 28, 2016.

21. "Bounty Culture" (cover story and special report), *SI*, March 12, 2012.

22. The Fainaru brothers told the story in *League of Denial*, 329–37. The Boston University group and the Omalu group both wanted Seau's brain for autopsy, but at the last minute Seau's family gave it to the National Institutes of Health (the NFL's choice), which sent tissue samples from three brains (one of which was Seau's) to three neuropathologists and two of its own. All confirmed the diagnosis of CTE in Seau, the most rigorous confirmation of the disease to date.

23. Everett J. Lehman, "Neurodegenerative Causes of Death among Retired National Football League Players," *Neurology* 79, no. 19 (November 6, 2012), 1970–74.

24. John Branch, "N.F.L. Tried to Influence Concussion Research, Congressional Study Finds," *NYT*, May 24, 2016.

25. Ken Belson, "N.F.L. to Spend $100 Million to Address Head Trauma," *NYT*, September 14, 2016.

26. Fainaru-Wada and Fainaru, *League of Denial*, 2.

27. Daniel J. Flynn, *The War on Football: Saving America's Game* (Washington, DC: Regnery, 2013), 2–3. Flynn quoted Obama's comments from Franklin Foer and Chris Hughes, "Barack Obama Is Not Pleased," *New Republic*, January 27, 2013.

28. Darlene Superville, "Obama Pushes for Expanded Research on Youth Concussions," *LH-Leader*, May 30, 2014. This is the Associated Press piece that appeared in much of the country.

29. Steve Almond, *Against Football: One Fan's Reluctant Manifesto* (Brooklyn, NY: Melville House, 2014).

30. Flynn, *War on Football*, 3, 15, 141.

31. Flynn, *War on Football*, 119, 131, 132, 134.

32. Flynn, *War on Football*, 12.

33. Flynn, *War on Football*, 106.

34. See Stephen T. Casper, "Punch-Drunk Slugnuts: Violence and the Vernacular History of Disease," *Isis*, June 1922, 266–88.

35. Flynn, *War on Football*, 3.

36. Youth football figures from the Aspen Institute's annual report "State of Play 2018" (www.aspeninstitute.org/wp-content/uploads/2018/10/StateofPlay2018_v4WEB_2-FINAL.pdf); high school participation from the annual report of the National Federation of State High School Associations (www.nfhs.org/sports-resource-content/high-school-participation-survey-archive); and high school population from census data (www.census.gov/data/tables/2013/demo/school-enrollment/2013 cps.html).

37. In its 2023 series "The Divided States of Football," the *Washington Post* quoted a longtime youth football coach in West Texas who attributed the decline of youth football in his community to the Will Smith movie, which got parents doing their research and saying, "You know, that's a lot of hitting for these young kids." Dave Sheinin, "In Football's Epicenter, a Shifting Landscape," *WP*, December 18, 2023.

38. Bennet Omalu, "Don't Let Your Kids Play Football," *NYT*, December 7, 2015; Nancy Armour, "Kannell Should Check Facts on CTE," *Des Moines Register*, December 9, 2015; Justin Tasch, "Ex-Giant Kanell and the 'Liberal' War on Football," *NYDN*, December 9, 2015.

39. "Trump: NFL Soft, Like Our Country" (AP), *Chicago Tribune*, January 11, 2016.

40. See, for example, Adam Kilgore and Abby Phillip, "Trump Goes to War with NFL, NBA," *Minneapolis Star Tribune*, September 24, 2017 (originally in the *WP*); Eugene Scott, "Trump, NFL in Culture War over Kneeling," *Hartford Courant*, October 22, 2017; Chris Morris, "Donald Trump's Nearly Four-Decade War with the NFL: A Timeline," *Fortune*, September 25, 2017, https://fortune.com/2017/09/25/donald-trump-attack-nfl/; Deena Zaru, "Donald Trump's Unrelenting War with the NFL," CNN, February 5, 2018, www.cnn.com/2018/02/03/politics/trump-super-bowl-tom-brady-football-colin-kaepernick/index.html; Ken Belson, "As Trump Rekindles N.F.L. Fight, Goodell Sides with Players," *NYT*, June 5, 2020.

41. Kevin Horrigan, "Football on the Brain," *St. Louis Post-Dispatch*, May 29, 2016.

42. Ben Guarino, "Trump Criticizes NFL Concussion Protocol," *Concord Monitor*, October 14, 2016 (reprinted from *WP*).

43. Christine Brennan (*USA Today*), "Trump Didn't Learn His Schoolyard Lesson," *Arizona Republic* (Phoenix), September 24, 2017.

44. Mark Leibovich, *Big Game: The NFL in Dangerous Times* (New York: Penguin, 2018), 11. Leibovich also described Trump's attacks on the NFL during the 2017 season for allowing the player protests.

45. Ken Belson, "Not Safe for Children? Football's Leaders Make Drastic Changes to Youth Game," *NYT*, January 31, 2017.

46. Ken Belson, "Football's True Believers Circle the Wagons and Insist the Sport Is Just Fine," *NYT*, January 30, 2018.

47. Ken Belson, "Family Sues Pop Warner over Suicide of Player Who Had Brain Disease," *NYT*, February 5, 2015.

48. Ben Strauss, "Concussion Lawsuits Rankle School Groups," *NYT*, May 20, 2015; Ben Strauss, "Concussion Lawsuit in Illinois Is Dismissed," *NYT*, October 28, 2015.

49. Ken Belson, "Pop Warner Settles Lawsuit over Player Who Had C.T.E.," *NYT*, March 10, 2016.

50. Jim Litke, "Youth Football Could Lose the Numbers Game" (AP), *Miami Herald*, November 21, 2013; Christopher Weber, "Teen Player Whose Injury Raised Safety Efforts Dies" (AP), *Montgomery Advertiser*, May 13, 2016.

51. The six Dolphins are Jim Kiick, Nick Buoniconti, Jake Scott, Bob Kuechenberg, Bill Stanfill, and Earl Morrall. See Ken Belson, "For N.F.L. Perfection, a Steep Price," *NYT*, February 21, 2022. These six are among twenty-one former Dolphins diagnosed with CTE, fifteen of them unidentified for privacy reasons. See Hal Habib, "Twenty-One Former Dolphins Had CTE, Boston University Research Study Reveals," *Palm Beach Post*, February 7, 2023.

52. Justin Block, "We Shouldn't Be Surprised When NFL Players Retire Early Anymore," *Huffington Post*, April 8, 2016, www.huffpost.com/entry/dbrickashaw-ferguson-nfl-early-retirement-no-surprise_n_5707c4d5e4b0c4e26a2273fa0.

53. Mike Lupica, "At 24, Niner Says NFL Not Worth It," *NYDN*, March 17, 2015; Glenn Dickey, "Choosing Health Is Smart with NFL Dream," *San Francisco Examiner*, March 24, 2015. Borland's decision was a huge story and widely respected but almost unfathomable for many.

54. Ken Belson, "For Ravens' John Urschel, Playing in the N.F.L. No Longer Adds Up," *NYT*, July 27, 2017.

55. A. J. Perez, "Survey: 100% of Parents 'Affected in Some Way by Concussions,'" *USA Today*, July 20, 2016. For the press release on the poll conducted by the UMass Lowell Center for Public Opinion, see "National Survey Finds Concern about Brain Injuries in Athletics from Youth to Pro," UMass Lowell, July 20, 2016, www.uml.edu/news/press-releases/2016/concussionpoll072016.aspx.

56. Austin Murphy, "Endgame: The End of Football," *SI*, August 29, 2016.

57. Ken Belson, "Pop Warner Is Facing a Class-Action Lawsuit over Concussions," *NYT*, September 2, 2016. The sport sociologist Daniel R. Morrison describes the "veil of standards" employed by NOCSAE that "conceal scientific uncertainty regarding the likelihood of confusion in football." See Morrison, "Football Helmet Safety and the Veil of Standards," in *Sociocultural Examinations of Sports Concussions*, ed. Matt Ventresca and Mary G. McDonald (New York: Taylor & Francis, 2020), 59–71 (quotation from 61). This is similar to helmet manufacturers' misleading claims about their products' protection against concussions and then denying responsibility when sued. See Kathleen

Bachynski, "'A Clear Conscience': Advertising Football Equipment and Responsibility for Injuries," in Ventresca and McDonald, *Sociocultural Examinations of Sports Concussions*, 41–58, adapted from Bachynski's book *No Game for Boys to Play*.

58. Archie and Cornell found each other online, and despite their legal setback, they launched a crusade on behalf of parents of sons brain-damaged from football. In 2019, they published a book with chapters by thirteen parents, including themselves, who became a community through online chat groups. See *Brain Damaged: Two Minute Warning for Parents* (USA Sport Safety Publishing, 2019); and Bachynski, *No Game for Boys to Play*, 210–11.

59. Ken Belson, "Concussion Lawsuit against Pop Warner Is Dismissed," *NYT*, December 28, 2019.

60. Jesse Mez et al., "Clinicopathological Evaluation of Chronic Traumatic Encephalopathy in Players of American Football," *JAMA*, July 25, 2017, 360–70. As the one who conducted the autopsies, McKee was a coauthor. See also Joe Ward, Josh Williams, and Sam Manchester, "111 N.F.L. Brains," *NYT*, July 25, 2017; and "The Scars from 'Bell-Ringing' Football Tackles" (editorial), *NYT*, July 29, 2017.

61. Zachary O. Binney and Kathleen E. Bachynski, "Estimating the Prevalence at Death of CTE Neuropathology among Professional Football Players," *Neurology* 92, no. 1 (January 1, 2019): 43–45. The authors took the total number of former players' deaths from annual lists on pro-football-reference.com.

62. "BU Finds CTE in Nearly 92 Percent of Ex-NFL Players Studied," *The Brink*, February 7, 2023.

63. Rachel Grashow, Douglas P. Terry, and Grant L. Iverson et al., "Perceived Chronic Traumatic Encephalopathy and Suicidality in Former Professional Football Players," *JAMA Neurology* 81, no. 11 (September 23, 2024): 1130–39.

64. Kent Babb, "They Watched Their Husbands Win the Heisman—Then Lost Them to CTE," *WP*, December 9, 2023. Babb describes the annual celebrations for former Heisman winners, where several others appear to have the disease as well. Wikipedia's "List of NFL Players with Chronic Traumatic Encephalopathy," accessed January 2, 2025, https://en.wikipedia.org/wiki/List_of_NFL_players_with_chronic_traumatic_encephalopathy#cite_note-196) includes a secondary list of "Living Former Players Diagnosed with CTE or ALS or Reporting Symptoms Consistent with CTE or ALS." The eighty-seven names include such stars as Harry Carson, Lance Briggs, Tony Dorsett, Joe DeLamielleure, Jim McMahon, Mark Gastineau, Leonard Marshall, Brett Favre, and Warren Sapp. Players who have died with suspected CTE but were not diagnosed, or the diagnosis has not been announced, include Otis Taylor, Conrad Dobler, Ralph Neeley, and Mike Curtis, all stars of their eras.

65. For an overview, see "NFL Health and Safety Related Rules Changes since 2002," NFL Player Health & Safety, March 29, 2024, www.nfl.com/playerhealthandsafety/equipment-and-innovation/rules-changes/nfl-health-and-safety-related-rules-changes-since-2002. The blocking and tackling techniques taught by Bear Bryant and Woody Hayes in the 1960s, which filtered down to high schools and youth football, were now explicitly banned by the NFL.

66. Steven Wise, "Committee to Decide on Tweaking Interference," *Cincinnati Enquirer*, May 23, 2019.

67. David Fleming, "Is the Oklahoma Drill a Rite of Passage or Everything to Fear about Football?," *ESPN The Magazine*, August 18, 2015.

68. Fleming, "Is the Oklahoma Drill a Rite of Passage?"

69. Matt Murschel, "NCAA Reducing Amount of Contact for Preseason," *Orlando Sentinel*, May 21, 2021.

70. See Sarah Effress, "Who Wears a Guardian Cap in NFL? Players Who Have Worn New, Protective Helmet in 2024 So Far," *The Sporting News*, October 27, 2024, www.sportingnews.com/us/nfl/news/guardian-cap-nfl-players-worn-protective-helmet-2024/c86c41078ob10a495e218do8.

71. Paul Newberry, "Guardian Caps Aimed at Reducing Head Injuries" (AP), *St. Louis Post-Dispatch*, August 5, 2022; "NFL to Allow Players to Wear Protective Soft-Shell Helmet Covers during Games" (AP), *WP*, April 26, 2024; Mark Maske, "Why Some NFL Players Are Wearing Guardian Caps in Preseason Games," *WP*, August 18, 2024.

72. Patrick Hruby, "'Junction Boys Syndrome': How College Football Fatalities Became Normalized," *The Guardian*, August 19, 2018; Rick Maese and Keith L. Alexander, "Report on Maryland Football Culture Cites Problems but Stops Short of 'Toxic' Label," *WP*, October 25, 2018.

73. Jacob Bogage and Emily Guskin, "Poll: Americans Mixed on Whether Tackle Football Is Safe for Children," *WP*, September 12, 2017.

74. Data are from the Aspen Institute's online annual reports on the "State of Play." The first year of publication, "State of Play 2017," has figures for 2008, 2010, and 2012–16 (www.aspeninstitute.org/wp-content/uploads/2017/12/FINAL-SOP2017-report.pdf). Subsequent reports have followed each year. For the latest, see "State of Play 2024," Project Play Aspen Institute, accessed February 3, 2025, https://projectplay.org/state-of-play-2024-participation-trends.

75. High school participation from the annual reports published online by the National Federation of State High School Associations.

76. Jerry Doby, "2024 Football Recruiting Hotbeds Aren't a Surprise," TheHype Magazine.com, April 30, 2024, www.thehypemagazine.com/2024/04/2024-football-recruiting-hotbeds-arent-a-surprise/.

77. Ken Belson et al., "Inside Football's Campaign to Save the Game," *NYT*, November 7, 2019, www.nytimes.com/interactive/2019/11/08/sports/falling-football-participation-in-america.html?searchResultPosition=1. The article is accompanied by a graph showing the decline in all fifty states.

78. Dave Sheinin, "California Lawmakers Take Step toward Banning Youth Tackle Football," *WP*, January 10, 2024; Albert Samaha, "California Lawmakers Pushed a Tackle Football Ban. Families Pushed Back," *WP*, January 20, 2024.

79. Ken Belson, "Football's Risks Sink In, Even in Heart of Texas," *NYT*, May 12, 2014 (also cited in the next paragraph).

80. Ken Belson, "Tackle Football Makes a Comeback in the Heart of Texas," *NYT*, December 4, 2016.

81. Ken Belson, "A Small Town Gave Up Tackle Football. It Came Storming Back," *NYT*, November 16, 2019.

82. The entire *WP* series was published online on December 18 and then in the print edition over consecutive days around Christmas. See Dave Sheinin and Emily

Giambalvo, "The Changing Face of America's Favorite Sport," December 18, 2023; Albert Samaha, "A Violent Clash of Football Haves and Have-Nots" (on rich and poor high schools in Sacramento); Dave Sheinin, "In Football's Epicenter, a Shifting Landscape" (on high school football in West Texas); Michael Lee, "Where Tackle Football Still Reigns" (on high school football in small-town and rural Mississippi); and Dave Sheinin, "In a Midwest Football Hotbed, an Economic Divide" (on high school football in poor urban and rich suburban schools in Dayton, Ohio). Samaha's article on the attempt to ban youth tackle football in California, cited above in n. 74, was a sixth installment in the "Divided States of Football" series.

83. Sheinin and Giambalvo, "Changing Face of America's Favorite Sport."

84. Sheinin and Giambalvo, "Changing Face of America's Favorite Sport"; Sheinin, "In a Midwest Football Hotbed, an Economic Divide." The *Washington Post*'s figures for flag and tackle football were from the source used for the Aspen Institute's "State of Play 2024" (see n. 74 above).

EPILOGUE

1. Rob Fleder, ed., *NFL 100: A Century of Pro Football* (New York: Abrams, 2019), 15.

2. Mike Ozanian and Christina Settimi, "The NFL's Most Valuable Teams 2021," *Forbes*, August 5, 2021.

3. Austin Karp, "NFL Sees Best Average Viewership since 2015," *Sports Business Journal*, January 9, 2024; Anthony Crupi, "NFL Ratings Dip 2% as TV's Biggest Draw Fends Off Political Raid," *Sportico*, January 8, 2025.

4. Anthony Crupi, "NFL Swallows TV Whole, with 93 of Year's Top 100 Broadcasts," *Sportico*, January 5, 2024. The seven broadcasts in 2023 that were not NFL games included three college games (nos. 58, 71, and 74), the State of the Union address (no. 23), the Thanksgiving Day Parade (no. 45), the Academy Awards (no. 60), and the Super Bowl Lead-Out (no. 92) (the program immediately following the Super Bowl, that is).

5. Anthony Crupi, "NFL Owns 72 of TV's Top 100 as Politics Loosens Sport's Grip," *Sportico*, January 3, 2025. In addition to sixteen nights of political programming, two nights of the Paris Olympics (nos. 82 and 89), four college football games (nos. 24, 34, 79, and 100), the NCAA women's (not the men's) basketball final (no. 76), and Game 5 of the World Series (no. 84) made the Top 100 (along with the usual Thanksgiving Day Parade, Academy Awards, Grammy Awards, and Super Bowl Lead-Out). In other words, without the quadrennial presidential election and the Olympic Games, the NFL would have had 90 of the top 100 programs, down slightly from 2023. With 25 million viewers, the College Football Championship trailed ten NFL regular-season games as well as all but one of the playoffs (on the streaming network Peacock with its smaller potential audience).

6. "Super Bowl LVIII Becomes Most-Watched U.S. Program Ever with 123.7 Million Viewers," *The Athletic*, February 13, 2024.

7. Richard Deitsch, "Eagles-Chiefs Super Bowl Sets Record with 127.7 Million Viewers," *The Athletic*, February 10, 2025.

8. Michael Schneider, "100 Most-Watched TV Series of 2023–24," *Variety*, May 28, 2024, https://variety.com/2024/tv/news/most-popular-tv-shows-highest-rated

-2023-2024-season-tracker-survivor-1236015844/. Ratings for 2024 were not yet available when the book went to press.

9. Thomas M. Talavage, Eric A. Nauman, Evan L. Breedlove, et al., "Functionally-Detected Cognitive Impairment in High School Football Players without Clinically-Diagnosed Concussion," *Journal of Neurotrauma*, February 15, 2014, 327–38 (from the Purdue group's measurements of high school football players in West Lafayette, Indiana).

10. Ann C. McKee et al., "Repetitive Head Impacts and Chronic Traumatic Encephalopathy," *Neurosurgery Clinics of North America*, October 2016, 529–35.

11. Julie M. Stamm et al., "Age of First Exposure to Football and Later-Life Cognitive Impairment in Former NFL Players," *Neurology* 84, no. 11 (March 17, 2015): 1114–20.

12. Ken Belson and Benjamin Mueller, "Collective Force of Head Hits, Not Just the Number of Them, Increases Odds of C.T.E.," *NYT*, June 20, 2023, based on a study of 631 brains in the Boston University brain bank. For the study, see Daniel H. Daneshvar et al., "Leveraging Football Accelerometer Data to Quantify Associations between Repetitive Head Impacts and Chronic Traumatic Encephalopathy in Males," *Nature Communications*, June 20, 2023, 1–14.

13. Ann C. McKee et al., "Neuropathologic and Clinical Findings in Young Contact Sport Athletes Exposed to Repetitive Head Impacts," *JAMA Neurology* 80, no. 10 (October 1, 2023): 1037–50.

14. Patrick Hruby, "Damage Assessment," *WP Magazine*, September 2, 2020.

15. Jeff Legwold, "Former Denver Broncos WR, Demaryius Thomas, 33, Found Dead in His Home, Police Say," ESPN.com, December 10, 2021; Ken Belson, "An N.F.L. Star's C.T.E. Diagnosis Offers Only Partial Insight," *NYT*, July 6, 2022.

16. Jonathan Abrams, "Phillip Adams Had Severe C.T.E. at the Time of Shootings," *NYT*, December 14, 2021.

17. John Branch, "N.F.L. Tried to Influence Concussion Research, Congressional Study Finds," *NYT*, May 24, 2016.

18. "Diagnose CTE Research Project: Aims, Methods and Designs," Diagnose CTE Research Project, accessed January 2, 2025, https://diagnosectedata.bu.edu/Review.aspx. Publications that have come from the research thus far are posted on the BU Research CTE Center website, accessed January 2, 2025, www.bu.edu/cte/tag/diagnose/.

19. Alan Schwarz, "Scans Could Aid Diagnosis of Brain Trauma in Living," *NYT*, December 2, 2010.

20. Michael Keefe, "Researcher Says in 5 Years, CTE Test Can Be Given to Living," *NYDN*, February 3, 2016; Bob Hohler, "A Step toward CTE Diagnosis in Living," *BG*, September 27, 2017; Felice J. Freyer, "BU Study Raises Hope of CTE Scans," *BG*, April 11, 2019; Alexi Cohan, "Boston University Scientists Getting Closer to Diagnosing CTE in Living People Using MRI," *Boston Herald* (online), December 12, 2021.

21. Ken Belson, "A Test for C.T.C. in the Living May Be Closer Than Ever," *NYT*, November 16, 2022.

22. Gina Digravio and Jessica Colarossi, "Researchers Are One Step Closer to Diagnosing CTE During Life, Rather Than After Death," *The Brink*, February 5, 2024 (this is a newsletter for BU research). The group's paper was published in Michael L. Alosco, Micaela White, Carter Bell et al., "Cognitive, Functional, and Neuropsychiatric Correlates

of Regional Tau Pathology in Autopsy-confirmed Chronic Traumatic Encephalopathy," *Molecular Neurodegeneration* 19, no. 10 (2024): 1–19. (McKee, Stern, Nowinski, and Cantu appear well down the long list of co-authors.)

23. Ben McGrath, "Does Football Have a Future?," *New Yorker*, January 31, 2011.

24. "NFL Report: Ex-Players Face Dementia" (AP), *Philadelphia Inquirer*, September 13, 2014.

INDEX